Trinitarian Grace and Participation

Trinitarian Grace and Participation

An Entry into the Theology of T. F. Torrance

Geordie W. Ziegler

Fortress Press
Minneapolis

TRINITARIAN GRACE AND PARTICIPATION

An Entry into the Theology of T. F. Torrance

Cover design: Alisha Lofgren

Hardcover ISBN: 978-1-5064-2339-5

Paperback ISBN: 978-1-5064-0683-1

eBook ISBN: 978-1-5064-0684-8

The paper used in this publication meets the minimum requirements of American National Standard for Information Sciences — Permanence of Paper for Printed Library Materials, ANSI Z329.48-1984.

Manufactured in the U.S.A.

This book was produced using Pressbooks.com, and PDF rendering was done by PrinceXML.

Contents

Contents

Acknowledgments

A great cloud of witnesses has participated in the birthing of this book, many more than can be named in this short space: Alan Torrance, for teaching the gospel in a way that grabbed my soul and for planting the seeds of a mid-life crisis worth sacrificing for; Paddy Ducklow, thank you for asking the question that set me free from fear of failure; Andrew Purves, for setting my call ablaze by preaching the gospel in a way that made the people cheer God; Eugene Peterson, for believing in the importance of this project for Christ's Church and for pastoring me through the schizophrenia of PhD life; Jim Arwood, for believing in me more than I believed in myself; the people of Fremont Presbyterian, for sending us out with your love and prayers and support; the people of Banchory, Scotland, for welcoming us into your world until it became ours as well; Jonathan and Vicky Harris, for trusting us with your home for four years; for the people of Columbia Presbyterian, for being God's unexpected gift; my various editors Gary Deddo, Robert Walker and Laurel Neal, for your patient and sacrificial encouragement chapter by chapter; Robert, for your fidelity to Uncle Tom's theological thought which, in the absence of T. F. himself, you have been the best substitute I could imagine or ask for!; Gary Deddo and Paul Molnar, for giving me a thesis topic; for the space and hospitality of the brothers of Pluscarden Abbey, St. Deiniol's Library, Mt. Angel Abbey and Monastery, Marissa's Cabin and the Frakes first floor; and Max, I'm sure you'll never see this, but thank you for your prayer when I was at the bottom; and Fitz and Scout, for your incredible gift of encouragement. You have been faithful icons of God's grace for me and I am deeply thankful.

Of course, humanly speaking, there are three more people to thank without whom this book would have remained dormant. First, my supervisor, the late John Webster: his patience, calmness, and attentiveness were unmatched. It truly was an immense privilege to have his voice and blessing throughout this long process—even after I'd returned to the States and he's moved on to another academic post. John's presence in this world is profoundly missed, though hopefully reflected in some way in those of us who had the privilege of being his students and following in his wake. Next, my parents: thank you for entering my world, and rejoicing and mourning in our rejoicing and mourning. Your encouragement and belief never faltered. And finally, of course, none of this would have happened without my wife Sharon and her 'up for anything' attitude, which allowed us to uproot and cross the world with our school-age children— Andrew, Brennan and KaiLi. Doing this together has made all the difference. You sacrificed by far the most in this process and along with me gained the most. You are my one thousand gifts.

But last and most, I must thank Jesus Christ—brother, Lord, priest, prayer-leader, Creator and Savior—for including me in your joy in the Father.

Abbreviations

Atonement	*Atonement: the Person and Work of Christ*
A&MO	"Atonement and the Moral Order"
Apocalypse	*The Apocalypse Today: Sermons on Revelations*
CNDDG	"Call for a New Discussion on the Doctrine of Grace"
CDM	*Calvin's Doctrine of Man*
CDG	*The Christian Doctrine of God: One Being Three Persons*
CFM	*The Christian Frame of Mind*
Consensus	"Doctrinal Consensus on Holy Communion"
CTSC	*Christian Theology and Scientific Culture*
C&A1	*Conflict and Agreement in the Church, vol. 1*
C&A2	*Conflict and Agreement in the Church, vol. 2*
DCO	*Divine and Contingent Order*
DM	*Divine Meaning: Studies in Patristic Hermeneutics*
DGAF	*The Doctrine of Grace in the Apostolic Fathers*
DJC	*The Doctrine of Jesus Christ*
GGT	*The Ground and Grammar of Theology*
GCM	*Gospel, Church and Ministry*
G&R	*God and Rationality*
G&DMCT	"The Goodness and Dignity of Man in the Christian Tradition"
Reply to Critics	"Relevance of the Doctrine of the Spirit for Ecumenical Theology: Reply to Critics"

Incarnation	*Incarnation: The Person and Life of Christ*
KBBET	*Karl Barth: Biblical and Evangelical Theologian*
Latin Heresy	"Karl Barth and the Latin Heresy"
Mission	"The Mission of the Church"
MOC	*The Mediation of Christ*
New Era	"The Church in the New Era of Scientific and Cosmological Change"
PCT	*Preaching Christ Today: The Gospel and Scientific Thinking*
PiC	"Predestination in Christ"
RP	*The Royal Priesthood*
R&ET	*Reality and Evangelical Theology*
R&ST	*Reality and Scientific Theology*
SOF	*The School of Faith*
S&PTP	"The Soul and Person, in Theological Perspective"
S&PUC	"Soul and Person, in the Unborn Child"
STI	*Space, Time and Incarnation*
STR	*Space, Time and Resurrection*
TCFK	*Transformation & Convergence in the Frame of Knowledge*
TF	*The Trinitarian Faith: The Evangelical Theology of the Ancient Catholic Church*
TiR	*Theology in Reconciliation: Essays Towards Evangelical and Catholic Unity in East and West*
TP	*Trinitarian Perspectives: Toward Doctrinal Agreement*
Tracts and Treatises	Tracts and Treatises
TRn	*Theology in Reconstruction*
TS	*Theological Science*
UE	"Universalism or Election"
WCCCA	*When Christ Comes and Comes Again*

Foreword

Although it is now widely acknowledged that T. F. Torrance was one of the most distinguished and original British theological thinkers in the second half of the twentieth century, his theology of divine grace has rarely been studied at any depth. The literature on his work—much of it pious summary, although the best of it engages in the kind of generous critical conversation which his writings surely deserve—has long devoted a great deal of attention to his understanding of the nature of theological knowledge and of its relation to non-theological conceptions of 'science'; and there have been some studies of a range of doctrinal themes in his work. But there remains a lacuna in interpreting and assessing his thinking about how God's active and merciful benevolence is at work in the world and shapes human life. In part, this is because much of what Torrance has to say on these matters is scattered across a large and varied corpus, never having been drawn together by him into a synthetic statement. In part, too, it is because he was curiously reluctant to commit himself to saying much about the moral-practical effects of the divine working, preferring to restrict himself to talk of the sanctifier rather than the sanctified (in this he stood at some considerable distance from his beloved teacher Barth). Yet, grace is as it were the ambience in which his thinking on all manner of theological topics moves from the very early book on the doctrine of grace in the apostolic fathers to the mature dogmatic writings on Trinity, Incarnation, Spirit and Church. It is this which the study that follows seeks to elucidate and assess.

The book's contribution to the interpretation and reception of Torrance's work is two-fold. First, it offers to its readers a patient, accurate and comprehensive presentation of Torrance's thinking about Divine grace, in its trinitarian, soteriological, ecclesiological and anthropological aspects. As it does so moreover it indicates how the theology of Grace provides a vantage-point from which the entirety of Torrance's thought can be seen and understood. The energy and speed and the sometimes associative style of Torrance's writing can be demanding for the interpreter, who needs to exercise a measure of determination to display the full scope and coherence of what Torrance has to say. Readers of this study will find here a thorough and perceptive interpretation of the matter in hand. Second, the book reflects throughout on the adequacy of Torrance's theology of grace. At the heart of the reflection is a set of questions about how he considers the relation of God and creatures. If Torrance's account of the forms and activities of human life under grace remains relatively underexplored, in his writings there is nevertheless a set of resources for a more ample theology of the Christian life and of churchly formation than he allowed himself to present.

In short: this is a full and perceptive study of an under-appreciated element in the work of a theologian of great stature, and an invitation to give thought to some central questions in the theology of the Christian life.

John Webster
University of Aberdeen

Introduction

> It was the concept of grace together with the internal structure of the Trinity and Christology which I felt would give me the grasp of theology in its inner scientific relations.[1]

Thomas F. Torrance (1913–2007) has been described as the greatest British theologian of the twentieth century, and by more than a few as the most significant English-speaking theologian of the second half of the twentieth century.[2] Regardless of rankings, the fact that Torrance was able to publish more than six hundred works during a career spanning six decades undeniably establishes him as a scholar's scholar and a theologian's theologian. The significance of Torrance's intellectual contribution is demonstrated by the steady appearance of scholarly analysis of his thought over the last three decades of the twentieth century. Furthermore, in the ensuing years since his death at the age of ninety-four, there has been a resurgence of interest in Torrance's theological thought with the publication of multiple academic books, scholarly essays, and research theses. There are now regular Torrance conferences,[3] a Torrance Society,[4] an annual Torrance lecture series,[5] and an online Torrance Journal,[6] not to

---

1. John I. Hesselink, "A Pilgrimage in the School of Christ – An Interview with Thomas F. Torrance," *Reformed Review* 38, no. 1 (Autumn 1984): 53.
2. Robert J. Stamps, *The Sacrament of the Word made Flesh* (Edinburgh: Rutherford House, 2007), xiii.
3. In 2010, Robert Walker began hosting bi-annual Torrance retreats at Firbush Outdoor Center on Loch Tay, dedicated to further reflection upon and dissemination of the teaching of both Tom and James Torrance.
4. The T. F. Torrance Theological Fellowship began in the United States in 2004. It can be found at: http://www.tftorrance.org/.

mention several presentations given on Torrance's theology each year at AAR and ETS.[7] Given this barrage of Torrance scholarly works, what justifies the addition of yet one more? Very simply, up to this point there has been no focused scholarly study on the subject upon which Torrance cut his theological teeth during his own post-graduate work under Karl Barth: the doctrine of Grace.[8]

Early Torrance scholarship tended to focus on his theological method and scientific theology.[9] While many studies have centered on particular aspects of Torrance's thought,[10] or the application of Torrance's theology to a particular field of knowledge,[11] others have sought to provide a general overview of Torrance's theological corpus.[12] While Torrance has been depicted as the champion of a variety of theological loci (trinitarian theology, eschatology, theological method, ecumenical dialogue, the relation between science

5. After Torrance's death in 2007, the annual Scottish Journal of Theology lectures were renamed the Thomas F. Torrance lectures.
6. *Participatio* began in 2009 and is published 1-2 times per year. It can be found at: http://www.tftorrance.org/journal.php.
7. American Academy of Religion, Evangelical Theology Society.
8. Throughout this book the term "Grace" will be capitalized when referring to Torrance's doctrine of Grace. This should serve to alert the reader to Torrance's conviction that Grace is none other than God's self-giving.
9. Some of these have been published: John Douglas Morrison, *Knowledge of the Self-Revealing God in the Thought of Thomas Forsyth Torrance* (New York: Peter Lang, 1997); Colin Weightman, *Theology in a Polanyian Universe: The Theology of T. F. Torrance* (New York: Peter Lang, 1995); Elmer Colyer, *The Nature of Doctrine in T. F. Torrance's Theology* (Eugene, OR: Wipf and Stock, 2001); Tapio Luoma, *Incarnation and Physics: Natural Science in the Theology of Thomas F. Torrance* (Oxford: Oxford University Press, 2002); Kettler, Christian D. *The Vicarious Humanity of Christ and the Reality of Salvation* (Lanham, MD: University Press of America, 1991; C. Baxter Kruger, "Participation in the Self-Knowledge of God: The Nature and Means of our Knowledge of God in the Theology of T. F. Torrance" (PhD diss., University of Aberdeen, 1989).
10. George Hunsinger. *The Eucharist and Ecumenism: Let Us Keep the Feast* (Cambridge: Cambridge University Press, 2008); Peter Cass, *Christ Condemned Sin in the Flesh: Thomas F. Torrance's Doctrine of Soteriology and Its Ecumenical Significance* (Saarbrücken, Germany: VDM Verlag, 2009); Graham Redding, *Prayer and the Priesthood of Christ in the Reformed Tradition* (London: T&T Clark, 2003); Stanley Stephen MacLean, *Resurrection, Apocalypse, and the Kingdom of Christ: The Eschatology of Thomas F. Torrance* (Eugene, OR: Pickwick, 2012); Robert Julian Stamps, *The Sacrament of the Word Made Flesh: The Eucharistic Theology of Thomas F. Torrance* (Edinburgh: Rutherford House, 2007); William Rankin, "Carnal Union with Christ in the Theology of T. F. Torrance" (PhD diss., University of Edinburgh, 1997); Phee Seng Kang, "The Concept of the Vicarious Humanity of Christ in the Theology of Thomas Forsyth Torrance" (PhD diss., University of Aberdeen, 1989).
11. Eric Gordon Flett, *Persons, Powers, and Pluralities: Toward a Trinitarian Theology of Culture* (Cambridge: James Clarke, 2012).
12. Elmer M. Colyer, *How to Read T. F. Torrance: Understanding his Trinitarian & Scientific Theology* (Downers Grove, IL: IVP, 2001); Alister E. McGrath, *Thomas F. Torrance: An Intellectual Biography* (Edinburgh: T&T Clark, 1999); Paul D. Molnar, *Thomas F. Torrance: Theologian of the Trinity* (Farnham: Ashgate, 2009).

and theology, to name but a few), only a small number of scholars have attempted to bring to the fore that which Torrance himself championed.[13]

While these studies have illuminated important aspects of the structure of Torrance's thought, this project lays claim to what could be considered a deeper strata of Torrance's theology: his doctrine of Grace, in which all other doctrines find their interior logic.[14] It is the unique assertion of this monograph that Torrance's doctrine of Grace, heretofore unexplored, is the central and controlling conceptual set which provides the fundamental organizing framework for his entire theological project.[15] Such a bold claim is simply an attempt to follow the lead of the one who knew Torrance the best, Torrance himself.

> Christology must always be the *centrum* of a Christian dogmatic. If therefore it can be said that a systematic treatment of theology will be one in which all the doctrines cohere and dovetail together . . . then we may look for certain material dogmatic norms within the body of theology which may act as a kind of interior logic throughout the whole, characterising as well the single doctrines themselves. *Without doubt we find that in Christology, or viewed from another angle one might well say it was the doctrine of Grace. How God deals with us in Jesus Christ, that must be the norm for all our theologising.*[16]

13. Of particular note here are Kye Won Lee's *Living in Union with Christ* (New York: Peter Lang, 2003). Lee makes the claim that "'Union and communion' is the central theme of Torrance's theology" (2). Myk Habet's *Theosis in the Theology of Thomas Torrance* (Farnham: Ashgate, 2009); Paul Molnar's *Thomas F. Torrance, Theologian of the Trinity*, and Dick Eugenio's *Communion with God: The Trinitarian Soteriology of Thomas F. Torrance* (Eugene, OR: Pickwick, 2014). While Grace is certainly a subject within each of these studies, none of them attempts to delineate the contours of Grace across the doctrinal spectrum. Perhaps the study which comes closest to the heart of Torrance's theological framework is Eugenio's with its dual emphasis on Torrance's trinitarian soteriology and soteriological Trinity. Yet Eugenio's fine work is not aimed at specifically illuminating Torrance's understanding of Grace in its own right.

14. Thomas F. Torrance, "Predestination in Christ," *Evangelical Quarterly* 13 (1941): 127-28. Hereafter, *PiC*.

15. An important case should be made against ascribing any theme or doctrine as *the* central aspect of Torrance's theology in light of the fact that Torrance himself consistently opposed the fixing of any principle over the personal reality of the living God. To raise one theme above all others would risk displacing the triune God by a system. Thus, even though Torrance's concept of grace ruthlessly refers to the personal self-giving movement of the triune God and the personal communion such a movement creates, it should never be described in impersonal terms that would fix it as a principle.

16. *PiC*, 127-28. Italics added.

In this book I endeavor to take Torrance at his word by viewing the movement of his thought via the lens of Grace. Accordingly, the working hypothesis of this book is that *Grace* is Torrance's basic theological centrum. My aim is to demonstrate that claim using Torrance's own words as documented by his writings—both published and unpublished—which span more than 60 years of his adult life. By lifting up and bringing to the fore Torrance's unique approach to the doctrine of Grace, I present it as a valuable resource in the theological conversation. Torrance (and the Athanasian tradition which he seeks to represent) stands apart as a consistent, robust, trinitarian and practical approach worthy of much wider appreciation and practice.

As we discipline ourselves to follow Torrance's lead, we will discover that Grace is not simply Christology alone, but the active soteriology which accompanies it and which cannot be thought of apart from the entire triune Godhead.[17] Grace for Torrance is nothing less than the self-giving of God for our salvation. This self-giving of God is an activity of the whole Trinity which moves *from the Father through the Son in the Spirit,* and *in the Spirit through the Son to the Father.* The ultimate purpose of this motion of Grace is fellowship with human creatures and the redemption of the whole created order.

Torrance Reception and Style

Before launching into our study it should be noted that there are particular challenges that Torrance's theology presents, which have influenced its reception as well as the scholarship that builds upon the foundations he has hewn. As Robert Walker who has spent much of his life interpreting and editing Torrance's works has observed: "Torrance's dogmatics combines an inner simplicity with a structural complexity"[18] such that what he offers is systematic but not a system. Much of the complexity comes from the fact that Torrance tends to think "stereoscopically," holding multiple concepts together at once,

---

17. In a footnote, Torrance notes that by *Christology* he also means *soteriology,* "for the Person of Christ can only be rightly interpreted functionally" (ibid., 139).

18. Thomas F. Torrance, *Incarnation: The Person and Life of Christ,* ed. Robert T. Walker (Nottingham: Intervarsity, 2008), xxv. Hereafter, *Incarnation.*

refusing to flatten into a neat system the diversity contained in the scriptures. Regardless of what doctrine or concept he exposits, each person of the Trinity must be acknowledged along with the full humanity and full divinity of Christ, as well as the humanward and Godward movements. This presents itself in a writing style which is not only complex and integrative, but also repetitive.

This repetitive or circular movement can be confusing as well as tiring. Torrance's writing is replete with shorthand terms preloaded with a world of meaning: *homoousion, hypostatic union, anhypostatic, enhypostatic, perichoresis* and *onto-relations* intersect and overlap as various stratified levels of knowledge mutually inform and impress upon one another.[19] The density of technical terms that Torrance wields can make for laborious reading. However, it is important to realize that the circling movement is not the sign of a random or disorganized mind, but is highly intentional. Torrance is convinced this wholistic approach is necessary if one is to prevent the creeping in of dualistic ways of thinking.

Torrance's wholism enables him perhaps more than most to keep his attention on the incredible acts of God in Christ and in the Spirit, and thus to maintain a mood in his theology which, while certainly analytic, is never far from praise and wonder. Yet Torrance's wonder is rarely poetic. Torrance is more naturally a scientist than a poet, a cartographer than an artist.[20] Given a literary style designed to present theology in a truly scientific form, simplicity of concepts are not to be found, which has posed difficulties to wide reception. Torrance's writings have been characterized as a semantically undisciplined "verbal jungle,"[21] "densely packed and replete with jargon,"[22] "a cobweb of different doctrines and notions,"[23] "dense to the point of obscurity,"[24] "stylistically turbulent,"[25] and full of "great intellectual

---

19. These terms will be explained and expounded in the course of this book.
20. Roger J. Newell, "Participatory knowledge: theology as art and science in C. S. Lewis and T. F. Torrance" (PhD diss., University of Aberdeen, 1983: 2 vol.), 538.
21. Donald M. McKay, "Review of *Divine and Contingent Order* by T. F. Torrance, ChrG 35, 2 (1982)," 38–39.
22. David L. Anderson, "Review of *Divine and Contingent Order* by T. F. Torrance, Bloomsbury, 2005," 502.
23. Lee, *Union*, 6.

constructions," which "make hard going and by the end seem to have lost their bite."[26] The difficulty for readers is so great according to Stamps that they may be inclined to disregard Torrance's doctrine "not for its sheer realism, but for its sheer complexity."[27]

Methodology and Approach

Unfortunately, Torrance's scholarship often suffers from the same pitfalls. It is not uncommon for studies on Torrance to fall into step with his laborious style, rendering them as difficult to read as Torrance himself! Those attempts which have been made to summarize Torrance's thought comprehensively have themselves been plagued by an overwhelming complexity in which they succumb to the role of 'tour guide' rather than interpreter.[28]

What this study seeks to offer is a translation by way of exposition of Torrance's theology which enables the reader to clearly grasp the core of his theology of Grace. To achieve this purpose will require a wide and wholistic approach involving the inclusion of a range of doctrines; and yet within each doctrinal locus I have sought to pare down the material in order to illuminate what is central to Torrance's theology of Grace. The reason for this dual approach (wide, yet exemplary) is the fact that, perhaps more than most, Torrance's theology is a kind of interlocking 'open system' which must be comprehended as a whole in order to grasp the parts properly. Each doctrine is so intimately and inherently related to the other that to isolate a single doctrine from the others would be by definition to distort it. Consequently in this monograph the whole will illumine the parts and the parts

---

24. Colyer, How to Read, 16.
25. Walter Thorson, "Review of Reality and Scientific Theology by T. F. Torrance," PSCF 38, no. 2 (1986): 212–14.
26. Ronald Lunt, "Review of Theology in Reconciliation by T. F. Torrance," Expository Times, 87 (1975–76): 379.
27. Stamps, Sacrament, 290.
28. Colyer and Molnar's works in particular suffer from this difficulty. While each stands as an excellent and indispensible overview map for gaining access to the key themes in Torrance's theology, neither leaves the reader with a clear architectonic picture or framework which has the power to guide the reader through the whole of Torrance's work. Alistair McGrath's "Intellectual Biography" is an easier read simply because it is more narratival and is primarily interested in Torrance's scientific theology rather than the whole of his dogmatic reflections.

will illumine the whole. As a strategy, this is plainly apparent in the structure of the book. Within each doctrinal area, I will materially restrict myself to discuss only those aspects of Torrance's theology which bear directly and significantly upon his theology of Grace. It is not the purpose of this study to engage deeply with secondary critiques of Torrance's writings.[29] Instead, I intend to demonstrate the logic of Grace which flows through Torrance's theology on its own merit and ground.

I begin in part 1 with 'Objective Grace': that is, with Grace as a movement of the Trinity, expressed in the economy of salvation which moves from the Father through the Son in the Spirit, and in the Spirit through the Son to the Father. Chapter 1 examines the dynamic ground which Torrance's doctrine of Grace finds in the inner life and love of the triune God, while chapters 2 and 3 address the manner in which this Grace is given through the Son and the Spirit. Part 2 of the book builds on the ground laid in part 1 and focuses on how the objective motion of Grace of the Trinity applies to the human person. Thus, part 2 examines the way in which human beings participate in Christ's Sonship through the Holy Spirit. Chapters 4, 5 and 6 examine this participation through the three concentric levels of anthropology, ecclesiology and personal formation in Christ by the Spirit.

Background to Torrance's Theology of Grace

Because of the historical nature of the development of doctrine, the manner in which orthodoxy is articulated is inevitably reactive—that is, it is designed to counter heterodoxy. Consequently, orthodoxy cannot be fully understood unless heresies are understood as well. While the concern of this book is neither to rehearse the doctrinal history of the theology of Grace nor to provide a comprehensive review of various theologies of Grace, before I present a positive account of Torrance's theology of Grace, it will be helpful to bring to light the

29. Though I do suggest that to the degree that others have not taken with sufficient seriousness what Torrance himself judges to be the centrum of theology, many of their critiques will miss the mark and be of diminished value.

versions of Grace which he understands himself to be combating.[30] In undertaking this, we first step back and review Torrance's early thinking on Grace as set forth in his doctoral research, which he commenced at the early age of just twenty-four.[31] This will provide us with a preliminary grid for inspecting the concerns he brings to his analysis of contemporary understandings of Grace.

Torrance dedicated his own doctoral thesis to an exposition of *The Doctrine of Grace in the Apostolic Fathers*.[32] This exposition primarily serves as an apologetic for a New Testament account of *charis* over against a degenerate form tainted—Torrance claims—by understandings of *charis* already present within the Judaistic religion and Hellenistic culture. According to Torrance, this resulted in "the great mistake" of "detach[ing] the thought of Grace from the *person* of Jesus Christ."[33] It is neither our purpose to defend the specific details of Torrance's doctoral thesis nor to exposit its full argument, yet the basic contours are worth observing because as Torrance argues the deficiencies in the understanding of Grace by the apostolic fathers have been echoed throughout the history of the doctrine's development.

---

30. Torrance heavily utilizes patristic and reformation sources in his own exposition, yet the interest of this monograph is not in Torrance as a historian. Therefore, when Torrance's ventures into historical reconstruction are included, they are presented as his own perspective and this present book generally will not attempt to either defend or critique Torrance's historical accounts.
31. While Torrance's doctoral work precedes by as much as sixty years his fully mature writing, there is no evidence that Torrance's thinking on Grace significantly changed over the course of his lifetime. The broad framework was set out early his life through the significance influence of his teachers Hugh Ross Macintosh and Daniel Lamont at Edinburgh and Karl Barth at Basel—not to mention Athanasius and Calvin. McGrath, *Intellectual Biography*, 29–46.
32. T. F. Torrance, *The Doctrine of Grace in the Apostolic Fathers* (Eugene, OR: Wipf and Stock, 1996). Hereafter, *DGAF*. Torrance's doctoral research began in 1937 with a year in Basil studying at the feet of Karl Barth. After multiple interruptions (a one year teaching post at Auburn Theological Seminary in New York [1938–1939], parish ministry in Alyth, Scotland [1940–1943] and service in the war as a military chaplain [1943–1945]), he finally completed his doctoral Rigorosum (examination) in 1946.
33. The purpose of his dissertation is stated in the preface: "It has been the purpose of the dissertation—by inquiring in the literature of the Apostolic Fathers—to probe into the early Christian understanding of Grace and to discern how and why there came about in the history of that doctrine so great a divergence from the teaching of the New Testament" (*DGAF*, v).

The New Testament Doctrine of Grace

Torrance surveys the doctrine of Grace by observing the Greek concept of *charis*, looking at its usage in classical Greek, Hellenistic Greek and Philo, and then examining the biblical concept of Grace through the Old and New Testaments. One of Torrance's key moves is his conviction that "in the New Testament *charis* (*xaris*) becomes a *terminus technicus*." That is, while he recognizes that other meanings of *charis* continue to be used (even in the New Testament),[34] "there is a special Christian sense of the word coined under the impact of Revelation to convey something quite unique."[35] In fact, "*charis* is such a new word . . . that it cannot be interpreted in terms of antecedent roots or ideas."[36] Torrance suggests that Paul actually coins the word *charis* (or at the very least gives it its distinctive sense) as the best term to describe God's self-giving in Jesus Christ through the cross.[37] This fact alone, Torrance asserts, "means that the Christian *charis* completely outdistances its etymological roots. There is doubtless a linguistic but no theological point of contact with *charis* in classical and Hellenistic Greek."[38]

Torrance does note that Paul uses *charis* in both a primary concrete sense and a secondary applied sense.[39] The primary sense of Grace "has to do with the divine act of intervention . . . *charis* is now the presupposition of all man's relations with God and constitutive of the whole Christian life."[40] This alters the entire basis of religion, for it undercuts any notion of divine reward based on ethical achievement.[41]

---

34. Torrance cites several examples of the contemporary usage of *charis* as general divine favor in the gospel of Luke: 1:30; 2:40, 52; 4:22; 6:32, 33, 34; 17:9.

35. *DGAF*, 20. Torrance is certainly not unique in recognizing the newness of Paul's usage of charis in the New Testament. See *Sacramentum Mundi 2*, where Klaus Berger describes *charis* as a sort of missionary slogan developed in particular by Paul.

36. Torrance notes that the LXX chose not to use *xaris* to render the Old Testament *hesed*, and suggests that its contrasting prolific usage in the New Testament indicates it must have undergone a "radical anakainosis" (*DGAF*, 20n2).

37. Ibid., 28.

38. Ibid., 21.

39. Ibid., 28–29.

40. Ibid., 29. Torrance lived in a time when 'man' semantically referred to both men and women. While this book will use inclusive language, for the sake of the integrity of Torrance's own writing, I will not alter the terminology of direct quotations.

Torrance admits that the move from the primary meaning of Grace to Grace in its applied sense "is more elusive." He insists that Grace is never "a transferred quality" or "a private possession," nor can Grace be "pocketed" or "handed on." It always acts upon men and women in an intensely personal manner—"as personal as Christ Himself."[42] Consequently, the Grace-grounded faith issues forth in "an intensely personal life in the Spirit," which Torrance describes as both charismatic and eschatological.[43] While the eschatological character of faith assures the believer that "Christ is his righteousness" such that "no striving will add one iota" to what he is in Christ,[44] Christ's personal presence also evokes personal transformation through a charismatic life in the Spirit.

The Non-Radical Concept of Grace in the Apostolic Fathers

When Torrance turns his attention to the Apostolic Fathers, his contention is that their theology "represents a corrosion of the faith . . . because the basic significance of grace was not grasped."[45] Torrance attributes this situation to the limited circulation of Paul's epistles in those first few generations. Once "its real implications began to be grasped, as in Irenaeus," then things began to change. "But meantime the whole Church had become thoroughly moralistic. Some of the implications of the Gospel, Grace particularly, were never recovered till the Reformation."[46]

In summarizing his evaluation of the Apostolic Fathers, Torrance makes three observations with regard to their faulty understanding of Grace. *First,* Grace was treated as a supplement rather than the ground and substance of the Christian life. Rather than being the decisive

---

41. *GAP*, 24. Torrance does go on to affirm the real place for rewards and punishments in the kingdom (Matt 6:19f; 10:41f; 10:28; Mark 10:21, etc).
42. *DGAF*, 32.
43. Ibid., 34.
44. Ibid., 35.
45. Ibid., 137. Torrance's thesis surveys several manuscripts which he dates from the first half of the second century CE, including: *The Teaching of the Twelve Apostles, The First Epistle of Clement, the Epistles of Ignatius, The Epistle of Polycarp, The Epistle of Barnabas, The Shepherd of Hermas and The Second Epistle of Clement.*
46. Ibid., 136.

motion of God's love and the presupposition of the whole Christian life, Grace was something to be acquired. They did not view the person and work of Christ as "a final act of redemption which undercuts all our own endeavours at self-justification."[47] As a consequence, Grace became related to the *continuance* of the Christian life. This resulted in the loss of the eschatological character that Grace has in the New Testament which sets the believer in a completely new world. As such, "they did not live from God so much as toward Him," and Grace was reduced to an *ad hoc* aid enabling believers to worthily strive after and attain sanctification.[48] Torrance's critiques are scathing and totalized: "The Gospel carries with it an eternal indicative, but post-Apostolic Christianity labored only under an imperative."[49] "[T]he Christian ethic was codified" and "the constraining love of Christ reduced to rules and precepts." The themes of their preaching were "law and obedience, reward and punishment."[50] In short, the Fathers had not slain "the basic urge of man for self-justification."[51]

Second, Grace along with the Holy Spirit was regarded sub-personally, as a force. "Grace was the gift of spiritual energy" that gave the believer understanding of truth and the power to resist evil.[52] Torrance notes that the association of Grace with the Holy Spirit "might not have been so mischievous, were it not for a parallel change in the understanding of the Holy Spirit, which by this time had largely lost the inseparable attachment it has to Christ and His work in the New Testament and came to be thought of in sub-personal fashion as pneumatic power," which could be infused into the worthy believer.[53]

Third, Grace was regarded as a commodity "committed to the care of the Church" as a "precious deposit."[54] Torrance perceives particularly in the writings of Ignatius a way of conceptualizing union with Christ as dependent upon the Church, which like other mystery religions of

---

47. Ibid., 138.
48. Ibid., 135.
49. Ibid., 134.
50. Ibid., 139.
51. Ibid., 134; cf. 137.
52. Ibid., 140.
53. Ibid.
54. Quoted on ibid., 76.

the time was believed to be "full of God."[55] From the Church, the means of Grace could be "dispensed in sacramentalist fashion."[56]

Pre-Reformation Interiorized and Commodified Versions of Grace

Nearly twenty years after the publication of his doctoral thesis we find Torrance repeating essentially the same critiques, yet now the target has broadened from the Apostolic Fathers per se, to the historical foundations which undergird and affect the whole Church of the West—Protestant as well as Roman Catholic.[57] The fundamental error has not changed in that the basic ailment continues to be the detachment of Grace and the Spirit from the person and work of Christ.[58] Once this detachment took hold, Grace and the Spirit collapsed into one another in what Torrance calls "spiritual grace"—that is, independent naturalized principles of pneumatic potency which could be interiorized and commodified.

The gap which this created between this world and the divine realm came to be filled by the Church and her clergy: the Church, as the mystical body of Christ herself endowed with the divine power of Grace; and her clergy, through the Grace causally conferred by virtue of ordination, who mediated divine Grace in what was effectively an ecclesiastical form of semi-Pelagianism. The Church emerged as a continuous extension of the incarnation, mediating the Grace which was entrusted to her and thus functioning as the divinely endowed bridge leading humanity across from nature to supernature.

Within this framework, Grace came to be understood as a *thing* to be ministered through legal definition and control,[59] which required *means* for its administration.[60] Torrance suggests that to the degree that Grace becomes impersonalized as a force, cause, potency or principle, it is likewise indefensibly susceptible to being used, acquired,

---

55. Ibid., 73.
56. Ibid., 141.
57. "The Roman Doctrine of Grace from the point of view of Reformed Theology" (*TRn*, 169–91).
58. Torrance notes that only twice in the NT is grace brought into connection with the Spirit: Heb 10:29 and Jas 4:6. Otherwise, the primary referent is Jesus Christ (*TRn*, 172).
59. Ibid., 179.
60. Ibid., 172.

achieved and earned. The legalistic expression of Grace resulted in a multitude of definitions and formulae for various applications and cases so that Grace would be properly dispensed. Whether the results can authentically be traced to Augustine is not important for our purposes.[61] What matters is that eventually Grace became *paired* with merit in such a way that Roman theology came to differentiate between "external and internal Grace," "actual and habitual Grace," "the Grace of operation and the Grace of co-operation," "sufficient Grace and efficacious Grace," and the like.[62] Torrance notes that the intention was simply to distinguish between Grace that is given and Grace that is actualized. However, the net effect was instead a distinction between free Grace and conditional Grace, for they introduced an element of co-operation and even co-redemption into the Creator-creature relation.[63]

The pietistic mystical commodification of Grace led to a notion of Grace which inheres in the human soul and affects even the physical human being. As Grace actualizing itself within the human creature, "created Grace" or "ontological Grace" elevates the creature to the "higher ontological order" of a "supernatural existence."[64] In this regard, Torrance finds particular fault with Basil's suggestion that Grace is a transferrable quality from human to human, such that "human souls who have Grace conferred on them by the Spirit may themselves emit Grace to others."[65] This clearly indicates a "weakening of the doctrine of grace," in which Grace itself is detached from God's

---

61. As a general rule, Torrance perceives a correlation between the proliferation of definitions and controls (i.e. legalism) and the growth of Pelagian notions of merit and duty (ibid., 179). While sincerely affirming that Augustine deserves the title of 'supreme doctor of grace', Torrance asserts that "his view of Grace as the interiorizing of a divine power within us, the inspiring of goodwill and the implanting of an ability to will and perform what is commanded in the divine law" has had "baleful" results (ibid., 173-74). According to Torrance, this aspect of Augustine's teaching on grace is "semi-Pelagianism in its heart."

62. I recognize that each of these 'kinds' of Grace is loaded with theological, contextual and historical meaning. Our purpose here is not to debate or exposit the details of these, but simply to note Torrance's concern that they introduce confusion into nature of the Creator-creature relation.

63. Ibid., 174.

64. Ibid., 180.

65. Cf. ibid., 225, where Torrance references *De Spiritu Sancto* 9.23. Torrance points out that this suggestion by Basil is in direct contradiction to Basil's own belief that the Holy Spirit must be divine in order to mediate any participation in the grace of God "for only God is a source of grace."

self-giving and replaced by a notion of mutuality between the creature and God—"and with it all the Arian and Pelagian notions of created grace and merited grace that go along with it."[66] In that last resort Torrance remarks, "Roman theology appeared to be subordinated to a philosophical ontology," and "a consistent system of ideas tended to displace real and historical conversation with the living God."[67]

Post-Reformation Return to Grace

Torrance praises Reformed theology for its rejection of the notion of 'created grace' or 'connatural grace,' which was inherent in the conception of the sacramental universe and for its embrace of the biblical framework of the covenant of Grace. This he suggests had the effect of restoring to theology the "dialogical" and "intensely personal" character, which is befitting to an understanding of Grace as a real living relationship with the triune God.[68]

Torrance perceives the crucial Reformed insight to be the rethinking of Grace as "an indivisible whole and a living reality interpreted through the *homoousion*."[69] It is this move in particular which he views as the critical corrective to the Church's proliferation of Graces.[70] For Torrance, the application of the *homoousion* to Grace is to recognize Grace as "the one indivisible self-giving of God in Christ."[71]

Yet in spite of these positive advances Torrance is quick to point out that the same errors and problems which plagued the Church before the Reformation reemerged afterwards; indeed Protestantism has shown an uncanny ability to replicate its own counterpart to nearly every flawed version of Grace which it opposes in Romanism. Torrance targets three particular snares which tend to besiege Protestantism: tendencies towards pietistic subjectivism, impersonal determinism and abstract extrinsicism.

66. Ibid., 225.
67. Ibid., 178.
68. Ibid., 176, 181.
69. Ibid., 190.
70. Ibid., 182-83.
71. Ibid., 225. I will address in more specifics the subject of the application of the term *homoousios* to grace in chapter 3.

Consequently, it was not long before the Reformed return to Grace suffered its own 'fall from Grace': Grace transmuted from its proper setting as the gift of the self-giving of God in Christ and Spirit was unwittingly co-opted for humanistic and pietistic purposes. Torrance assigns responsibility for these specious forms of "Protestant subjectivist pietism" to a tangled multiplicity of sources: "notions of common Grace, Arminian notions of Grace, and the blending of 'the Grace of the Spirit' with the graciousness of the godly or the infused sanctification that the Westminster theology is so infected with."[72]

Subjectivistic and impersonal tendencies were accentuated and hardened by the dogmatic location where Grace was assigned within Protestant theology. Torrance notes the observation of Risto Saarinen, that while the Grace of God certainly continues to be a central theme, "contemporary Protestant dogmatics rarely treats the doctrine of grace as a chapter in its own right."[73] Torrance suggests that this reduction of Grace to the status of servant within the doctrine of justification was an attempt to correct the Mediaeval way of thinking of Grace instrumentally as means or end. While the Reformers recognized the inappropriateness of the categories of means and end, by reacting against the instrumentalization of Grace they solidified the functionality of Grace even more by reducing Grace to a subcategory of justification. As a result, Grace became strongly identified with the forensic language of acquittal and the extrinsic model of imputation.

In view of this confusion and misuse of the doctrine of Grace throughout the history of the Church, Torrance made it his deep and life-long concern to rescue the doctrine of Grace from the incessant pull of naturalism and legalism. What Torrance offers is a Protestant Reformed way of conceptualizing Grace—not as a doctrine sublated to anthropology or to justification but as the core of the gospel itself—in a way that involves *all* of God and *all* of human persons. This trinitarian form of Grace is neither inherent to the creature by nature, nor is it definitive of the Creator-creature relation merely because the human

---

72. *Reply to Critics*, Q27.
73. Risto Saarinen, *Religion Past & Present: Encyclopedia of Theology and Religion*, ed. Betz, H. D. (Leiden, Brill, 2007), 556.

is a sinner. Grace rooted objectively in the divine life and love is the very ground of the human's being, God's free, personal (pre)covenanted favor.

It is the argument of this book that this self-giving-for-participation movement of triune Grace functions as *the* presuppositional and all-encompassing context materially undergirding and methodologically guiding the formulation of all of Torrance's theology. Like leaven, Torrance's concept of Grace permeates the whole and forms the basis upon which all other doctrines have their sustenance.

T. F. Torrance and the Revival of Trinitarian Theology in the Last Decades of the Twentieth Century

In the final two decades of the last century, a massive shift took place in English-language theology, whereby "trinitarian doctrine came to be considered not a problem but a resource." No honest account of this resurgence of trinitarian doctrine could be narrated that did not view T. F. Torrance's contribution as fundamental.[74] From the 1950's forward, Torrance was a powerful and consistent force to be reckoned with.

Indeed, the 'comeback of trinitarian theology' is evident in the plethora of treatises, commentaries, articles and applications of 'trinitarianism' that have inundated the market during the last twenty years of the twentieth century and which shows no sign of abating as we continue through the twenty-first. In a competitive milieu where it is fashionable to be 'more trinitarian than thou,' the doctrine is appealed to and coaxed into shoring up both sides of just about any contested issue faced by contemporary theology with the Trinity serving as a 'model' for anything to which one can attach the number

---

74. John Webster, "Thomas Forsyth Torrance, 1913–2007," *Biographical Memoirs of Fellows of the British Academy* 13 (2014): 430. Torrance wrote three primary works on the Trinity: *The Trinitarian Faith* (1988); *Trinitarian Perspectives: Toward Doctrinal Agreement* (1994); and *The Christian Doctrine of God* (1996). He personally was most pleased with *The Trinitarian Faith* (Michael Bauman, *Roundtable Conversations with European Theologians* [Grand Rapids, MI: Baker Book House, 1990], 117). While his major writings on the Trinity did not appear until well after his retirement in the 1980's and 1990's, the essential structure of all Torrance's dogmatic thinking and teaching was thoroughly trinitarian.

'3.' The bandwagon of trinitarianism has spawned a mixed bag of theologians establishing their own relevance through creative (and not-so-creative) attempts to rescue the doctrine of the Trinity from irrelevance![75]

In contrast to many, Torrance did not approach the Trinity as a doctrine to be 'used' or 'made relevant,' but as a reality around which all else must find its center:

> It is not just that the doctrine of the Holy Trinity must be accorded primacy over all the other doctrines, but that properly understood it is the nerve and centre of them all, configures them all, and is so deeply integrated with them that when they are held apart from the doctrine of the Trinity they are seriously defective in truth and become malformed.[76]

Through his own attempt to think through the implications of all things in relation to the triune God, Torrance has provided discriminating and helpful controls for the church. There is the consistency and depth with which Torrance undertook this task, and there is also his methodological and scientific commitment to critical realism. One area within Trinitarian theology which is notorious for creating problems and spawning theological disagreement is exactly how the axis between God *in se* and God *pro nobis* is to be navigated. Post-Rahnerian theology has tended toward denial of any meaning to the immanent life of God apart from salvation history.[77] Similarly, social-trinitarian impulses act to blur the distinctions between creaturely and uncreated categories. For Torrance, such "historical positivism cannot be Gospel."[78] In this season of overabundance and 'trinitarian theology gone wild,' Torrance has done some important groundwork for the flourishing of theological reflection on the Trinity

---

75. Catherine LaCugna's statement is a case in point: "the doctrine of the Trinity is ultimately a practical doctrine with radical consequences for the Christian life" (Catherine Mowry LaCugna, *God For Us: the Trinity and Christian Life* [New York: Harper, 1993], 1).
76. *CDG*, 31 (italics added).
77. Catherine Mowry LaCugna's *God For Us: The Trinity and Christian Life* is a case in point.
78. *CDG*, 6.

by charting out a ground and grammar[79] which has proven instructive to multiple theologians across a variety of doctrinal loci.[80]

Torrance's abiding significance to the discipline of Trinitarian theology is exemplified in the recent publication, "Trinitarian Theology after Barth," in which no other post-Barth theologian receives more references than Torrance.[81] The long-term relevance of Torrance's trinitarian theology is largely the result of his methodology. Torrance was a traditionalist in the deepest sense of the word. His great concern was to mine, recover and display the theological foundations of the Gospel as discovered by the best representatives of the early church. For this reason, Torrance did not spend a lot of time interacting with modern theologians. Even Barth only gets three very brief passing mentions in Torrance's major treatise on the Trinity, *The Trinitarian Faith*. Rather, Torrance's points of reference tend to be classical—especially patristic—texts. In the estimation of John Webster, "Torrance was ... the British *ressourcement* theologian." As such, he was "a performer of the Christian tradition, not a composer."[82]

---

79. Fred Sanders describes Torrance's important role within this resurgence as that of a 'restrictor.' (Fred Sanders, "The Image of the Immanent Trinity: Implications of Rahner's Rule for a Theological Interpretation of Scripture" [PhD diss., Graduate Theological Union, 2001]).

80. One important example is John Webster, who explicitly follows Torrance's trinitarian approach in how he reads Scripture as an item in the divine economy: "the centre of a theology of the canon must be an account of the action of Father, Son and Spirit" (John Webster, *Word and Church: Essays in Christian Dogmatics* [Edinburgh: T&T Clark, 2001], 28–29).

81. *Trinitarian Theology After Barth*, ed. Myk Habets and Phillip Tolliday (Eugene, OR: Pickwick, 2011).

82. John Webster, "Editorial," *IJST*, 10, no. 4 (Oct 2008): 370. While he does not mention Torrance directly, Stephen Holmes has critiqued the late twentieth-century trinitarian and patristic revival as less a return to the Fathers than a rehearsal of contemporary preconceptions and commitments (Stephen R. Holmes, *The Holy Trinity: Understanding God's Life* [Milton Keynes: Paternoster, 2012]). Jason Radcliff argues that Torrance is not guilty of Holmes' charge and points out that Holmes and Torrance are doing substantially different things: "Holmes exposits the Fathers whereas Torrance reconstructs the Fathers" (Jason Radcliff, "T. F. Torrance in the Light of Stephen Holmes's Critique of Contemporary Trinitarian Thought," *Evangelical Quarterly* 86, no. 1 [2014]: 28). Torrance's project is less historical theology than it is constructive systematic theology and as such he offers "a Christologically conditioned reconstruction of the Fathers in light of the Reformed and evangelical tradition" (ibid., 37). This difference leads to discrepancies between Torrance and Holmes in their respective readings of the patristic material as well as their construction of the patristic era in general. In the final analysis, Radcliff argues the two approaches complement one another.

Torrance and the Orthodox East

It is this quality of Torrance's—his vigorous commitment to return to the well of the patristic fathers—that allowed him to be the catalyst around whom dialogue with the Eastern Orthodox church could not only build mutual trust and appreciation, but also create a space for critical engagement. Torrance masterfully drew upon the best elements of the Orthodox church as material for his critiques and correctives of the Roman and Protestant churches, while at the same time reminding (and boldly reframing for) the Orthodox what he deemed to be the most important aspects of their own theology and practice.[83] Most prominent and persistent was his continued plea for a "Christological correction" of the doctrines and Ministry of the Church in accordance with "the essential nature and form of the ancient Catholic Church."[84] Torrance's vision was for "the rehabilitation of Nicene theology and of theological thinking in Britain" through the vehicle of a fresh and thorough engagement with the Ancient Creeds and Councils. To achieve this end, closer relations and dialogue with the Orthodox Church would be essential to the task.[85]

The exchange Torrance developed with Eastern Orthodoxy was informal and personal, decades before it became formalized in 'dialogues' and publications. Many students including George Dragas travelled from Greece to Edinburgh to study under the guidance of

---

83. George Hunsinger notes the impact which Torrance's engagement with the Eastern Orthodox has had on their own theology: "Like the Roman Catholic reception of Barth by Balthasar and his heirs today, the contemporary Orthodox reception of Torrance's construal of Barth and his legacy . . . is testimony to the ecumenical character of Torrance's theology and its immense promise for the future" ("Forward," *T. F. Torrance and Eastern Orthodoxy*, ed. Matthew Baker and Todd Speidell [Eugene, OR: Wipf & Stock, 2015], iv).

84. T. F. Torrance, "The Foundation for Hellenism in Great Britain – The Orthodox Church in Great Britain," in *Texts and Studies*, vol. 2, ed. Methodios Fouyas (London: Thyateira House, 1983), 254.

85. Ibid., 255. Torrance argued that an inherent similarity existed between the Reformed tradition and the Orthodox churches, arguing that the Reformed Church is essentially a prophetic movement of reform within the Catholic Church, and simply sought "to restore to it the face of the ancient Catholic and Apostolic Church" (*Conflict and Agreement in the Church: Volume I: Order & Disorder* [London: Lutterworth, 1959], 76). Torrance's appropriation of Eastern Orthodox theology in order to enrich his own Reformed tradition bears similarities to the way in which Hans Urs von Balthasar "raided Barth" in order to re-shape and enrich his own Roman Catholic theology (George Hunsinger, "Forward," *T. F. Torrance and Eastern Orthodoxy*, ed. Matthew Baker and Todd Speidell [Eugene, OR: Wipf & Stock, 2015], iii).

Torrance[86] and his friendship and influence extended to such important figures as George Florovsky, John Zizioulas, Methodios Fouyas, Chrysostom Constantinides, Constantine Dratsellas, Nikos Nissiotis, Angelos Philippou and many others.[87] Such was Torrance's appreciation and respect within Orthodox circles that he was given the unprecedented title of "honorary protopresbyter" by the Greek Orthodox Patriarch of Alexandria, Nicholas VI.[88]

These relationships, forged and faithfully nurtured over several decades along with his official position as Moderator of the Church of Scotland (1976–77), placed Torrance in the unique position among Western theologians of being able to initiate an official international Reformed-Orthodox dialogue. Perhaps unlike other ecumenical dialogues, the conversations Torrance engaged in were always marked by their *dogmatic* weightiness. This has led to a significant deepening and refining of trinitarian theology among both Eastern and Western theological traditions.[89] While one might be tempted to conclude that the dialogues were fruitless—since the conclusions of the official dialogues were never adopted by the holy synods of the Orthodox autocephalous churches—this conclusion would fail to recognize the organic (unofficial) development of theology and theologians. Perhaps the truest test of the value and significance of someone's work is not so much what took place during their lifetime but how that work is carried on into the future. Orthodox scholars continue to find that direct engagement with Torrance's theology is an important discipline and this fact is testimony to the magnitude of Torrance's impact on trinitarian theology well into the twenty-first century.[90]

86. Matthew Baker, "Interview with Protopresbyter George Dion. Dragas regarding T. F. Torrance," *T. F. Torrance and Eastern Orthodoxy*, ed. Matthew Baker and Todd Speidell (Eugene, OR: Wipf & Stock, 2015), 2–3.

87. Ibid., 8.

88. Methodios Fouyas presented Torrance with the pectoral cross of a protopresbyter to mark the occasion. Matthew Baker, "The Correspondence between T. F. Torrance and Georges Florovsky (1950–1973)," *T. F. Torrance and Eastern Orthodoxy*, ed. Matthew Baker and Todd Speidell (Eugene, OR: Wipf & Stock, 2015), 319.

89. It was Torrance's suggestion that any Orthodox and Reformed theological dialogue should begin with the doctrine of the Trinity and proceed from there. See the "Minutes from the visit of the delegation from the World Alliance of Reformed Churches to the ecumenical patriarchate in Istanbul, July 26–30, 1979" in the Thomas F. Torrance Manuscript Collection. Special Collections, Princeton Theological Seminary Library, Box 170.

Torrance and the Catholic and Protestant West

Torrance's impact on late twentieth century and early twenty -first century trinitarian theology is also evident in the fact that his writings consistently continue to appear in the bibliographies of contemporary theologians.[91] In a volume of essays entitled, "Trinitarian Theology After Barth," no less than 10 of the 16 essays draw on Torrance directly.[92] It is widely recognized that Karl Barth is the most influential theologian of the modern era. If Karl Barth were to be considered a "father" of the church (as some have suggested), then Torrance might be thought of as his adopted son. Torrance's role as one of Barth's leading interpreters and his significant part in making Barth more accessible to the English speaking world, is undeniable. Torrance himself rejected the label of "Barthian," declaring instead that if anything he should be recognized as an "Athanasian."[93] Like many, Torrance follows in Barth's footsteps both as a faithful disciple and a developer and refiner of Barth's thought. Both impose tremendous dogmatic weight upon the second article, yet Torrance's theology does so with a more integrative and more thoroughly personal dynamism than Barth's—and therefore loses sight of the first and third articles less often. Indeed, trinitarian theology 'after Barth' would not be nearly as grounded were it not also 'after Torrance.' The uniqueness and significance of Torrance's incorporation of and fluency with each of the major streams of the Christian Church are reflected in the following comments by Fr. George Dragas:

> [T. F. Torrance is] a theologian who is at the same time Orthodox, Catholic and Reformed because he seeks to build up his theology on the one, historical common ground of all three traditions and because he is prepared at the same time to confess in full modesty and sincerity their historical particularities and fortify himself only with their positive

90. See the recently published volume, edited by Matthew Baker and Todd Speidell, *T. F. Torrance and Eastern Orthodoxy*. "The theological dialogue begun by this great Scotsman and his Orthodox friends ought to continue, and move to a deeper level" (Matthew Baker, "Introduction," x).
91. Colin Gunton, Ray Anderson, Myk Habets, Fred Sanders, and Thomas Weinandy to name but a few.
92. Edited by Myk Habets and Phillip Tolliday (Eugene, OR: Pickwick, 2011).
93. See Michael Bauman, *Roundtable Conversations with European Theologians* (Grand Rapids, MI: Baker Book House, 1990), 111.

forces. Is this not what ought to be commended today across the boundaries of the Christian traditions when Patriarch and Pope and Reformed theologian have been united in reminding the world about the Gift of God's boundless Love, Grace and Truth in and through Christ and His Church?[94]

Whether one affirms or opposes Torrance's formulations, history is proving the fact that Torrance's trinitarian theology is a force that must be reckoned with by those who seek to do trinitarian theology in the century that follows Karl Barth. Theologians certainly exist who by ignorance or choice do not engage with Torrance's trinitarian theology, but these are exceptions to the rule.[95] What one may miss by neglecting Torrance perhaps most significantly is his doctrine of Grace as reflected in the pages of this book. The best theologians in the coming decades will be those who have read, understood and appreciated Torrance, and who then demonstrate a capacity to integrate his thoughts into their own projects in ways that are constructive, respectful and creative.[96]

94. George Dion. Dragas, "The Significance for the Church of Professor Torrance's Election As Moderator of the General Assembly of the Church of Scotland," ΕΚΚΛΗΣΙΑΣΤΙΚΟΣ ΦΑΡΟΣ LVIII, no. III–IV (1976): 226.
95. Robert Jensen is a prime example. Neither in his book, The Triune Identity, nor in his two volume Systematic theology, does he draw on T. F. Torrance at all.
96. John Webster is a case in point.

PART I

The Objective Agent
in Grace—
the Triune Persons

There is only one grace . . . and one Spirit. . . , for God himself in the fullness of his triune being is present in all his acts of creating, revealing, healing, enlightening and sanctifying.[97]

For Torrance, Grace is the self-giving of the life and love of God (a self-giving which arises out of God's own eternal fullness as Father, Son and Spirit), so that his creation might share in a creaturely way the *koinonia* of the triune life.

In the first part of this book, chapter 1 will examine the dynamic ground Torrance's doctrine of Grace finds in the inner life and love of the triune God, while chapters 2 and 3 address the manner in which this Grace is given through the Son and the Spirit in the economy of salvation.

97. T. F. Torrance, *The Trinitarian Faith: The Evangelical Theology of the Ancient Catholic Church* (Edinburgh: T&T Clark, 1995), 328–29.

1

The Motion of Grace from the Trinity

> The Holy and blessed Triad is indivisible and one in himself. When mention is made of the Father, there is included also his Word, and the Spirit who is in the Son. If the Son is named, the Father is in the Son, and the Spirit is not outside the Word. For there is one grace from the Father fulfilled through the Son and in the Holy Spirit.[1]

The triune God exists eternally in the fullness of his life and love. The extension of this triune life and love beyond itself is a creative act, a mission whose sole purpose is to share God's life and love with that which is other than God.

The following chapter on the immanent Trinity is laid out in three progressive sections. Because it might not be self-evident for some readers as to how Torrance can speak with any level of confidence regarding the immanent Trinity, we begin with a discussion of the source and nature of knowledge of God. For Torrance, the source of revelation is the triune God himself, and the nature of the triune revelation is that it establishes and invites participation. From here we give our attention to the perichoretic tri-unity of the Godhead, noting that for Torrance "there is only one divine activity" and "there

---

1. Athanasius, *Ad Ser.*, 1.14.

is only one grace."[2] Torrance emphasizes that for Grace to be conceived properly the unity must be seen *through* the Trinity—that is, through the intrinsic personal relations. Thirdly, we consider creation, grounded in Torrance's doctrine of God, as a free and non-compelled movement of Trinitarian Grace which has its purpose and origin in the love of God. In creation, God establishes an all-embracing framework of Grace within which and through which he shares with human beings the fellowship of his love.

The Source and Nature of Knowledge of God

On what basis and by what right do we speak of God? For Torrance, knowledge of God is utterly dependent upon a dynamic movement of divine Grace. Only God can properly and fully reveal God. Thus, our only access to God in his internal relations is through the Father-Son relation revealed in the incarnation. Because this self-revelation takes place ontologically in the creaturely sphere, true knowledge of God is both objectively possible and objectively controlled by this concrete actuality. This means that knowledge of God has its ground in the Christ-event, which in turn sends us back to God himself in the tri-unity of his immanent life. Thus, knowledge of God comes from the Father, through the Son in the Spirit and returns to the Father through the Son in the Spirit. Caught up in the all-encompassing context of this gracious movement, knowledge of God takes place *within* the context of the active presence of God; Grace is known from *within* Grace. The entire universe is stamped by the order and pattern of this Grace, which by nature makes knowledge of God inescapably personal and requires of the would-be knower personal participation in the gracious movement of God in his triune relations.

This chapter begins with a discussion of revelation and its source not for the purpose of laying out the history of revelation or of offering a full account of Torrance's doctrine of revelation, but with a much

---

2. Thomas F. Torrance, *The Trinitarian Faith: The Evangelical Theology of the Ancient Catholic Church* (Edinburgh: T&T Clark, 1995), 309; Hereafter, *TF*. *TF*, 328–29; Cf. Thomas F. Torrance, *The Christian Doctrine of God: One Being Three Persons* (Edinburgh: T&T Clark, 1996), 108. Hereafter, *CDG*.

more modest goal: simply to note that for Torrance all discussion of the immanent life of God arises from God's revelatory acts in the economy, and that the acts of God in the economy are grounded in the immanent life of God. Describing the manner in which this gracious movement of God among creatures takes place involves a complex web of interdependent, mutually reinforcing concepts. There are six major epistemological moves that Torrance commonly makes. These moves are not sequential but operate in a dynamic back and forth movement where each move acts as both a ground for and a result of the others in the web.[3] While Torrance does not slavishly make all these moves every time he makes one of them, each move is implicitly present in and with the others and forms the basic structure of his thought. Our purpose in this context is not to offer yet another comprehensive analysis or description of Torrance's epistemology,[4] but to point out the way the logic of Grace permeates the manner in which he orders his doctrine of revelation. Torrance's major epistemological moves are:

1. The Christ-event reveals the Father-Son relation.[5]
2. The motion of Grace of the Father-Son relation revealed in the Christ-event is the epistemological and ontological axis between the Creator and creatures.
3. The Father-Son relation revealed in the Christ-event is one which falls within the life and being of God and is revealed to be a triune perichoretic reciprocal relation.
4. The Father-Son relation revealed in the Christ-event is the form and content of the triune Grace of God.

---

3. Torrance's epistemology is heavily influenced by Michael Polanyi. Cf. *Personal Knowledge: Towards a Post-Critical Philosophy* (London: Routledge and Kegan Paul, 1958); and "The Place of Michael Polanyi in the Modern Philosophy of Science," *Transformation and Convergence in the Frame of Knowledge: Explorations in the Interrelations of Scientific and Theological Enterprise* (Grand Rapids: Eerdmans, 1984), 107–73.

4. See especially Morrison, *Knowledge of the Self-Revealing God*; and Kruger, "Participation in the Self-Knowledge of God."

5. Torrance uses the phrase *Christ-event* as a way of referring to the "indivisible whole" of "the Word made flesh . . . which includes the life, teaching, death, and resurrection of Jesus Christ." Torrance, *Conflict and Agreement in the Church*, vol. 2: *The Ministry of the Sacraments of the Gospel* (London: Lutterworth, 1959), 156. Hereafter, *C&A2*.

5. The entire natural universe is stamped by, and caught up in, the order and pattern of this gracious movement of the triune God.

6. Knowledge of God takes place within the movement of Grace and is thus inescapably personal, requiring personal participation. This order/pattern of Grace extends to all our forms of knowing.

Unpacking this set of concepts will occupy the following section of material.

The Christ-Event Reveals the Father-Son Relation

The first epistemological move focuses on the Father-Son relation revealed in the historical actuality of the incarnate Jesus Christ. God "crosses the boundary between himself and us" personally and uniquely in this concrete form, a form in which the Son knows, is known by, and makes known the Father: "*No one knows the Father except the Son and anyone to whom the Son chooses to reveal him.*" (Matt 11:17) Jesus Christ is the actual embodiment of "the mutual knowledge which the Father and the Son have of one another."[6] For Torrance, the epistemological significance of the Father-Son relation revealed in the history of Jesus cannot be over-emphasized.

Of greatest interest epistemologically for Torrance in the Christ-event is this: the mutual relation of knowing it reveals between the Son and the Father and the Father and the Son implies a corresponding mutual relation in being. The Son is only the Son in relation to the Father, and the Father is only the Father in relation to the Son. "Knowledge of God the Father, then, and knowledge of God the Son are coincident."[7] As the eternal Son Jesus is the image of the Father, to see him is to see the Father (John 14:9). Furthermore, this mutual relation of being, Torrance asserts, is "not only between the eternal Son and the Father but between the incarnate Son and the Father."[8] In the human history of Jesus the eternal Word of God becomes personal

6. *TF*, 55.
7. Ibid., 60.
8. Ibid., 59.

event among us. This means that the presence and revelation of the Son in our space and time is at the same time the revelation of the Father, for the Son is (and always was) the eternal Word (mind and rationality) of the Father. Thus, to know Christ is to know God, for Christ (the Son) is the Word and mind of the Father. In other words, on the creaturely side of the Creator/creature divide, there is one (the Son) *who not only knows God, but is God as one of us ontologically.* Thus, "the mutual relation of knowing and being between the Father and the Lord Jesus Christ constitutes the ontological ground for our knowing of God, for in and through it our knowledge of God the Father is objectively rooted in the eternal being of God himself."[9] This critical principle for Torrance is expressed by Athanasius' dictum, "It is more pious and more accurate to signify God from the Son and call him Father, than to name him from his works and call him Unoriginate."[10]

The Epistemological and Ontological Axis

Because the motion of Grace of the Father-Son relation revealed in the Christ-event contains both a mutual relation of knowing and of being, it constitutes an exclusive and controlling epistemological and ontological axis between the Creator and creatures.[11] That this relation of knowing and being is the controlling central axis represents a second fundamental move in Torrance's epistemology. The motion of Grace in the event of Jesus Christ is properly described as the epistemological and ontological *central axis* because it is the one point of contact "grounded both in the reality of God and in the realities of our world."[12] As the one *place* in our space and time which spans both sides of the Creator/creature divide, creaturely truthful knowledge of God is given objective possibility. As such, the movement Grace takes in the Christ-event operates for Torrance as a kind of scientific control within the web of theological doctrines, and Torrance's careful and deliberately *scientific* attention to this movement could appropriately

9. Ibid., 59.
10. Athanasius, *Con Ar.* 1.34; Cf 1.16.33; *De decr.* 31.
11. *CDG*, 30.
12. Ibid., 30.

be described as "the science of grace."[13] As a field of knowledge, theology must operate, according to Torrance, under strict scientific controls appropriate to the uniqueness of its object. Theology's object is a subject who gives himself to be known in the historical actuality of the incarnate Jesus Christ, and thus theological knowledge pivots upon that which is *given*.[14] "Theological thinking," Torrance reminds us, "is *theo*-logical, thinking not just from our own centres, but from a centre in God, from a divine ground."[15] God and his Grace towards us always comes first.[16] "A real revelation of God to us must be one which God brings about through himself."[17] Thus, the first principle which Torrance adopts following the Church Fathers, and in particular Irenaeus, is the maxim *"without God, God cannot be known."*[18]

This represents the great epistemological divide for Torrance governing everything else in the Christian faith.[19] Jesus is the "exclusive language of God to mankind" and also the "faithful response in knowledge and obedience of humanity to God."[20] As Jesus is "the one place in space and time" which embodies the mutual knowing of the Father and the Son, and the only "revelation of God in which he himself is its actual content," all "doctrinal statements about God are possible and true only when Christologically grounded" and thus bear this "Christological pattern."[21] In Jesus Christ, God identifies himself as "the Father, the Son and the Holy Spirit." This self-identification is not accidental to God's being, but intrinsic. That is, *Trinity* is not just a "way of thinking about God," but is *what and who* God actually and intrinsically is, "and cannot be truly conceived otherwise."[22] The form and shape of the objective reality of the being of God gives form and

13. Thomas F. Torrance, *Theological Science* (Oxford: Oxford University Press, 1969), 281.
14. Ibid., 32. Cf. Thomas F. Torrance, *Space, Time and Resurrection* (Edinburgh: T&TClark, 1998), 72–73. Hereafter, *STR*; Thomas F. Torrance, *Transformation and Convergence in the Frame of Knowledge* (Grand Rapids: Eerdmans, 1984), 294. Hereafter, *TCFK*.
15. Ibid., 29.
16. Thomas F. Torrance, *Theology in Reconstruction* (Grand Rapids: Eerdmans, 1965), 9. Hereafter, *TRn*.
17. *CDG*, 77.
18. *TF*, 54. For Torrance's discussion of the exclusivity of God's self-naming in the Old Testament, see *CDG*, 121–24.
19. Thomas F. Torrance, "Karl Barth and the Latin Heresy," *SJT* 39 (1986), 464. Hereafter, *Latin Heresy*.
20. *CDG*, 17.
21. Ibid.
22. Ibid., 15.

shape to the range of statements and actions which can be truthfully said and done in reference to that object. The uniqueness of the Christ-event as the "great axis" makes it *materially* non-substitutable.[23] As such, Torrance asserts, "The one trinitarian way of thinking of God forced upon us through the incarnation calls into question and sets aside at the same time any alternative way of thinking of him. . . . To admit any other than a trinitarian way of thinking about God is . . . to set aside the Gospel."[24]

This exclusive epistemological and ontological central axis of revelation revealed in the person of Christ is the means by which "we have access by one Spirit unto the Father" (Eph 2:18). In Torrance's view, this "amounts to the greatest *revolution in our knowledge of God*."[25] In an effort to explore this center "in all its depth,"[26] Torrance borrows the concept of a stratified understanding of truth from Einstein and Polanyi. In doing so, Torrance is not seeking to impose an alien epistemological theory upon our knowledge of God but simply "to articulate the stratified way our knowledge of God has actually emerged as a result of our encounter with Jesus Christ."[27]

The Three Levels of Theological Knowledge

Torrance's stratified structure of theological knowledge is articulated in three levels.[28] While each level moves farther up the scale of theological abstraction and formalization, this increase in refined conceptuality is not at the expense of its grounding in concrete reality. One never leaves behind the hard factuality of the history of Jesus but rather penetrates ever more deeply into it in an effort to grasp "reality in its depth."[29] In reflecting upon knowledge of God in a stratified way, one sees how the concrete form of Grace revealed in the incarnate

---

23. *TS*, 273.
24. *CDG*, 24.
25. Ibid., 3.
26. Thomas F. Torrance, *The Ground and Grammar of Theology* (Charlottesville: University Press of Virginia, 1980), 35. Hereafter, *GGT*.
27. Ben Meyers, "The Stratification of Knowledge in the Thought of T. F. Torrance," *SJT* 61, no. 1 (2008): 15.
28. *CDG*, 84.
29. *G&G*, 35.

history of Jesus Christ provides the ontological and epistemological axis around which knowledge of God arises in a circular, back-and-forth pattern which corresponds to the form or motion that Grace has taken.

The first level of theological knowledge concerns the way Grace meets us in ordinary religious experience; in the intuitive and informal apprehension of God through our basic Christian involvement within the worship, teaching and fellowship of the Church.[30] Here we encounter Jesus Christ through a threefold act in which God turns towards us as Father, Son and Spirit. We recognize the Grace of the Lord Jesus Christ, the love of God the Father and the fellowship of the Holy Spirit yet not in a way that we can spell out clearly or comprehensively.[31]

In the second level of knowledge, which Torrance refers to as the theological (or scientific) level of the economic Trinity, we come to see that in God's threefold self-giving "revelatory and ontological factors are indivisibly integrated."[32] Here we grapple with the recognition that in our evangelical experience with Jesus Christ and the Spirit "we have to do directly with the ultimate Reality of God."[33] We recognize that the incarnate Jesus Christ spans both sides of the Creator/creature divide and is thus the *epistemic bridge* between humans and God, grounded in the Being of God yet also anchored in the being of humanity. At this level, the epistemological and ontological axis of the Christ-event is given expression through explanatory terms like *hypostatic union* and *homoousion* in order to reflect the relation of being and agency between Jesus Christ and the Father.[34] Here the basic insight is that "what *Jesus Christ* is toward us . . . he is inherently in himself in his own divine Being."[35] In short, *Jesus is God*.

Finally, in the third level, which Torrance calls the higher

---

30. Ibid., 156–57.
31. *CDG*, 89.
32. Ibid., 92.
33. Ibid., 99. Torrance claims this movement from the evangelical to the theological level is the kind of movement which took place at the Council of Nicaea.
34. Cf. *CDG*, 93.
35. Ibid., 99.

theological level of the ontological Trinity, we have the recognition that *God is Jesus Christ*. As with the transition from the first to the second level, the transition from second to third level is made again via the truth of the *homoousion* and its "cognate conception," the *hypostatic union*.[36] The insight here is that "what God is toward us in Christ Jesus, he is inherently and eternally in himself in his own Being."[37] As a result, we can say, *God is Jesus*; and we can have real, objective knowledge of God.

Torrance repeatedly reminds us that the immanent relations of the ontological Trinity must continually undergo what he calls "cross-level coordination" if they are to serve a refining function for the rest of the doctrinal corpus. Cross-level coordination functions as a system of 'checks and balances' in which theological concepts (levels two and three) are guarded from mythological projection by being empirically correlated with the actual history of Jesus and the ground level of our evangelical experience (level one). We do not leave behind either the economic Trinity or our evangelical experience of the triune God, nor can we do so and continue to remain in the truth. The necessity of this move is theologically secured for Torrance by the doctrine of the ascension in which the human and divine Jesus is taken up into the very heart of the Godhead and "belongs for ever[sic] to the ultimate Truth of the one Triune God." The doctrine of the Trinity has "its material content" in and through "the crucified Jesus, risen again, and now forever lodged in the heart of the Triune Being of God."[38] The purpose of theological reflection upon the ontological Trinity is therefore not a movement away from Jesus, but a movement further *into* Jesus. Thus, Torrance asserts that we must approach God simultaneously from below (what God is toward us: the economic acts of Christ and Spirit) and from above (what God is in himself: the ontological Trinity): "for it is in the light of what we learn from below that we appreciate what derives from above, and in the light of what

36. Cf. *CDG*, 94, 98, 101; *G&G*, 165.
37. *CDG*, 99.
38. *CDG*, 110.

derives from above that we really understand what we learn from below."[39]

This stratified structure is misunderstood if it is imagined to be a pyramid-like edifice, constructed by objectively-minded scientific theologians seeking to create order and simplicity out of the messy details of history.[40] For Torrance, the stratified structure cannot be properly understood "from the bottom upward, but [only] from the top downward in accordance with God's self-revelation to us."[41] While the truth may be empirically derived from below as we encounter God in the history of salvation, in fact it is ontologically constituted from above. "This transcendent origin must not be forgotten even when . . . we may begin from below with our basic experience and knowledge of God."[42] Thus, the purpose of the second and third levels is "to relate Jesus Christ and our redemption in and through him intelligibly to the inner life of God," for without an objective referent in God, Torrance observes, "faith withers away."[43] At present, our immediate task is to consider the ontological Trinity from which the Christ-event receives its grounding from above.

The Life and Being of God is a Triune Perichoretic Reciprocal Relation

The third important epistemological move Torrance makes is the recognition that the motion of Grace in Jesus Christ is fundamentally a triune perichoretic movement. While the order of knowing begins with Christology, Christology itself is intrinsically Trinitarian in form and content: the Son is only the Son in relation to the Father and the Spirit. As such, the doctrine of the Trinity (both the economic Trinity and the ontological Trinity) arises from the Christ-event. In addition, Torrance's understanding of the Father and the Spirit is inseparably

39. Ibid., 114.
40. *G&G*, 171–72; Cf, Meyers, "Stratification," *SJT* 61, no. 1 (2008): 10.
41. *CDG*, 87.
42. Ibid.
43. Ibid., 91.

bound to the historical event of Jesus Christ. Because of this Torrance is best described as a 'Christocentric Trinitarian.'[44]

With regard to the relation of Christology to the doctrine of God, Torrance wants to establish two points. In sum, we only know the Father and the Spirit through the Son, and we only know the Son within his relation to the Father and the Spirit. First, our knowledge of the Father and the Spirit is controlled by and grounded in our knowledge of the Son: we only know the Father and the Spirit through our knowledge of the Son. This is Torrance's second point: we do not know the Son in isolation from the Father and the Spirit, for there is no independent Son to know. God is only known as a whole, that is, as Trinity. "Knowledge of the Father, knowledge of the Son, and knowledge of the Holy Spirit cannot be separated from one another, for God is known only through the one movement of self-revelation from the Father, through the Son and in the Holy Spirit."[45] This recognition—of the oneness between the economic Trinity and the transcendent or ontological Trinity—calls for a "thorough refinement" of all our theological doctrines.[46]

The essential truth here which calls for a reorganization of our theological thinking is that the incarnation falls *within* the life and being of God. "While the incarnation falls within the structures of our spatio-temporal humanity in this world, it also falls within the Life and Being of God."[47] The economic activities of the triune God are not external activities to God's being, but are the very being of God in action.[48] If the concepts of the *homoousion* of the Son and the Spirit, along with the *hypostatic union*, are truly allowed to govern our thinking, we will have to speak also of *perichoresis*—the mutual containing, coinhering or co-indwelling of the triune persons. By these terms we give articulation to the recognition that "the coinherent relations of the Father, the Son and the Holy Spirit, revealed in the

---

44. Thomas F. Torrance, *Theology in Reconciliation: Essays Towards Evangelical and Catholic Unity in East and West* (reprint; Eugene, OR: 1997), 241. Hereafter, *TiR*.
45. *TF*, 204.
46. *CDG*, 107.
47. *GGT*, 160.
48. Cf. *TiR*, 236–37.

saving acts of God through Christ and in the Spirit, are not temporary manifestations of God's Nature, but are eternally grounded in the intrinsic and completely reciprocal relations of the Holy Trinity."[49] In order to emphasize this critical point, Torrance even coins a new term—*onto-relations*—in order to complement perichoresis while emphasizing more forcefully that these eternal relations are *being-constituting* relations.[50] The consequences and importance of this affirmation cannot be underestimated. Because of the mutual indwelling of Father, Son and Spirit, in Jesus Christ we are actually in touch with God and thus with "the trinitarian relations of love immanent in God."[51] These *perichoretic* relations are the "ultimate constitutive relation in God" and thus constitute "the ground upon which the intelligibility and objectivity of all our knowledge of God finally repose."[52] Thus, a refinement here opens the way for "a thorough refinement of all our theological beliefs and truths."[53] Consequently, Torrance has applied much of his theological muscle to this point, in an effort to uncover the very 'ground and grammar' of the entire theological enterprise.[54]

The Form and Content of Triune Grace

The next epistemological move for us to consider makes explicit what has been implicit until now in our discussions: the form and content of God's Grace *is* a dynamic *perichoretic* triune relation. In the previous move our concern was the intrinsically triune (perichoretic) nature of the Christ-event and that the incarnation falls within the being of God; in this move our focus is the form and content of the Grace we have come to know through the Christ-event. We can also restate this again using terminology which echoes our discussion of the stratification of knowledge.[55] In the former we spoke at the level of the economic

49. *CDG*, 102.
50. Cf. Lee, *Union*, 70.
51. *CDG*, 108.
52. Ibid., 107.
53. Ibid.
54. Myers, "Stratification," 11. Cf. *CDG*, 31.
55. See p. 9ff.

14

Trinity, showing how Jesus Christ is the expression of the triune Grace. Here we speak at the level of the ontological Trinity to show how the triune Grace is expressed (perichoretically) in Jesus Christ.

The triune perichoretic relations have a particular form or movement which is expressed in the Father-Son relation. The coinherent relations of the Trinity are not external to God's acts in the economy; they *are* the acts. Thus, when God communicates himself to us, it is *as* and *through* himself that he communicates. The communication (revelation) does not come from another source or ground, but *in* and *through* the reciprocal relations of the triune God. In other words, "divine revelation is intrinsically trinitarian in its content, movement and structure."[56] The action of revealing and the being of the revealer are one and the same; form and content coinhere in one another. Thus, another of Torrance's central maxims: *"the Gift and the Giver are of one and the same Being."*[57]

To 'follow the way of Grace,' theology requires a dynamic way of thinking which is reflective of the circularity of the movement of Grace itself. In this movement, "all exposition moves from God to God, from his revelation to us back to himself, and from himself to his revelation, from what he is for us to what he is in himself, and from what he is in himself to what he is for us."[58] For Torrance, this cross-level coordinating movement is necessary because God's self-revelation "is a self-enclosed *novum* which may be known and interpreted only on its own ground and out of itself."[59] All this means that in a faithful account of the doctrine of the Holy Trinity "our thought cannot but engage in a deep circular movement from Unity to Trinity and from Trinity to Unity."[60]

Torrance considers Athanasius's description of the pattern of God's interaction with us (*"from the Father, through the Son and in the Spirit and to the Father, through the Son in the Spirit"*) to be an exercise in

---

56. *CDG*, 32.
57. Ibid., 21.
58. Ibid., 28.
59. Ibid., 27.
60. Ibid.

cross-level coordination at its finest. Athanasius sought to coordinate the pattern taken in the history of Jesus with the inherent order of the triune relations in the Godhead. The result was the development of an organic structure in theological understanding of God that is "at once Christocentric and theocentric."[61] For Torrance, this organic pattern that Athanasius discerned is the very form of Grace itself. Grace has a form and content: the onto-relational perichoretic triune movement from the Father through the Son in the Spirit, to the Father through the Son in the Spirit. Torrance's claim is that there is no other movement of God than this circular movement; therefore all God-talk (i.e., *theology*) must adhere to and be grounded in this movement.

The Order and Pattern of the Natural Universe

The next move we must consider in Torrance's epistemology has to do with the relation of the order or pattern of triune Grace and the natural universe. Here, as with each of our preceding observations, it is the act of God in the economy through Jesus Christ that provides "a basic clue . . . of the essential pattern of truth."[62] In Trinitarian terms, since there is no other movement of the triune God than that which is *from the Father, through the Son and in the Spirit and to the Father, through the Son in the Spirit,* this same dynamic provides the context and ground of the entire created universe. While it is outside of the scope of this project to offer a full analysis of Torrance's engagement with natural theology, we will briefly consider five implications for the natural universe followed by a short introduction to his "new natural theology."

First, all created existence is brought into being by the triune movement of Grace. As Grace is a gift, it implies both an otherness and a continuous contingence in creation.[63] Second, this otherness and contingence extend to all aspects of the created order, such that even creation's inherent intelligibility is conferred upon it by God's

---

61. *TiR*, 251.
62. Ibid., 260.
63. Ibid., 219.

free determination. Third, the rationality of creatures participates in a mutable and dissoluble fashion in the transcendent rationality of God *only by God's Grace*. Fourth, this participative rationality, which is only by Grace, runs deep within the very fundamental structures of the created order. Torrance asserts, creation "must be regarded not only as having taken place through the Logos but *in* the Logos which nevertheless remains utterly transcendent over it all."[64] Thus, while the order and rationality which God gives to creation are not necessary or inherent, *by Grace they are natural*. Order is derived from the Logos.[65]

Finally, it is worth observing that this movement of thought reflects Torrance's rejection of any kind of cosmological or epistemological dualism and is simply the application of his refusal to abstract form from being, or structure from substance. This again is his way of faithfully following "the way of grace."[66] Creation and redemption share the same center of reference (*skopos*). In reaching back to the creative center in God, an integrating light is thrown upon all theological relations and connections.[67] "The entire universe of visible and invisible, celestial and terrestrial, realities is a cosmic unity due to the all-embracing providential and integrating activity of the divine Logos, so that a single rational order pervades all created existence contingent upon the transcendent rationality of God."[68] By Grace, the order of the Logos freely pervades his creation.

Torrance's *New* Natural Theology

Torrance's approach to the relation of nature and Grace is sometimes referred to as his "new natural theology." While vigorously rejecting traditional natural theology and its attempt to ground humanity's being in an *analogia entis* between Creator and creature, Torrance also rejects a simplistic dialectical relationship between nature and Grace (and creation and redemption) which would pit them as opposite poles

---

64. Ibid. Italics added.
65. Ibid., 263.
66. Ibid., 250.
67. Ibid., 256.
68. Ibid., 258.

over against one another.[69] What makes Torrance's approach unique within much of Reformed theology, and of particular relevance to our proposal, is not so much his articulation of this relation in christological (creation/covenant) terms, but his choice of metaphorical descriptors. Thus, rather than describing the relation between creation and covenant such that the covenant is seen "as the inner ground and form of creation, and creation is seen as the outer ground or form of the Covenant,"[70] Torrance prefers to shift the metaphor away from static spatial terms ('inner/depth'; 'outer/ surface') to the more dynamic language of the 'downward motion of Grace', which is revealed and fulfilled in Jesus Christ. It is from within this *dynamic perspective*, which as we will come to see has its source in his concept of trinitarian Grace that Torrance affirms the Reformed outlook which posits a distinction without a dichotomy and which challenges the notion, embedded in traditional natural theology, of reversibility in the relations between God and humanity. Torrance speaks of this "non-dichotomous distinction" as the irreversible relation of Grace which is not explainable from the side of the creature. It is this "logic of grace,"[71] which sets the basic terms for Torrance's 'new' natural theology.

The relation between God as such and creation is not inherent, but is based purely upon the gracious decision of God. It is a God-determined relation of *covenant-correspondence*.[72] Thus, by Grace, God gives

---

69. Torrance follows Barth in his general approach to natural theology, and the relation of creation to God as an *analogia relationis* (not *entis*). See p. 42, "Analogy of Relations–All of Creation bears the imprint of the Trinity." While both would agree that a traditional natural theology which claims that God can be known outside of faith and apart from revelation must be rejected, Torrance departs from Barth's absolute opposition by claiming that natural knowledge of God can be known, *albeit by Grace as well*. This affirmation, that there is a natural form of knowledge which is freely grounded in Grace, creates space for science to do its work reliably within an intelligible universe. Barth would not accept this claim on the basis that "any claim to knowledge of God based on the intelligibility of the universe could just as easily be knowledge of the devil as knowledge of the triune God." (Paul Molnar, "The Role of the Holy Spirit in Knowing the Triune God," in *Trinitarian Theology After Barth*, ed. Myk Habets and Phillip Tolliday [Eugene, OR: Pickwick, 2011], 4).

70. *TS*, 68. Cf. CD 3.1.§41.

71. Ibid., 206–7. The technical way Torrance uses *the logic of Grace* will be discussed in chapter 2, *Downward (Hypostatic Union): 'The Word became flesh. . .'*

72. Ibid., 68. Torrance also refers to Barth's expression "created correspondence" in *The Christian Frame of Mind: Reason, Order and Openness in Theology and Natural Science*. (Colorado Springs: Helmers and Howard, 1989), 23. Hereafter, *CFM*.

humanity the intelligence and authority to dominate and order the rest of creation. Yet that primacy and dominion cannot migrate from the "realm of nature" to the "realm of grace" for Grace "is neither explainable from the side of the creature nor logically definable."[73] In both realms, "man is created and called to be a partner in covenant with God, to be a subject in communion with God, to live in dependence upon Him and in obedience and love toward him."[74]

It is on this basis that Torrance asserts that natural theology is a denial of Grace, for it determines to gain knowledge of God apart from Grace. Furthermore, since the created order exists by Grace and is thus an object of Grace (which is to posit an irreversible relation), Torrance condemns natural theology as fundamentally unscientific: "natural theology may offer the greatest hindrance to natural science and to scientific theology alike."[75] Thus, for Torrance, the problem with natural theology is methodological, not metaphysical.[76] Torrance happily affirms that there is "a form of natural knowledge" in which God may come to humanity *through* nature. What he rejects is the idea that God comes to humanity *by* nature, and so he strongly asserts that true scientific theology rejects any "attempt to treat 'natural theology' as a foundation upon which positive theology can be made to rest, or to use it as a criterion by which to assess the content of what we apprehend through divine 'revelation.'"[77]

---

73. Ibid., 66.
74. Ibid., 68–69.
75. Ibid., 103.
76. Torrance spent much of the 1960's in an exploration of the methodological relations between the natural sciences and Christian theology. Although he "remained anxious to show the continuity of this work with that of his Basel teacher," this engagement in the field of 'theological science' "took him beyond anything that Barth had attempted." (David Fergusson, "Torrance as a Scottish Theologian" in *Participatio: Journal of the Thomas F. Torrance Theological Fellowship*, vol. 2 [2010], 84).
77. Ibid., 104. Torrance's approach to natural theology separates him in significant ways from Pannenberg's claim that "Dogmatics . . . cannot begin directly with the reality of God" (*Systematic Theology 1*, 61). Where Pannenberg starts with a human generated notion of God, and builds a series of rational arguments on that starting point, Torrance (with Barth) begins with the reality of God revealed in his Word and by his Spirit as an act of witness (see CD 1.2, 817f). Torrance describes the form theology takes as most properly "recognition-statements," which is to say that genuine theological knowledge begins in acknowledgement and, as such, is neither creative nor inventive (*G&R*, 182).

Knowledge of God Requires Personal Participation

The final critical epistemological move which Torrance makes concerns the extension of this order or pattern of triune Grace to all our forms of knowing. We do not think autonomously, but in participation with Christ in the Spirit. This participation in the movement of Grace is grounded in the historical actuality of the incarnate Jesus Christ and becomes lived in us through the present activity of the Spirit.

As I have already noted, for Torrance, theological knowledge is impossible apart from the incarnation. Yet the type of theological knowledge which the incarnation yields is not simply the *revelation* of theological knowledge, but also its *reception*. The incarnation provides the establishment of both a revelation of truth *to* humanity and a reception of truth *by* humanity.[78] Thus, for Torrance, the fundamental content of revelation is two-fold: the objective reality of the Word revealed in the incarnate Christ *and* the subjective actualization of the reception of that Word in the obedient Humanity of Christ.[79] The same Spirit in and through whom the incarnate Christ lived his life of communion with the Father now draws us into participation in this same triune movement of Grace. While the Christ-event is the established source of the 'grammar of Grace', and the exclusive objective ground of the possibility of our knowledge of God it remains apart from the present activity of the Spirit, only a possibility for us. Torrance calls the Spirit's activity in the actualization of this participation "the epistemological relevance of the Spirit."[80]

I will have more to say about knowledge of God in later chapters. At this point my purpose is simply to gesture towards the general contours of Torrance's thought by highlighting the significance of Jesus's obedient humanity in communion with the Father, and our pneumatic repetition of that communion through a corresponding participation in the triune movement.

78. Ibid., 51.
79. *CDG*, 147ff.
80. Thomas F. Torrance, *God and Rationality* (Edinburgh: T&T Clark, 1997), 165–94. Hereafter, *G&R*.

Conclusion

The task of this book is to display the organizing role that Grace plays in Torrance's theology; to analyze its inner consistency; and to consider its usefulness both for understanding Torrance's theological project and for Christian living. In section 1 I have begun with a consideration of the source and nature of knowledge of God in which I have sought to show the relation of God's revelatory and reconciling acts in the economy to the immanent life of God. I have observed that knowledge of God is utterly dependent upon a dynamic triune movement of divine Grace. The controlling center of this knowledge is the Christ-event and its revelation of the Father-Son relation.

In the next section I will consider Torrance's doctrine of God proper: the immanent Trinity. What follows will be neither an historical analysis of the development of the doctrine of the Trinity, nor a comprehensive exposition of Torrance's theology of the immanent life of God. Rather, the focus of attention will be on Torrance's assertion that "there is only one divine activity," and I will demonstrate the way in which this principle is fundamental to his theo-logic of trinitarian Grace.

The Godhead's Processions

Torrance's main argument in this section centers on the essential unity of God's self-giving. Rather than approaching the three and then the one, or the one and then the three, Torrance insists upon approaching the "Trinity in unity and unity through the Trinity," asserting that "there is only one divine activity" and "there is only one grace."[81] This approach secures for Torrance the fundamental grounding point that the Gift and the Giver are identical, for it means that God's word and act inseparably inhere in God's being. Since God is encountered in his being and activity together, Trinitarian language is most helpful (and least speculative) when its primary concerns are ontological and soteriological.

81. *TF*, 309; *TF*, 328–29.

From this standpoint, Torrance emphasizes that it is critical that the Trinitarian employment of the concepts of *ousia* and *hypostasis* be understood *through* the lenses of *homoousios* and *enhypostasis* and not apart from them. That is, the unity must be approached through the Trinity, such that *ousia* consists of intrinsic personal relations, and the *hypostaseis* are understood *perichoretically*, as distinct ontologically-constructed relations. In Torrance's understanding, this was the Nicene solution which sought to avoid the problems generated by the Cappadocian constructions. The critical issue for Torrance is to secure the basic point that the gift of the love of God is the gift of God *himself*, the very God who is love. This self-gift, and nothing else, is Grace. Misunderstandings at this point have implications for how both the East and the West have traditionally been led to conceive of Grace.

Naming the Terrain: the Case for "a Measure of" Apophatic Ontology

From Torrance's perspective, to speak of the immanent life of God is to traverse upon holy ground.[82] The claim that, as finite creatures, we can have objective knowledge of the immanent Trinity raises many questions. First and foremost, how much of the economic Trinity can be read back into the immanent Trinity? Torrance speaks emphatically, and typically without qualification, that the God we know in Jesus Christ is the only God there is. And yet, when pushed for further clarification, he draws limits as to how far back into the immanent being of God one can read the acts of God in the economy. It is just these limits that Torrance finds missing in the kind of collapsed ontology represented in Rahner's axiom "the economic Trinity is the immanent Trinity and the immanent Trinity is the economic Trinity."[83]

Torrance cautions that the more concretely we conceptualize a

---

82. Thomas F. Torrance, *Trinitarian Perspectives: Toward Doctrinal Agreement* (Edinburgh: T&T Clark, 1994), 87. Hereafter, *TP*.

83. Karl Rahner, *The Trinity* (London, 1970), trans. J. Donceel, 317–401. By collapsing the distinction between the immanent and the economic Trinity, one simultaneously collapses the distinction between God and this world. With Barth, Torrance views the proper relation to be one of correspondence such that there is a 'unity-in-distinction', but not a 'dialectical identity.' Again, with Barth, the economic Trinity is secondary and contingent upon the immanent Trinity which

oneness between the immanent Trinity and the economic Trinity, the greater the need for "a real measure of *apophatic theology* grounded in the *homoousion*." That is, while Torrance boldly affirms that what God is towards us and for us in the incarnation he is inherently and antecedently in himself, he also stresses that in order to correctly understand what this means, "we must learn what is proper to read back into the eternal Being of God and what is not proper to read

is primary and constitutive. "God would be no less God if he had created no world and no human being" (CD 1/1: 139).

This 'breach' in the use of Rahner's rule indicates a watershed departure within various doctrines of the Trinity. Three significant Protestant theologians, Moltmann, Pannenberg and Jungel, all fall on the far side of Torrance and Barth at this point. Moltmann, in his attempt to secure the unity of the divine life by means of the doctrine of perichoresis, not only leaves himself open to tritheism, but views 'God for us' and 'God in himself' as two sides of the same coin. God's eternity is simply a transcendent dimension of history. (Moltmann, *The Trinity and the Kingdom* [New York: Harper & Row, 1981], 151). Pannenberg, for his part, locates God's immanent life in a relation of teleological contingence upon history. God's unity is "realized in relation to the world." (*Systematic Theology*, vol. 1 [Grand Rapids: Eerdmans, 1991], 445). God in himself is not perfect and self-sufficient, but in some sense codependent with the world. Such Hegelian sensibilities lead Pannenberg to write, "[God] has made himself dependent on the course of history." (Pannenberg, *Systematic Theology*, vol. 1 [Grand Rapids: Eerdmans, 1991], 129). Jungel also fails to resist the slide from a 'unity-in-distinction' to 'dialectical identity'. Whereas for Barth and Torrance, the Trinity's self-repetition in history is a free and non-necessary movement, Jungel surrenders the Trinity's eternal antecedence such that "God's being is in coming." (Jungel, *God's Being Is in Becoming* [Grand Rapids: Eerdmans, 1983], 380). God only becomes himself ("comes to himself') by coming to, or with, man. Accordingly, Jungel asserts that God cannot be thought of as God "without thinking of him simultaneously as the Crucified" (39).

Over against such 'radicalizers' of Rahner's Rule, Torrance functions necessarily as a 'restrictor'. While Torrance is clear that the economic Trinity is more than simply "a real reflection" of God's life *in se* (CDG, 198), his affirmations are measured: the economic "is grounded in . . . , inseparable from . . . , and actually flows from" the immanent. (CDG, 198). Where Rahner would assert that the immanent is inseparable from the economic, and Moltmann would argue that the immanent flows from the economic, Torrance refuses to reverse the relationship. And yet, as Fred Sanders points out, Torrance also refuses to push God's freedom *in se* so far that we speculate counterfactually on what God might have done had he not done what he did. Such hypothetical arguments, which Sanders detects in Molnar (Sanders, *The Image of the Immanent Trinity: Implications of Rahner's Rule for a Theological Interpretation of Scripture*, [Dissertation, GTU, 2001], 196), would call into question the revelatory authenticity of God's acts in Christ and the Spirit "so that in fact God remains ultimately unknown to us" (CDG, 199).

For a fuller discussion of Torrance's use of the *homoousion* in the context of Rahner's rule, see "Theological Problems with Identifying Grace as Homoousion" in chapter 3 (pp. 132–41). There I specifically compare and contrast Torrance's approach with that of both Rahner and Barth, demonstrating that Torrance's theology of Grace provides a framework which offers important restrictions as well as clarity to the relation of the economic and immanent Trinity. In short, while Torrance enthusiastically affirms that the economic Trinity must be the "norm for all our thought and speech about God," he cautions against the undifferentiated way in which Rahner himself puts his maxim to use. (*Trinitarian Perspectives*, 78) Rahner reverses the downward flow of Grace "on the altar of a transcendentally subjective natural theology" (190). Barth also contradicts the flow of Grace by pushing Grace back into the immanent life of God as one of the perfections. In Torrance's view, both teeter on panentheism at this point. (see also chapter 1, "How: in Freedom" [p. 37].)

23

back."[84] Torrance clarifies that this does not imply a preference for a negative theology over a positive one, for that would suggest that God's acts in the economy are simply accidental to his eternal being. Rather, the centrality and normativity of the *homoousion* anteriorly grounds all apophatic impulses in the *positive* affirmation that the incarnation falls within the life of God. Torrance calls this kind of *homoousion*-grounded apophatic knowledge "the positive ineffability of God."[85] It is positive in that God really does make himself known to us through the Son and in the Spirit. It is also positive in that through the Son and in the Spirit God opens us up and out for union and communion with himself.

It is worth noting that the ontological implications of this "positive ineffability" of the *homoousion* can be helpfully differentiated with reference to the Son or the Spirit. As one takes the *homoousion* of the *Son* seriously, the economic Trinity is related to the ontological Trinity in such a way that we have secure grounds to assert that what God is towards us he really is in himself; and that who God is in the internal relations of his transcendent being is the same Father, Son and Spirit who encounters us in his revealing and saving activity. In addition, as one takes the *homoousion* of the *Spirit* with the same seriousness, all dualist structures of thought (often manifested in social Trinitarian constructions) which would separate God's energies from his essence are abandoned. The activity of the Spirit *is* the real presence of God directly bearing upon us. It is often under-appreciated that Torrance's pneumatology, which is robustly informed by the *homoousion*, actually leads to the full integration of his Trinitarian theology with his doctrine of Grace, thereby forming the spring from which all other doctrines have their source.

And yet the positivity of this *homoousion*-grounded apophatic knowledge is also ineffable, for our minds are unable to grasp God's infinite transcendence, and the participation in God into which we are drawn is a communion that far exceeds the limits of our finite creaturely existence. However, Torrance's *apophatism* is not blind

---

84. *TP*, 85.
85. Ibid., 87.

vacuity, but the super-abundance of life. It is an *apophatism* of plenitude; not a sheer abstract plenitude, but the infinite dynamic fullness of personal loving communion. Thus, for Torrance, the call for apophatic restraint is not the same thing as crying 'mystery'; rather, it is part of the gospel. It is, as we shall soon see, an integral and necessary aspect of his theology of Grace.

Constructing a Soteriological Apophatic Ontology of Grace[86]

Two aspects of this super-abundance of life ground and orient Torrance's theology of Grace in a register that is at once soteriological and ontological. First, the ground and source of all God's ways and works in creation and redemption go back to the love that God is in his innermost being as God. There is no antecedent ground which might explain God's being or actions other than this. There is no triune life behind the love of God which is not also this very same love.[87] God's life *is* his love. "His Love is his Being in ceaseless triune movement and activity."[88] For Torrance, this is the very heart of the gospel—this love is *who* God is. God's *is-ness* is an ever-living and acting communion of loving and being.

This leads to Torrance's second fundamental orientation point: God *is* as he *does* and *does* as he *is*. In God, being and action completely cohere; there is no separation. Thus 'God *is* love' (a statement of *being*) and 'God *loves*' (a statement of *action*) are equivalent statements, for the love that God gives is *himself*. That is, the one who is eternally loving in himself, and whose love moves unceasingly within his eternal life as God, *loves through himself.* For God to love is for God to give himself. These two points (that God is a communion of love and that God gives himself), when taken together, enable Torrance to assert that the gift

---

86. Stanley Grenz makes a helpful distinction between an *onto-theology* built upon a narrative which assumes Greek metaphysics and a *theo-ontology* grounded in the God's trinitarian self-revelation. See Stanley J. Grenz, "The Named God and the Question of Being: A Trinitarian Theo-Ontology," *The Matrix of Christian Theology Volume 2* (Louisville: Westminster John Knox, 2005), 119.
87. *CDG*, 108.
88. Ibid., 5.

(of the love of God) is identical with the giver (the God who is love) of the gift.

We can consider both of these points simultaneously by posing and answering the question, "What is the eternal triune motion and how should it be described?" According to Torrance, the eternal triune motion is "the Communion of his own eternal Life and Love."[89] This communion, while containing differentiation and diversity, is not divisive or dividable. It is ever and always only *one* life and *one* love. When this communion of life and love 'moves' beyond itself, what 'moves' is the very communion. When this communion reveals itself and gives beyond itself, what is revealed and given is the very same communion. The love-gift *is* the Giver-who-is-love. This can be said only if God's being inheres in his acts such that there is only one divine activity and not three. Thus, the eternal divine activity is the movement of this love, and Grace is the movement of this love outside of God's-self. Torrance's ontology of Grace is built upon his ontology of the triune life and love. To put it another way, the one activity *in* God of love is the one activity *of* God of Grace. Or, more tersely, the love *in* God is the Grace-gift[90] *of* God. Grace, by definition, is nothing less (or more) than the *self*-giving of God. When laid out in this fashion, one begins to see the foundational building blocks which make up Torrance's ontology of Grace.

There is One Divine Activity

So how does Torrance go about relating the one to the three and the three to the one? Again, our purpose here is not to summarize Torrance's complete theology of the Trinity, but to note a few of the key concepts which play a significant role in his theology of Grace. These include his careful attention to the terms *ousia* and *hypostasis*, which are properly understood within and through the Nicene *homoousion*. According to Torrance, within Nicene orthodoxy, *ousia* and *hypostasis* undergo a "profound reconstruction" from their traditional

89. Ibid., 220.
90. I use the phrase *Grace-gift* to emphasis that Grace is the gift of God's love *ad extra*.

usage within Greek thought. For Torrance, the resulting clarity and refinement of these terms open the way for "a thorough refinement of all our theological beliefs and truths."[91] In fact, these terms become foundational to the way Torrance views the dynamic movement of triune Grace. It is important to understand how they function in Torrance's theological framework and doctrine of God, which we do now by examining how Torrance distinguishes his "Nicene Athanasian" view from that of the Cappadocians.

It is well known that Torrance unashamedly claimed Athanasius as his theological mentor and hero.[92] What attracts Torrance to Athanasius is both his theological conclusions and the stratified way in which he arrives at these conclusions such that soteriological and ontological factors are integrated throughout.[93] Athanasius begins with the saving and revealing acts of God in the incarnation. This leads him to a recognition of the oneness of being between the Father and the Son, and then finally to the ultimate ground of this oneness in the immanent Trinity.[94]

By Torrance's account, it is the theology of Athanasius which fundamentally 'wins out' at Nicaea and thus underlies its creedal formulations. However, in Torrance's view the important nuances of Nicaea have not been sufficiently appreciated. Particularly relevant are Torrance's critiques of the Cappadocians's conceptualization of the triune life. In his estimation, their theological motivations are approached in a distinctively devotional style reliant upon "doxological and liturgical arguments," rather than out of the same deep soteriological and ontological convictions as those of Athanasius.[95] While not all the Cappadocians shared all of these views and some even changed their positions over time, noting the

---

91. *CDG*, 107.
92. Questions have been raised as to the historical accuracy of Torrance's reconstruction of Athanasius's theology at several levels. For the purpose of this proposal, I will not try to prove or defend Torrance's position, though it should be recognized that scholars are of differing opinions here.
93. *TF*, 263.
94. Colyer, *How to Read*, 292f; Cf. *CDG*, 83ff.
95. *TF*, 313–14.

viewpoints which Torrance finds conceptually costly will help illuminate his doctrine of Grace.

The basic fault in the Cappadocian formulation was that they operated with a more abstract generic model of the *ousia* of God (*physis* [φύσις]), and thus excised the real meaning of the *ousia* of God as *"being in its internal relations."*[96] Because they separated *ousia* and *hypostasis* into two different levels—one generic and one particular—all the pressure of describing the relations of the persons fell to *hypostasis*, and all the pressure of describing the being of the Godhead fell to *ousia*. In this way, the Cappadocians united the three *hypostaseis* through the *monarchia* of the person (*hypostasis*) of the Father.[97]

In the end, Torrance faults the Cappadocian formulation as seriously ambiguous, for while it intended the rejection of subordinationism, this "non-subordinationism" was secured by the imposition of a hierarchical structure within the Godhead. For Torrance, this represents a "strange lapse" from the Nicaean notion of the unity and triunity of God and consequently a theological shift in approach which "opened up the way for serious misunderstanding and division."[98]

Personalist Ontology and Dynamic Soteriology

It is our task now to follow the train of Torrance's logic of Grace and note how *he uses core concepts to relate the one to the three and the three to the one.* By attending to these core concepts and the various nuances associated with them, one can grasp the divine ontology, which underlies Torrance's theology of Grace. In contrast to the Cappadocian

---

96. Ibid., 317.
97. On this critique of the Cappadocians (and St. Basil in particular), George Dragas suggests that Torrance was reacting more against the explicit position of John Zizioulas rather than the implicit position of the Cappadocian Fathers. Zizioulas claimed, "rather unwarrantedly" in Dragas' opinion, that the person (*hypostasis*) of the Father is the cause of the common divine *ousia*, thus subordinating the divine ousia to the *hypostasis* of the Father. As Dragas points out, nowhere does Basil teach that the person of the Father is the cause of his own essence. (Interview with Protopresbyter George Dion. Dragas regarding Torrance in *T. F. Torrance and Eastern Orthodoxy: Theology in Reconciliation*, ed. Matthew Baker and Todd Speidell (Eugene, OR: Wipf & Stock, 2015), 16–17. It is for this reason that Radcliff suggests Torrance's critique of the Cappadocians says more about the 1980s than the 380s. (Jason Radcliff, "Torrance and Reformed-Orthodox Dialogue" in *T. F. Torrance and Eastern Orthodoxy*, 46.)
98. *TF*, 319.

approach, Torrance advocates a personalist, dynamic, soteriological ontology as the basis for developing adequate theological thought: that is, theological thought which relates the unity to the Trinity and the Trinity to the unity, while resisting the slide into preconceived abstract metaphysical concepts. From Torrance's perspective, this is the Nicene solution, properly conceived. How does this play out in Torrance's theological conceptual network?

The Divine *Ousia* is *Enhypostatic Ousia*

In order to correspond with the reality of the object and to maintain conceptual clarity, Torrance insists that *ousia* and *hypostasis*, as theological terms need to be viewed *through* homoousios and *enhypostasis*, and not apart from them. Doing so recasts the way *ousia* is used in theological language, from a kind of static *is-ness*, to *being* "in respect of its internal reality" (which may indeed be dynamic).[99] It recasts the way *hypostasis* is theologically understood: from *being* as 'independent subsistence' to *being* in its "objective otherness" (which, necessarily, is defined by relatedness).[100] Rather than distinguishing *ousia* from *hypostasis* through categories of the general and the particular, they can be understood either as *being* considered in its internal relations or inward reference, or as *being* considered in its otherness or outward reference.[101] In other words, each of the persons may be considered "absolutely *in se* as *ousia* and relatively *ad alium* as *hypostasis*."[102] God's being, his *ousia*, is not isolated *ousia*, but is *ousia* for others. That is, God's *ousia in se* is *ad alios*. "For God to *be*, is to be for himself in himself, that is, . . . to be *for one another* in the onto-personal relations of the Holy Trinity."[103] Thus, God's being is inherently communion, "being-for-others" or "being-who-loves."[104] The divine *ousia* is *enhypostatic ousia*. It is not a physical substance, nor is it an

---

99. *CDG*, 130.
100. Ibid.
101. Torrance notes that this is a distinction expressed by G.L Prestige, *God in Patristic Thought* (London, 1952).
102. *CDG*, 131.
103. Ibid.
104. Ibid., 104.

abstract essence (as the unfortunate Latin translations, *substantia* and *essentia*, suggest); rather, the most fundamental revelation we have is that the being of God is essentially personal, dynamic and relational.[105]

Eternal, Reciprocal, Being-Constituting Onto-Relational Personhood

It is here that the concept of *perichoresis* is so helpful, for it effectively holds *homoousios* and *enhypostasis* together under one dynamic conceptual umbrella. Perichoresis asserts on the one hand the full equality of the three, while on the other hand it affirms the real distinctions between them through their hypostatic relations with one another.[106] *Perichoresis* reinforces the fact that God makes himself known to us through himself and in himself as a whole—i.e., as Father, Son and Holy Spirit.[107] Torrance argues that if we get *perichoresis* right, it is clear that the Godhead is constituted not by the Father only, but also in the Son and Spirit. The Monarchia is the interlocking of "Unity and Trinity, Trinity and Unity."[108] The Spirit proceeds, not from the Person (*hypostasis* or *prosopon*) of the Father, but "from the Community of Being of the Father and the Son, or from the Communion (*koinonia*) between the Father and the Son, which the Holy Spirit himself is, and the three Divine Persons are."[109] As I have noted, because of this intrinsic wholeness, we can only speak of the Trinity by engaging in a deep circular movement from Unity to Trinity and from Trinity to Unity. "God is known only in a circle of reciprocal relations."[110] There is

---

105. Ibid., 124; Cf. Ibid., 104.
106. For Torrance's discussion on the origin of the term and its irreversible migration from Christology to Trinity, see *CDG*, 102ff.
107. Ibid., 173.
108. Ibid., 185.
109. Ibid., 192. Torrance's own convictions on how to articulate the procession of the Spirit from the Father and the Son appear to have developed over time. In his 1959 *SOF* he writes, "He is God Himself personally present in this way, distinct from His Person as Father and distinct from His Person as Son, and yet as proceeding personally from the *person* of the Father and the *person* of the Son in the unity of the One God, and in the indivisible operations of the Trinity." (*School of Faith* [London: Camelot, 1959], xcvii. Hereafter, *SOF*. italics mine). However, in his final word on the procession of the Spirit in *CDG*, he overtly advocates Epiphanius' position that "the procession of the Spirit is from the Being of the Father, and *not* from the Person (ὑπόστασις) of the Father, in distinction from his Being" (Ibid., 188; italics added).
110. Ibid., 174.

no part of this circle, which is not to be understood 'homoousially', even the inner relations themselves. To give expression to this *homoousial enhypostatic* reality, Torrance coins the term *onto-relations* in order to emphasize the ontological significance of the relations between the divine persons.[111] The interrelations themselves are to be understood as *substantive* in the sense that they belong to or make up what each of the distinctive hypostases essentially is in itself. "Thus the Father is Father precisely in his indivisible ontic relation to the Son and the Spirit, and the Son and the Spirit are what they are as Son and Spirit precisely in their indivisible ontic relations to the Father and to One Another."[112] Consequently, in what has profound implications for Torrance's doctrine of Grace, "'Person' is an onto-relational concept."[113]

If person is an onto-relational concept, how then does Torrance conceive of the three divine persons when specifically identified as *Father, Son,* and *Holy Spirit*? First, he asserts that all analogies which might be drawn from the visible world (such as, human fatherhood, human personhood) must be set aside, and we "must think of 'Father' and 'Son' when used of God as *imageless relations.*"[114] What Torrance means by this (and here he intends to follow Gregory Nazianzen) is that "*Father* . . . is the name of the *relation* in which the Father stands to the Son, and the Son to the Father."[115] *Person* then refers to a dynamic stance towards another. For the Father to be the *Father* is for him to be Father of the *Son.* It is his *belonging to* and *being for* the Son. The stance itself is substantial or constitutive of their being. The *person is*

---

111. Ibid., 157. Torrance himself coined the term *onto-relations* to give expression to the mutual indwelling or reciprocal containing of one another contained within the term perichoresis. While the English term onto-relations is Torrance's own, the basic concept is already present in Gregory of Nazianzen in his concept of the divine Persons as *substantive relations*, which was intentionally meant to contrast with the Cappadocian notion of *modes of being.* Substantive relations means that the relations between the three divine Persons belong to what they essentially are in themselves in their distinctive hypostasis. They are hypostatically interconnected with one another. Conceptually, the two terms (perichoresis and onto-relations) refer to the same reality though from differing angles: perichoresis emphasizing the co-inhering of the three and onto-relations emphasizing the substantiality (the hypostatic reality) of the co-inhering.

112. Ibid.

113. Ibid.

114. Ibid.

115. *CDG*, 157–58.

the stance, not as an accidental appendage, but constitutionally and substantively.[116] In the Godhead there are not *persons*; only *persons-in-relation*. Each dynamic person is not without unique and particular content, and yet the 'content' that makes the Father *Father*, the Son *Son*, and the Spirit *Spirit* is realized precisely *through* their reciprocal relations. In this sense, the concept of *perichoresis* actually serves to deepen and strengthen our understanding of the hypostatic distinctions within the Trinity.[117] It secures that each of the divine persons has incommunicable characteristics, and that these incommunicable characteristics constitute the communion, which God is.

These distinctions are also more than 'modes of being,' but are inherently personal so that a real sense of consciousness can be appropriated to each of the persons. Torrance argues that *perichoresis* allows for "each divine Person in virtue of his distinctiveness [to share] in [the divine consciousness] differently and appropriately," such that the "one indivisible God" can appropriately be said to consist of "three conscious Subjects in mutual love and life and activity."[118] Torrance believes that the concept of *perichoresis* allows him to speak this way without sliding into tri-theism, for it brings "into the concept of the person a deeper ontology according to which a person precisely as person is understood to be free to go outside of himself while remaining in himself in relation to others what he distinctively is."[119]

Procession and Generation in the Light of Perichoresis

When Torrance turns his attention upon the procession of the Spirit and the generation of the Son, it is the *perichoretic* doctrine of the coinherence of the divine persons that is determinative. Following Athanasius, Torrance states that "the procession of the Spirit from the

---

116. The specific term *stance* is not Torrance's word, but I believe it captures the sense of what he wants to say regarding dynamic substantial relations.
117. *CDG*, 175.
118. Thomas F. Torrance, *Trinitarian Perspectives: Toward Doctrinal Agreement* (Edinburgh: T & T Clark, 1994), 97. Hereafter, *TP*; Cf. *TF*, 321.
119. *TP*, 98.

Father is inextricably bound up with 'the generation of the Son from the Father.'"[120] The Spirit is *in* the Word and is thus *in* God through the Word, for the Spirit is never "outside the Word."[121] For the purposes of this discussion, what is important with regard to Torrance's doctrine of Grace is this: he locates the procession and generation, not in an activity of the *hypostasis* of the Father, but of the *ousia* of the Father which the Son and the Spirit share in as God. This is not to deny the meaningfulness of the *hypostasis* of the Father, but to limit its agency to *enhypostatic* differentiation and not to the causation of the being of the Son and the Spirit. Where in his view the Cappadocians create a dualist rift between the *ousia* and the *hypostasis*, Torrance emphasizes that God is no less personal in his *ousia* as whole God than he is in each person.[122] Thus, properly understood, the divine processions issue not from the Father alone but from the Monarchy, for none of the triune persons is properly itself apart from the other two.[123] It is for this reason that Torrance insists that the unity of the Godhead is "in the identification of the **Monarchia** with the **Triunity** of God."[124] This is an argument for the consubstantial Trinity which he claims follows an Athanasian, Epiphanian, Constantinoplitan and Cyrilian line of descent.

Implications of an Ontology of Grace

We are now in a position to answer the question at hand: "How does a personalist ontology, contextualized by a dynamic soteriology, *function* in Torrance's theology of Grace?"

Ontologically, *Grace is ultimately personal*. It cannot be reduced to a logical system. It cannot be logically supposed, projected or extended. This pushes against certain proposals, which attempt to use systematic and logical inference as a method for explaining the triune life. Torrance has recently been critiqued by Bruce McCormack for privileging the persons over the work.[125] This is a critique Torrance

---

120. *TF*, 235. Quoting Athanasius, *De decre.*, 12.
121. Athanasius, *Ad Ser.*, 1.14.
122. *CDG*, 161.
123. Ibid., 192.
124. *TF*, 340 (bold original).

would gladly receive, for to do otherwise threatens the very foundations of Grace as he understands it. If removed from the register of soteriology, Grace becomes something other than Grace. If systematized into necessity or emanation or universal law or self-constitution, the *gift* which is given loses its character as *gift*. Thus, Torrance refuses to push beyond the bounds of revelation to inquire as to *how* the processions take place, choosing with the Church Fathers the position of humility and reverence. This resistance to speculation, even when *logically* warranted, is part of Torrance's stratified structure of theological knowledge:

> Each level is open to consistent and deeper understanding in the light of the theological concepts and relations operating at the next level, and that the top level, and indeed the whole coordinated structure with it, while open-ended and incomplete in itself, points indefinitely beyond itself to the ineffable, transcendent Mystery of the Holy Trinity.[126]

Here we see Torrance's appeal to what he calls *ontic explanation*.[127] 'Ontic explanation' recognizes the fact that in the immanent Trinity, as well as in the economic Trinity, we are dealing with transcendent religious realities which cannot be subjected to logical dissection. It refers to his insistent privileging of the reality of the Agent over abstract logical analysis. Thus, all concepts which we use as descriptors of God (for example: person, relation, being, truth) must *be derived ontologically from this intra-trinitarian communion of love, and not logically*.

In developing what is in effect an 'ontology of Grace,' Torrance intentionally resists dualistic ontologies which would create a divide in the God-world relation, as well as synthesized ontologies (constitutional, emanating, 'historical ontology') in which God realizes (or becomes) himself through events in time. Contemporary theologies often lean in the direction of 'onto-history,' in which history itself is metaphysically primary. These approaches tend to emphasize an

---

125. See McCormack: "Abandoned by God: The Death of Christ in Systematic, Historical, and Exegetical Perspective," Croall lectures, University of Edinburgh, Jan. 2011.
126. *CDG*, 113.
127. *TP*, 92ff. Torrance borrows this phrase from Rahner, though his employment of it is his own and by it he intends exactly what *homoousion* is meant to convey.

actualism which identifies the economic and the immanent Trinity without remainder. They would pose challenging questions of Torrance as to whether he finally contradicts his repeated assertion that there is no God behind the back of Jesus Christ. Does Torrance's theology really allow us to unequivocally assert that the human Jesus is the same person as the divine Logos? Is the extra-Calvinisticum a known or unknown extra? In what sense can the *Logos asarkos* be the same *person* as the *Logos ensarkos* if it does not share the same experiences as the human Jesus? These are serious questions and some thoughtful theologians put these to Torrance as fatal flaws. What if anything does Torrance put in place to defend against the accusation that after all his efforts to remove the wedge between the economic and immanent Trinity, he has at the last retained the split?

While we do not have the luxury of knowing exactly how Torrance would respond to the contemporary theological issue, the trajectories of a reply are fairly well set out. For Torrance, an 'onto-historical' approach to the Trinity by definition is not Grace, but self-actualization on God's part. Torrance would caution that we cannot go behind Grace or soteriology in order to analyze or systematize either God's being or the logic of the eternal decision of election. It is not our purpose to pursue this debate in any detail in this book. However, as we enter the realm of the economic Trinity in the final section of this chapter and the two chapters which follow, we will begin to see how Torrance's ontology of Grace works itself out in the missions of the economy; and we will discover an overall theological framework which holds together not only consistently and very satisfactorily, but also provides a firm basis for human ethical action.

Conclusion

Grace is the triune movement of God's self-giving towards creation. This motion is the *why*, the *how* and the *what for* of all things. In the following section, I examine the way this movement from the triune life *in se* to the triune activities *ad extra* is carried out in Torrance's doctrine of creation. Our concern is to note how his doctrine of Grace

sets the tone and focus of this transition from the ontological to the
economic Trinity. This will also begin to address some of the questions
raised at the end of the previous section regarding a possible gap
between the immanent and the economic Trinity in Torrance's
account.

Creation and the Missions

When Torrance turns his attention from his doctrine of the immanent
Trinity to his doctrine of creation, he does not leave behind for an
instant his logic of Grace. At every point the argument is the same:
free Grace. This Grace is the very same perichoretic onto-relational
inward movement, *now turned outward* in a corresponding perichoretic
onto-relational movement. Because God's being inheres in his acts, the
one activity *in* God (ontologically) becomes the one activity *of* God
(economically), "so that they are not only Triune in Being but are
Triune in Activity."[128] Torrance calls this the "perichoretic coactivity of
the Holy Trinity."[129]

Who: the Whole Trinity

The triune activities in the economy are inseparable from, grounded
in and actually flow from the pattern of coactivity of the Father, Son,
and Spirit in the ontological Trinity.[130] Within his personalist ontology
in which *ousia* and *hypostasis* are not dualistically segregated, all God's
activities, creation included, can be seen to arise from God's "undivided
activity as Father, Son and Holy Spirit, one God *from* whom and *through*
whom and *in* whom are all things."[131] Certainly the persons have
distinct modes of operating from within these collective activities
(indicated by the prepositions, *ek, dia* and *en*), but the primary
affirmation must be the unity of the *ousia* and the *energeia*.[132] This is a

128. Ibid., 197.
129. Ibid., 198.
130. Ibid.
131. *TF*, 93; see 2 Cor 8:6; Rom 11:36. Torrance liberally references Athanasius on this subject in *TRn*,
215–16.
132. *Ad Ser.* 1.30; *TRn*, 216.

fundamental principle in Torrance's logic of Grace. As I have already observed, establishing that there is essentially one activity *in* and *of* God is a premise for Torrance's assertion that there is only one Grace which flows from the one communion of God. Stated differently, *because the communion of the three is ontologically significant, it is also soteriologically (i.e., economically) significant.*

How: in Freedom

How does God create? While Torrance emphatically asserts that there is an ontological correspondence between the being and activity of God *in se* and *ad extra*, this does not detract from his insistence that the *ad extra* of creation is an utterly new event *for God*. The acts of God *ad extra* are acts of God's will, whereas the activity of God *ad intra* in the generation of the Son and the procession of the Spirit are eternal activities of God's nature. Creation is neither eternal in the way that God is eternal, nor is it necessary. Thus, there is no logical link between creation and generation. Because creation is brought into being by a definite act of God's will and freedom, it must be affirmed as *ex nihilo*. God "does not beget out of himself but wonderfully brings into being out of nothing."[133] The newness of the act of creation is in fact an integral element in the logic of Grace.

This means that while God has always been *Father*, he is not always *Creator*. Creator is something (and consequently *someone*) God *became*. At this juncture, the important point to emphasize in Torrance's thought is that God's ontological becoming does not mean ontological

---

133. *CDG*, 220. Here Torrance differs strongly from Moltmann who interprets the 'creatio ex nihilo' as a thing itself which God created by withdrawing his presence: "The space which comes into being and is set free by God's self-limitation is a literally God-forsaken space. The *nihil* in which God creates his creation is God-forsakenness, hell, absolute death . . . (Jürgen Moltmann, *God in Creation: A New Theology of Creation and the Spirit of God*, trans. Margaret Kohl [New York: Harper and Row, 1985], 87). For Moltmann, creation is a 'contraction' of God's being such that "the existence of the universe was made possible through a shrinkage process in God." (Jürgen Moltmann, *The Trinity and the Kingdom, The Doctrine of God*, trans. Margaret Kohl [New York: Harper & Row, 1981], 109–10). For Moltmann, creation and God are mutually conditioning and so he can say, "the idea of the world is already inherent in the Father's love for the Son" (*Trinity and Kingdom*, 108). Torrance rejects this form of reciprocity between God and creation because it ultimately means that, in some sense, God needs the world. This is a line Torrance refuses to cross. Blurring the distinction between the inner life of God and the outer acts of God for him would be an abandonment of Grace (cf. Molnar, *Thomas F. Torrance: Theologian of the Trinity*, 79–82).

change. Ontology is not constituted by or dependent upon soteriology. God's ontology is such that "without ceasing to be what he eternally is" he is free *"to be other than himself,* and to bring into being what is entirely different from what he has done before."[134] Because God's acts are his acts-in-being and his being-in-action, for God to do new *acts* implies that his *being* is "always *new* while always remaining what it ever was and is and ever will be."[135] In this sense, Torrance can affirm with Jüngel, that "[God's] eternal being is also a divine becoming."[136] Yet for Torrance the language of becoming is not to evoke potential or development, but the overflow of God's eternal fullness.[137] The act of creation does not expand God's being, for he is life in himself. Yet as life and aliveness, God's being is also dynamic. Thus for God becoming is fitting, but not necessary; free, yet not arbitrary.

Thus the newness of the act of creation does not imply its strangeness. In all of its non-necessity, creation is entirely fitting. Because it is as the Father that God is Creator, and not visa versa, creation can be understood truly as an act of love. God's power to create flows from his intrinsic nature as love; the eternal Father freely shares the fullness of his love in fellowship with that which he creates.[138] As *Father,* God is "essentially generative or fruitful in his own Being, and it is because he is inherently productive as *Father* that God could and did freely become Creator or Source of all being beyond himself."[139] The work of creation "is activated" and "flows freely" out of the Father's eternal love of the Son, that is, from the life and love of the eternal God. In this sense, creation (*and incarnation*) cannot be said to be an after-thought. Creation is a free act of God's will. Thus, the motion of Grace *ad extra* is fitting to who God is inwardly.[140]

At this point an important difference between Torrance and Barth arises—one that has significant implications within contemporary

---

134. Ibid., 217. (italics mine)
135. Ibid., 208.
136. Ibid., 242.
137. Ibid., 59.
138. Ibid., 209.
139. Ibid.
140. Cf. CD II/I, 317, 358.

theology. While Torrance affirms the fittingness of the motion of Grace *ad extra* to who God is inwardly, he does not consider Grace *per se* to be an activity of the immanent Trinity. God in himself is not Grace to himself. Grace itself is not a divine perfection. The Father is not gracious to the Son, nor the Son gracious to the Father, nor is the Spirit the communion of Grace between the Father and the Son. What the triune persons share among themselves in the eternal communion of their life is more appropriately defined as *love*, not Grace. Grace specifically is that eternal movement within the Trinity *turned outward beyond the Trinity*. For Torrance, to blur this distinction, and to insist (as Barth does) that Grace as such is one of the divine perfections, is to deny the gospel of Grace itself. Grace by necessity cannot be necessary.

Why: Out of Love

If creation is not generation or emanation,[141] or a necessary self-constitution, why then does God create? For Torrance, the reason for creation and "why it exists at all, but also why it is what it is and not something else" is "the ultimate Love of God."[142] This love is the very communion of love which constitutes the inner life of God as Father, Son and Holy Spirit. As such, love of God is also free and in his freedom God purposes not to live for himself alone, but to give life to a creaturely realm with which he can share the communion of love which he is. God is not remote, unknowable, aloof, or isolated from us. We are created from and for love and communion.

Because the love that God is, is not a *thing* but a *person*, it is "inflexible" in the sense that this love is "the Law of his own divine Being and Activity."[143] Torrance also refers to this as the "law of God's Love *for* the universe," which "bears in a commanding ontological way upon it."[144] As the intransigent love, which is the law of God's being and activity, God's love is intrinsically *holy* love. This love then is the ultimate ground for the created order, yet it is also a "commanding

141. *DCO*, 71.
142. *CDG*, 212.
143. Ibid., 213.
144. *CFM*, 17.

ground" which judges all disorder and evil that opposes it.[145] This holy lawful divine love "withstands and negates all that is contrary to God's Love, judges all that resists it, and inexorably condemns it."[146] The creaturely realm, which the holy love of God brings into being is intended to reflect his glory by sharing in the freedom of this communion of love through an analogous free and exclusive self-giving on the part of the creature.

Because creation arises out of the Father's eternal love of the Son, Torrance asserts that God's relation to his creation is "completely positive"—he is always creatively and continually loving, upholding, blessing and coordinating its creaturely existence with his uncreated existence as its ultimate source.[147] The fittingness and positivity of God's relation vis-à-vis creation leads Torrance to engage in further reflection regarding the proleptic relation of creation and incarnation—reflection, which he admits verges on speculation. With a degree of holy fear and trembling, he says, "without knowing what we say, we may nevertheless feel urged to say that in his eternal purpose the immeasurable Love of God . . . would have become incarnate within the creation *even if we and our world were not in need of his redeeming grace.*"[148]

The compulsion to speak in this way is for Torrance a further application of his logic of Grace. Torrance reasons: the incarnation of God's love within his creation is simply the historical manifestation of the Love that God eternally is in himself (i.e., the Father's eternal love of the Son).[149] Because God's creative activity flows from the love that God eternally is, we can and should say that God loves us with the same love that he is—that is, with a loving movement that is unceasing and ungrudging, and most astonishingly revealed in the gift of his Son on the cross.[150] The 'destination' of creation has always been its relation

---

145. Ibid.
146. *CDG*, 213.
147. Ibid., 211.
148. Ibid., 210; italics mine.
149. Ibid., 5–6.
150. Ibid., 5. Torrance also quotes his beloved professor H.R. Mackintosh who, with great rhetorical flourish proclaims: "God loves us better than he loves himself" (ibid., 209–10; H.R. Mackintosh, *The Person of Jesus Christ* [London, 1912], 91). Properly speaking, of course, God loves himself perfectly

to God through God's own incarnate expression of his love within it. The sharing of this love which God is constitutes a larger category than redemption itself, and redemption has its ultimate purpose in freeing the creature for this love.[151]

What: an All-Embracing Framework of Grace

Thus far in this section we have observed the *who, how* and *why* of the movement of the triune persons from their eternal life *in se* to their perichoretic co-activity *ad extra*. This motion of Grace is a willed activity of the whole Trinity, which is both fitting and new—an act which has its ground in the holy love and freedom of God's life in himself. As I have noted, the 'fittingness' of the divine act of creation is more than superficial. In the willed act of creation, God freely brings into being a created realm which corresponds to the inner divine relations. The force of this claim (which Torrance takes from Barth) is that as *love* is the all-inclusive ground and essence of the relation between the Father and the Son, so *Grace* is the all-inclusive ground and essence of the relation between the Creator and his creation. The love of the Father encounters creation as the Grace of the Son in the communion of the Holy Spirit. In short, the movement of God's holy love meets creation in the form of omnipotent Grace.[152]

Torrance reads Ephesians 1:3–14 as a pronouncement that God has "established between himself and the creation an *all-embracing framework of grace* within which and through which to share with humanity the fellowship of his Love."[153] The all-encompassing nature of this framework of Grace spans two general 'levels', which correspond to the processions and the missions. On the one hand, this framework can be described by focusing upon the Father-Son relation as that which "constitutes the central axis round which the whole universe is made to revolve."[154] On the other hand, this framework

and his loving of us is not at cost to his self-love. The main point is that God's love for himself is not self-absorbed, and God does not spare himself but gives himself for our sakes.
151. Ibid., 210.
152. Ibid., 214.
153. Ibid., 219.

may also be considered by focusing on the "relation between the faithfulness of God and the created order, or the relation between *covenant* and *creation*."[155] I will take these two levels in order, recognizing that the covenantal relation falls within the ontological.

Analogy of Relations—All of Creation Bears the Imprint of the Trinity

Given that creation arises out of the dynamic life and love of the triune persons, Torrance does not find it surprising that "creation and its history should bear the imprint of the Trinity upon it."[156] Following Barth, creation is "a 'temporal analogue,' taking place outside of God, of that event in himself by which God is Father of the Son."[157] A correspondence exists between God and his world such that there is a kind of 'sacred economy' in the universe.[158] However, this *analogia* is emphatically *not* an *analogia entis.* The Creator and his creation are absolutely ontologically disparate, *and yet,* in the freedom of God's love he wills the universe to be a kind of 'created counterpart' of the movement of the eternal triune love. This 'created correspondence,' which is by no means natural or automatic, but by Grace (i.e., the free will and act of God) can be envisaged as an analogy of relation (*analogia relationis*).[159] The two terms of this analogy are: first, "the relationship between the eternal generation of the Son within the life of the Holy Trinity (begotten, not made)," and, second, "the relationship between the creation of the universe (made, not begotten) outwith the life of the Holy Trinity."[160] While the qualifying phrases pile up ('freely posited,' 'created correspondence,' 'not necessary,' 'not natural, but by grace') in an effort to preserve the freedom of the correlation,

---

154. Ibid.
155. Ibid.
156. Ibid.
157. Ibid., 219. Torrance's reference to Barth is from *Dogmatics in Outline* (London: SCM, 1949), 52.
158. Torrance credits Gregory Thaumaturgus for this phrase, In *Origenem*, 8.
159. For Torrance, the doctrine of *creatio ex nihilo* precludes the sacramental universe, for God freely and creatively brings into being a creation which is utterly contingent and distinct from himself. God creates in freedom by an act of his will, i.e. by Grace. *TRn*, 272–74.
160. *CDG*, 220.

Torrance still insists that the analogy is *ontological* and not merely conceptual. This pattern of the Father-Son relation is ontologically embedded in the creation. However, speaking of ontology in reference to the Creator and the creature is to speak of two completely different things. There is no 'real' ontological continuity from one to the other, for ontologically, creation is an 'opposite' of God; the two exist at 'cross-levels' and must be differentiated. Because of this fundamental ontological distinction, creation can be seen and understood as no more than a reflection or "a shadowing forth of the inner divine relationship between God the Father and the Son."[161]

The ontological correspondence of creation with its Creator is secured by the fact that creation takes place through Christ and is held together in Christ and the Spirit. Jesus Christ is "the incarnate correlate of the ἀρχή that God is in his triune being"[162] and thus he is the economic form which the divine ἀρχή [the triune pattern/ movement] takes in all God's sustaining and redeeming activities towards us. More attention will be given to this in the following chapter on Christology; our concern here is to highlight that Torrance makes Christ's headship over all creation both thoroughly Trinitarian and also structurally significant. Because it is structurally significant, the implications of Christ's headship over creation move in two directions. On the one hand, Christ reveals to us the dynamic and personal motion of the Trinitarian life of God. On the other hand, Christ lives the form of human life which corresponds to the triune movement of Grace. All the ways and works of God in creation are to be understood through the form of Christ incarnate.[163] Christ is the "uncreated *Autologos*" or "Self-Word," in contrast to whom and upon whom all other *logoi* ("rational forms pervading the universe") are shown to be contingent, and derived from, his antecedent Word. Yet, as the uncreated *archē* becomes 'created,' the incarnate Christ constitutes "the Beginning of a new beginning within the creation."[164] Therefore,

---

161. Barth, *Dogmatics in Outline*, 52.
162. *TF*, 83.
163. Ibid., 83–84.
164. Ibid., 83.

Torrance speaks of Christ as the *fundamental principle* and *archetypal pattern* of God's Grace. With God in Christ entering creation as the new *archē* of it, creation is renewed and sanctified in him "to be a creaturely correlate of the fellowship, communion and faithfulness which are manifested in God himself."[165]

Because creation takes place through and in the Logos and has its form and *archē* in him, Torrance does not have a problem with thinking of creation's reflection of the inner divine life as a kind of "created participation."[166] In his use of the language of participation, Torrance intends to bring attention to the contingent nature of our existence, which cannot fulfill its created purpose of correspondence apart from the gracious activity of God upon it. Things created out of nothing, in fact, are "intrinsically unstable." It is only through the preserving activity of God's Grace that created things are kept from lapsing back into nothingness. As there was no necessity for creation to exist in the beginning, so also is there no basis for the continued existence of creation were it not sustained in its creaturely reality through the abiding presence of the Word and the Spirit. Humankind's turning away from God towards self-determination threatens human-being with the prospect of being-no-thing, for our existence has no continuing basis other than that which is graciously given by God. Sin then is fundamentally not against an impersonal law, but against Grace itself—against God's loving, holy will and being. Torrance's emphasis on participation importantly emphasizes both the utter contingency of our existence and the non-naturalness of the Creator-creature correspondence, which leaves creatures absolutely dependent upon God's agential intervention if we are to reflect or echo his inner existence.

Nevertheless, within the ontological reality which creation has been given, God wills it to correspond to the mystery of his uncreated being. In describing this correspondence, Torrance notes several interrelations incorporated within this all-embracing framework of

165. *TF*, 94.
166. Ibid., 103; Cf. *CDG*, 219.

Grace, including but not limited to: God's uncreated life and the creaturely life of human beings; the uncreated time of God and the created time of our world; uncreated light and created light; the transcendent communion of the three divine persons and the communion of persons in the Church; and God's uncreated rationality and intelligibility and the rationality of creatures.[167] This framework of Grace is so basic, so fundamental that it permeates absolutely every fiber of the created order, such that the ultimate meaning and order of creation is "locked into the mystery of the Holy Trinity."[168] Torrance writes, "It is this Holy Lawful Divine Love that constitutes the ultimate invariant ground of all rational and moral order in the created universe, and it is under its constraint that all physical and moral laws functioning within the universe operate and are in the last resort to be recognized and formulated."[169] In other words, Grace (that is, the holy divine love towards us) is everywhere, providing the rationality, order and organization of every facet of the universe. This has profound implications for how Torrance locates the moral field which consequently must be grounded, constrained, recognized and formulated accordingly. I will address these issues in chapters 4 and 6.

God's Covenantal Relation with Humanity

The imprint of the triune processions, which indelibly marks the created order, serves as the medium within which the coactivity of the triune missions operate. Within this created ontological relation there is also a willed covenantal relation. This covenantal relation refers to the "relation between the faithfulness of God and the created order, or the relation between *covenant* and *creation*."[170] This covenanted relation constitutes "the inner ground and form of creation," and creation provides "the outer ground or form of the Covenant."[171] The all-embracing framework of Grace, which is the holy divine love of God's

---

167. *TF*, 103-4, *CDG*, 220f.
168. *CDG*, 140.
169. Ibid., 213.
170. *CDG*, 219.
171. *TS*, 68. Cf. CD 3.1.§41.

being as it operates *ad extra,* is purposeful. It is *for fellowship* in the form of a two-way covenanted relation. Thus, "while Grace asserts that the relation between God and the creation is irreversible, it does nevertheless insist that the relation between God and the creature is a two-way relation."[172] The Creator-creature relation is irreversible in that it is one which is established completely and freely from the side of God "out of pure grace."[173] It did not and does not have to be. And yet, just as the ontological *analogia relationis* between the Trinity and the created order is non-necessary, so also is the covenantal relation non-necessary and purely by Grace. These relations are not reversible or to be confused, nor are they to be separated or dichotomized.

Again, while grounded in creation, the correspondence of human beings with God is not 'natural.' Covenantal correspondence is by Grace alone. While opposites, human beings correspond in our creaturely onto-relations analogically—*by the power of the Spirit.* "The Spirit is the creative and sanctifying Source of all things made by God through Christ."[174] It is by the ongoing presence of the Spirit that we are given to share in the communion of the Father and the Son. We are only able to reflect by Grace something of the uncreated life of God because of the creative, energizing, and personalizing power of the Spirit. I will address the way Torrance understands this Spirit-effected correspondence as a movement within the all-embracing framework of Grace in chapter 3. Our reason for raising it here is to point out that the Holy Spirit is never absent or inactive in the movement of the triune missions outward in creation. As the eternal Word is active in both creation and recreation, so also is the Spirit. Torrance pulls these various strands together in one concise statement:

> God does not withdraw his activity from the world which he has once for all brought into being, but . . . continues to conserve the creation in a covenanted coexistence with himself. He interacts positively and constructively toward it and within it, in a life-giving and preserving activity in which he cares for it and supplies all its needs out of his

172. Ibid., 67.
173. Ibid., 66.
174. Ibid., 227.

limitless grace, constantly upholding all things by the Word of his power and through the presence of his Spirit.[175]

Election in the Context of Grace

When Torrance directs his attention towards the divine decision to relate to creation in the form of this all-embracing framework of Grace, he regularly uses the language of election, but with several significant caveats. Election (and its correlate, predestination) is a doctrine that Torrance warns can be very damaging to a theology of Grace if it is not viewed from within the sphere of Grace. In fact, all doctrines can be properly conceptualized only when viewed through the lens and logic of Grace. The way Torrance handles the doctrine of election provides a model case study, demonstrating how his theological methodology is guided by his theology of Grace.

In Torrance's account then the doctrine of election emphasizes first that *election does not precede Grace, but is grounded upon it*.[176] There is no higher will or fact in God than Grace. The *pre* of predestination is for the purpose of grounding election in an act of God himself. Grace arises from the divine aseity, and pre-destination is simply the positive purposeful movement of creative Grace in the communion of the Holy Spirit.[177] Similarly, to describe this act as an 'eternal decree' is simply to make reference to the life of the Godhead—that is, to the personal relations of the Trinity. This decree is the decision God makes to elect, a decision which he makes in his freedom and which has himself as its sole author, instrument and ground. This ground is himself the triune Grace, which Torrance specifically identifies as Christ.[178] Torrance's emphasis here is less on the *act* of God (for to speak of an act in the Eternal can only be done analogically) than it is on the personal triune life of God which acts. In other words, what matters with regard to

---

175. *CDG*, 223.
176. Torrance accuses Calvin (and the traditional doctrine of predestination) of a weakness here in making election precede Grace. Thomas F. Torrance, "Predestination in Christ," *Evangelical Quarterly* 13 (1941): 109. Hereafter, *PiC*.
177. *PiC*, 115, 116.
178. It is significant that in this context Torrance uses the terms *Christ*, *Grace*, and *the eternal decree* synonymously.

election is that our salvation is to be referred to the will of *This One*, and all *acts* that issue from This One by definition have Grace as their antecedent.

Election also emphasizes that the relation between God and creation is *personal*. Creation and redemption are both by God's Word, which Torrance interprets as an indication that God's dealings with human beings are utterly personal. Torrance sees this same truth communicated by the fact that all human relations with God are in Christ. The personal nature of God's relations with humanity is shown in that "God's action toward men is identical with Jesus Christ."[179] Election is through the Word and in Christ. That election has its origin in this personal Word means that God does not manipulate human beings, but calls them to decision that is all-embracing. God speaks his Word and his speaking of it to human beings makes us response-able—and consequently truly personal.

Because the relation between God and creation is personal, it is also free. It is free because it is personal, and it is personal because it is free. Torrance interprets election as the way that faith affirms "that God's action of predestination is a choice or decision."[180] It is not determined by some immanent process or necessitated by cause and effect; nor is election a spontaneous overflow of God's nature absent from a personal free decision. Neither is Grace (i.e., election) reducible to God's answer or response to human sin; primarily it is God's free purpose of creating human beings for communion with himself. For Torrance, God's freedom in election does not raise the specter of possible counterfactual decisions God might have made, nor does it imply randomness in God's choices. In his view, to make election a form of determinism, or of self-constitution in God, is to put something prior to Grace and thus to deny the love of God itself.

179. PiC, 111.
180. Ibid., 116–17.

Conclusion

In this chapter we have seen how Torrance's doctrine of Grace arises from the dynamic ground of the inner life and love of the triune God. This exploration was presented in three successive sections. First, the source and nature of knowledge of God was considered, revealing that the source of knowledge of God is God himself, and the nature of that knowledge is that it creates communion. Second, I drew out salient features of Torrance's conception of the immanent Trinity were drawn out, with the weight of attention falling upon the intrinsic personal relations which cohere to form a dynamic understanding of the Trinity as a *perichoretic* tri-unity. Third and finally, we followed the movement of God's love in himself as it flows out freely, yet fittingly towards a creation by establishing an all-embracing framework of Grace within and through which the triune life and love is shared with humanity.

Our objective has been to establish and illuminate the Trinitarian foundations, which undergird Torrance's theological framework and to show the way Torrance understands the triune life as the free, yet fitting source and substance of Grace. Throughout I have sought to demonstrate the central and organizing role that the concept of Grace plays within Torrance's theological material and method. We have seen that for Torrance "there is only one divine activity" and "there is only one grace," which is another way of asserting that that which God gives is not to be separated from God, for the gift of the love of God is the gift of God *himself*, for God *is* love.

Yet how does the communion, which the Father and the Son share in the Spirit, become an inclusive communion without absorbing or overwhelming human creatures? What prevents God's Grace from being done 'over the heads' of human beings or more naturally from becoming absorbed by human beings as an aspect of their own immanent existence? Torrance is committed to finding a means of conceiving the divine-human relation so that inclusion in the divine communion is realized, while human freedom is honored and enabled. This way is expressed in a covenanted two-fold relation, which is objectively fulfilled in the Son and realized in the Spirit. This is a movement *by* God that is *from* God and also *to* God, yet a motion in which human creatures are included. It is the movement of Grace in the economy of salvation.

2

———

The Motion of Grace Through the Son

The Truth of God in Jesus Christ is Grace. Grace is the turning of God toward us in His mercy and love, His self-giving to us and His action for us, whereby He establishes us in union and communion with Himself and so gives us a true place in relation to the Reality of God. As such Grace is identical with Jesus Christ. He is Grace and Truth in Himself, and therefore Grace and Truth for us.[1]

The following chapter examines the trinitarian activity of Grace in the economy. To accomplish this goal, the material that follows possesses a four-fold shape. **First,** I will outline the basic form of Grace in this world as a unilateral covenant initiated and fulfilled by God himself. God creates and situates humans within an all-embracing framework of Grace and calls Israel to be a people whom he will train in the way of Grace. **Second,** I will call attention to the way this loving movement of Grace is poured out upon humanity for their redemption as the Son, sent from the Father in the Spirit, takes human form ("the Word became flesh . . ."). This dynamic insertion of divine-human communion in and through the Holy Spirit is simultaneously and importantly an incarnational union, a personal union and an atoning

---

1. Thomas F. Torrance, *Theological Science* (Oxford: Oxford University Press, 1969), 155. Hereafter *TS*.

union ("and dwelt among us"). **Third,** I will unpack in greater detail the nature of this atoning union ("for us and for our salvation") in which the Son-become-human is the substitute and representative for humanity's covenant obligations and as such is the means by which God ultimately realizes his covenant relation with creatures. **Finally,** in observing the shape of the reconciling event of Christ's life, I will note that Torrance places the obedience and faithfulness of the Son within the larger context of the prayer and worship of the Son. This christological trinitarian perspective will shape how reconciliation, justification and sanctification—and thus Grace itself—are understood as fundamentally onto-relational realities.

It is important to bear in mind that all the christological material in this chapter must be integrated into the following chapter on the Spirit where the union accomplished in Christ himself is expounded as the union with Christ accomplished *in us* through the Spirit. That is, in this chapter we speak of a hypostatic, personal and atoning union, in which Christ incorporates himself into us; in the following chapter we speak of a pneumatic union in which we are incorporated into Christ. Grace cannot be understood apart from both realities for Grace by definition includes our actual participation.

The Covenant as Servant of Grace

Turning from our consideration of the immanent Trinity to the economic Trinity, we encounter the essential shape of Torrance's concept of Grace. The form and content of this meeting, which Torrance summarizes as a *downward two-fold single movement* of Grace, provides the interior logic of all his theological doctrines.[2] After briefly setting the parameters of this movement, I will attend to how it takes shape within as covenant.

Torrance understands Grace to be a fundamentally *downward* movement: that is, it comes *down* to us from *above*.[3] As the self-giving of God's presence to creatures, Grace by definition is unidirectional

2. Ibid., 206–7.
3. Sermon on 2 Corinthians 13:14, preached November 1940.

and irreversible. Its downward movement emphasizes its soteriological basis and is also befitting of its ontological structure.[4] However, Torrance's use of the spatial idiom of 'downwardness' in no way conflicts with his assertion that triune Grace takes on a two-fold motion in relation to creation—a humanward movement (or mission) *from* the Father through the Son in the Spirit and its complementary Godward movement *to* the Father through the Son in the Spirit. Both the humanward movement and the Godward movement are agentially *downward*, since both are the work of God; the activity of Grace. Finally, this two-fold downward movement of Grace is a *single* movement. That is, the motion of Grace is a *perichoretic* activity—one activity in which is united, yet differentiated according to the persons of the Trinity. While Torrance's language does not slavishly call attention to the ceaseless interplay of the triune *perichoretic* co-activity, this dynamic is perpetually in his mind. Indeed, in order to read properly any of Torrance's theology, one must hold together the three core elements which Torrance himself so relentlessly holds together: Christology, the internal relations of the Trinity and the movement of Grace. For Torrance, none of these can be understood apart from the other two and all are necessary for our salvation.[5]

Israel

The creation itself provides a theater, an "outer ground or form," in which God's will for fellowship with humanity finds expression. This will of the Father to share his life and communion with his children is the "inner ground and form" of the creation and is expressed in the covenant, "I will be your God, and you will be my people."[6] The term *covenant* is a way of describing the all-embracing framework of Grace in God's personal and dialogical relation with his creation.[7] As

---

4. Thomas F. Torrance, *Theology in Reconstruction* (Grand Rapids: Eerdmans, 1965), 99. Hereafter, *TRn*.
5. Thomas F. Torrance, *The Mediation of Christ*, rev. ed. (Edinburgh: T&T Clark, 1992), 65. Hereafter, *MOC*.
6. *TS*, 68. Cf. CD 3.1.§41. For Torrance's discussion of the Reformed concept of *covenant* in contrast to the Roman conception of a sacramental universe, see *School of Faith* (London: Camelot, 1959), lff. Hereafter, *SOF*.
7. Cf. *SOF*, li.

the expression of Grace in history, the covenant relation between God and his people is effectively the history of Grace. As such, it is both irreversible and two-way: always an act of God which also creatively calls forth a corresponding human response.

The covenant of Grace embraces not only humanity but the whole of creation, for all creation "is made to be the theatre of God's glory and the sphere of his revelation."[8] Within the context of this universal range, the covenant of Grace takes concrete form in three historical expressions: among the people of Israel; in its fulfillment in the incarnation; and in the founding of the Church in Christ.[9] The history of this relation is a dialogue or conversation between humans and God in which God speaks personally and historically within the covenant of Grace. Thus, Grace in the form of covenant is intensely *personal*, and humans are considered *partners* with God, personally *addressed* and called to respond in worship and love, trusting that God will fulfill his promises.[10]

With the fall and rebellion of humanity, God's covenant purpose was not abandoned but took on a redemptive function. With the communion of God and humanity perverted and broken, God elected the people of Israel to be the "mediator of the restoration of God's covenant purpose in creation."[11] Through this long historical dialogue between Israel and God, Israel would be a community of reciprocity before God and thus be capable of mediating divine revelation and reconciliation to all peoples and nations.[12]

Torrance develops God's election of Israel along two lines which reflect two general emphases: "Israel was called to be the Servant of the Lord . . . ," and "Israel was called to be the bearer of the Messiah. . . ."[13] Thus for Torrance the history of Israel is a kind of 'pre-history' of the incarnation. The continuity between Israel and Christ is

---

8. *TRn*, 181.
9. Thomas F. Torrance, *Conflict and Agreement in the Church*, vol. 2: *The Ministry of the Sacraments of the Gospel* (London: Lutterworth, 1959), 120–21. Hereafter, *C&A2*.
10. *SOF*, 1; *TRn*, 181.
11. C. Baxter Kruger, "On the Road to Becoming Flesh" (Perichoresis.org, 2007), 6.
12. David W. Torrance, *The Witness of the Jews to God* (Eugene, OR: Wifp & Stock, 2011), 88.
13. *TRn*, 196–98.

more than racial genetics or prophetic anticipation, but a provisional embodiment of "the new and living way" of Grace in her midst.[14] This way as expressed in the covenant reflects the downward two-fold movement of divine Grace as it takes concrete historical form within God's creation.

Law and Liturgy

Fundamental to Torrance's understanding of Israel's identity as servant of the Lord is her identity as a people *constituted by address*. Israel only exists as a *response* to the Word of God. However as the *servant* of the *Lord* this response was both dictated by the Lord to his servant and provided by the Lord for his servant.[15]

The covenanted way of response took the form of two types of obedience: obedient conformity to God's will (law) as laid out in the covenant; and, when Israel failed to uphold her side of the covenant, obedient conformity to God's way (liturgy) of cleansing and restoration of fellowship. These two aspects of covenant faithfulness—obedience and sacrifice—found expression in God's self-giving to Israel through the unity of the law and the cult.[16]

The covenant partnership called for a perfect correspondence between God and his chosen people and was expressed in God's declaration: "you shall be holy, for I am holy."[17] As God had given himself unconditionally to Israel, Israel was to give herself unconditionally to God through the obedience of a servant and the faithfulness of a son.[18] This motif of sonship is intrinsic to Israel's call to sacrificial obedience and the call always has sonship in mind.[19]

This covenanted way of response was set out in Israel's cultic liturgy.[20] As Baxter Kruger points out, for Torrance, one of the critical

---

14. Thomas F. Torrance, *Conflict and Agreement in the Church*, vol. 1 (London: Lutterworth, 1960), 307. Hereafter, *C&A1.*
15. See Kruger, "On the Road to Becoming Flesh," 9ff, for a detailed analysis of Torrance's conception of the covenanted way of communion as expressed in Israel.
16. *C&A2*, 16; cf. Thomas F. Torrance, *Incarnation: The Person and Life of Christ*, ed. Robert T. Walker (Nottingham: Intervarsity, 2008), 46. Hereafter, *Incarnation.*
17. Lev 11:45; 1 Pet 1:16.
18. *MOC*, 26–27.
19. Ibid., 75.

features of the law and the liturgy as the obedient way of response is this: in both instances (obedience and restoration), not only is the response divinely prescribed, it is also divinely *provided*.[21] Torrance refers to this divinely provided response as *covenanted* or *vicarious* response, for it functions as a *third dimension*[22] or *middle term*[23] between the polarities of the two parties of the covenant. Thus, "the sacrifices and oblations were not regarded as having any efficacy in themselves, but . . . were designed to point beyond themselves to God's will to be gracious and to pardon. They were essentially *witness* and were performed within the Tabernacle of Witness."[24] They did not act upon God but were simply a way of acknowledging and bearing witness to God's testimony of himself in the covenant. In the Old Testament, "the priestly cultus is designed to answer to [God's] act and bear witness to [God's] cleansing of the sinner," for God himself is always the Subject (and never the object) of expiation or reconciliation.[25]

Since both sides of the covenant relation were established and maintained by God's Grace, Torrance appropriately distinguishes God's covenant from a contract. God *himself* pledges to fulfill both sides of the covenant, so its validity does not depend upon the contractual fulfillment of its conditions on the part of Israel.[26]

But the fact that God provided the way of response also highlighted the judgment side of Grace. The provision by God of the way of cleansing (sacrifice) carried with it a condemning verdict upon all self-made offerings of Israel's own devising. Thus, the covenant partnership of sinful Israel with God meant escalating conflict: Israel's patterns of thought, understanding and speech had to undergo the suffering of purifying fire, in which God would burn away all that was in conflict with his holiness, mercy and truth. As a result, again and again Israel shatters herself on God's unswervingly persistent truth

20. Thomas F. Torrance, *Royal Priesthood* (Edinburgh: T&T Clark, 1993), 3. Hereafter, *RP*.
21. Kruger, "On the Road to Becoming Flesh," 10.
22. *C&A2*, 15.
23. *MOC*, 74.
24. *RP*, 3.
25. Ibid.
26. *MOC*, 28.

and love. Yet, it is in and through this very struggle that the way of Grace is forged into our human condition. Torrance writes, "To be the bearer of divine revelation is to suffer, and not only to suffer but to be killed and made alive again, and not only to be made alive but to be continually renewed and refashioned under its creative impact. That is the pre-history of the crucifixion and resurrection of Jesus in Israel."[27]

And yet, while the cultic liturgy provided a means for Israel's grateful acknowledgement of her restoration to fellowship, this arrangement was not to last forever. In spite of her unfaithfulness, God's declaration to Israel—"you shall be my people"—increasingly pointed toward a Messianic figure: one who would embody the obedient conformity to God's law and also sacrificially bear in his body the judgment upon the people's sins. What was symbolized in the cult would be realized in the Servant, who would be both offerer and offering: *representing the many* in fulfilling the covenanted obedience, while also *substituting for the many* by bearing the sins of the people, so that they might be restored to fellowship with God.[28] God himself would provide the response he required of his covenant partner in the very flesh of her history.

Incarnation

Throughout the Old Testament, it is God's unswerving and steadfast love that surrounds Israel in spite of her unfaithfulness. God will not let Israel go, persisting in his love for her in spite of her adulterous ways (Hosea 3:1). In the incarnation, God steps into the conflict himself in Jesus Christ, concretely fulfilling his covenant of Grace.[29] In this way, what was provisional and ostensive in Israel becomes abiding and eternally real in Jesus Christ for all humanity. Because the covenant is objectively and permanently realized in Christ, Torrance frames God's covenantal atoning and saving action under ontological categories.[30] Christ himself is the concrete universal, the reality which the covenant

---

27. Ibid., 11.
28. *TiR*, 196.
29. *MOC*, 39–45.
30. Thomas F. Torrance, *Divine and Contingent Order* (Edinburgh: T&T Clark, 1998), 135. Hereafter *DCO*.

system has always pointed toward and serves. Thus for Torrance the concept of covenant in the economy of Grace is completely subordinated to the concrete reality of the person of Christ, rather than the other way round. *Christ does not serve the covenant, the covenant serves Christ.*

It is this insistence on the central place of the person of Jesus Christ that gives a conceptual mobility to the form of Torrance's theology. Rather than a system of theology with its ground and grammar organized around an alien structure, his arrangement seeks to receive its ground and grammar from the Son who exists in eternal communion with the Father through the Holy Spirit. The relation God establishes between himself and humanity does not have its essence in forensic or cultic covenantal categories. While legal and forensic categories hold an important place in Torrance's theology, he repositions them within a larger ontological and filial context. These conceptual structures are only accommodated pointers towards the reality of which they speak—a reality which finds its concretization in Jesus Christ.

For Torrance, the incarnation literally possesses cosmic significance: the historical covenant God established with Israel now through Christ achieves universal validity which includes not only all humanity but the entire created order. Similarly, the vicarious representative and substitutionary role that Israel had within the covenant for the nations, Christ now has with respect to the rest of creation and yet importantly "in an entirely new way."[31] Now, "the covenant will of God for fellowship with man was translated into eternal actuality,"[32] for

> in Christ a creative centre of healing and integration has been set up within the structure and density of human contingent being, which cannot but affect the whole created order with which man has to do.[33]

31. Ibid., 134.
32. Thomas F. Torrance, "The Atoning Obedience of Christ," *Moravian Theological Seminary Bulletin* (1959): 71.
33. *DCO*, 136.

The Rhythm of Grace

For Torrance, the hypostatic union of God and humanity in Christ is the heart of the gospel and the essential and foundational paradigm of Grace. The virgin birth is the outward sign which bears witness to this reality. It does so not as a biological proof that God became human, but by its correspondence to the nature of the mystery of Christ. As such, "it is the analogical form of the thing signified."[34] Thus, far from downplaying the necessity of the virgin birth to Christian belief, Torrance considers the virgin birth of archetypal importance. It is "more than a sign—it is a determinative act of God,"[35] setting the pattern and charting the way which the saving Grace of God takes with our fallen humanity.[36] As such, it is the *archetype* of Grace.[37] This way of Grace is two-fold: "God as the creator and redeemer actually with us in our estranged human existence," and "God bringing out of our fallen and sinful existence a new humanity that is holy and perfect."[38] As the archetype of all God's acts of Grace, the virgin birth is not only an embodied sign which reveals the form of Christ's entry into the world, it also "proclaims analogously the mode of his entry into all who believe in him."[39] That is, the virgin birth is a sign of the manner of Christ's *continuous* coming to his people in a world burdened by sin—a coming which proclaims the possibility of our salvation and proclaims it as arising from God's side and not our own.

It is very significant to Torrance that this movement of Grace is a *creatio ex virgine* and not a *creatio ex nihilo*.[40] God neither bypasses the first creation nor limits himself to its natural processes. The incarnation is an event which breaks in and interrupts. It initiates a new creation out of (not merely in the midst of) the fallen old creation.

---

34. *Incarnation*, 96. See Torrance's discussion of the virgin birth and the resurrection as twin signs in which the veiled miracle at Bethlehem points to the same unveiled miracle of the resurrection.
35. Ibid., 103.
36. Ibid., 101.
37. Ibid., 103.
38. Ibid., 98.
39. Ibid., 104; cf. Thomas F. Torrance, *Doctrine of Jesus Christ* (Eugene, OR: Wipf & Stock, 2002), 119. Hereafter, DJC.
40. Ibid., 100; DJC, 119.

Thus, the way of God's Grace is a recreation within our human existence, which involves our human existence in the creative action of God. Every human response of faith in the gospel so to speak is a virgin birth: an empty womb in which Christ comes to dwell, conceived in our hearts and minds by the Holy Spirit.[41]

Thus in the case of Mary God takes the initiative in electing Mary and telling her of his decision for her. It is a free and sovereign act of God. While Mary is involved, she is neither the subject nor the lord of the event, but its predicate. Her part is simply to receive the word—a receiving which itself is given to her by the Holy Spirit. She submits and surrenders to the decision of God already taken on her behalf: "Behold, I am the handmaid of the Lord; let it be to me according to your word." (Luke 1:38) The holy and free love of God acts not in synergistic cooperation with human beings, but sovereignly *includes* them in his action. The entire movement is uni-directional and irreversible—from God to humanity. Thus, the way of Grace manifested in the virgin birth and correspondingly in the hypostatic union is paradigmatic of how Grace operates in all creation. The movement is downward as the Creator meets his creature in the midst of his creation and out of which he creatively begets a new humanity in the creative power of the Spirit.

One of the ways Torrance discusses these two aspects of the way of Grace is under the general heading of "the logic of God." As a descriptive tool, he differentiates the logic of God into "two different but related points of view": *the logic of Grace* and *the logic of Christ.*[42] What Torrance calls "the logic of Grace" describes the basic *direction* of this logic, while the logic of Christ refers to its *pattern*. Together, they speak of Jesus Christ who is "the logic of God's Grace and truth toward us."[43] These are not two different logics or two different movements, nor is one about Grace and the other about Christ. Rather, they are the same reality regarded from different angles and *together* they bear witness to the dynamic movement of the Grace of God in Christ and the Spirit.

41. Cf. ibid., 101–2; *DJC*, 119.
42. *TS*, 214ff.
43. Ibid., 206; John 1:14.

It is these two aspects of the logic of God, personally and historically embodied in the God-human Jesus Christ, which form the mode of all theological knowledge, description and action. Consequently, the rhythm of this logic will effect and constitute the arrangement of our ongoing exposition of Torrance's doctrine of Grace.

Downward (Hypostatic Union): "The Word became flesh . . ."

The logic of Grace is the basic direction the Truth of God takes in condescending to become incarnate and meeting us in the trenches of our fallen and guilty flesh; it expresses the "unconditional priority of the Truth and the irreversibility of His relationship to us."[44] This downward movement of Grace is most vividly captured in the Apostle John's report that in the incarnation "the Word became flesh" (John 1:14). It is an irreversible, uni-directional movement of pure freedom and love in which the triune God elects to make himself known within the created realm. Torrance does not use the language of downward spatially, but in terms of origin or ground: downward underscores that all God's works originate, and derive freely and creatively, from God himself. In this sense, downward does not temporally precede the two-fold movement of the logic of Christ, but encompasses and defines it. Thus, "downward" can be read as 'originating from the Triune Life and Love of God,' with "two-fold" referring to the movement of the Son, who through the Spirit is from the Father and returns through the Spirit to the Father. In this way, the downward two-fold motion is the motion that proceeds from the immanent life, into the economic activity, and back to the immanent life. Dogmatically, the logic of Grace is the doctrine of election, in which God is always Subject and Lord in his action in relation to us, thus undergirding all of our present decisions for him: "you have not chosen me, but I have chosen you"; and "we love because he first loved us" (John 15:16; 1 John 4:19). It is this logic of Grace which defines the ontological conditions within which the gospel of Grace functions.

---

44. Ibid., 206–7.

For Torrance, a biblically faithful exposition of the hypostatic union of God and man must involve three dynamically related components: the *assumption* of a fallen human nature; the *sanctification* and condemnation of that fallen humanity through a life of perfect obedience; and the sacrificial *offering* of that perfect life to the judgment of the Father. These three components of assumption, sanctification and offering (or *incarnational union, personal union,* and *atoning union*) should not be separated from one another as if they are referred to as three sequential moments in the history of Christ; rather, they are the same event seen from different angles, which together comprise the incarnation concept of *atoning exchange.* If any one is left out, then the ontological conditions required by the logic of Grace (and essential to salvation itself) are compromised.

The first ontological condition inherent in the logic of Grace relates to the incarnation of the Son of God as a human. In what sense, if any, is it appropriate to describe Jesus's humanity as authentically *fallen?* Acutely aware of what is at stake, Torrance reads the apostle John's *sarx egeneto* [ὁ λόγος σὰρξ ἐγένετο] as an assertion that "the Word fully participates in human nature and existence."[45] The Word as flesh is not God *in* a human, but God *as* a human. For Torrance, whatever *flesh* the Word assumes must be the very same flesh that we are. It cannot be just *part* of our flesh (our body, but not our mind or will). Nor can Jesus's humanity be a *neutral* version of our fleshly existence: it must, like ours, be understood as a *fallen* humanity. Torrance finds fault with the Council of Chalcedon's ambiguity with regard to the status of Christ's human nature and asserts that it should have used Athanasius' phrase that Christ's human nature was "under the servitude of sin."[46] For Torrance, this is critical—both exegetically and soteriologically. Since our situation as *fallen* has perverted the whole of who we are, he concludes that Christ needed to assume our whole human nature—body, mind, will and soul: "the whole man had to be assumed by Christ if the whole man was to be saved."[47] In this regard Torrance

45. *Incarnation,* 61.
46. Ibid., 201.
47. *MOC,* 39.

is fond of quoting Gregory of Nazianzen, "if Jesus Christ did not assume our fallen flesh, our fallen humanity, then our fallen humanity is untouched by his work—for '*the unassumed is the unredeemed.*'"[48] Our salvation requires an ontological solidarity with Christ in respect to his human nature.

For Torrance, the stakes are high. If Christ does not assume fallen humanity ontologically, then the reconciliation he achieves on our behalf can only be understood in terms of external forensic relations. The result of this in Torrance's view is a static hypostatic union in which the union is the product of a mechanistic and extrinsic *deux ex machine*, rather than a dynamic fleshing out of the incarnation within the whole life of Christ.[49] By contrast, Torrance views sanctification (salvation) as an internal ontological healing and re-creation. Consequently, and critical to his exposition, *Christ's humanity is an object of his atoning work* and not simply a subjective or instrumental aid toward that end.

Since 'fallen flesh' has been interpreted in a variety of ways depending on one's anthropology, it is important to clarify Torrance's use of the term, for which he utilizes a wide variety of descriptors: 'in estrangement,' 'depraved,' 'in bondage,' 'at enmity with God,' 'in alienation,' 'laden with sin and guilt' and 'diseased in mind and soul.' The overarching depiction is of humanity as fallen and fleeing from relationship with God, and, as a result, "under the divine judgment." In other words, *fallen* is primarily a relational rather than a substantive category; and whatever ontological *substance* can be meaningfully attached to human fallenness exists only by virtue of humanity's *relation*, or lack thereof, to its Creator. Thus, fallen humanity is humanity in onto-relational estrangement from its Creator, an

---

48. *Incarnation*, 62. Torrance goes so far as to call this phrase "the cardinal soteriological principle of the ecumenical Church" (Thomas F. Torrance, "Karl Barth and the Latin Heresy," *SJT* 39 [1986], 477. Hereafter, *Latin Heresy*). Torrance's assertion that the early Church Fathers largely believed that Christ took on fallen flesh is strongly questioned by much modern scholarship. For a contextual history of the debate, as well as an insightful look at the argument and terms employed, see Kelly Kapic, "The Son's Assumption of a Human Nature: A Call for Clarity," *IJST* 3, no. 2 (2001): 154–66.
49. Cf. *MOC*, 40f. •

estrangement which is both radical (fundamental) and total (permeating every aspect of the creature).[50]

As Torrance develops it, "fallen human existence" has two basic characteristics: it is both "under the judgement of the law of God" and "under the dominion of sin."[51] The first characteristic refers to our relational status before God as condemned and guilty. The second describes how we actually live—to what we *do* in the flesh (i.e., we *sin*). *Fallen* is both ontologically what we are and phenomenologically, what we will be. Together these determine the way Torrance speaks of Christ appropriating our fallen humanity "under the judgment of God."[52] What separates Christ's humanity apart from the rest of humanity is that his 'fallenness' does not lead to 'sinfulness;' that is, *what* Christ is, as full participant in our fallen human flesh, is not the final determinate of *who* he will be in his relation to the Father.[53] Christ's *hypostasis* (person) is not driven or controlled by his (fallen) human condition; rather, his fallen nature is determined by what he in his *hypostasis* does in it. Because his *hypostasis* is the second person of the Trinity, he can 'possess' a fallen nature and in possessing it not sin. Unlike we who, under the bondage of sin, continually act out that bondage, Christ, though sharing our condition, does not do what we do. Whether Torrance's explanation renders the category of fallenness unrecognizable, is a valid question.[54] Yet his concern is not to systematize sin (after all, it is illogical by definition), but to articulate the dynamic nature of sanctification. Sanctification is not a static or 'once and for all' state of being, but is ongoing throughout Jesus's incarnate life. Christ condemns sin in the flesh by overcoming it at every point. He resists sin's alienating, downward drag and converts

---

50. See Torrance's discussion of J.A. Jungmann, *The Place of Christ in Liturgical Prayer* (London: Chapman, 1965), on the post-Nicene tendency toward monophysitism in *Incarnation*, 198ff; *TiR*, 142ff.

51. *Incarnation*, 63.

52. *MOC*, 41.

53. I am indebted to Ian A. McFarland's insightful essay "Fallen or Unfallen? Christ's Human Nature and the Ontology of Human Sinfulness," *IJST* 10, no. 4 (2008): 409–12. In particular, his observation that "A nature can be damaged (and thus fallen); but a nature cannot sin because sin is ascribed to agents and thus is a matter of the hypostasis" (413).

54. It deserves to be noted that the ambiguity which exists in Torrance's usage of the term *fallen* is not unlike that found in much of the teaching of the Church Fathers on this subject.

it back in himself to obedience towards God. This "converting it back in himself" is what Torrance calls *sanctification*.[55] Of course, all humans apart from Christ do actually sin in their fallen state under original sin. Since that is the reality of our human condition, reconciliation and atonement must meet us at both the phenomenological and the ontological level. Soteriologically, both the fruit (sins) *and* the root (original sin) need to be addressed in Jesus Christ if he is to be the living atonement between God and humanity.

Two-Fold (Personal Union): " . . . and Dwelt Among Us . . . "

The second ontological condition inherent in the logic of Grace is the sanctification of fallen flesh. While the Son assumes human nature in its fallenness, he does not leave it in that state but sanctifies it both upon assumption and throughout the whole course of his life.

Christ's sanctification of our humanity has two aspects and these correspond to the two characteristics of fallen flesh which we have already observed. As human fallenness is both a relational position (who we *are* relationally as those under God's judgment) and an actual practice (what we *do* as those under the dominion of sin), the sanctification worked out in Christ's person addresses both. Torrance describes these as sanctification through incarnational union and sanctification through the personal union of Christ's active and passive obedience. Both sanctifying unions are viewed by Torrance as dynamic and on-going throughout the life of Christ. In the previous section, we considered the downward aspect of the incarnation event in which Christ really becomes what we are, yet, without sin. In this section, we will consider the dynamic nature of that union as continuous and personal. Where previously the logic of Grace took the foreground, now the logic of Christ will assume that position.

---

55. *Incarnation*, 205.

The Continuous Personal Union—the Logic of Christ

The movement from the logic of Grace to the logic of Christ within our larger discussion of the Person of Christ is a movement from a focus on incarnational union *per se* to personal union. Here, the life and work of Christ is considered as a union of God and humanity which takes place *within the person* of the Son as a human being. That is, the life of Jesus is viewed as a subjectively enacted life, dynamic and personal rather than static or abstractly metaphysical. It is not merely a hypostatic union but a hypostatic *uniting*. Jesus is the true Son of the Father because he acts as true Son through a faithful life of worship and service to the Father. Correlatively, Jesus acts as the true Son of the Father because that is who he is—that is the truth of his being. In Jesus Christ, being, action and relation cohere and cannot be torn apart. As one of us, as a real human being, Jesus Christ lives as the Son of the Father.

The task of relating the ontological aspect of the sanctification of Christ's human flesh to the *noetic* (or lived) aspect calls for a more detailed analysis of Christ's humanity.[56] How is it within the medium of fallen humanity that Christ is able to turn toward the Father? How is it that Jesus can be just like us (a human), and yet so *unlike* us (a sinless human)? In delving into the details of the hypostatic union of God and humanity in Christ, we find ourselves at the very heart of the mystery of Christ where Grace assumes its most basic form. Here we encounter a matrix of fundamental concepts which provide the form and substance of Torrance's theology of Grace: specifically, *anhypostasia, enhypostasia,* and vicarious humanity. This collection of terms, set within their trinitarian context, also gives definite expression to the dynamic nature of Torrance's paired concepts of *the logic of Grace* and *the logic of Christ*.

As a corrective to the limitations of the static metaphysical categories of Chalcedon and in an effort to do justice to the fact that

---

56. Torrance has a somewhat uncharacteristic way of employing the term *noetic* as a way of referring to the *non-ontic* aspect of Christ's human life. *Noetic* should be understood to include all that involves the Spirit's agency—i.e., Jesus' active and passive obedience, not just his mind. Cf. *SOF,* lxxxi-lxxxiii; Thomas F. Torrance, *Atonement: the Person and Work of Christ,* ed. Robert T. Walker (Milton Keynes: Paternoster, 2009), 161–64. Hereafter, *Atonement.*

the incarnation is not a state but a history, Torrance harnesses the theological algebra[57] of the *anhypostasia* and *enhypostasia* couplet as a way of dynamically apprehending Christ as two natures in one person. At the impressionable age of twenty-five while furiously writing his theology lectures at Auburn Seminary in New York, Torrance was profoundly influenced by his encounter with this couplet in Barth's just-released CD 1.2. He recollects,

> I was gripped by the way in which he resurrected and deployed the theological couplet *anhypostasia* and *enhypostasia* to throw into sharp focus 'the inner logic of grace' (as I called it) embodied in the incarnation, with reference to which . . . all the ways and works of God in his interaction with us in space and time may be given careful formulation.[58]

In Torrance's view, the logic of the couplet (if not the couplet itself) was fundamental to the theological intuition of those theologians, beginning with Cyril of Alexandria, who represents a *third way* within Christology.[59] As we will see, Torrance employs this *theologoumenon*

57. *TS*, 269.
58. *Karl Barth: Biblical and Evangelical Theologian*, 125 (hereafter, *KBBET*). The couplet was originally used by Leontius of Byzantium (485–543 CE), after Chalcedon to address confusion caused by varying usages of the term for nature (*physis*). Its intention was to affirm that the humanity of Christ had no personal reality on its own (*anhypostasia*), but had personal reality (*enhypostasia*) in the person of the eternal Son. This was Leontius's effort to pave a middle-way between the Nestorian doctrine that Christ's human nature had an independent hypostasis (center of subsistence) and the Alexandrian rebuttal which argued for the *anhypostatic* humanity of Christ. Together the *an/en-hypostasia* effectively complement and enrich the doctrine that Jesus Christ is fully God and fully human, consubstantial with God and with fallen humanity (cf. *Incarnation*, 211–12). I am indebted to Robert Walker's exposition of Torrance's usage of the *anhypostasia* and *enhypostasia* for my own understanding and development here (cf. Editor's introduction in *Atonement*, lxxii–lxxix). It should be noted that this reading of Leontius is contested by LeRon Shults ("A Dubious Christological Formula: From Leontius of Byzantium to Karl Barth," *Theological Studies* 57 [1996], 431–46), but Shults's own conclusions are countered by U.M. Lang "Anhypostatos and Enhypostatos: Church Fathers, Protestant Orthodoxy and Karl Barth," *Journal of Theological Studies* NS 49 (1998): 630–57; M. Gockel, "A Dubious Christological Formula? Leontius of Byzantium and the Anhypostasis-Enhypostasis Theory," *Journal of Theological Studies* NS 51 (2000): 515–32; Davidson, "Theologizing the Human Jesus," 138–41; and W. Pannenberg, *Jesus - God and Man*, trans. L. L. Wilkins and D. A. Priebe, 2nd ed. (Philadelphia: Westminster, 1975), 337–44.
59. Thomas F. Torrance, *The Christian Doctrine of God: One Being Three Persons* (Edinburgh: T&T Clark, 1996), 160. Hereafter, *CDG*. For Torrance's account of the various 'schools' or traditions which existed in the early Church's understanding of the relation of Christ's humanity to his divinity, see *Incarnation*, 206–11; and "Athanasius: A Study in the Foundations of Classical Theology," in *TiR*, 215–19. See also "The Place of the Humanity of Christ in the Sacramental Life of the Church," in *Church Service Society Annual* 26 (1956), 3–10; reprinted as "The Humanity of Christ in the Sacramental Life of the Church," in *Gospel, Church and Ministry, Thomas F. Torrance Collected Studies I*, ed. Jock Stein (Eugene, OR: Pickwick, 2012), 86. Hereafter, *GCM*. Torrance's basic claim is that Athanasius represented a middle path in patristic thought between Alexandrian and Antiochene

for creative applications rarely advanced in the history of the Church. While his application of the couplet is certainly innovative, it represents a concerted attempt to allow the Grace of God in Christ to govern all aspects of theological reflection and action—or, in Torrance's words, "to work out . . . the scientific sub-structure of Christian Dogmatics."[60]

As Torrance employs it, the *an/en theologoumenon*[61] seeks to express biblical teaching regarding the union of God and humanity in Christ: "the presence of full and perfect humanity does not impair or diminish or restrict the presence of full and perfect deity, and the presence of full and perfect deity does not impair or diminish or restrict the presence of full and perfect humanity."[62] The Word does not absorb the flesh but assumes it in such a way that the union of the two does not create a 'third thing,' which is neither divine nor human. Jesus Christ is *homoousion* with both God and humanity. This is a critical point for Torrance, for it means that God can become a human without overwhelming or taking away our humanity. Using this pair of concepts, the action of God in the incarnation can be seen to be an act which was wholly the work of God's Grace (corresponding to the *anhypostasia*), and yet an act which results in a full and real human act (corresponding to the *enhypostasia*). In this way, the *an/en* couplet brings a dynamism to the Chalcedonian *inconfuse, immutabiliter, indivise* and *inseparabiliter,* which Torrance otherwise finds problematically absent. When understood within the context of Torrance's concept of onto-relations, the an/en couplet serves to "deliver the Chalcedonian doctrine of Christ from the tendency involved in the Greek terms to state the doctrine of Christ statically and metaphysically."[63]

---

extremes. R.V. Sellers, *Two Ancient Christologies* (SPCK, London, 1940) appears to be his primary historical source. (For a critique of Torrance's approach, see Habets, *The Danger of Vertigo*, 94; and Anatolios, *Athanasius: The Coherence of his Thought*, 70–73, 138–46.)

60. *KBBET*, 125.

61. The abbreviation of the *anhypostasia* and *enhypostasia* couplet to *an/en* is not found in Torrance's writings. The use of *an/en* in this book is both for the purpose of simplification and also to highlight the fact that the *anhypostasia* can never be abstracted from the *enhypostasia* and vice-versa.

62. *Incarnation*, 191.

63. Ibid., 85.

The Hypostatic Union is a Personal Union

By calling our attention to the *hypostasis*, the *an/en* couplet helpfully sheds light on the *what* and the *way* of the hypostatic union.[64] As Ivor Davidson points out, the purpose of the *an/en* couplet is not to logically explain how there can be two natures in one person; rather, "What it is about is specifying the way in which what Jesus does as a man is the action of God, which transforms but does not eliminate or suppress the human in its own sphere." By directing attention away from categories of substance metaphysics and towards personal presence, *an/en hypostasis* serves to enhance the Chalcedonian formula by bringing to the fore the personal dynamism of the union. The hypostatic union is a *personal* union, not in the psychologized sense of the joining together of two personalities, but in the sense that it is "a union within the *one* person of the Son."[65] In this way, the *an/en theologoumenon* is best understood as a means of fixing our attention upon the agent of Grace himself. Through the *an/en* couplet, the logic of God, expressed in the logic of Grace and the logic of Christ, is given concrete material focus in the person (*hypostasis*) of Christ as an agent.

By conceptualizing the hypostatic union as a personal union, Torrance is able to view the movement of Grace from multiple angles and in the midst of a variety of doctrinal debates, while keeping his focus on the proper object. In this monograph I will highlight only the doctrinal decisions Torrance makes which are most relevant to his theology of Grace. In light of the fact that Grace involves an identical correspondence between the Gift and the Giver, we will focus our attention on the question, "Who is the agent of Jesus's life?" Or, to put it differently, "who gets the credit for Jesus's holy life?" Specifically, we will look at the way Torrance employs the *an/en-hypostasia* couplet to answer this question, as well as how he conceptualizes the functional relation of the two wills of Christ.

---

64. Ivor Davidson, "Theologizing the Human Jesus," 147.
65. *Incarnation*, 207.

Agency in Jesus Christ

Who is the agent of Jesus's life? Is it the Logos (his divine nature), Jesus of Nazareth (his human nature), the Holy Spirit, or some combination of these three? In approaching this question, Torrance leads with the assertion that "grace must be understood in terms of his human as well as his divine nature."[66] While this is basic Chalcedonianism at work, it helpfully accentuates the significance of Jesus's humanity alongside the obvious importance of his deity. God the Son does not simply come *in* a human, but *as* a human. When the Son assumes the form of a servant, he does not merely *resemble* a servant by the servant–like way he lives his life; he actually takes on the concrete form of real human existence and possesses a real human agency. But *how* is this so? How can we best understand and express the reality that the Son/Logos has assumed our humanity for us and for our salvation? How are we to understand the relation between Christ's divinity and his humanity in terms of agency?

In Torrance's view, the *an/en* couplet opens up conceptual space for a dynamic way of describing divine and human agency in Christ that illuminates the key features of the motion of Grace, which Chalcedon's negative assertions fail to capture.[67] While the person of the Son remains the single *hypostasis* or agent of the God-human, the human Jesus is no mere instrument in the hand of God, but a full human person with human body, mind, reason, will and soul.[68] For Torrance, the doctrine of two wills (2nd Council of Constantinople [680AD]) is a critical move which discloses the ontological nature (as well as the nature of the ontology) at the inner heart of the atonement.[69] Were Christ to only have one will there would be no historical (lived) means for the divine Word to reorient that will. Here in the will of Jesus Christ, the divine will and the human will coexist without confusion or separation and in that onto-relational coexistence, the will of

---

66. *TiR*, 183.
67. See Bruce McCormack, *Karl Barth's Critically Realistic Dialectical Theology*, 364.
68. Thomas F. Torrance, *Incarnation*, xliii.
69. Ibid., 212.

estranged man is bent back into oneness with the divine will through the sanctifying obedience of Christ. Through the concept of the *an/ en hypostasia* combined with the doctrine of two wills in the Person of Christ, Torrance is able to hold incarnation and atonement together such that atonement takes place within the person of Christ himself as he personally mediates the two natures.

Combining the *an/en* with the biblical material, the pattern can be expressed in the following way: as triune Grace is always both downward *and* two-fold and always both *anhypostatic* and *enhypostatic*, so also is the life of Jesus—always *simultaneously*, the Son sent from the Father in the Spirit and the Son in the Spirit offering his life to the Father. Importantly, Torrance never abandons the priority of the downward movement of Grace and conceptually, it is within that circle and upon that field that the activity of the Spirit takes place in humanity. Thus, just as the downward and *anhypostatic* movement always informs and clears the space for the two-fold and *enhypostatic* movement, so too the incarnational union of human and divine nature is an act of the Son through the Spirit which provides the platform upon (or circle within) which the active and passive obedience of the Spirit-enabled Son has existence.

This is the basis for Torrance's doctrine of the vicarious humanity of Christ which I will examine in the next section of this chapter. In our present context, what impinges most directly is Torrance's observation about space in relation to the hypostatic union of God and humanity in one person. It is to his conception of space that we will now turn.

Relational and Receptacle Notions of Space and the Kenosis of the Son

A major barrier Torrance identifies as inimical to a proper understanding of Grace is the structural dualism inherent in container notions of space and time. In this vein he critiques the Lutheran principle *finitum capax infiniti* for leading to a Monophysite fusion of the two natures of Christ. If the divine is subject to space-time limitations, then the incarnation is necessarily a fusion of divine and human natures: that is, the divinization (change) of human nature into the divine. Or to use the language of gift and giver, the Giver completely overwhelms the Gift, displacing it into non-existence. Either way, the hypostatic union is compromised into a hypostatic fusion which is no longer *homoousios* with God or humanity. The following section lays out Torrance's critique of receptacle notions of space and describes how rethinking time and space as predicates of their occupant allows a way forward for a proper theological ontology and consequently a proper notion of Grace.

The Aristotelian receptacle notion of space and time which defines place as "the immobile limit within which a body is contained,"[70] postulates a relation of interdependence between the container and its contents such that "*what contains and what is contained are inseparable or interdependent.*"[71] For this receptacle view, there can be no void or empty space since all that exists has its existence *within* space. From within the space-as-receptacle framework and its inherent dualistic assumptions, the *kenosis* of the Son of God could only be viewed as "the emptying of the Son of God into a containing vessel."[72] However, this view of *kenosis* fails to give due consideration to the intent of Nicene theology: that the incarnation was meant to be Christ's full presence with us in space and time yet without ceasing to be present to the Father. Applying the receptacle notion to *kenosis* effectively destroys the *perichoretic* interrelations between the Son and the Father.

By contrast, Torrance points out that because God is the Creator of all things visible and invisible, he transcends all of space and time which he brought into being out of nothing. From this "It follows that the relation between God and space is not itself a spatial relation."[73] God exists in a creative not spatial relation to time and space. Accordingly, Torrance contends for a conceptual rethinking of time and space; not as receptacles which exist on their own apart from

---

70. Torrance implicates Aquinas in perpetuating the container view. See *Space, Time and Incarnation* (Edinburgh: T&T Clark, 1997), 7ff. Hereafter, *STI*.
71. *Incarnation*, 217 (italics original).
72. Thomas F. Torrance, *Space, Time and Resurrection* (Edinburgh: T&T Clark, 1998), 124. Hereafter, *STR*.
73. *STI*, 2.

bodies or forces, but as functions and forms of events in the universe, which take their form and function from "the nature of the force that gives them their field of determination."[74] Speech regarding God's own 'time' and 'place' must receive its meaning and definition strictly from the uncreated and creative communion of the divine life.[75] Thus, rather than attempting to *spatialize* the relation between God and creation, Torrance advocates *relationalizing* the concept of space by regarding space as "a predicate of the Occupant."[76] On this account, *kenosis* does not refer to a diminution or self-limitation of God's infinite being within space and time, but to the mystery of his abasement and impoverishment in his willing human-becomingness. The *kenosis* of the Son is a positive rather than a negative act; "a kenosis by addition, not by subtraction."[77] The Son's assumption of fallen human flesh "does not mean the self-limitation of God or the curtailment of his power, but the staggering exercise of his power within the limitations of our contingent existence in space and time."[78] Thus Christ's life is one of "continuous *kenosis* in which he refused to transgress the limits of the creaturely and earthly conditions of human nature."[79] The Son does not give up his divinity in becoming human, nor is the human nature altered (i.e., divinized) through its assumption. It is "a strictly dialectical union," a unity in differentiation.[80]

Torrance praises Reformed theology (in contrast to Lutheran) for incorporating the patristic recognition of what the incarnation teaches: that God is not boxed in by the limits of our finite conditions and that the finite does not contain the infinite *without remainder*.[81] The Reformed solution was to view the assumption of human nature into the divine *person* (not nature) of the Son,[82] in whom there was

---

74. *STR*, 130.
75. Ibid., 130–31. Cf. *STI*, 15; Torrance, *Divine Meaning: Studies in Patristic Hermeneutics*, 361ff. Hereafter, *DM*.
76. *STI*, 15.
77. *DM*, 361.
78. *CDG*, 214–15.
79. *Incarnation*, 187; cf. *CDG*, 214; *STI*, 14.
80. Ibid., 228. This non-confused asymmetrical participation is also evident in the way Torrance talks about time being taken up into eternity.
81. *STI*, 35.
82. *Incarnation*, 228.

an indirect (mediated) union between the two natures by the Spirit. That is, "there was a *unio immediata* between the human nature and the person of the Son, but a *unio mediata* between the divine and human natures through the Spirit."[83] In this way the Reformers could speak of a communion between the two natures without mutual inter-penetration. God became human in Christ, but humanity did not also become God. Human nature was not divinized, but only raised into union and communion with God through the Spirit. To suggest otherwise, as in the Lutheran *communicatio naturarum*, "makes nonsense of the incarnation and reconciliation."[84] By locating the union of two natures in the *person* of the Son and understanding space as a predicate of its occupant, Jesus Christ is able to be understood as the *place* or *space* "in our physical world of space and time where God and man meet, and where they have communion with one another."[85]

According to Torrance, it was the combination of this relational notion of space and time with the active bringing together of the *an/ en-hypostasia theologoumenon* which enabled the Reformed theologians to make a real advance over the Patristic usage of these concepts.[86] Together they create the ontological space needed for the union of divine and human natures to take place appropriately; and, as will become more apparent in the next section, they clear the conceptual ground for Torrance's doctrine of Grace to flourish.

Pneumatology within Christology

In the discussion thus far of the personal union of God and humanity in Christ, I have shown that in Torrance's theology the sanctification of fallen flesh in the person of Christ trades heavily upon a particular matrix of essential concepts. To this end we have considered his employment of *anhypostasia* and *enhypostasia*, the doctrine of the two wills of Christ and finally the importance of a relational rather than

83. Ibid., 222.
84. Ibid., 223.
85. *STR*, 128.
86. For Torrance's exposition on the way Reformed theologians parsed the relation between the two natures of Christ, see *Incarnation*, 225–33.

a receptacle notion of space and time. The final indispensable piece of the jigsaw is the role pneumatology plays within Torrance's Christology.[87] In fact, it is not overstatement to assert that everything thus far is logically incomprehensible without a thoroughgoing pneumatology in play. Accordingly, before we can proceed to this chapter's next major section on the vicarious atonement of Christ, the groundwork must be laid which sets Christ's atoning activity within its basic pneumatological context. A discussion of the relation of the Spirit to the incarnate Christ rounds out the ontological conditions which form the basis of the gospel of Grace.

In discussing receptacle notions of space and time, I have already noted that the application of the container view to the incarnation effectively denies the continuing *perichoretic* interrelations of the triune persons. This is because the dualism inherent in receptacle notions of space and time render God incapable of being present in history. Torrance views this dualism as a primary culprit in the detachment of the acts of God from his being, and of the being of God from his acts and concludes: "the loss of ontology has proved quite fatal."[88] This "loss of ontology" threatens to dislodge—or at the very least cast doubt upon—the truth that the God we meet in Jesus Christ is the very same *perichoretic* onto-relational God whose acts are co-acts and thus indivisible.[89] The link between the ontological and the economic Trinity calls for a relationship between the Father and the Son and the Spirit in the economy that corresponds to the relationship of the Persons in the immanent Trinity. Since the Sonship (and thus divinity) of Jesus is the unbroken history of his filial relationship to God the Father mediated by the Spirit, what is needed is a Christology that is wholly theocentric and pneumatological, and a pneumatology that is genuinely christological and theocentric.[90] The Son's mission from the Father in time corresponds to his eternal generation. The Spirit's

---

87. Thomas F. Torrance, "The Church in the New Era of Scientific and Cosmological Change," in *Theological Foundations for Ministry*, ed. Ray Anderson (Edinburgh: T&T Clark, 2000), 775. Hereafter, *New Era*.
88. *New Era*, 769.
89. *MOC*, 65.
90. See Harold Hunter, "Spirit Christology: Dilemma and Promise," *Heythrop Journal* 24 (1983).

communion of love which bonds the Father to the Son and the Son to the Father in time corresponds to his eternal spiration and procession. Consequently, if we are to reflect on how Jesus of Nazareth is both fully God and fully human, we are on firmer theological ground when we see the incarnation in its essential triune coactivity, rather than treating the union as a purely christological problem.

The Incarnate Son's Continuing Koinonia with the Father is through the Spirit

Ivor Davidson has observed that too often the heirs of Barth have been insufficiently overt in their articulation of the Spirit's action in, upon and towards the human Jesus.[91] While it is true that Torrance's treatment of the Spirit-led historical life of Christ is lacking in detailed attention, it is also the case that the pneumatological resources for a more robust account are indeed present.[92] However, working against such description is the fact that his pneumatological allusions are often presented via christological terms, for example: the humanity of Christ, *enhypostasia*, active and passive obedience, holiness, sanctification, consecration, and the like. Unfortunately, Torrance's vigilant refusal to separate his doctrine of the Spirit from his Christology leaves his pneumatology open to misinterpretation, obscuring the way pneumatology informs his Christology. Yet for Torrance the life of the historical Jesus is inexplicable apart from the continued indwelling and empowerment of the Spirit. The incarnation of the Son is a dynamic hypostatic uniting, and, as such, the human Jesus is not a *state* arrived at, but a life lived and a person personalized. Thus, apposite trinitarian reflection will not only perceive an essential pneumatic role in the constitution of the incarnate Son, but will also appreciate the continuous essential empowerment of the Spirit in the endurance and perdurance of the hypostatic union.[93]

Thus, the coming-and-presence of the Being of God among us in

---

91. Davidson, "Theologizing the Human Jesus," *IJST*, vol. 3 (July 2001): 151.
92. *SOF*, xcviii. See Habets' critique, 83.
93. Cf. *SOF*, xcviii; Calvin, *Institutes of the Christian Religion*, 2.16.19.

Jesus Christ is actually a *double* movement of both the Son and the Spirit. All that has been said thus far about the dynamic movement of God the Son is also necessarily a dynamic movement of God the Holy Spirit; and just as the Son's movement is both humanward and Godward, so the activity of the Spirit in the Son is also both humanward and Godward. In its humanward movement of revelation, the Holy Spirit mediates the life of the Son, from conception to baptism to resurrection. In his Godward movement of reconciliation, the Son of God in his assumed humanity vicariously receives the Holy Spirit and so lives as the Son he is by the Spirit, who is always active within him. In fact, the Spirit participates in all of Christ's vicarious and intercessory activities.[94] This *koinonia* of mediation and reception holds the humanward/Godward movement together throughout the life of Christ. For Torrance, nothing less than the very integrity of Jesus's human agency is at stake, for if the divine Logos displaces the human rational soul of Jesus Christ, the human Jesus is reduced to a mere instrument in the hand of God, and the salvific relevance of his humanity is shattered.[95]

Essential in Torrance's application of pneumatology to Christology is his appropriation of the *an/en theologoumenon*. There is a distinct development between his 1938–1939 Auburn lectures and his later Edinburgh lectures which can be attributed to Torrance's reading of Barth's CD 1.2 and making what would prove to be a life-changing discovery of the heuristic power of the *anhypostasia* and *enhypostasia* theological couplet.[96] In his early Auburn lectures Jesus succeeds in his struggle with sin solely by virtue of his being the eternal Son/Word, and while Torrance insists that the humanity of Christ is necessary and significant, his emphasis on the direct (unmediated) agency of *the Word* as this human being obscures the coherence of what it could tangibly mean for Jesus to be authentically human. And while Torrance repeatedly asserts the necessity of holding Christ's person and work

---

94. *CDG*, 153; cf. *TRn*, 246f; *MOC*, 118.
95. *TiR*, 116.
96. *KBBET*, 124–25.

together, the person so dominates that the work of Christ's actively obedient life is virtually absent from the discussion.

However, by the time of the Edinburgh lectures and beyond, new possibilities for christological description began to open up in his teaching, and it seems, in his understanding of the human enabling (participatory) aspect of Grace. This more developed account of pneumatology, which we might call a *pneumatic-Christology*, shows itself most clearly and consistently in the way that Christ's human and *noetic* existence is attributed to the work of the Spirit. As we will see in the following section on atoning union, by making a formal distinction between the *ontic* and the *noetic*, Torrance develops Christ's active and passive obedience as *noetic* activities which involve the Spirit's agency. In particular, Torrance draws upon the term *proekopte*[97] as a way of unpacking and giving real force to the activity of Christ's active obedience before the Father.

Atoning Union: *"for Us and for Our Salvation"*

In the previous section, I examined four key concepts which together provide what I am asserting are the basic ontological conditions underlying Torrance's doctrine of Grace: *anhypostasia/enhypostasia*, the two wills of Christ, a relational notion of space and time and a pneumatically understood Christology. These four concepts establish the essential basis and form for Torrance's understanding of the vicarious humanity of Christ, whereby incarnation and atonement interpenetrate one another in such a way that atonement takes place within the person of Christ himself.

Within Torrance's theology, all that is said of Christ's humanity as a hypostatic or a personal union gets recast and restated as an atoning union. *Atoning union* is the form that hypostatic union takes in a sinful and alienated humanity. In arguing that incarnation and atonement are internally linked, Torrance is asserting that

---

97. Luke 2:52, "And Jesus increased (*proekopten*) in wisdom and in stature, and in favor with God and man." Cf. *Atonement*, 64.

... atonement is not an act of God done *ab extra* upon man, but an act of God become man, done *ab intra*, in his stead and on his behalf; it is an act of God as man, translated into human actuality and made to issue out of the depths of man's being and life toward God.[98]

Torrance commends this ontological understanding of the vicarious life of Christ as of significant interpretive importance in providing an intrinsic coherence and wholeness to the overall doctrine of the atonement. He suggests that a failure to appreciate the coinherence of incarnation and atonement inevitably results in a fractured interpretation of the various aspects of Christ's death in terms of external relations, along with a corresponding variety of theories.[99]

In his actual exposition of the atonement, Torrance draws upon two sets of language which we might classify as material and formal. Materially, Torrance appeals to the biblical language of covenant and expounds atonement as the fulfillment of the covenant within the substitutionary and representative life of the Son.[100] Formally, he follows the downward two-fold movement of Grace by attending to atonement as a dynamic ontological (*ontic*) and subjective (*noetic*) reality, such that "it was carried through his conscious personal relations as well as his union in being with God."[101]

Within Torrance's theology, these atonement metaphors are not to be viewed as strict categories or parts or divisions, but more like portals or entry points which reveal the same truth of salvation from a particular angle. Each overlaps with the others and defies strict schematization. Consequently, "none of these aspects can stand alone or become the major basis of a doctrine of atonement without serious dislocation of the biblical understanding and failure to appreciate the fullness of Christ's saving work."[102] Rather than organizing his concept

---

98. *TF*, 158–59.
99. Thomas F. Torrance, "Atonement and the Moral Order," in *Universalism and the Doctrine of Hell*, 250. Hereafter, *A&MO*.
100. Torrance draws upon and inter-relates multiple biblical metaphors such as: the dramatic/dynamic (*pdh*), the cultic/priestly (*kpr*), and the ontological/incarnational (*g'l*). (Cf. *Atonement*, 27–62 and *TF*, 170–80.); Christ's three-fold office of the prophet, priest and king. (Cf. *SOF*, lxxxvii–xcv.) Throughout them all, the incarnational/ontological undergirds and grounds the atoning acts.
101. *Atonement*, 162. Torrance does not distinguish in any meaningful way between *ontological* and *ontic* or between *subjective* and *noetic*. Context generally determines which pair comes to the fore.

of atonement around a particular theory or metaphor, the multiplexity of christological themes is given coherent expression through the dynamic and personal language of worship. Thus, overarching Torrance's use of material and formal terminology, Torrance views the entire atoning union of Christ as the movement of the Son's worship of the Father through the Spirit in which we are given to share. Redemption's true context is one of worship realized through a union of divine and human agency in the person of Christ.[103] Set in the framework of worship, the movement of Grace enacted in the life of Jesus Christ is seen as both a humanward movement and a Godward movement, in which the covenant is fulfilled in our place and on our behalf.

Atonement as Covenant Fulfillment

Since Torrance's doctrine of atonement is set materially within the context of the covenant, whatever is to be said about the vicarious humanity of Christ must be understood from within this framework—the "all-embracing framework of grace."[104] Thus, an apprehension of the mystery of Christ's atoning life requires an understanding of God's covenant relationship with Israel.[105] As was noted at the beginning of this chapter, the concept of covenant is pre-historical, going back to God's purposes in creation. After the fall, Israel was elected as a people to be the mediator of the restoration of this covenant. Yet, as God pressed nearer and nearer to his people, the conflict between God and sinful Israel only intensified.[106]

This escalating conflict reached its climax in the coming of Jesus, who stepped into the place of Israel as the mediator of the (new) covenant.[107] As the new Israel—God's new covenant partner—Jesus fulfills Israel's role in himself and through his person and work, he is

---

102. Ibid., 53.
103. *TF*, 154.
104. *CDG*, 219.
105. Thomas F. Torrance, "Salvation is of the Jews," *Evangelical Quarterly* 22 (1950): 167.
106. *TRn*, 195–97.
107. *MOC*, 32–33.

the final mediator of revelation and reconciliation. Where Israel was called to be the bearer of the Messiah, a corporate prophet who in her embodied existence was to be a kind of clothing for the Word of God to wear, Jesus *is* the Messiah bearing the Word *in himself*.[108] Likewise, where Israel was called to be the servant of the Lord embodying in her flesh the covenanted way of communion through the law and liturgy, Jesus *is* the covenanted way of communion providing *in himself* the covenanted way of response through his obedience to the divine Word and by offering the divinely provided liturgical response to the Word.[109]

As the covenanted or 'vicarious way of response,' Jesus enacts reconciliation between God and humanity with himself as the 'living bond.'[110] In and through his vicarious life, death and resurrection, "Jesus drew the covenant partnership between God and Israel, and between God and humanity as a whole in Israel into his own relation as incarnate Son to the Father, thereby anchoring it forever in his own Person as the Mediator."[111] From this standpoint, the heart of atonement is embedded in his union of agency.[112] *Vicarious, in other words, refers to the historical anchoring of the covenant between God and humanity in the person of the Son,* and so also in Torrance's phrase, "into the very life of God."[113]

From this perspective, it is the dominant and ever-present motif of Jesus's Sonship, within the context of covenant, which sets the terms for how atonement as a whole is to be understood. For Torrance the atonement fundamentally is not a legal or legalistic problem solvable by a clever lawyer or merciful judge, but the anchoring of a relation of love in a movement of worship.[114] What Jesus does, he does as the Son. His active and passive obedience in his Father's house and his priestly mediatorial activities have their true grounding and meaning in his

---

108. Thomas F. Torrance, *God and Rationality* (Edinburgh: T&T Clark, 1997), 147. Hereafter, *G&R*.
109. *RP*, 3.
110. *MOC*, 77.
111. Ibid., 41.
112. *Atonement*, 75.
113. *TRn*, 248; *TF*, 155, 183–84.
114. *Incarnation*, 82; Cf. *A&MO*, 253.

identity as the Son. This framework gathers the material aspects of the salvation narrative together into a form which casts a particular color or light upon the way atonement is understood as an outflow of Grace.

Justification as Total Substitution

Certainly one of the major doctrinal loci where different visions of Grace most radically expose themselves is in the area of justification. When Torrance turns to the specific task of expounding the doctrine of justification, he takes his lead from the Scots Confession of 1560, out of which he gleans three "important facts" that he thoroughly integrates into his own exposition.[115] *First*, he notes that there is no separate article on justification in the confession, for justification belongs to the "inner texture" of the gospel and therefore does not belong on its own. Accordingly, in constructing his own doctrine of justification, Torrance resists the narrow definitions which would restrict its scope to exclusively forensic categories.[116] It is in fact the more spacious *motion of Grace which provides the basic framework for how justification is understood*—justification is by *Grace* alone. By expanding justification in line with his larger doctrine of Grace, it is given central importance—but *as a servant of Grace, not as its master*. *Second*, Torrance observes the absolute centrality of the person and work of Jesus Christ and our "fraternity," or union with him. In this regard, he highlights Knox's observation that the prayer of Jesus was part of his atoning obedience and oblation to God.[117] This observation directs our understanding of union with Christ as a sharing and participating in Jesus' life of worship of the Father. It is through union with his worshipping life that we are clothed with Christ's name and holiness, and are thus well-pleasing to the Father. The *third* observation Torrance makes is that the accent lies strongly on the positive side of salvation—that is, upon the saving humanity of Christ's "positive obedience and filial life in our flesh."[118] Rather than justification being

---

115. *TRn*, 151.
116. Cf. Matthew Baker, "The Place of St. Irenaeus of Lyons in Historical and Dogmatic Theology According to Thomas F. Torrance," *Participatio* 2 (2010): 28; *TF*, 168ff.
117. John Knox was the primary author of the Scots Confession.

exclusively oriented toward forgiveness of sins through Christ's death on the cross, Knox links justification with the resurrection and ascension of Christ, in which we share through union with him. Justification is essentially *personal*—it is by Christ alone who personally secures it in the incarnation and personally bestows it in the ascension (1 Cor 1:30). Those who are justified look to Christ rather than themselves that they might live out of him alone.[119] As Torrance's doctrine of justification unfolds, we will observe his fidelity to these aspects of Knox's thought.

According to Torrance, justify (*dikaioun*) essentially means "to put in the right, to put in the truth," and justification means the fulfilling of righteousness or the enactment of the truth.[120] Thus, depending on the truth of the matter for one to be justified (i.e., for justice to be accomplished), could mean either condemnation or vindication. In the gospel, "the justification of the ungodly" (Rom 4:5) paradoxically carries both meanings: for in the condemnation of Jesus Christ, the truth is enacted against the guilty by judgment (condemnation) and also by making the guilty righteous (vindication).

This two-fold sense of justification in which righteousness is fulfilled and the truth is enacted is linguistically distinguished—yet held together—by Torrance's conception of *objective* and *subjective* justification. Objective justification places the focus upon *the God who justifies*, embodied in God's justifying act in Jesus Christ; subjective justification places the focus on the side of *the justified human*, embodied in Jesus's human appropriation of the truth through the Spirit (1 Tim 3.16).[121] Justification then as Torrance frames it is the objective act of God's self-giving *and* the subjective actualization of that act of response from within alienated human existence.

Alongside this general distinction between objective and subjective justification, another layer of Torrance's thought tracks the relationship of justification and sanctification by equating subjective

118. *TRn*, 151.
119. Ibid., 161.
120. Ibid., 153; cf. *STR*, 51ff.
121. Ibid., 157.

justification with sanctification.[122] Or, more accurately, subjective justification is a subsection of sanctification. By speaking of sanctification via the language of subjective justification,[123] Torrance is able to secure two important aspects in his doctrine of atonement. *First*, it highlights the essentially redemptive character of the obedient life of Jesus. Christ's humanity is not external to the atonement for in fact Jesus Christ "*is* our human response to God."[124] Jesus's actualization of the divine act of righteousness accomplished by yielding to it and actively making it his own throughout his life and death is an appropriation in which he vicariously stands in our place as substitute and representative.[125] *Second*, this terminology serves as a corrective to the classic Protestant *ordo salutis* in which justification and sanctification were assigned to successive stages within a process of salvation. By contrast, Torrance's reading of the biblical material positions sanctification alongside justification as realities which are complete in Christ and imputed to us by free Grace.[126]

Like justification, so too does sanctification correspond to the downward two-fold movement of Grace. Thus, sanctification *first of all* refers to the sanctification of human nature through the divinely enacted union of fallen human nature and divine nature in the person of the Son. Torrance describes the sanctifying nature of this union: "in his holy assumption of our unholy humanity, his purity wipes away our impurity, his holiness covers our corruption, his nature heals our nature."[127] Viewed from this angle, the incarnation itself (which includes his crucifixion and resurrection) is a fundamentally redeeming and sanctifying event, which effects a kind of ontological healing at the roots of human nature. This downward movement of sanctifying Grace, which Torrance identifies as addressing humanity's need at the level of original sin, provides the *ontic* ground for the two-

---

122. Ibid.
123. Ibid., 156–58.
124. *MOC*, 90.
125. *TRn*, 156–57.
126. Ibid., 158. Torrance finds support for this view in his reading of Knox and Calvin. See especially Calvin's *Inst.* 2.16.19.
127. Ibid., 155–56.

fold motion of sanctifying Grace—Grace which is worked out *noetically* in the active and passive obedience of Christ and which addresses humanity's *actual sin and its penalty.*[128] This ordering is "supremely important" for Torrance, for it enables justification to be apprehended as "more than a merely forensic non-imputation of sin," and the humanity of Christ to be recognized as having saving significance throughout the whole life of the historical Jesus.[129]

Viewed in this comprehensive and vicarious way, justification is a broad concept in Torrance's atonement theology. He uses it to describe the entire movement of God's atoning mediation in Christ as a movement of descent and ascent: an *ontic* movement *into* human existence as well as a *noetic* movement *from within* human existence back to the Father. Upon the ground of this saving and sanctifying union, we are given to share not only in the negative righteousness through the forgiveness of sins, but also in the positive righteousness of Christ's obedient and perfect filial relation lived on earth with the heavenly Father. What remains to be demonstrated in this section is just how Christ's active and passive obedience is deemed to have atoning significance in Torrance's theology.

Positive Righteousness through Active Obedience

In his active obedience, Jesus the Servant-Son lives a life of perfect filial relation to the Father, obediently hearing, answering, trusting and living by faith in God's Word. By responding in total faithfulness to the love of the Father and actively making the Father's word and will his own, Jesus is the covenanted way of response. This he does in our name and on our behalf, as our representative.

As a way of describing and asserting the human authenticity of Christ's active obedience, Torrance draws attention to the term the gospel of Luke uses (2:52) to describe Jesus's increase [*proekopten*] in wisdom and stature.[130] Torrance translates *proekopte* literally, picking

---

128. Ibid., 156. Torrance's work contains little in the way of an extended consideration of ancestral sin and its relation to human nature.
129. *Incarnation*, 82.

up on the term's original nautical sense, and uses the phrase "cut his way forward" to emphasize that Jesus's growth was a making headway stroke by stroke, beating his way forward and progressively forging ahead. In our flesh and as one of us Jesus bears within his body the burden of our alienated humanity, pressing forward toward the Father throughout his life on earth. It is only in and through *this* way that he opens up *in himself* a new way for humanity to rise to true knowledge of the Father. In emphasizing *prokōpe* as an important descriptor of the struggle involved in the incarnate Son's human existence, Torrance is giving pneumatology a critical role in his doctrine of atonement. As was noted in the previous section, Torrance asserts that it was through the power of the Spirit that Jesus makes this headway [*prokōpe*], stage by stage willing by the Spirit to live *enhypostatically* as the Son that he is *anhypostatically*. As the Spirit is "the perfecting cause" bringing creatures to their fulfillment in God, so the incarnate Son is perfected through the Spirit.[131] In this way, Jesus' identity—his personhood as the Son of God—is confirmed even as it is forged "with loud cries and tears."[132]

Torrance's exposition of *prokōpe* vividly displays the theological weight he assigns to the human obedience of the Son to the Father. The filial obedience of Christ in the flesh is a faithfulness which must be understood, not merely in external terms as a sort of moral conformity to the legal requirements of the law, but also as an active obedience which issues out of the depths of the human heart and mind. It is the obedience of intimate fellowship ("the prayer of obedience"[133]), which is inseparable from prayerful dependence, communion and devotion, thanksgiving and worship.[134] It is in this way that the incarnate life of the Son is a life of perfect sonship, restoring the covenant-breaking creation to communion with God; yet this restoration occurs *from deep within our broken and shattered existence.*[135]

---

130. Torrance attributes this insight about *prokōpe* to Basil the Great. (*Prokōpe* is the noun form, while *proekopten* is the past form of the verb.)
131. *TRn*, 39. Quoting Basil, *De Spiritu Sancto*, 16.38.
132. Heb 5:7 (referred to by Torrance in *Incarnation*, 64).
133. *Incarnation*, 120.
134. Ibid., 114ff.

Through his Spirit-enabled perfect and unbroken fellowship with the Father, which spans the entire course of his life from birth to death to resurrection, Jesus's active obedience condemns sin in the flesh. The hard won praying and worshipping life of the Son before the Father is at the heart of his atoning activity. In addition to his praying and worshipping, Christ's teaching ministry and imparting of the word are equally aspects of his active *noetic* fellowship with the Father.[136] By life and word the truth of God asserts himself into the midst of human sin and error.

Negative Righteousness through Passive Obedience

In addressing Christ's passive obedience, Torrance focuses his attention upon the substitutionary aspect of atonement as it is given biblical expression through the language of law and cult. This is certainly the most common battle zone where themes and theories of atonement take their stand, very often garnering a life of their own that is disassociated from the doctrine of Grace. Here our concern is with Jesus's willing submission to the Father's judgment upon sin by offering himself in our place, as our substitute. Torrance observes that the New Testament draws upon the imagery of both law (Paul) and cult (Hebrews) and develops each of these in their distinctiveness as complementary approaches.[137] Paul's letters tend to emphasize the mediation of the Word (what the epistle to the Hebrews refers to as Christ's *Apostleship*) and speak of atonement primarily in terms of justification and expiation before the Word or Law of God. The epistle to the Hebrews is mainly concerned with the liturgical witness to that Word and therefore speaks of atonement primarily in terms of Christ's high-priestly self-offering and intercession. That is, where Paul stresses reconciliation through expiation and substitutionary exchange, Hebrews focus upon reconciliation through sacrifice and cleansing from sin.[138] Their complementary unity is seen precisely in

135. *TiR*, 116.
136. *Incarnation*, 122.
137. *Atonement*, 33–35.
138. Ibid., 77.

Christ as the high priest who confesses the righteousness of the divine word of judgment by offering himself up to the Father. Torrance insists that the forensic and cultic concepts of redemption must not be allowed to be separated since within the covenant they overlap in their significance and application. The covenant expresses God's will for communion with his people, as well as the form of their actual existence before God and in the world. Since, for Torrance, covenant language is filial language (Israel is God's firstborn son), redemption refers most basically to the restoration of sonship.[139] Breaches in the covenant are opposed by God, for God has affirmed Israel as his child and has determined himself to be Israel's God. As we will see, this framework places the concept of penal substitution firmly within the context of the Father-Son relation, in which "the Son submits himself to the Father's judgement and is answered through the Father's good pleasure."[140] I will look at the forensic and then the cultic approach, noting how Torrance weaves the two together in his doctrine of atonement in a form consistent with the downward two-fold motion of Grace.

Atonement and the Law of the Covenant

Torrance's hamartiology recognizes a double character in sin as revealed in the Gospel. Sin is rebellion against God, but it receives its ontological objectivity through God's resistance to it. God and humanity are alienated one from another—God (objectively) from humanity, by his wrath and judgment of sin; and humanity (subjectively) from God, in our rejection of God's love and rebellion against his covenant.[141] This situation, in which God's opposition gives human rebellion its ontological concretion, determines the nature of what is meant by justification. Torrance writes: "If sin is qualified as sin by the attitude of God against it, then *it is the divine will that must be maintained and justified in the death of Christ.*"[142] Justification

139. Ibid., 38.
140. Ibid., 72.
141. Ibid., 71–72; cf. *STR*, 61.
142. Ibid., 75. Italics mine. Cf. ibid., 111.

then has as its primary referent the righteousness of God's will, which has been crossed and scorned by humanity. God's righteousness is God's utter truthfulness and faithfulness to himself in his nature as pure, holy love.[143] In order for peace to be restored in divine-human relations, what opposes God's love must be judged and righted, and so God comes himself both to absorb that opposition and to realize a righteous human confession and obedience before God. This oneness of relation between the person of the Son and his work in our flesh and between the incarnate Son and the heavenly Father, is fully consummated on the cross; and *"it is that oneness which constitutes the inner heart of the atonement."*[144] Atonement then for Torrance is ultimately not a legal status, but a reality, *an event*, which is as real and objective on the side of God as it is real and subjective on the side of humanity. Reconciliation of God to humanity and of humanity to God involves a real "oneness of will and mind between man and God."[145]

This double character of sin is reflected in the two-fold character of justification spoken of earlier. Because God objectively opposes sin, sin must be objectively justified—that is, condemned and made right on God's side. Its objective character (rooted in God's opposition to all that is not love) requires a justification which is not only in name or status, not simply declarative or juridical, but *in subjective actuality*. That is, sin must be understood from within the context of the covenant of Grace and not as an independent reality *in abstracto*.

Torrance notes that the act of salvation through Christ is described by Paul as both "under the law" and "apart from the law" (Gal 4:3-5; Rom 3:19-22). Justification is *under the law*, for even though the law came about as a response to sin and even though sin turned the law into humanity's very bondage, the law had divine validity as a real expression of God's *"No"* against all sin and evil. Thus in Christ God enters the world as one under the full bondage of the law, and there

---

143. Torrance preached on this topic in a sermon delivered 13th Dec, 1964, "What is God like?—God in Judgment." Advent series. Thomas F. Torrance Manuscript Collection, Special Collections, Princeton Theological Seminary Library, Box 47.
144. *Atonement*, 75 (italics original).
145. Ibid.

God's righteousness is fulfilled by his final judgment against sin on the cross.[146] In this way through the medium of the law humanity is set free both from the bondage of external law as well as from the self-imprisonment of condemnation of its own conscience.[147]

Justification is also *apart from the law,* for in Christ "God steps out from behind the law and confronts humanity face-to-face."[148] Here the law no longer condemns (Rom 8:1) because the righteousness of God has been personally fulfilled by the faithfulness of Jesus (Rom 3:19–22). God is *satisfied.* The promise of the old covenant, which is founded upon and administered through law, is fulfilled by a new covenant founded upon and administered on the wholly new basis of Grace. "The cross of Christ," Torrance writes, "represents an interruption of the ethical order of the fallen world."[149] This idea of an *interruption* or *suspension* of ethics is in no sense a compromising of God's will as expressed in the law, but the fulfillment of the law and its subsequent replacement with a new grounding in what Torrance calls "God's holy love."[150] In this way, God's love bypasses and supersedes all abstract or detached legal relations between God and humanity.

Atonement and the Cultic Liturgy

While Torrance views the juridical act of expiation as a kind of external transaction, the priestly act of propitiation is concerned with the restoration of fellowship and peace between God and humanity ("the internal *at-one-ment*").[151] Torrance writes, "This is where we see that oneness of mind between God and man, and man and God is at the heart of atonement; yet it is not a oneness of mind that is detached from the actualization of it in manward and Godward ways."[152] Whereas the cultic liturgy of Israel was nothing more than a *witness* to the Truth, and the sacrifices bore no efficacy in themselves as they

---

146. Cf. *STR,* 61.
147. *Atonement,* 116.
148. Ibid., 117.
149. Ibid. Torrance recalls Kierkegaard's phrase, "teleological suspension of ethics" (quoted on 118).
150. Ibid., 119.
151. Cf. ibid., 68.
152. Ibid., 69.

were simply "liturgical acknowledgment of what God has done and spoken in His grace,"[153] both anticipated a real historical fulfillment. That fulfillment takes place in the historical life of Jesus, which is not just cultic or forensic symbolism, but at-one-ment in *actuality*. What was symbolized in the Old Testament rites is no longer merely symbolic in the New Testament, but the thing itself.[154] The priestly actions of Christ are the gospel *happening*-not simply being announced or pointed to, but *actually present in the present*. As actualized propitiation, the ancient cultic liturgy has its fulfillment in a *concrete reality* which Torrance insists is both "concrete historical reality" and also "eternal spiritual reality."[155] In the concrete historical event of the cross, a new and living way to the Father has been opened up by Christ who through his ascension ever lives before the face of the Father as our priestly intercessor: "for there He confesses us before the face of God as those for whom He died, as those whose names He has entered as members of His Body."[156]

Torrance describes this actualization of divine and human propitiation in the life of Jesus in terms of prayer. In so doing, he subsumes Christ's priestly mediation into what he calls "the prayer of priestly self-sacrifice."[157] Christ prays for us, not only with his words, but with his very life.[158] His passive and active obedience is essentially a "prayer translated into his physical existence" which he lives out before the Father. With profound sorrow, he passively acquiesces to the Father's verdict upon our sin; with perfect trust, he actively converts the mind and will of alienated humanity back to God. It is in this way that Torrance understands repentance as fundamental to what it means for Christ to be our high priest. We cannot justify ourselves by our own repentance—all we can do is cast ourselves on Christ. He writes, "It is at the point of vicarious repentance that we

---

153. *RP*, 9.
154. Ibid., 13. Cf. ibid., 9.
155. Ibid., 13.
156. Ibid.
157. *Atonement*, 71.
158. A cognate term which Torrance relates to Christ's priestly prayer and intercession is "confession" (*homologia*) which is used three times in Hebrews (3:1; 4:14; 10:23). Like prayer, confession is "not in word only but in deed and in life, in action and in concrete reality" (ibid., 89).

really face up to the radical notion of the priesthood of Christ—priest in our place—in vicarious sorrow and anguish, in vicarious trust and faith, in vicarious worship and thanksgiving."[159] It is this priestly life of prayer that Christ then pours out on the cross and which he continues to offer as he presents himself (and us in him as those he has "brothered, redeemed and consecrated in himself") to the Father.[160] This "saving efficacy of the prayer-life of Jesus" is an emphasis which Torrance observes in Calvin's writings and Craig's catechism, though he bemoans the later neglect of this doctrine in the generations that followed.[161] As Torrance understands it, the whole concept of propitiation in the New Testament takes place within the filial context of the prayer of the Son before the Father. All the concepts associated with propitiation such as elements of wrath, judgment and forgiveness are drawn into the personal Father-Son relationship. This framework carries profound implications for how Torrance conceives of human participation in Grace.

The Only True Response to the Father

The previous sections have focused on the atoning significance of the active and passive obedience by the Son as a life of total substitution, lived for us and on our behalf. Here, I have drawn attention to the exclusive and inclusive nature of this substitution. In laying out his doctrine of atonement, Torrance chooses a form which attempts to exclude in the strongest language possible any possibility of salvation being a human work, which can be achieved or earned in any way from the creaturely side. Thus for example the Reformation cry, "justification by faith alone," is interpreted by Torrance as a gloss on "by the grace of Christ alone," for "faith is but an empty vessel to be filled by the covenant mercies and faithfulness of God in Christ."[162] For Torrance then the phrase "justification by faith alone" is simply the

---

159. Ibid., 71.
160. Ibid.; Cf. 117ff.
161. *SOF*, lxxxi. Torrance notes this in John Craig's catechism: "Q. How did He satisfy God's wrath for us? A. By His obedience, prayer, and everlasting sacrifice" (ibid., 111).
162. *TRn*, 161. Cf. *Inst*. 3.2.24.

inverse of "justification by works." It serves as a negating function by asserting the truth that we are not justified by ourselves. Its positive content is purely the absence of any self-justifying content. Because of this, he is critical of the legalism and self-righteousness that creeps in under the idea of "justifying faith," for this shifts the emphasis away from Christ to ourselves and our act of trust or belief. Christ does not just *enable* us to be saved (by our own act of faith); Christ actually saves us by his own faith—for us and in our place. Thus, union with Christ is not a reward for faith, but faith's *foundation*. The point Torrance wants to secure is that *nothing* (neither faith nor actions) can be put forth as a condition for salvation in addition to what Christ has already done for us and in us through his incarnational union with us. "It is through union with Him that we enter into the blessing of justification because it was through His becoming one with us first in His Incarnation that Christ wrought our justification for us."[163] Torrance believes it is the clear tendency of Westminster theology to reverse this order, viewing "justifying faith" as the entryway into union with Christ.[164] For Torrance, justification is secured by Christ's incarnational union with us. Faith is therefore not a *justifying work* that gets outsiders in but rather a *communing work* which enables us to enter what we already have. Justification by the Grace of Christ alone places the focus squarely upon Christ and his faith, thereby excising the whole question of assurance of personal salvation by rendering it unnecessary. By contrast, *justifying faith* allows an uncertainty to creep in regarding the worthiness of our repentance and faith before God. On this point, Torrance will not budge or bend: salvation (and thus atonement) is, from first to last, by *Grace* alone.

Critiques of Torrance's theological project have often focused on his unwavering insistence on *Grace alone*—specifically his strong emphasis upon the vicarious humanity of Christ, in which Torrance asserts that Christ exclusively is "our language to God" and "the only true response to the Father" such that all other forms of response are "displaced."[165]

---

163. *SOF*, cx.
164. In his exposition of Craig's Catechism, Torrance shows how Craig explicitly relocates the 'problem' of salvation from its traditional location in the Westminster *ordo salutas* (ibid., cxi).

Such dogmatic language understandably prompts Tom Smail to challenge, "[Certainly], it is not enough that a response to God should be made for me by Jesus, but what he has done for me, I need to go on and do for myself."[166] This leads Smail to make a more generalized accusation: "Torrance's failure to distinguish clearly enough between Christ's response to God made for us and our response to Christ made for ourselves" is symptomatic of "a wider failure to distinguish between the work of the Spirit and the work of Christ."[167] As a preferred alternative, Smail recommends that a distinction be made between the work that Christ does *for* us and the work that the Spirit then does *in* us enabling our response to Christ. This is succinctly summarized in his catch phrase that we respond *"for* ourselves, but not *by* ourselves." In Smail's view, Christ's vicarious response to God on our behalf exists in a polar relation to our need to respond *for ourselves* to what Christ has done. This concern (which is certainly not exclusive to Smail) will be approached by examining the conceptual background and basis which undergirds Torrance's discourse in the register of human response. In the process, it will be discovered that for Torrance exclusivity in the realm of justification, while unconditionally qualifying and re-establishing human response, does not preclude or undercut the reality and appropriateness of human activities which correspond to the way of Grace. Human responses within the movement of Grace—*while displaced are not unplaced*—for they are given a real and secure place *with* Christ's as (re-established) responses that are joined to and participate in his.

Response as Witness

Human responses within the movement of Grace are firstly witness to the truth of the divine Word. They are not witness to a word which fades into the past, but to a living Word. Jesus' priestly witness to the truth is the liturgy of his life. His confession is not in word only,

---

165. *G&R*, 151.
166. Thomas Smail, *The Giving Gift, The Holy Spirit in Person* (Lima: CSS Publishing, 1998), 111.
167. Ibid.

94

but is historically *actualized confession*. "At the Cross it becomes the actual judgment of God, and the actual submission of Christ in perfect obedience to the point of death."[168] This "fulfilled liturgy of Word and Oblation" is a "concrete reality" in Christ which has opened up "a new and living way to the Father." Ascended "before the face of the Father . . . He confesses us before the face of God as those for whom He died."[169] Our response now is to take his confession as *our* own, "and in His Name to go boldly before the throne of grace," holding on to that confession as our one hope.[170] The Church's praise and thanksgiving to God stems from and echoes the confession of her high priest and as such it is understood as witness.

As noted earlier (3.1), for Torrance, the activity of human response to God, while most appropriately understood through the language of priestly witness, is situated within the overarching category of sonship.[171] In light of this framework, Torrance emphasizes "three facts of cardinal importance" concerning Christ as our *leitourgos* (intercessor).[172]

First, Jesus Christ fulfils both aspects of biblical priesthood 'in his Sonship and on the ground of his Sonship.'[173] Priestly activity is composed of two aspects: apostolic (Mosaic), bearing the Word of God to the people; and priestly (Aaronic), bearing witness to that word through liturgical offerings.[174] His enactment of his priesthood does not operate independently or outside of his Sonship (Heb. 5:5f). In other words, as the one who is both Apostle and High Priest, Christ's priesthood is part of his Sonship.[175] Person and work are not separable. His priestly actions bear witness to his royal word *as the Son* and not to something else or other that God does, for he *is in himself what God does*. As the Son, his word is kingly action; thus, his priesthood is a *royal priesthood* in which the offering is identical with the person of the

168. *RP*, 13.
169. Ibid.
170. Ibid.
171. Ibid., 11.
172. Cf. ibid., 14ff.
173. Ibid., 14 (italics mine).
174. Cf. ibid., chapter 1, "The Royal Priest," 1–22.
175. Ibid., 11.

offerer. The voice of judgment and the voice of love are the same voice of the royal priest, the one in whom we have "the coincidence of Grace and Omnipotence."[176]

Second, omnipotent Grace means that both parts of priesthood are fulfilled *for us, as our substitute*. Torrance insists that Christ's substitutionary priesthood does not merely perfect and complete our imperfect offerings, but *displaces them by his completed self-offering*. Thus, "in him our human answer to God . . . is already completed."[177] Christ's confession and offering "is also our confession."[178] He is our Word (our obedience, response, witness and amen) offered to God once and for all and on our behalf; and he is our Word in such a way that we can offer no Word *on our own* any longer (no obedience, response, witness or amen, nor even any worship or prayer). Consequently, that which we offer has *already* been offered on our behalf. This situation relocates the nature of our acts towards God out of the realm of justification and into that of the only mode appropriate—prayer, thanksgiving and praise.

Third, and equally important, Christ has ascended *"wearing our humanity" and ever lives as our intercessor*. The human life of Jesus, which in its sinlessness and perfection is a new creation, is made permanent in the resurrection. For Torrance, the ascension of Christ into his heavenly session as a new reality bears profound ontological implications. In this event, human *being* is healed and restored in relation to the creative Source of all being.[179] In the resurrection, the human creature is re-established on a wholly new basis "in a reality that does not crumble away into the dust or degenerate into nothingness or slip into the oblivion of the past."[180] What was by nature "the closed circle of the inner life of God" has now been "extended to include" or "made to overlap" with human life in and through Jesus.[181] This fact that "human nature is now set within the Father-Son

176. Ibid., 14.
177. Ibid.
178. Ibid., 13.
179. *STR*, 79.
180. Ibid.
181. *TRn*, 241.

relationship of Christ"[182] is pointed to in the Pauline language of our adoption and constitution as joint heirs with Christ (Rom 8:14-17, 29; Eph 1:3-14; Gal 4:4-7).

Response as Fellowship

What then remains for us to *do*? Torrance is very careful to define the location (*place*) of human responses such that Christ's continuing priestly humanity retains its ongoing relevance within the life of God. At the same time, Christ's permanent priesthood does not leave us unplaced. The heart of atonement is *union of agency, not replacement of agency*.[183] However, the language of *vicarious* and *representation* if not carefully defined can be taken to suggest—at least in their connotations—"extrinsic replacement." Christ's vicarious humanity does not mean he is human *instead* of us, but refers rather to the inclusive nature of his humanity. *Inclusion* indicates personal involvement and emphasizes that his response involves the sinner at every step.[184] Thus, *vicariousness is not graspable as a complete concept in Torrance's thought apart from the cognate concepts of inclusion and participation.*

The point is, because *he* is truly human, *we* are human with him. We are included in Christ's priestly acts, which are enduringly for us. Thus, Torrance declares, "We are with Jesus beside God, for we are gathered up in him and included in his own self-presentation to the Father."[185] As such, he is the leader of all aspects of our worshipful response to God. Grace, by definition, involves participation; in fact, Grace is not Grace apart from this inclusion. Yet inclusion does not mean repetition or imitation. Its proper *modus* is sharing. Consequently, when Torrance

---

182. *STR*, 69.
183. *Atonement*, 75.
184. J. B. Torrance does in fact use this term in his book, *Worship, Communion, and the Triune God of Grace*, where he refers to the "all inclusive humanity" of Christ. (Downers Grove: InterVarsity, 1997), 50–51.
185. *STR*, 135–36. Another term which connotes the assymetrical and irreversible aspect of creaturely participation in God is *incorporation*. This book continues to use the language of participation—both because it is more commonly used by Torrance and it emphasizes the personal force of Grace, which summons human beings to a response of faith. Not to 'answer' the summons, is itself a form of participation *by negation*.

does speak about the human response to Grace, he maintains that these responses indeed possess no traction of their own. Our responses *to* Jesus Christ are *through* and also *with* Jesus Christ. Human responses possess no *independent* existence, for there is no human relation to God outside of that which is joined to Christ, who is the *all significant middle term* of divine-human relations.[186] The ascended Lord in his *continuing vicarious humanity* is *the living objective basis* for human participation *in* and fellowship *with* God. The life we live, we live on the wholly new basis of his faithfulness (Gal 2:20). Given this framework, it should now be clear that for Torrance an absence of autonomy does not entail an absence of responsibility, for we must live. Human being—even a *perfect* human being—has no autonomy.

Because the issue of response is of fundamental relevance to Torrance's concept of Grace, this theme will be returned to again and again throughout the remainder of this book. Chapter 4 will detail the onto-relational being of human beings, which mirrors and echoes God's own onto-relational reality. Chapters 5 and 6 will address the particularities of the form that Grace takes in the Church, which shares in Christ's continuing humanity as one Body with him.

Before moving on to discuss the third article (i.e., pneumatology) and Grace in the next chapter, one more big picture look at Torrance's theology of atonement will be taken posing the question, "*What actually justifies?*" At the risk of blasphemously attempting to 'look behind the veil,' there are a number of things that can be said about Torrance's position in light of his doctrine of Grace.

Onto-Relational Eschatological Justification

Asking this question is an attempt to get as close as possible to the heart of what exactly justifies or reconciles men and women to God. How precisely is the personal and atoning union which takes place in Christ also inclusive of other human beings? Several models of justification have already been observed that Torrance clearly and

---

186. *G&R*, 145.

consistently rejects. Most prominently, Torrance rejects the idea that salvation is purely legal or externally won from the outside. By the same token, he rejects a salvation which is internal yet impersonal, such as one that is effected automatically or mechanistically through some kind of sheer metaphysical union of God and humanity in the person of Jesus. Torrance also distances himself from liberal protestant forms of justification that are purely relational or moral along with their "rather Pelagian" notions of sanctification construed as "the spontaneous response" of humans to God's forgiveness.[187] Finally, Torrance is committed to steering clear of 'Roman' notions of justification, for these problematically suggest a kind of ontological infusion of righteousness (or of Grace) which effectively confuses the divine and human natures.[188] Given that Torrance finds all of these approaches deficient, what actually makes the event of Jesus an effectual expiation/propitiation of sin? For Torrance, the fix must fit the problem.[189] If the diagnosis is that humanity is "diseased in mind and soul," "enslaved to sin" and "depraved," then no external solution can be deemed adequate. Atonement must address not only "actual sin," but *original* sin as well. Given the multiplex nature of the problem, Torrance's answer to the question of how Christ's righteousness is made our own is not a simplistic choice of one option or theory over against the others. Justification is multi-faceted in the person of Christ and as such involves ontological, relational and eschatological factors. That which holds all the facets of justification together is a real union by the Spirit with the risen humanity of Christ.

The Logical Fallacy of Universalism

One can gain insight into how these three factors interpenetrate in Torrance's thought through the way he discusses the wholeness of the new creation in Christ, as well as the issue of universalism within his doctrine of reconciliation. Torrance unequivocally asserts on purely

---

187. *C&A1*, 64.
188. *TRn*, 174–80.
189. That is, the problem *which is revealed through the incarnation of the Son of God as a human being.* Torrance's hamartiology is determined by his Christology, not the other way round.

ontological grounds the universal extent of redemption in and through Christ. Since the Creator Word became flesh, he argues, "we must think of the being of every man, whether he believes or not, as grounded in Christ and ontologically bound to his humanity."[190] At the same time, ontology does not imply necessity. While affirming both the sufficiency and the efficiency of Christ's death for all, Torrance rejects any strand of determinism that would insert a logico-causal relation of necessity between the death of Christ and the salvation of human beings.[191]

He addresses this theme in many of his writings, though most directly in a 1949 article in *SJT* in which he critiques the doctrine of universalism as the attempt to turn a possibility into a necessity.[192] Torrance's argument depends strongly on his insistence that "sin has a fundamentally surd-like character."[193] Any attempt to convert the "mystery of iniquity" into a rational explanation which overlooks the fundamental discontinuity that sin and evil introduces into God's world, is to force a coherence where none can exist. Any resolution to the contradiction between "the bottomless reality" of human guilt and the holy God can only be anticipated eschatologically; so exactly how the contradiction will be dealt with, has still to be revealed.[194]

> The connection between the atoning death of the Lord Jesus and the forgiveness of our sins is of an altogether ineffable kind, which we may not and cannot reduce to a chain of this-worldly logico-causal relations. To do that comes very near to sinning against the Holy Spirit.[195]

As is clear from the severity of his warning, Torrance takes this point extremely seriously and as a result finds damning fault with both the doctrine of limited atonement and universal salvation. Together, they are the "twin heresies which rest on a deeper heresy" of logico-causal explanations for why the death of Christ avails or does not avail.[196]

---

190. *Latin Heresy*, 481.
191. Ibid., 482.
192. PiC. Torrance's primary target and occasion for his article is a refutation of John Robinson's arguments which were laid out in the previous edition of *SJT*: "Universalism—Is it Heretical?," *SJT* 2, no. 2 (1949): 139–55.
193. Thomas F. Torrance, "Universalism or Election," *SJT* 2, no. 3 (1949): 313. Hereafter, *UE*.
194. *UE*, 314.
195. *A&MO*, 247.

Here in Torrance's refusal to be trapped in the polarities of limited atonement or universal salvation, we find a significant manifestation of the triumph of his doctrine of Grace over theological systems. Even the cherished Reformed doctrine of the sovereignty of God is subsumed by the personal meeting of Grace. For Torrance to do otherwise would be to sin against God himself. Thus, "the most rational thing reason can do" is to "accept the way of humility" and "suspend judgment" rather than force "a closed system of thought upon the actual facts of existence."[197]

Torrance is able to break the logico-causal necessity of universalism by recollecting his doctrine of God, which asserts that, "because the love of God is . . . a Person—Jesus Christ—the eternal election of God has become encounter, acutely personalised in the midst of our choices and decisions, demanding response and decision."[198] Thus, while Torrance can assert that "every man's being is bound up forever with the one and indivisible act of God's love in Jesus Christ," this reality does not render human freedom impotent and meaningless. By conceiving of election as "a living act that enters time and confronts us face to face in Jesus Christ," rather than an abstract principle recalling some distant point in a timeless eternity, Torrance is able to hold together two seemingly contradictory realities: in Jesus Christ, God has universally chosen all men and women such that "no one can ever elude the election of His love";[199] and yet, this event of election in Jesus Christ comes in the form of an encounter which demands an "answer of love," an answer which we are given the capacity to make by virtue of being "apprehended" by that love.[200] Thus, rather than universal election adversely cutting across human decision, for Torrance, election is inseparable from personal encounter and response to Jesus Christ. Here one can see Torrance's doctrine of Grace

196. Ibid., 248.
197. *UE*, 314.
198. Ibid., 315.
199. Ibid.
200. Ibid., 316.

in operation, as he strongly rejects the forced juxtaposition of God and humanity such that "all of God" logically excludes "anything of man."

One might argue that Torrance himself operates with his own version of logico-causality, in that he assumes: (a) because the Creator Word became a human being; therefore (b) all human beings are ontologically caught up in the new creation. While it is true that ontological categories provide the substructure of Torrance's doctrine of atoning reconciliation, he refuses to allow ontology to be separated out as a principle unto itself. By wedding ontological discourse to personal being, Torrance is able to conceive of reconciliation as always a free act of God (a declaratory act), yet a declaratory act which accompanies the actualization of what is declared. It is an act in which Truth becomes event or, rather, an event becomes Truth. In the Christ event, the covenant is fulfilled but the covenant itself trades upon God's active will to affirm its truthfulness. That is, God is not subject to the covenant; he is the author of it. His commitment to the covenant is therefore not forced upon him, but his to keep. For Torrance, justification (and reconciliation) can never be understood as something done *to* God, but something from beginning to end which God effects *himself*. The motion of Grace can never be reduced to an impersonal force. Thus, the notion of causality which is most proper to Grace, as it meets humanity in justification and reconciliation, is not one of necessity or logic but *personal causality*. God's keeping of the covenant is thus not the end product of a legal machine or extrinsic mechanism, but a *personal* act befitting his character. God remains true to himself and nothing can prevent him from acting 'in character.' This is the freedom of God. The point of the covenant is not to turn the personal act into a forensic obligation, but rather to express God's promise to us that we might place our trust and confidence in his faithfulness.

A Soteriology that Befits the Onto-Relational Eschatological Nature of Human Creatures

Because reconciliation is not subject to the logic of causality but is essentially the self-presentation of the Son to the Father *on our behalf*, it cannot be thought of as strictly ontological or imputational, although most appropriately as ontological *and* relational. While our being by Grace is ontologically bound to Christ, this bond involves an encounter and response, and a teleological purpose. While Torrance describes justification as sufficient, effective, declared and actualized for all, he still insists that it requires an active relation to Christ in which individuals actually share in his righteousness through regeneration and renewal. Justification then must be *realized* through participating in the regenerative, sanctifying and healing power of the resurrection. Here one might recall the term *onto-relations*, which Torrance coins to describe the nature of the relations shared among the three hypostases of the Trinity. By invoking it here, I emphasize the fact that neither ontology nor relations exist autonomously, but have their existence and reality in correlation with each other. While Torrance himself never refers directly to onto-relations in his dogmatic material on justification or atonement, he does appropriate it analogously with respect to Creator-creature and creature-creature relations. Specifically, he makes use of it as a way of understanding sanctification as the *humanization* or *personalization* of humans by virtue of their relation to Christ—humans become finally and properly the human persons they are created to be through their union with Christ.[201] Viewing justification onto-relationally also fits Torrance's insistence that justification is not a *state* we achieve, but "a continuing act in Christ, in whom we are continuously being cleansed, forgiven, sanctified, renewed and made righteous."[202]

We can now extract a bit more clearly these three senses of justification (ontological, relational and eschatological), noting their

201. Cf. *MOC*, 47–49.
202. *STR*, 64.

natural interpenetration as they follow the logic of Christ and the logic of Grace. **First,** Torrance insists that "justification has ontological content." That is, the "substance of justification is *a real and substantial union with Christ*."[203] Jesus Christ is not simply the agent of justification, but *its whole substance.* On the ground that "he became our very brother, bone of our bone and flesh of our flesh,"[204] we are actually included in what he did; we are offered *with* him and accepted by God *in* him. Justification or the new righteousness in Christ must be understood "in terms of the concrete righteousness of the new Man—the *eschatos Adam*—who dwells in our heart by faith and whose Epiphany waits for the last day."[205] Righteousness has its location and substance in the risen humanity of Christ. Atonement *is a person.* That is, "atonement is not just an act of judgment, but active truth in the form of personal Being."[206] Thus, as Paul declares, "Christ was raised for our justification" (Rom 4:25).

This is where Torrance locates the penal-substitutionary aspect of atonement. Penal and forensic categories (*kipper*) do not stand on their own ground, but have their place within what Torrance calls "the *goel* notion" of redemption. The work has its place within the person; therefore Torrance writes, "We are not saved by the atoning death of Christ ... but by Christ himself who in his own person made atonement for us. He is the atonement who ever lives and ever intercedes for us."[207] For Torrance, the New Testament speaks of penal-substitutionary atonement in terms of the larger story line of "the intimacy of the Father-Son relation, in which the Son submits himself to the Father's judgement and is answered through the Father's good pleasure."[208]

Second, the ontological reality of the resurrected new humanity of Christ "demands as its complement," "an active and an actual sharing" in Christ's righteousness through an active relation to him.[209] The two

---

203. *C&A1*, 64.
204. Cf. Eph 5:29–32; Gen 2:21–24.
205. *C&A1*, 65.
206. *STR*, 68. Jesus says as much in his "I am the resurrection and the life."
207. *Atonement*, 73.
208. Ibid., 72.

events and thus the two doctrines (justification and sanctification) are inseparably related: in light of the resurrection, justification "is a creative event in which our regeneration or renewal is already included within it."[210] Through his Spirit, the living Christ continues to draw us into the circle of his life that we might know experientially our identity in Christ. Jesus Christ is both God's "*No*" to sin and evil and God's "*Yes*" to real fellowship with his creatures.

Third, Torrance nevertheless asserts that *imputation* in justification must also be understood as having an eschatological dimension, "for there is certainly a time-lag . . . between the resurrection of Christ, the Head of the Body and of us who are members of his Body."[211] However for Torrance eschatological does not mean *not-in-the-present* or *wholly future*, for "through the power of the Spirit we have union with the risen Christ here and now and in that union taste already the powers of the age to come."[212] While the reality of the ascension of Christ forces us to take seriously this "eschatological suspension," the fact of Pentecost means that "here and now between the times through the power of the Spirit . . . we are made to participate in the power of the resurrection and God himself is at work creatively in our midst, regenerating, sanctifying and healing."[213] Torrance's eschatology shifts the emphasis from defining people by the dialectic of *in or out*, to the dynamic tension of the *already, but not yet*. That is, we are righteous here and now, yet it is only eschatologically that that is completely fulfilled in us.[214] Thus, while justification is a completed reality, it awaits disclosure; and until that day when it is finally revealed, imputation holds together the two moments of what already is and what is yet to come.[215]

It is because of this eschatological dimension that justification cannot be thought of as a *moment*, but only as a reality which *is already*

---

209. *STR*, 63; *TRn*, 111.
210. Ibid., 63–64.
211. Ibid., 64. Torrance notes that this is particularly the case with respect to the use of forensic terms, which should be understood eschatologically rather than legalistically (*C&A1*, 63).
212. Ibid.
213. Ibid., 64–65.
214. *TRn*, 186.
215. *Atonement*, 134–36.

fully realized and which *continues to be realized in us* in sanctification, as it unfolds and is continually nourished and maintained within the body of Christ. Sanctification then is not a response of men and women that must be *added* to justification, it is the continual realization of the justification we have received through union with Christ. As such, sanctification "involves us in His death and resurrection, for we cannot become one with him without participating in His death and resurrection that is without mortification and regeneration."[216] Thus, union with Christ is not a static state, but a *living* union which grows and increases as the bond of fellowship with Christ grows in communion on a daily basis. Torrance writes, "unless the doctrine of justification bears in its heart a relation of real union with Christ . . . Christ would remain as it were—inert or idle."[217]

This final section has demonstrated the way in which justification for Torrance centers around a real union with the risen humanity of Christ, which consequently involves ontological, relational and eschatological elements. This personal framework, which is rooted in Jesus Christ, is the critical groundwork for how Grace becomes worked out in the actual sanctification of God's people in the Church.

Conclusion

In this chapter, we have observed the trinitarian activity of Grace in the economy with a focus on its christological form—the form where the love of God takes in the person of Jesus sent from the Father through the Spirit. While the focus has been on Christology, we have seen throughout that Christology never operates in isolation from the triune co-activity of the Father and the Spirit. All that Christ does is a motion from the Father in the Spirit, which returns to the Father through the Spirit. Throughout this exposition of Torrance's thought, the fundamental form that Grace takes has been seen to follow a downward two-fold movement. This movement is so basic to all God's relations with human creatures that Torrance denotes it *the logic of God*,

216. *C&A 1*, 65.
217. *STR*, 63.

with *the logic of Grace* emphasizing the downward *direction* of this logic, and *the logic of Christ* describing the two-fold *pattern* of this logic.

This basic logic was seen to be personally and historically embodied in the God-human Jesus Christ. Jesus emerged out of the womb of the long dialogue which God initiated with Israel. In this ongoing dialogue, the law and the liturgy functioned as language tools through which God's covenant love could be communicated and also bore witness to within her lived existence. In the person of Jesus, the divine-human union and communion was seen to be a union that is at once incarnational, personal and atoning. I also noted that the atoning aspect of this union is specifically realized in the substitutionary and representative manner in which Jesus fulfils the human side of the covenant through his historical lived existence. Throughout I have pointed out that, for Torrance, the obedient life of Jesus is the primary datum, for it manifests the communion relation shared by the Son with the Father through the Spirit. The centrality of the relation of communion means that the life of the Son is most properly understood through the lens of prayer and worship.

Our objective has been to demonstrate that for Torrance, God is always Subject and Lord in his action in relation to human beings, yet in such a way that human subjectivity is given a true voice of its own. It has been suggested that the texture of this Grace-relation in Torrance's theology can be viewed through the lens of three 'ontological conditions:' the incarnational assumption by the Word of fallen flesh, the sanctification of that fallen flesh through a continuous personal union, and the pneumatic context of Christ's human existence. Through these conditions the way that incarnation and atonement interpenetrate one another in Torrance's understanding of the meaning and reality of the person of Christ has been evident. On this basis, atonement was seen not to be an act of God performed *upon* a human, but an act of God performed *as* a human—and as such an act which issues out of the depths of humanity's own being and life toward God.

In the coming chapters, a more direct look at the dynamics of how sanctification works itself out in the life of the believing community will be taken. We will continue to see Torrance's disciplined commitment to locate covenant fulfillment completely in God's activity, yet not in such a way that human activity is rendered meaningless or irrelevant. While Christ's humanity is relentlessly vicarious, it is always vicariously inclusive of our own, thereby freeing us for real fellowship with the Father through the Son in the Spirit.

3

The Motion of Grace through the Spirit

In its application of the homoousion to the gift of grace, Nicene theology rejected entirely the idea that grace is a created medium between God and man. Rather is grace to be regarded as the self-giving of God to us in his incarnate Son in whom the Gift and the Giver are indivisibly one.[1]

Pneumatology has been an intrinsic component of this project, playing an essential role in Torrance's treatment of the Trinity (chapter 1) and also in his christological material (chapter 2). In the previous chapter we spoke of a hypostatic, personal and atoning union in which Christ incorporates himself into us; our present interest is to speak of a pneumatic union through which we are incorporated into Christ. Grace cannot be understood apart from *both* realities, for Grace *by definition* includes actual human participation and also the means of that participation, which is *by the Spirit*. While it is true that pneumatological concerns have been before us all along, this chapter will attend to the Spirit's identity and activity more directly. Our concern is not to offer a complete treatment of Torrance's doctrine of

---

1. Thomas F. Torrance, *The Trinitarian Faith: The Evangelical Theology of the Ancient Catholic Church* (Edinburgh: T&T Clark, 1995), 140; Hereafter, *TF*.

the Holy Spirit, but to demonstrate the overall shape of triune Grace in Torrance's doctrine of the Spirit.

The abundance of pneumatological material in Torrance's writings arguably reflects his abiding concern for proper foundations in our approach to the doctrine of the Spirit.[2] Torrance views misunderstandings of the doctrine of the Spirit as a potential threat to the doctrine of Grace. If the doctrine of God's Grace is going awry, this will be exposed as Torrance believes in the doctrine of the Spirit.[3] Torrance shares the same concern and caution as his Doktorvater Karl Barth, who pointed out that because the Spirit in revelation is both the Spirit of God *and* of humanity, great care must be taken to insure "that the qualitative and not just quantitative distinction between God and man is not abrogated," for this distinction is the very "presupposition of fellowship between God and man."[4] The gift of the Spirit cannot be abstracted from its Giver, for even as the Spirit is imminent in human beings he remains transcendent over them.

Thus, Torrance sets out to combat what he perceives to be the common error arising from doctrines of the Spirit which do not complement the doctrine of justification by Grace alone. He identifies varying expressions of this contradictory effect, most notably within classic Roman formulations, but also in ascetic and interiorizing notions of the Spirit which were imported into pietistic versions of Protestantism from mediaeval monasticism.[5] If Pneumatology does not complement and correspond to Christology, it will subvert Christology

2. Cf. Thomas F. Torrance, *Theology in Reconciliation: Essays Towards Evangelical and Catholic Unity in East and West* (reprint; Eugene, OR: 1997), 12. Hereafter, *TiR*. Torrance's writings on pneumatology are quite extensive. His most concentrated treatment is found in a series of essays in *Theology in Reconstruction* (Grand Rapids: Eerdmans, 1965). Hereafter, *TRn*. Additionally, significant portions of *Trinitarian Faith, Christian Doctrine of God, School of Faith,* and *God and Rationality* (chapter on "The Epistemological Relevance of the Spirit," 165–92) and the section in *The Mediation of Christ*, "The Communion of the Spirit," (115–19) are also dedicated to an exposition of the Holy Spirit.
3. Cf. *TRn*, 225–28.
4. CD 1.2, 488.
5. "The Relevance of the Doctrine of the Spirit for Ecumenical Theology (Reply of Professor Thomas F. Torrance to his Critics)," Q38. (Edinburgh, Scotland, November 20, 1963). Thomas F. Torrance Manuscript Collection, Special Collections, Princeton Theological Seminary Library, Box 135 (hereafter, *Reply to Critics*). This document, marked "for private distribution only" was an extended written response of 68 paragraphs which Torrance penned to address specific concerns and critiques to his Schlink-Festschrift article. German text, Oekumenische Rundschau, 1963. Reprinted in *Theology in Reconstruction*, 229–39.

by taking the focus away from Christ. In fact, Torrance blames the weakness of modern Protestantism's understanding of God's Grace on its anemic doctrine of the Spirit. This failure is most apparent to Torrance in the way "'the Spirit' has come to mean little more than our subjective awareness of God or our religious self-understanding, and has very little if anything to do with the objective reality of the Being and living presence and action of God himself in the world."[6] In the face of this, Torrance presses for a recognition of the *objective* reality of God with respect to the doctrine of the Spirit. His solution is to lift up the foundational truth of the *homoousion* of the Spirit; only on this basis does he believe we can think correctly of the relationship of humanity to God.

Having introduced the problem and its essential relation to Torrance's doctrine of Grace, we will first examine Torrance's solution through a thoroughly objective pneumatology. Following this, we will address the manner in which the Spirit is active in the world, the church and individuals.

Objective Pneumatology

Torrance considers the application of the *homoousion* to the Spirit by the post-Nicene Fathers to be one of the most important decisions in the history of the Church. In so doing, the Church affirmed the objectivity of the Spirit and thus confirmed the theological structure of the trinitarian understanding of the Godhead. This opened the way to an objective and trinitarian understanding of Grace.

Torrance notes that the doctrine of the Spirit was derived "not merely from biblical statements, nor from doxological formulae alone, but from the supreme truth that God reveals himself through himself and therefore that God himself is the content of his revelation through the Son and in the Spirit."[7] The critical movement of thought, as Torrance describes it, was for the Church to articulate clearly "the lordly freedom of God in his Spirit and Word over against all that is

6. *TiR*, 270.
7. *TRn*, 202.

not-God." In this way God is sovereignly free to make himself present to the creature, giving and sustaining the creature in its being, yet in a way that maintains "its utter distinctness from himself."[8] This was the same move the Church had explicitly made in its doctrine of the Son: in which for us and our salvation God sovereignly and freely enters creaturely existence as a human, yet without ceasing to be eternal God; as a result, the Church already had the basic tools to assert the doctrine of the *homoousion* of the Spirit. In recognizing the intimate relation between Christology and pneumatology, Torrance observes that it became clear to the Church "that the doctrine of the Son requires the doctrine of the Spirit, and the doctrine of the Spirit requires the doctrine of the Son."[9] It is not our purpose here to trace the development of the doctrine of the Spirit; it is to highlight the fact that the identification of the Spirit as *homoousios*, along with the Son, affirmed both the lordship of the Spirit and the intimate relation of Christ to the Spirit, and consequently established how the person of the Spirit is to be understood. Torrance argues that a lack of clarity about the lordship and Christ-relatedness of the Spirit has been one of the grave errors the Church has struggled with throughout its history. This struggle is revealed most prominently perhaps in the doctrine of the procession of the Spirit from the Father *and the Son* (*filioque*). For Torrance, this phrase of the Western creed and the doctrinal issues which surround it are critically illuminative for understanding how the Spirit is "God of God" and also the intensely personal God. Consequently, most of what Torrance says about the Spirit is grounded in the trinitarian framework inherent in this phrase of the creed. We will briefly touch on the lordship of the Spirit before developing the implications of the Spirit's intimate relation to the Son.

The Spirit is Lord: the Lordship of the Spirit

Torrance asserts that the procession of the Spirit from the *Father* affirms that *the Spirit is Lord*—that is, the Spirit is none other than

8. Ibid., 212.
9. Ibid., 213.

112

"God in all his glory, majesty and sheer Godness."[10] The lordship of the Spirit is the lordly (i.e., transcendent and objective) presence of God over the whole of his creation, whereby God governs, directs, curbs and restrains evil, so that all might serve his glory.[11] The Spirit's lordship is "the royal freedom of God to be present to the creature" in a manner which realizes (sanctifies) and brings to completion (perfects) the creative purpose of God in the life of the creature.[12]

While the procession of the Spirit affirms the *homoousion* of the Spirit with the Father and the Son, *procession* notes and assumes a distinction as well. The Spirit is *homoousios* in a different way from the Son, "in a manner appropriate to his distinctive personal reality and nature as Holy Spirit,"[13] for the Spirit's lordship is different in mode and operation from the lordship of the Son or the Father.[14] As Torrance points out, the Spirit is not knowable in his own distinctive person (*hypostasis*), for he is not embodied in our world of space-time. "The Holy Spirit is God of God but not man of man."[15] The Spirit exercises his lordship according to his nature, which is to hide himself "behind the Face of the Father in the Son and the Heart of the Son in the Father."[16] As such, the movement of our thought cannot be directed to knowing him after the mode of being of the Father or the Son. Rather, we can only know the Spirit properly in accordance with his mode of being as *Spirit*, "as he who utters the Word and illumines the Son of the Father." This entails that in our knowing of the Spirit, we must make our starting point, not his external manifestations, but his internal relation within the Godhead to the Father and the Son.[17] In an effort to prevent the Spirit's translucence from provoking its displacement by the visible yet created realities of Church and world, Torrance takes a thoroughly objective, realistic and trinitarian approach to

10. Ibid., 230.
11. Cf. *School of Faith* (London: Camelot, 1959), xcvii. Hereafter, *SOF*.
12. *TRn*, 221–23.
13. Thomas F. Torrance, *The Christian Doctrine of God: One Being Three Persons* (Edinburgh: T&T Clark, 1996), 100. Hereafter, *CDG*.
14. Cf. Graham Tomlin, *The Prodigal Spirit* (Alpha International, 2011), 20.
15. *CDG*, 101.
16. *TRn*, 226–27.
17. *TF*, 208.

comprehending the Spirit's lordship. In this he follows many of the Church Fathers, who carefully maintained that Spirit in us is also God beyond us. Thus, Torrance affirms Epiphanius's approach that we cannot know the Spirit apart from the context of his "inner '*enhypostatic*' relation to the triune being of God"; nor can we know the Spirit apart from his dwelling in us.[18] That is, knowledge of God and of the Spirit only takes place *from within* human *koinonia* with God's *koinonia*.[19] Torrance remarks that Gregory Nazianzen even speaks of the relation that God establishes with us through his Spirit "as a relation of himself to himself."[20] Since God can only be known through God, the Spirit "who is God and dwells in God" enables us to share in the inner communion (the "closed circle of knowing") between the Father and the Son and the Son and the Father.[21] The Spirit does this by creating in us "beyond all creaturely or human capacities the ability to know the unknowable God."[22] From this perspective, the Spirit of whom we partake inwardly through his dwelling in us is "an objective inwardness grounded in the mutual indwelling" of God himself.[23] Thus, "for us to be in the Spirit or to have the Spirit dwelling in us means that we are made partakers of God beyond ourselves and even share in the inwardness of God himself."[24] This is the miracle of Grace in which the triune God "draws near to us and draws us near to himself."[25]

For Torrance, it is only on the objective basis and creative ground of this participatory *koinonia* that we can then move to an articulation of the doctrine of the Spirit.[26]

---

18. Ibid., 208.

19. Even though the language of *koinonia* is used both of creaturely relations with God and the inner divine life, Torrance is clear that creaturely involvement in *koinonia* is purely "analogous to and grounded in" the eternal communion which God has in himself. Thomas F. Torrance, *Incarnation: The Person and Life of Christ*, ed. Robert T. Walker (Nottingham: Intervarsity, 2008), 179. Hereafter, *Incarnation*.

20. *TF*, 229.

21. *MOC*, 116.

22. *TRn*, 226.

23. *TF*, 208.

24. *TiR*, 208–9. In support, Torrance references John 20:22; 1 John 4:12f; John 14:6.

25. *MOC*, 119.

26. *Reply to Critics*, Q34.

The Spirit of the Son: the Intimate Relation of the Spirit to Christ

That the Spirit processes not only from the *Father* but also from the *Son* indicates, as Torrance interprets it, that the Spirit is the *intensely personal* presence of God to his people. The *filioque* clause gives expression to the intimate relation between the Word and the Spirit, so that we cannot think of the Spirit's creative work independently of that of the Son. Torrance asserts,

> We cannot speak of the Spirit as poured out and as operative among men as if the Incarnation had not taken place, as if the Incarnation made no difference to His work, as if He may now operate behind the back of Christ. . . . [A] theology faithful to Christ and to the relation of the Spirit to Him, is prevented from thinking of a relation of the Spirit to the creation or to men except in and through the Person and Work of Christ the incarnate Son.[27]

Just as the life of the incarnate Son is "through the Spirit,"[28] so all that the Spirit does in and among creation as "the Lord, the Giver of Life" is through the Son. There is an inseparable relation of the Spirit to Christ in creation and redemption. While Torrance agrees "that the doctrine of the Spirit should not be just an adjunct of the doctrine of Christ," he is adamant that "it is the doctrine of Christ, in particular the relation of the Incarnate Son to the Father and of the Father to the Incarnate Son that controls our knowledge of the Spirit."[29] Specifically, for Torrance, this means that the creative work of the Spirit is "proleptically conditioned by that of redemption," so that the Spirit's work takes place contextually as a sanctifying and perfecting operation.[30] Thus, the Spirit is present to us in the Son in God's self-giving to humanity in the incarnation—and the Son is present to us in the Spirit.[31] For Torrance, "it is as we take seriously the utter lordship and deity of the Spirit . . . that we take seriously the very Being of God in his self-giving to us in the Incarnation; and it is as we

27. *SOF*, xcviii.
28. Basil, *De Spiritu Sancto* 16.39.
29. *Reply to Critics*, Q34.
30. *TRn*, 217.
31. Ibid., 215–16.

take seriously the utter lordship and deity of Christ . . . that we take seriously the direct and intensely personal activity of God in his self-giving to us at Pentecost."[32] Torrance describes the uniqueness of their inseparable relation by commenting that the two share a "homoousial bond" such that "the Spirit is sent by the Son in the Father."[33]

One of the aspects of this doctrine which bears special ecumenical significance is "the transcendently personal yet implacable objectivity" of the Spirit's presence and activity in the Church.[34] This combination of the utter objectivity and intensely personal nature of the Spirit's mode of presence and operation is a product of Torrance's staunch refusal to allow a wedge to be driven between the ontological Trinity and the economic Trinity. In this regard, Torrance perceives in many Eastern theologians a dualism which he traces to Origen: that "to know God in the Spirit [ἐν πνεύματι] is not to know God in his divine Being."[35] Even the well-known Irenean image of "the two hands of God" dangerously implies that the Spirit (along with the Son) is merely instrumental in the hands of God.[36] For Torrance, the "homoousial relation" of the Holy Spirit to God necessarily implies that the sending of the Spirit by the Son in revelation and faith is "grounded immanently in the eternal being of God." In other words, the historical mission of the Spirit from the Son is not simply descriptive of the divine energies of God; it is the objectively real and personal presence of God himself as he is "in the intrinsic relations of his eternal being."[37] For Torrance, any other position indicates a failure to take seriously the Nicene concept of identity of being and a replacing of *homoousion* with *homoiousion*.[38] Torrance's realist conception of the *homoousial* and *perichoretic* interpenetration of the triune persons will not allow this kind of dualistic apophatic move.[39] Torrance admits that "not everything that took place in the historical economy can be read back

32. Ibid., 230.
33. *CDG*, 197.
34. *TRn*, 231.
35. *CDG*, 187.
36. *SOF*, xcvii; cf. *TRn*, 230.
37. *CDG*, 186–87.
38. Cf. ibid., 187. Torrance notes that the notion of likeness in being (*homoiousion*) is the error that Athanasius attacked in his *Letters to Serapion on the Holy Spirit*.

into eternity"; he also asserts that "the intrinsic oneness between the coactivity of the Father, Son and Holy Spirit in the economic Trinity and their coactivity in the ontological Trinity are soteriologically and epistemologically absolutely essential."[40] For Torrance, the odious judgment of dualism is cast upon any dogma which would threaten to disrupt the oneness of identity between the divine Giver and the divine Gift. Understanding that "in the Holy Spirit God communicates *himself* to us, not just something of himself in his uncreated energies" is Torrance's abiding concern.[41]

Several negations and affirmations follow from Torrance's approach to the *filioque*. We will take them in turn.

Negations: Any Natural Theology or Immanent Principle

Negatively, the *filioque* "implies the renunciation of a so-called natural revelation or natural theology."[42] Its objective and personal framework means that the Spirit is neither *natural* nor *impersonal*, but always tied to the person of Christ. Therefore, the Spirit "cannot be interpreted in terms of immanent principles or norms within the creaturely processes,"[43] for the Spirit is the very power and presence of the transcendent God, *who also abides in and issues from the incarnate Christ.* There is no other Word of God which the Spirit can reveal apart from this Word, so it is exclusively this Word of God that the Spirit utters and reveals and creates communion with. For Torrance, "the *filioque* is another way of saying *solo Christo, solo verbo, sola gratia, sola fide*."[44]

Affirmations: Objective/Real Agency

Positively, the *filioque* framework affirms the category of agency. In

---

39. For support of this position and against Vladimir Lossky, Torrance cites Gregory Nazianzen (*Orationes*, 40.41). Cf. *CDG*, 187n90.
40. *CDG*, 198–99.
41. Ibid., 188.
42. *SOF*, xcix. See chapter 1, *The order and pattern of the natural universe*, for Torrance's rejection of viewing the Creator-creature relation through an *analogia entis* in which knowledge of God could be gained apart from Grace.
43. Ibid., xcvii.
44. Ibid., xcix.

fact, Gary Deddo asserts that Torrance restores the category of *agency* to an essential function in theological discourse through his resistance of impersonal, causal and instrumental explanations for God's Grace.[45] For Torrance, the Holy Spirit is the answer to all *how* questions of Grace. Or to phrase it differently, the answer to the *how* is a *Who*. Agency is a function of the Agent. However, because the Spirit by nature *"hides and effaces himself, and directs all our attention to Christ as Lord and Savior,"*[46] we will never be able to "go behind the back of the Holy Spirit and find out how God 'really' did something."[47] Consequently, while opacity is an abiding and basic characteristic of the Spirit's activity in creatures, this hiddenness does not come at the expense or atrophy of the Spirit's christological and personal moorings.

On this basis, Torrance argues for a corresponding objectivity of human agency. He is emphatic that "notions of 'irresistible Grace' . . . can have no place in biblical, evangelical or Reformed theology."[48] The activity of the Spirit as the ultimate agent of Grace in creation, can never be resolved as a natural product of the created order or reduced to an impersonal force, which overwhelms and disrespects the created freedom of creatures. Rather, the Spirit is transcendently present with creatures as the Spirit of the Father and the Son. For Torrance, this objectivity of the Spirit provides the ground for a corresponding objectivity of human agency.

While noting the pneumatological negations and affirmations to which the *filioque* attests, Torrance critiques an ongoing disconnection of the doctrine from practice which has "often led to serious error."[49] Lacking clarity and a realist notion of the Holy Spirit's objectivity, our attention becomes absorbed by the fallen human spirit, which we have confused with the Holy Spirit; and we identify the Church, or the human heart, or religious affections, or moral rectitude, or immanent

45. Cf. ed. Elmer Colyer, *The Promise of Trinitarian Theology: Theologians in Dialogue with T. F. Torrance* (Lanham: Rowman & Littlefield, 2001), 106.
46. Ibid., 311.
47. Ibid., 313; cf. *Alive to God*, "The Spiritual Relevance of Angels," 133.
48. Ibid.
49. *TRn*, 172.

principles of creation with the Spirit of God. On this issue Torrance remarks,

> ... the failure to take the *homoousion* [of the Spirit] seriously has tended to throw up a notion of event-grace, in which the centre of gravity is translated to man's own decisions and acts, so that Pelagian notions of co-operation and co-redemption are still rife within Protestantism. This involves a failure to distinguish the objective reality of grace from the individual believer's subjective states, and so a tendency, if it may be so expressed, to replace the *filioque* by a *homineque*.[50]

Torrance describes a parallel version of this tendency in the Church as the replacement of the *filioque* by an *ecclesiaque*, conflating the Spirit of God with the spirit of the Church. Whether this propensity finds its expression through a falsely objectified subjectivity in the individual ("the error of Neo-Protestantism") or through a legalized institutional structure in the Church ("the error of Romanism"), the loss of proper objectivity is equally damaging.[51] Displaying his rhetorical flair, Torrance likens this tendency of modern humanity (and, presumably of post-modern humanity) to a "serious mental disorder": since a confusion of the objective and subjective is the primary mark of irrational behavior and mental disorder, "religious man is in desperate need of some kind of spiritual psychiatry."[52] What appears to be lost all too often, in spite of creedal affirmations to the contrary, is the intimate relation that exists between the Spirit and the person of Christ. For Torrance, the truth that the Holy Spirit never acts autonomously can never be overstated. He notes that in the New Testament, "when the Spirit comes to dwell in us, He directs us away from ourselves to Christ"; so "even when we think of Christ as dwelling in us through His Spirit, we are nevertheless directed to Christ away from ourselves, and find ourselves in Him."[53] As support, Torrance points to the exegetical preponderance of *in Christ* in comparison to

---

50. Ibid., 190.
51. For Torrance's discussion of the conflation of spirit and reason in the German word *Geist*, see ibid., 231f.
52. Ibid., 231; 271.
53. *Reply to Critics*, Q67. Torrance notes that he finds Calvin's Ascension-theology to be of great importance here.

Christ in us in the New Testament. This he suggests should demonstrate to us that believers first and foremost have their life *in Christ* who is with God and in God. Torrance says little regarding the Charismatic movement; but since the Spirit of Christ is not an interior feeling of 'God in us,' he does venture to critique what he describes as "the danger point" in many charismatic movements: "when an emphasis on the Holy Spirit incompatible with the coinherent nature of the activity of the Triune God can become unbiblical and heretical."[54] Torrance's perception of a proper relation of humans to the Spirit is marked by a profound "objective inwardness"[55] that is irreducible to psychological subjectivity or sacramental externality. In the objective *otherness* of the Spirit's presence within us, space is created for true fellowship and consequently for true transformation in which the Spirit personalizes us by humanizing us.

In this section we have explored the theological implications of the *filioque* in the Western creed. Torrance however holds no personal stake in the perpetuation of the clause itself. What he does insist upon though is the preservation of the truth to which the *filioque* clause refers: the inseparable relation of the Spirit to Christ in creation and redemption. In fact, Torrance asserts the non-necessity of the *filioque* clause in light of the fact that "the teaching of all the great Eastern Fathers up to Theodoret" was to affirm: a) the unity of the divine *ousia* in the Holy Trinity; b) the consubstantial communion of the Father, Son and Spirit; and c) the impossibility of conceiving of the hypostasis of the Spirit apart from the revelation of God in Christ and his mission from Christ.[56]

> This being so we can forget about the *filioque* clause – it was entirely wrong to introduce it into the Ecumenical Creed without the authority of an Ecumenical Council – but we cannot allow to slip away from us the Athanasian teaching of the *homoousion* of the Spirit, and therefore of his full place in the one creative and redemptive activity of God through Jesus Christ.[57]

54. *Promise*, 312.
55. Cf. *TiR*, 234; *TF*, 208; Torrance, *Divine Meaning: Studies in Patristic Hermeneutics*, 197–98.
56. *TRn*, 218–19.
57. Ibid., 219.

We turn now to the manner in which the Spirit is active in the world, the Church and the individual.

The Communion of the Father and the Son

Torrance approaches the work of the Spirit from a profoundly ontological standpoint. The fundamental building block of this ontology is denoted by the communion (*koinonia*) of the Spirit, which we encountered in chapter 1 under the terminology of *onto-relations*. It is the particular work of the Holy Spirit to be the agent through which the being-constituting relations of the Triune persons exist. For Torrance, the Spirit is not simply the bond of love between the Father and the Son, but the one through whom the love of the Father and the Son is bonded. The Spirit is active, not as the harmony of the Trinity, but as the harmonizing One. "The Spirit . . . realizes and actualizes the power of the Godhead to be one with God in the identity of his eternal Being."[58] As Torrance perceives it, the Holy Spirit *is* the very communion of the Father and the Son, and the communion of God *is* the Holy Spirit. As such, Torrance refers to the Spirit with many ontologically-associated terms: the Spirit is the "*homoousial* bond," the "ontological connection," the "onto-relationalizer," the "personalizing being," the "hypostatic communion . . . between the Father and the Son," and the one who constitutes being-in-relations.[59] Taking his lead from the threefold distinction given in Patristic theology, Torrance recognizes three levels in which being-constituting relations through the Spirit operate: 1) the *consubstantial communion* of the Triune relations; 2) the *hypostatic union* between the divine and human natures of the person of Christ; and 3) the *koinonia* of the Spirit, which is the love of God poured into our hearts from the Father through the Son.[60]

These three levels are coterminous and non-competitive, such that the Holy Spirit is the ontological connection between the Father and the Son in their trinitarian life, as well as between the divine Son and

---

58. *TiR*, 235.
59. Cf. *Reply to Critics*, Q34. Torrance claims the phrase "hypostatic communion" comes from the tradition, though he does not cite who or where.
60. Thomas F. Torrance, *Space, Time and Resurrection* (Edinburgh: T&T Clark, 1998), 70. Hereafter, *STR*.

his human nature in the incarnation. Additionally, this same Spirit is also the bond between the Church and the incarnate Son. The eternal relationship between the Triune persons, the historical hypostatic union of the Son in the Spirit, and the present relation Christ's body has with him through the Spirit are all the workings of one life and one reality—though, in various forms. As the communion of the Spirit fans out from the immanent life of God to the incarnate Son and to the Church in the world, the perichoretic relations of the Godhead never cease: they take a form appropriate to each of the terms involved in the relation.

The Spirit and the Constitution of the Hypostatic Union

In chapter 2, we observed that the Spirit is active in and throughout the Son's assumption of a human nature; and indeed, that the being of God in the life of Jesus Christ is recognized as a double movement of both the Son and the Spirit. When the eternal Son becomes the incarnate Son in hypostatic union, the Father also sends the Spirit to accompany and effect the act of the union of natures in the one *hypostasis*. While Torrance never neglects the priority of the Son in the assumption of human flesh, he does not do so at the expense of the trinitarian *koinonia*. Thus, "the *hypostatic union . . . takes place through the operation of the Holy Spirit who is the Love of God.*"[61] In this way, the Spirit grounds and continually upholds the Son's divine-human union within the consubstantial communion of the Holy Trinity.[62] Through the Spirit, the communion of the Father and the Son is not an other-worldly reality which must desist during the Son's incarnate existence; rather, through the Spirit, the *incarnate* life of the Son is as much a part of the overall trinitarian movement, as the Son is *eternally* in God. No contradiction exists between the Spirit being active with the Son in the consubstantial communion of the Triune persons, and simultaneously being active in sanctifying the human Jesus. As Torrance says, "the eternal relations within the Triune God have assumed an economic

61. Ibid.
62. *MOC*, 65.

form within human history, *while remaining immanent in the Godhead*, thus opening out history to the transcendence of God while actualizing the self-giving of God within it."[63]

Torrance presses for further clarification and detail by asserting that the Spirit's relation to the Son must also be apprehended according to his divine and human natures—in ways appropriate to the whole nature of the Father-Son relation.[64] Thus, while Christ as the eternal Son is never without the Spirit, in his vicarious historical mission as the incarnate Son, Christ needs to receive the Spirit. Here we recall Torrance's use of the *an/en-hypostasia* for comprehending the dynamic movement of the Son's assumption of human flesh; and in particular the Spirit's personal activity in conceiving, anointing, indwelling, empowering, sanctifying, raising and glorifying the Son. This work of the Spirit in co-establishing and perfecting the incarnate Son enables the human Jesus to live his actual human life (*enhypostatically*) as the Son of the Father that he is. The Spirit personalizes the human Jesus in the person of the *Logos*, enabling the hypostatic union to perdure and endure in and through fallen time. Now we can rephrase this around the communion of the Spirit: as the communion of the Father and the Son, the Spirit continually upholds the communion of the Son with the Father, and the communion of the Father with the Son, *even as* the Son becomes subject to the alienating conditions of fallen humanity. The human Jesus always remains *in* (communion with) the Father, and the Father remains *in* (communion with) the Son. Jesus receives the Spirit in such a way that everything he does "is in a humanly appropriate mode."[65]

As a vicarious act, Christ's life in the Spirit is not merely exemplary, but ontologically significant: it constitutes the healing of the very depths of human existence. In this communion of fallen humanity with the holy God, humanity in its alienated condition is confronted and, is consequently, judged, cleansed and atoned through Christ's

---

63. *TiR*, 102. Italics added.
64. *TRn*, 246.
65. Canlis, *Calvin's Ladder: a Spiritual Theology of Ascent and Ascension* (Grand Rapids: Eerdmans, 2010), 98.

Spirit-enabled obedience. Plumbing the depths of this vicarious act even further, Torrance invokes Irenaeus's idea that in the incarnate Son's reception of the Spirit, the Holy Spirit "became accustomed to dwell in humanity."[66] Torrance writes, "in the union of divine and human natures in the Son the eternal Spirit of the living God has composed himself, as it were, to dwell with human nature, and human nature has been adapted and become accustomed to receive and bear that same Holy Spirit."[67] This idea of human nature becoming adapted and accustomed to receive and bear the Holy Spirit is consistent with Torrance's view of the incarnation as a real forging of *the place* where God and humanity unite in communion with one another. Jesus Christ then is the one place where God dwells in a human being, and where a human being *learns* to receive God and becomes accustomed to God dwelling in him. Through the Spirit's sanctifying, consecrating, healing, adapting work in Jesus Christ, an historical and actual place or location for the new creation is objectively established.[68]

This gratuitous and vicarious act is extended in and through the ascension. In the ascension of the incarnate Son to the right hand of the Father, a new *place* has been established in Christ where humanity and God live in communion. This *place* is the creation of a new relation between God and human beings on the entirely new basis and ground of God's self-commitment.[69] In his heavenly exaltation, the vicarious humanity of Christ endures as the living objective basis for human participation *in* God and fellowship *with* God. Having received the Spirit vicariously as one of us, Jesus lives in the power of the Spirit (which is his communion with the Father) as the incarnate ascended Christ. He does so in order that we by the Spirit might share with the Son in his relation to the Father. The Spirit whom Christ received, he now shares, for until this new mediatorial *place* was established in the form of the incarnate Son, the divine Holy Spirit could not be poured out

66. Irenaeus, *Adv. Haer.*, 3.18.1, vol. 2, 92; 3.21.2, 107. Referenced by Torrance in *TF*, 189.
67. *TRn*, 246.
68. As we noted in chapter 2, this *space* or *location* is not geographic or latitudinal, but relational, yet in an ontologically significant sense (i.e. onto-relational).
69. Thomas F. Torrance, *The Doctrine of Grace in the Apostolic Fathers* (Eugene, OR: Wipf and Stock, 1996), 29. Hereafter, *DGAF*.

upon sinful humanity. The presence of God and the Spirit in human beings is possible only through the mediating presence of Christ before the Father; otherwise, the fallen and willful humanity would be unable to bear the consuming holiness of the love and goodness of God, and would thus be destroyed by it. For Torrance, the historical necessity of Christ's life, death, resurrection and ascension is fundamentally and foundationally important in releasing the presence of the Spirit in the Church:

> *Until* he had sanctified himself and perfected in our human nature his one offering for all men, *until* he had made once and for all the sacrifice to take away sin, *until* he had vanquished the powers of darkness and overcome the sharpness of death, *until* he had ascended to present himself in propitiation before the Father, the Kingdom of Heaven could not be opened to believers and the blessing of the divine Spirit could not be poured out upon human flesh or be received by sinful mortal men. *Only with* the enthronement of the Lamb, *only with* the presence of our Surety and the continual intercession of our High Priest before the face of the Father, *only with* the taking up of the glorified Humanity of Christ our Brother into the unity of the Blessed Trinity, could the Holy Spirit be released in all his sanctifying and renewing agency to dwell with man.[70]

The Spirit as Gift

In and through Pentecost, Jesus, the bearer of the Holy Spirit becomes the mediator of the Spirit.[71] In keeping with his objective and person-emphasizing pneumatology, Torrance considers the gift of the Spirit to be an enduring relation, not a once-for-all-act. Our receiving of the Spirit is not only objectively grounded in Christ's (substitutionary and representative) reception of the Spirit; it is also objectively grounded in Jesus Christ's *continuing* incarnate existence as the enthroned lamb of God who bore away the sins of the world and as our high priest who lives to make intercession for us.[72] This emphasis on Christ's continuing humanity is of utmost importance in Torrance's theology. By virtue of his continuing humanity, Christ is able to mediate the

---

70. *TRn*, 247 (italics mine).
71. Ibid., 241.
72. Ibid., 249.

Spirit to his body and the Church: having transferred to himself what belongs to us (our wayward humanity), and having transferred what is his (his faithful Spirit-enabled humanity) to our human nature in union with him. Thus, the Spirit who is mediated to us by Christ is mediated "through the human nature and experience of the Incarnate Son." The Spirit comes then, "not as isolated and naked Spirit, but as Spirit charged with all the experience of Jesus."[73] In this way, "the Spirit comes as the Spirit of a Manhood wholly offered to God in perpetual glorification and worship and praise."[74]

Torrance is careful—particularly in discussions which involve human agency—to consistently establish the asymmetrical yet contrapuntal nature of Christ's relation to the Spirit and of our relation to the Spirit.[75] As this is the case, we do not know the Spirit in the same way as Jesus did; yet there is an intimate relation between the two. The Spirit in Jesus taught him to look to the Father; the Spirit in humanity teaches us to look away from ourselves *to Christ*. In the incarnate Son, the Spirit was the *koinonia* between him and the Father; in us, the Spirit is the *koinonia* between us and the incarnate Son and, through the Son, with the Father. Torrance's language here is quite particular: we have fellowship with God the Father through (by virtue of) the *humanity* of the Son by the Spirit.[76]

The rule which guides Torrance's understanding of our relation to the Spirit is a carefully nuanced articulation of the Creator-creature distinction. Using the hypostatic union as a rubric, he maintains this distinction without confusion or separation and it is in this way that Torrance is able to retain a profound intimacy in our relation to Christ through the Spirit, while ensuring that God's gift of himself to us never becomes our possession. To put it another way, the Spirit who resides/dwells in us is *objective* to us.

Accordingly, Torrance draws a firm line in both Christology and

---

73. Ibid., 246–67.
74. Ibid., 248.
75. Cf. *STR*, 122 for Torrance's use of contrapuntal. Also see Flett's creative appropriation of this term in relation to the work of the Spirit in culture: *Persons, Powers, and Pluralities: Toward a Trinitarian Theology of Culture* (Cambridge: James Clarke, 2012), 168–69.
76. *TRn*, 184.

anthropology between *koinonia* with the Creator Spirit and *methexis* —where *methexis* refers to participation in eternal realities and *koinonia* to participation in personal relationships.[77] With respect to the Church, Torrance emphasizes that *koinonia* does *not* refer to a union of divine and human elements. Creaturely union with God in the Spirit is *not* comparable to the union of divine and human natures in Christ; indeed, such a comparison only serves "to obscure the understanding of the hypostatic union."[78] Torrance ventures a more nuanced description of the analogical relationship: while human deification is clearly not the same thing as the hypostatic union of the incarnate Son, he suggests that the *logic* of the hypostatic union should serve as a controlling guide to how we formulate the human relation to (or participation in) the divine. Torrance states it this way: "*as divine and human natures are related in Christ, so in the Church Christ and human nature are related.*"[79] The Church participates in Christ, in whom divine and human nature are united; she therefore participates in the incarnate Son *by virtue of his human nature.* "Grace is . . . such a self-giving act that he unites us to himself and makes us share in his human nature and in him share in the very Life and Love of God himself."[80]

While maintaining the Creator-creature distinction is of utmost importance to Torrance, he does recognize a significant spatio-temporal overlap between the Son and the Spirit. This has led some to criticize him for collapsing the Spirit and the Son and to charge that he eliminates any distinction between them.[81] However, the unity and distinction between the Son and the Spirit can be seen in the way Torrance conceives the Spirit's work as primarily *communication* and *communion*, and the Son's as *mediation* and *union*. It is this distinction between Son and Spirit which enables finite and fallen human beings to participate in the life of God. Properly speaking, we do not commune *in* the Spirit, but *in Christ through the Spirit*. Because Christ shares our

77. Ibid.
78. Ibid., 185.
79. Ibid.
80. Ibid.
81. Smail, *The Giving Gift*, 92.

nature, we can be in full union with him in his humanity. However, because the Spirit did not assume human nature, the Spirit remains an *other* to us and as such is not an endowment we can possess, an instrument we can wield, or a logico-causal relation we can ever presume upon. It is not *our* Spirit; it is the *Holy* Spirit of the Holy Trinity, who shares the same essence and Being (*homoousion*) of God. Thus, even though we are not united with the Spirit[82] because the Spirit is objectively an other in relation to human beings, we can be in communion with the Spirit and indwelt by Him.

The asymmetry of Christology and anthropology within Torrance's theology sets the framework within which the language of deification receives its meaning. The deifying content of atonement is located specifically in the Spirit-filled incarnate Son and in the atonement itself. This atonement took place within the ontological depths of human being in and through the Son's own vicarious life. In other words, the deifying content of the atonement is the Father-Son relation lived out in our humanity through the Spirit. As such, it is strictly controlled by the boundaries of the hypostatic union, without confusion or separation.

This gives us a helpful rubric for how to understand Torrance's frequent positive use of the language of participation and deification, *theosis* and *theopoiesis*. Properly speaking, the treasures of salvation are never possessed by the Church; they are only hers through union with Christ. Salvation cannot be detached from—and, in fact, has no reality apart from—communion. In the *koinonia* of participation the human creature is reaffirmed and recreated in her human nature. Now as a creature, she shares as a creature, and in a creaturely way in the Father-Son relation through the *koinonia* of the Spirit.[83] Everything that is Christ's in and through his incarnation as the human being for us actually becomes ours through our spiritual union with him. This includes his *justification* (1 Tim 3:15), *adoption* (Rom 1:4), *sanctification* (Rom 6:9-10), and *glorification* (1 Cor 15:20, 42-44). The New Testament

82. Cf. Thomas F. Torrance, *God and Rationality* (Edinburgh: T&T Clark, 1997), 168. Hereafter, *G&R*.
83. *TRn*, 186.

attributes all these to the activity of the Spirit in and upon Christ; and through our spiritual union with Christ, we are given to share by Grace "in saving acts that are abruptly and absolutely divine."[84] Therefore, "our 'deification' in Christ is the obverse of his 'inhomination.'"[85] Deification then as Torrance employs the term *theopoiesis* has nothing to do with being *less* human; it involves being lifted "up in Christ to enjoy a new fullness of human life in a blessed communion with divine life."[86] As the Spirit is the one who underpins, enables and preserves the humanity of Christ, our participation in that same Spirit also preserves and enhances our humanity.[87] Through the Spirit, the Church is given to live by the faith-(fullness) of Christ, so that his faith becomes her faith as with him she cries, "Abba, Father."

As the mode of God's presence by which God brings his relations with creation to their proper end and perfection, the Spirit "goes forth from God and returns to God" mediating the Church's response to Christ.[88] As the Spirit of the incarnate Son, the indwelling Spirit echoes the movement of Christ, replicating the same self-offering to the Father which Christ made through the Spirit.[89]

Again, to frame this according to our thesis, we can say that following and grounded upon the objective historical motion of Grace in Christ, a *corresponding objective* motion is repeated in the mission of the Spirit.[90] Since for us to have the Spirit is to share in the Son's union and communion with the Father, the shape that communion takes will correspond to its form in the historical life of Christ. In this way, the motion of the Spirit answers or echoes the two-fold work of the Son, which we recall is both humanward (in assuming human flesh) and Godward (in offering that sanctified humanity to the Father). At Pentecost, the Spirit repeats that humanward and Godward movement, descending upon the Church in order to lift it upward in faith and

---

84. Ibid., 243.
85. *TF*, 189.
86. Ibid.
87. See Canlis on this same point in Calvin's theology, *Calvin's Ladder*, 100.
88. *TRn*, 248.
89. *TF*, 190.
90. *TRn*, 235–36.

worship.[91] "Pentecost," Torrance remarks, "was the counterpart on earth to wonderful things done within the veil."[92] In line with this, Torrance makes statements that come across as quite radical: in Christ, "the closed circle of the inner life of God was made to overlap with human life, and human nature was taken up to share in the eternal communion of the Father and the Son and the Holy Spirit. . . . The inner life of the Holy Trinity which is private to God alone is extended to include human nature in and through Jesus."[93] And again, accompanied by a warning of "the danger of vertigo:"

> The ascension means the exaltation of man into the life of God and on to the throne of God. . . . There we reach the goal of the incarnation. . . . We are with Jesus beside God, for we are gathered up in him and included in his own self-presentation to the Father. This is the ultimate end of creation and redemption revealed in the Covenant of Grace and fulfilled in Jesus Christ. . . . We ourselves are given a down-payment of that, as it were, in the gift of the Spirit bestowed on us by the ascended man from the throne of God, so that through the Spirit we may already have communion in the consummated reality which will be fully actualized in us in the resurrection and redemption of the body.[94]

In this movement, the Spirit answers the prayer and intercession of the ascended Christ by echoing the continual prayer and intercession of Christ in the church. This action of the Holy Spirit in and with the Church is also Christ himself, who is "acting for us not only from the side of God toward man but acting in us from the side of man toward God."[95] There is no aspect of our response to God that is not realized through the communion of God mediated by Christ. Through the Spirit, the prayers and obedience of the Church are echoes of the praying life of Christ who "prayed with his life, and prayed with his death," and who continues to "offer himself up" in an on-going living form of embodied intercession.

91. Ibid., 248.
92. Ibid., 249.
93. Ibid., 241.
94. *STR*, 135–36.
95. *TRn*, 250.

130

The *Homoousion* Applied to Grace

Torrance's pneumatology is striking in one more respect. Because the Trinity completely governs Torrance's pneumatology and his doctrine of Grace, many of the theological decisions and distinctions he makes regarding these two doctrines are nearly identical. Thus, to live *in the Spirit* is to live *in Grace*. This can at times make distinguishing the Spirit from Grace ambiguous if not impossible. Similar ambiguity pervades Torrance's Christological treatments, where Grace appears to be identified with Jesus Christ, if not indistinguishable from him.[96] Yet, notably, these identifications are not without remainder and the differentiation is theologically significant. Notice the way Torrance nuances the similarities with qualifying distinctions:

> It is not inappropriate to relate the movement of grace to the Holy Spirit, provided we remember the inseparable relation between the Spirit and Christ, and that the Spirit proceeding from the Father operates in and through the Son and thus proceeds from the Son as well as the Father. This connection is not inappropriate for it helps to deliver theology from construing the operation of grace as some form of causality. Grace is as sovereignly free as the Spirit of God and yet as free from arbitrariness as the Persons of the Trinity in whom it is grounded and from whom it cannot be separated.[97]

Thus, the movement of Grace is the movement of the Holy Spirit, *but not only so.* Just as the Spirit is inseparable from the Son and the Father, so too is Grace. Grace in effect is Torrance's shorthand way of speaking of a movement of *the whole* Trinity—a movement which is as free as the Spirit, as personal as the incarnate Son, and as transcendent as the very life of God *in se.* This is the basis on which Torrance aggressively applies the Creator-creature distinction and the logic of the hypostatic union as controlling guides to the concept of Grace. Yet, Torrance pushes further and argues that because Grace is God's personal self-giving the

---

96. Thus, "grace is Jesus Christ." *TRn*, 183; cf. Thomas F. Torrance, *Theological Science* (Oxford: Oxford University Press, 1969), 155. Hereafter, *TS.*
97. *TRn*, 187.

homoousion must be applied to our understanding of Grace as it was with the Spirit.[98]

Since Torrance only asserts this application of the *homoousion* to the understanding of Grace in two of his published writings, both critics and proponents should exercise restraint.[99] Yet, one cannot help but see the logical consistency of such a move given Torrance's overall theological framework. Practically speaking, nothing new is being asserted and no new ground is being claimed beyond the foundation that has already been laid. However by invoking the *homoousion* in relation to Grace Torrance consolidates his argument: it makes explicit the ultimate inner logic and unshakable ontological foundation of Grace within the very being of God.

In order to assess the helpfulness of this sort of appropriation of creedal language, we will now attempt to clarify the theological points Torrance is attempting to secure. First we show how identifying Grace as *homoousial* fits within Torrance's overall theological project; then we will evaluate the fitness and potential problems of this kind of extension of classical trinitarian language.

Theological Reasons to Identify Grace as *Homoousial*

First, in asserting the *homoousion* of Grace, Torrance is highlighting and clarifying two key aspects of Grace: (1) Grace is intensely personal and implacably objective. In an unpublished response to his critics, Torrance explains the movement of his thought in more detail:

> What [the Reformers] did, then, was to apply the homoousion also to the acts of God, to revelation and grace, and to insist that what we have in the Word is God speaking personally, and what we have in grace is not something detachable from God, some sort of created grace or Arian

---

98. Ibid., 182.
99. Torrance's most developed application of the *homoousion* to Grace is in his "The Roman Doctrine of Grace from the Point of View of Reformed Theology," in *TRn*, 182–91. He restates the argument in a different context in "Spiritus Creator: A consideration of the teaching of St Athanasius and St Basil" (*TRn*, 225) and again in *Preaching Christ Today: The Gospel and Scientific Thinking* (Grand Rapids: Eerdmans, 1994), 20–21, though he uses the cognate term *consubstantial* rather than *homoousion*. In his unpublished writings, he defends his doctrine of the Spirit and reaffirms the application of the *homoousion* to Grace in "The Relevance of the Doctrine of the Spirit for Ecumenical Theology (Reply of Professor Thomas F. Torrance to his Critics)," *Reply to Critics*, Q27.

entity, but very God of very God. They emphasized that the Word of God is God speaking Himself to us, that the Grace of God is total, God giving Himself unreservedly to us. *This created in the most intense way personal relationships on the one hand*—destroying the impersonalism and the objectivism of mediaeval theology—*and yet emphasized the implacable objectivity of God on the other hand*, for it is the sheer majesty of His Being, His ultimate Self-giving that we encounter in His Word and Grace.[100]

For Torrance, Grace is the personal self-giving of the Triune God through Christ and the Spirit, by which creatures are given to share in the Father-Son relation. Grace is not a nebulous divine 'good will,' but has real content: "for what God communicates to us in his grace is none other than himself. The Gift and the Giver are one."[101] The application of the *homoousion* to Grace is to recognize Grace as "the one indivisible self-giving of God in Christ."[102] Grace is not therefore something abstract, an impersonal force, or a generalized divine favor; nor is it a generic term for the gratuitous character of all God's gifts. Grace is irreducibly personal; in fact, Grace has a name. Torrance writes,

> Grace is not something that can be detached from God and made to inhere in creaturely being as 'created grace'; nor is it something that can be proliferated in many forms; nor is it something that we can have more or less of, as if grace could be construed in quantitive terms. This is the Reformation doctrine of *tota gratia*. Grace is whole and indivisible because it is identical with the personal self-giving of God to us in his Son. It is identical with Jesus Christ. Thus it would be just as wrong to speak of many graces as many Christs, or of sacramental grace as of a sacramental Christ, or of created grace as of a created Christ.[103]

While Grace is not to be generalized, it cannot be delegated to just one member of the Trinity's activity either, for that would reduce it to a purely economic and instrumental function. Thus as we have observed and argued throughout Torrance roots Grace in "the living relations of the Persons of the Holy Trinity"; which in freedom and love issue

---

100. *Reply to Critics*, Q27 (italics added, underlines are original). Cf. *TRn*, 182.
101. *TRn*, 182.
102. Ibid., 225.
103. Ibid., 182–83. Torrance's phrase *tota gratia* appears to be his own rephrasing of *sola gratia* with an emphasis on the christological nature of Grace which makes it irreducible and indivisible.

forth through the missions as a movement from the Father, through the Son in the Spirit, and which return in the Spirit through the Son to the Father.[104] Thus,

> Between its going forth from God and its coming out upon the creature grace at no point ceases to be what it is within the Trinity, in order to become what it was not, some impersonal entity or causality. Grace can never be regarded in an instrumental sense, for from beginning to end in grace God is immediately present and active as living Agent.[105]

Torrance will not abide any break between the being of God and his activity, for that would involve the trading of impersonal instrumentalities for real relations of communion.

Practically speaking, the recognition that Grace is irreducibly personal and objective and raises strong objections to the "impersonal determinism" of some Protestant doctrines of election. By construing the operation of Grace according to some notion of causality, "the *sui generis* movement of grace" is converted into "causal terms," which "can then appear to be only quite arbitrary."[106] Equally problematic in Torrance's estimation is the Augustinian notion of irresistible Grace. He suggests that the doctrine deleteriously introduced an internal connection between *Grace* and *cause*, which made way for the more general view of Grace "as a divine mode of causation at work in the universe."[107] Torrance argues that at least partially the development of the notion of irresistible Grace is an anthropomorphic projection of pragmatism upon the Divine: God *uses* Grace to administrate his salvific agenda for humankind and in that way God's use of Grace mirrors human means of Grace.

The **second** overt concern which underlies and motivates Torrance's argument is the intimate relation between the doctrine of Grace and the doctrine of the Spirit. As we have already noted, Torrance views this relation as completely appropriate; yet, the pervasive tendency throughout the history of the Church has been for both doctrines to

104. Ibid., 187.
105. Ibid.
106. Ibid.
107. Ibid., 173.

lapse into anthropology or subjectivism. Whereas Romanism tends to confound the Spirit with the spirit of the Church, Protestantism tends to confound the Spirit of God with the human spirit. Torrance warns, "just because the human partner is given his full place by God as knowing subject over against God as his proper object, he is always being tempted to assume the major role in the theological conversation."[108] He views the Protestant "notion of *event-grace*" (where what really matters is the individual believer's own decisions and acts rather than the objective reality of Grace) as a direct result of a failure to take the *homoousion* seriously.[109] Here the stress falls upon religious inwardness and immediacy: the *truth* of one's salvation is lodged within the religious subject, in which the Holy Spirit fails to be distinguished from the depths of the individual's own spirituality and personality. Personalism, if not balanced by a proper objectivism, can easily lapse into "the fatal weakness" of an anthropology in which the objective reality of Grace is indistinguishable from one's own subjective states. So begins the slippery slope in which Grace is first *humanized* and then *secularized,* until Protestantism simply has in a new form "the old notion of *created grace* . . . with its attendant notions of co-operation and co-redemption."[110]

Thus as Torrance perceives it the *homoousion* reminds us that while Grace is intensely personal, it cannot be subsumed into human nature; and, as that which cannot be assimilated into creaturely beings, Grace's mode of operation is irreducibly creative (*sui generis*) and grounded as it is in the living relations of the Trinity.[111] Grace then can only properly be understood by upholding the foundational connection between the Spirit and Christ and by thinking of the Spirit as the Spirit who proceeds from the Father with the Son.[112] For Torrance, to affirm the *homoousion* of the Spirit but not to apply that understanding to Grace, is to drive a wedge between the two doctrines, effectively

---

108. Ibid., 181–82.
109. Ibid., 190.
110. Ibid., 182.
111. Ibid., 186–87.
112. Ibid., 187.

voiding Grace from its personal and objective content. The practical outworking of his approach as Torrance envisions it is this: Grace will maintain its personal and creative character and will also be protected from reduction to either of the twin errors of external causality or inner subjectivity.

Theological Problems with Identifying Grace as *Homoousion*

We can certainly appreciate the importance of the theological points Torrance is seeking to secure. Nevertheless, we must go on to ask whether this bending of theological language is appropriate. This is neither the first time nor the last that we have noticed Torrance's creativity and flexibility with theological terms. Torrance boldly and creatively fashions new terms to convey his meanings, often in a manner that requires his readers/hearers to acquire a new—*Torrancian*—dialect. His coinage of *onto-relations* as a way of speaking of the Triune relations, his expansive use of *an/en-hypostasia* and his innovative manipulation of 'personalogical' terminology[113] are just the tip of the iceberg. For Torrance, language and concepts are never meant to be rigid, for their truth is not in themselves but in the reality to which they refer. While this perspective is certainly to be appreciated, it could be argued that language is usage: when terms loaded with a particular meaning, context and purpose within the tradition are diverted or expanded to serve another function, the short-term payoff may not justify the long-term erosion such a move can precipitate. In this case, *homoousios* has been an important and helpful term within theological discourse for talking about the Son and the Spirit and their relation to the divine essence. However, Grace by definition is externally oriented. Appropriating the *homoousion* outside of its original context and usage creates a potential danger: namely, that it begins to lose its proper shape and as a result, abdicates its technical ability to say what it needs to be able to say within the dogmatic corpus.

---

113. For an example of Torrance's use of *personalogical* as a form of theological description, see ibid., 189.

In Torrance's defense, Grace is not a doctrine which lies somewhere far downstream in the overall dogmatic scheme. Rather, Grace holds a place within first principles. For Torrance, the Trinity must certainly govern and shape all other doctrines; at the same time, he would stress that the converse is equally true: if one gets Grace wrong, the Trinity falters. This integrative understanding of the Trinity, Christology and the Christian life lived in Grace is a fundamental characteristic of Torrance's over all theological program, providing its shape and trajectory. The interweaving of these core doctrines is evidenced in Torrance's concluding remarks on the *Roman Doctrine of Grace and Reformed Theology*:

> So far as the doctrine of grace is concerned the following would appear to be of paramount importance: the *homoousion* with equal stress upon the Being of God in his Acts and upon the Act of God in his Being, participation in the new Humanity of Jesus Christ the crucified and risen Saviour, with the rejection of every form of monophysitism, and, behind all, the living and life-giving communion of the Persons of the Holy Trinity, with the rejection of every form of nominalism.[114]

Within Torrance's integrative approach, the logic holds together. Yet we must press further and question whether Torrance is in danger of hypostatizing Grace as a reference to the Godhead *ad extra*. Does the operative principle that "the Gift and the Giver are one" tempt one to confuse God-in-himself with God's acts *ad extra*?[115] That is, is Torrance in danger of conflating the divine missions with the processions?

We will approach this question by considering briefly how Torrance's thinking on the relation of the immanent and the economic Trinity agrees with and differs from the thinking of Karl Rahner and Karl Barth.

With respect to Rahner, Torrance initially and enthusiastically endorsed Rahner's axiom that "the immanent Trinity is strictly identical with the economic Trinity and visa versa";[116] he did so

---

114. Ibid., 191.
115. *TF*, 328–29. This is the very error Torrance perceives in the Apostolic Fathers usage of the concept of Grace (*charis*), as it tended to relapse to current Hellenistic usage. He claims that charis became "regarded as pneumatic and divinizing power and at times was more or less hypostasized and made into a distinct divine or supernatural entity" (*DGAF*, 141).

because he found himself in complete agreement that the economic Trinity should be the "norm for all our thought and speech about God."[117] However as Molnar has shown Torrance and Rahner operate with irreconcilable differences: for Torrance, God's self-revelation in Christ and the Spirit is absolutely definitive; but Rahner's transcendental method "begins with our experiences of self-transcendence and posits the existence of God as the nameless, silent whole or horizon surrounding us, [and] effectively allows God's oneness to be defined and understood without specific reference to God's self-communication in Christ and the Spirit."[118] Torrance also maintains an *apophatic* reserve, which respects God's mystery and resists reading back subjective experiences of God into God's eternal being in an inappropriate way. Nor will Torrance abide any *analogia entis*, or possibility of thinking about our relations with God as mutually conditioned or mutually conditioning; for the economic Trinity as known only in God and in Christ "is and remains normative for all that is said about God and us."[119] From this standpoint, Rahner's vice-versa is a violation of Grace, for in Rahner's scheme Grace sacrifices its downward movement on the altar of a transcendentally subjective natural theology.

In contrast to Barth, Torrance does not identify Grace among the divine perfections. Grace is not a way of God's being with and toward himself within his eternal Triune perichoretic existence. For Torrance, to push back Grace as Barth does into the immanent life of God is to deny the existence of Grace altogether as well as to risk rejecting the freedom of God to be truly *for* the *other*. If God's self-giving to his creation is not free but is a necessary expression of his being, then the God-world relation dangerously drifts towards a naturalized means of God's own self-constitution or fulfillment. In this panentheistic

116. Karl Rahner, "Theology and Anthropology," *Theological Investigations*, vol. 9, trans. Graham Harrison (New York: Herder and Herder, 1972), 28–45, 32.
117. Thomas F. Torrance, *Trinitarian Perspectives: Toward Doctrinal Agreement* (Edinburgh: T&T Clark, 1994), 78. Hereafter, *TP*.
118. Molnar, *Theologian of the Trinity*, 69.
119. Ibid., 70. Cf. Rahner, "Reflections on Methodology in Theology," TI, 11, 68–124, 87.

account, Grace is rendered unrecognizable; it morphs from being sacrificial self-giving love to being predominantly self-expression.

This, albeit brief, comparison of Torrance's position with the positions of Rahner and Barth demonstrates that Torrance is not in danger of conflating the divine mission with the processions. However, it does leave us with another no less important concern. If Grace is *not* one of the divine perfections and thus not fundamental to God's life *in se*, should it be identified by the term *homoousios*—a term specifically designed within the tradition to assert the full personal reality of Godness in each of the persons and thus to differentiate the immanent life of God? Is there a latent inconsistency here, whereby Torrance denies that Grace is proper to the immanent life of God, and yet commandeers a theological term specifically designated to relate the three persons of the Trinity to one another within the divine essence? A related critique is the risk that Torrance's language of Grace might problematically generalize trinitarian language that ought to be allowed to stand in its own proper specificity. Rather than specifically naming the activity of the Father or the Son or the Spirit, Torrance often just says *Grace*. This is particularly true with respect to the Holy Spirit, who may at times seem to fade silently out of the picture.[120] Certainly the work of the Trinity *ad extra* is undivided; but this should never be allowed to obscure the fact that the activity of the Trinity has a particular shape—a taxis—which we meet not in some generic sense, but in the modes of Father, Son and Spirit. We only know persons, not *essences*; or, rather, we do not know God's *ousia* detached from *hypostasis*. God's *essence* does not *act in abstracto*, but only in the persons as Father, Son and Spirit. Substituting the term *Grace* in lieu of the more personal language of Father, Son and Spirit is to speak in more general terms of the whole nature of God's action towards us without linking

---

120. This tendency is particularly noticeable in Torrance's chapter in *Theology in Reconstruction* on "The Roman Doctrine of Grace and Reformed Theology" (169–92). In a chapter specifically devoted to the subject of Grace, the Holy Spirit gets only one brief mention: "it is not inappropriate to relate the movement of grace to the Holy Spirit . . ." (*TRn*, 187). However, it should also be noted that the apostle Paul does the same thing, speaking of Grace at times in lieu of the Spirit. (For example, whereas in Ephesians the Spirit plays a very prominent role, in Colossians the Spirit is less overtly prominent.)

it to any one person in particular. It may be argued that this risks obscuring the personal and relational reality that God is. Of course, Torrance's concern is precisely the opposite: in the light of the prevailing tendency throughout the history of the Church to detach Grace from its objective and personal ground in God himself, he seeks to make the attachment overtly and irreducibly *seamless*. For Torrance, to allow a gap of any sort between Grace and the Spirit is to chip away at this proper grounding.[121]

Finally, there is one more question which forces itself upon us. If Grace can be *homoousial*, what is there to prevent the *homoousion* from being extended to other aspects of God's being-in-action? Can we say that God's love (or his wisdom, life, holiness, etc.) is *homoousial* as well? Certainly, all that God does is *homoousial* in the sense that God's acts can never be disassociated or abstracted from his being; they are ever personal and objectively rooted in who he is. Yet, the fact that this question can even be posed points us perhaps towards a broader issue: that terms can subtly (and problematically) gain a life of their own in detachment from God, even as they are being used in reference to God. Once a term is reified and abstracted from God himself, it becomes a tool at the mercy of the winds of theological willfulness. In fact, love or any descriptor of God employed in the service of theology, must be defined *by God*, not by other creaturely categories.[122] Nothing can be allowed to replace the real referent. Regarding this issue, Torrance points out that theologians within the Church create various distinctions in order to serve their modes of thinking and speaking about Grace, and that these distinctions in actuality lack any objective correspondence to the true reality of Grace itself. This is what Torrance

---

121. Torrance's concerns regarding the naturalization of Grace and the naturalization of the Spirit run parallel. This is particularly noticeable in his discussion of *theosis*, where it is most often evoked for the express purpose of asserting the true Godness of the Holy Spirit. See *TRn*, 242ff where in the section, "The New Coming of the Holy Spirit at Pentecost Was a Coming in the Utter Godness of God." Torrance makes a special plea for a reconsideration of *theosis* stating: "*Theosis* was the term the Fathers used to emphasize the fact that through the spirit we have to do with God in his utter sublimity, his sheer Godness or holiness. . . . God in the most absolute sense, God in his ultimate holiness or Godness."

122. Torrance frequently made this point in his writings. Cf. "Christian Thinking Today," 12. (Unpublished Moot Paper [1941], John Baillie Collection, New College Library, Edinburgh.)

means by his assertion that we must not "ever imagine that any hypostatized entity is the equivalent of the self-giving of God in the Person of the Son."[123] Thus for Torrance the *homoousion* can exclusively be applied to Grace, because Grace is *uniquely* descriptive of the *actual* self-giving of God in the Son sent from the Father, together with the Spirit. Given this framework, far from positing a fourth hypostasis in addition to Father, Son and Spirit, Torrance retains the mystery inherent in the Church's participation in Christ. God's presence in and among creatures does not come at the cost of vacating God of his Godness, or creatures of their creatureliness. Positive assertions about the Church's participation must be governed by both the Chalcedonian doctrine of the hypostatic union and the Chalcedonian adverbs (without confusion, change, division or separation). The Church in other words while really united to the incarnate Son, partakes in him in a creaturely appropriate mode, of the Father-Son *koinonia* through the Spirit.[124] "The mystery of grace is the mystery of Christ; by keeping ourselves within the great Chalcedonian adverbs we allow that mystery constantly to declare itself to us and impose itself upon us."[125]

Conclusion

Our objective in this chapter has been to display the integral relation in Torrance's theology between Grace and the doctrine of the Spirit. We have observed that many of the threats which lay siege to the doctrine of Grace, also challenge pneumatology. Consequently, a weakness in one will necessarily compromise the other. We have seen that Torrance's thoroughly objective pneumatology combined with the inseparable relation between the Spirit and Christ provides an essential foundation for an understanding of Grace as fundamentally and essentially participatory in nature. Grace *entails* inclusion. Through the Spirit, who includes us in the *koinonia* of the Father and

---

123. *TRn*, 183.
124. Ibid., 186.
125. Ibid.

the Son, we are given to share in divine activities, creatures though we remain.

PART II

Human Participation in the Motion of Grace

[G]race . . . is thus the presupposition of the whole Christian life, not one principle which (along with others) works within that life.[1]

The remaining task of this book is to apply Torrance's theology of Grace directly to the human subject. We have already observed that the doctrine of Grace holds ontological implications for human creatures. As created subjects who have their being within the two-fold motion of the Trinity, and who have been created to share in the communion of the Spirit in which the Father and the Son share, our human identity and formation are intimately bound up with our relation to the triune persons.[2] This relation is grounded by the objective ontological reality of redemption in Christ—a reality which also calls forth the subjective fulfillment of salvation through the Spirit in Christ's body, the Church.[3]

The ongoing argument of this book has been that the motion of Grace includes human participation in the New Humanity of Christ. I have also argued that the concept of Grace in Torrance's thought is a particularly comprehensive term, linking who God is and how God acts

---

1. Thomas F. Torrance, *The Doctrine of Grace in the Apostolic Fathers* (Eugene, OR: Wipf and Stock, 1996), 30. Hereafter, *DGAF*.
2. Thus the preceding three chapters are not optional material, the unnecessary precursor to the more important subject matter of ourselves.
3. Thomas F. Torrance, *Theology in Reconstruction* (Grand Rapids: Eerdmans, 1965), 186.

in the world with human involvement in that activity. In light of its pervasive organizing force, the dynamic of Grace supplies a decisive component of the underlying logic of Torrance's entire dogmatic project. Grace is a heuristic or interpretive key for all other doctrines: the very motion of our theological thought, if it is to align at all with reality, must literally move *from Grace to Grace*. I have further argued that the logic of Grace plays a determinative role—both methodologically and materially—in all doctrines which seek to order the relation of God and humans.[4]

In the coming chapters, we broaden our doctrinal scope and enter what is in effect a secondary level of theological reflection, moving from the economic missions of the Triune persons to the creaturely fellowship re-created by those missions. That is, we move from specific attention to the Triune God as he gives himself to human creatures in Christ and the Spirit (chapters 1-3) to the way the New Humanity fully achieved in Christ is extended by the Holy Spirit through communion and union and therefore participation in Christ's Sonship (chapters 4-6). In attending to the human subject, we never leave behind the person or work of Christ, for his perfected and continuing humanity is crucial to our treatment of the Spirit in the Church. A formalized division of 'what God does' and 'what we do' is neither possible nor desirable. Here as before we find that the logic of Grace serves as "a sort of category which describes the peculiar relatedness found throughout the whole body of theology."[5]

Given this is the case, we will consider the relation between the triune persons and the human subject in the communion of the Spirit on three concentric levels: the anthropological *context*; the ecclesiological *form*; and the personal *way or mode* of the doctrine of Grace, as it confronts the human being. These will form the following three chapters.

Chapter 4 will attend to the implications of Torrance's doctrine of Grace for a theological anthropology. Here, we consider the actual

4. Cf. ibid., 114.
5. Thomas F. Torrance, *Theology in Action*, Lecture. Date unknown. Thomas F. Torrance Manuscript Collection, Special Collections, Princeton Theological Seminary Library, Box 22, p. 35.

context in which Grace takes place among human creatures; creatures who are united to the incarnate Christ by virtue of their existence as human beings. Torrance notes an irreversible ontological relation between the Creator and all human beings through Christ. In this light, we consider Torrance's appropriation of the *imago Dei* as expressive of the human response to Grace. This consideration will engage us in the following relevant topics: the constitution of human personhood; the effects of sin upon the image; and the implications of the constancy of God's Grace for human creatures, who *are* not what they *ought* to be and consequently are creatures under judgment.

Chapter 5 will consider the relation of Torrance's doctrine of Grace to ecclesiology. Here we consider the *form* Grace takes in the human sphere, among those who participate in the new humanity of Christ through the Spirit. As the particular locus within human history in which people gather together under the name of Christ, Torrance views the Church as "the supreme object of divine grace."[6] In the Church, Grace takes the *form* of a community of people who are one body with Christ—a form which is corporate before it is personal —or rather, is corporate *because* it is essentially personal. Within the sphere of this corporate body, the union between God and humanity in Christ creates a corresponding personal fellowship among human beings in their relations with one another. This corresponding *koinonia* is the manner in which men and women share in the life and love of the Trinity (i.e., in the communion of the Spirit). The basic motion of the Church's life is to serve her head by sharing in his ministry to the world. The living Christ empowers her for this task through the ongoing nurture of Word and sacrament. The existence of the Church is one of incorporation and participation in Christ, for in the Church there is only one body and, thus, only one worship and one ministry.

Chapter 6 brings the focus up close by looking at the relation of the doctrine of Grace to individual Spiritual formation. Here we consider the *way* in which Grace becomes particularized and personalized among human beings. The Spirit's work in God's people

6. *TRn*, 192.

is to actualize subjectively in them what has been accomplished for them objectively and ultimately all in the Incarnation. Through the communion of the Spirit, Christ does not relate generically to the Church; he confronts each individual person personally in his love, calling for an ultimate decision. The way of transforming Grace in the individual is the love of Christ, which heals and restores humanity through "a meeting of the minds"—that is, through renewing our mind with the mind of Christ in a life of baptismal self-abandonment and Eucharistic service.

These chapters—each in its own sphere—are different ways of addressing the same key existential question: the relation between the objective ontological reality of redemption in Christ and the subjective fulfillment of humanity's salvation in the Spirit.[7]

7. Ibid., 186.

4

Anthropology—Grace Has a Context

[M]an never attains to a true self-knowledge until he has previously contemplated the Face of God, and come down after such contemplation to look into himself. . . . It is upon this downward motion of God's grace that the very being of man is grounded.[1]

This chapter sets out to examine anthropology as the context of Grace and Grace as the context of anthropology.[2] Theological anthropology receives its form and meaning from the doctrine of God: "there can be no true knowledge of man except within our knowledge of God."[3]

---

1. Thomas F. Torrance, *Theology in Reconstruction* (Grand Rapids: Eerdmans, 1965), 99. Hereafter, *TRn*. Torrance begins by quoting from Calvin, *Inst.* I.1.2.
2. For Torrance's theological anthropology see: Thomas F. Torrance, "The Word of God and the Nature of Man," in *Reformation Old and New: Festschrift for Karl Barth*, ed. F.W. Camfield (London: Lutterworth, 1947), 121–41, reprinted in *Theology in Reconstruction*, 99–16; *Calvin's Doctrine of Man* (London: Lutterworth, 1949), hereafter, *CDM*; "Man, Priest of Creation," in Thomas F. Torrance, *The Ground and Grammar of Theology* (Charlottesville: The University Press of Virginia, 1980), 1–14. Hereafter, *GGT*; "The Goodness and Dignity of Man in the Christian Tradition," *Modern Theology* 4 (1988): 309–22 (hereafter, *G&DMCT*); "Man, Mediator of Order," in *The Christian Frame of Mind*, 29–48. Hereafter, *CFM*; "The Soul and Person in Theological Perspective," in *Religion, Reason, and the Self: Essays in Honour of Hywel D. Lewis*, ed. S.R. Sutherland and T.A. Roberts (Cardiff: University of Wales Press, 1989), 103–18. Hereafter, *S&PTP*; *The Soul and Person of the Unborn Child* (Edinburgh: Handsel Press for the Scottish Order of Christian Unity, 1999), hereafter, *S&PUC*; and *The Being and Nature of the Unborn Child* (Edinburgh: Handsel Press for the Scottish Order of Christian Unity, 2000).
3. *TRn*, 99.

As such, "the very being of man is grounded" upon the "downward motion of God's grace."[4]

In the resurrection of the incarnate Son, the atonement is established as a permanent reality in the new creation. Torrance describes this elevation of the human creature to a permanent reality as the most profound form of "Christian humanism."[5] Because of the seismic significance of the resurrection and ascension of Christ, Torrance asserts that theological anthropology must begin with atonement: "It is precisely in Jesus . . . that we are to think of the whole human race, and indeed of the whole creation, as in a profound sense *already* redeemed, resurrected, and consecrated for the glory and worship of God."[6] This new relation with the incarnate Son is a deepening of the ontological relation which all of humanity shares with Christ by virtue of creation.[7] Now, on the basis of his work in life and death, and on the ground of his person as mediator,

> the whole of creation is now put on a new basis with God, the basis of a Love that does not withhold itself but only overflows in pure unending Love. . . . That applies to every man, whether he will or no. He owes his very being to Christ and belongs to Christ, and in that he belongs to Christ he has his being only from Him and in relation to Him.[8]

Humans can be properly understood only within the context of the circle of the Triune Life, by whom and through whom creation and redemption take place.

Thus it is from within this all-embracing framework of Grace that Torrance approaches his doctrine of humanity. To be a human creature is to be caught up in this situation of participation in the Triune life. There are not two kinds of humans: those in the circle of the Triune life and those outside. To be human is to exist within a willed covenantal

---

4. Ibid.
5. Thomas F. Torrance, *Space, Time and Resurrection* (Edinburgh: T&T Clark, 1998), 79. Hereafter, *STR*.
6. Thomas F. Torrance, *The Trinitarian Faith: The Evangelical Theology of the Ancient Catholic Church* (Edinburgh: T&T Clark, 1995), 183; Hereafter, *TF*. Italics added.
7. Torrance is emphatic that the ontological relation of humanity to God in creation is purely by grace (i.e. non-necessary, irreversible/asymmetrical).
8. Thomas F. Torrance, *School of Faith* (London: Camelot, 1959), xciv. Hereafter, *SOF*; cf. Thomas F. Torrance, "Atonement and the Moral Order," in *Universalism and the Doctrine of Hell*, 244. Hereafter, *A&MO*.

relation—freely and personally elected and teleologically constituted for fellowship. Creation, as such, provides the historical space and time in which the relation between the faithfulness of God and human creatures unfolds.[9]

In this light, the purpose of this chapter is two-fold: (1) to establish the constitution of human beings as creatures of Grace, created as the image of God for fellowship with God; and (2) to explore the perverting effects of sin upon the *imago Dei*, and the resulting tensions due to the constancy of God's Grace towards the human being, who is now inescapably under judgment.

The *Imago Dei* as Participation in Grace

Given these foundational concerns, it quickly becomes apparent why Torrance finds the biblical metaphor of the *imago Dei* so attractive, for it fits perfectly within the shape of his theology of Grace.[10] In Torrance's exposition, the *imago* is an exact reflection of the downward two-fold motion of Grace at work among human creatures. Since the Creator-creature relation is fundamentally a relation of Grace, the *imago Dei* effectively functions as another way of speaking of the dynamics of Grace among human creatures.

As creatures of Grace, human beings are constituted by the following primary characteristics: first, the human being is a creature *addressed*; second, the human being exists by virtue of a spirit/Spirit relation with God and as such is essentially an *onto-relational* being; third, *co-humanity* as man and woman is fundamental to the structure of the human creature; and finally, the human being is the image of God through *participatory lordship* over its fellow creatures in the world. While an orderly treatment of these concepts might suggest clear lines of separation, this is not at all the case. The human being is an integrated whole; and it is the whole of the human person, "as body of his mind and mind of his body," with which we are concerned.[11]

---

9. Thomas F. Torrance, *Theological Science* (Oxford: Oxford University Press, 1969), 68. Hereafter *TS*.
10. Cf. *TRn*, 102; CD III.2, 203.
11. Thomas F. Torrance, "The Soul and Person in Theological Perspective," in *Religion, Reason, and the Self: Essays in Honour of Hywel D. Lewis*, ed. S.R. Sutherland and T.A. Roberts (Cardiff: University of

The Human Being is a Creature Addressed

If a priority must be assigned to the various aspects which constitute the human person, the basic fact that the human is *addressed* or *called* into being must take precedence. This quality of being addressed sets human beings apart from the rest of creation. They are not only commanded into existence (in the sense that all things come into being by God's command), but are also *called* into a relationship with the Creator through his Word. Here we can clearly see the contours of the downward two-fold movement of Grace already set forth.

In distinction from Barth (stylistically, not theologically) and in line with his overall preference for personal imagery, Torrance tends to prefer Calvin's language that speaks of obedience to the *Word* of God, rather than obedience to the *command* of God. God's "direct personal address" is the very life-pulse of human persons around which every other aspect of their being has its reason and purpose.[12] Thus, their "special duty is to give ear to the Word."[13] Life flows to them solely in the form of the Word of God; they possess life only as they acknowledge the One from whom life comes. Summoned to communion by God's intimate address, they are also *response-able*: the light of intelligence is given to them that they might answer the Word by living "in a thankful fashion corresponding to the motion of grace."[14] Thus, human beings are uniquely what Robert Jensen calls, "the praying animal," teleologically constituted for communion with God "in such a way that the Word of God is made to echo in the innermost being of man as man."[15]

Wales Press, 1989), 105. Hereafter, *S&PTP*; cf. Thomas F. Torrance, *Atonement: the Person and Work of Christ*, ed. Robert T. Walker (Milton Keynes: Paternoster, 2009), 438. Hereafter, *Atonement*.

12. Thomas F. Torrance, "The Goodness and Dignity of Man in the Christian Tradition," *Modern Theology* 4 (1988): 310. Hereafter, *G&DMCT*.

13. *Inst.* 1.6.2.

14. *CDM*, 32.

15. Thomas F. Torrance, *Incarnation: The Person and Life of Christ*, ed. Robert T. Walker (Nottingham: Intervarsity, 2008), 60. Hereafter, *Incarnation*; *G&DMCT*, 310. The phrase "praying animal" is from Robert Jenson's *Systematic Theology vol. 2* (Oxford: Oxford University Press, 1999), 58–61.

The Human Being as an Onto-Relational Being

The second aspect which constitutes the human being as a creature of Grace is the nature of the human's *being*. Torrance seeks to follow what he understands to be Greek patristic anthropology by observing that in creation God gives being and life to the human creature in such a way that "body and soul form a single living entity."[16] As a unitary whole of physical and rational being, the human creature lives and moves and has being in God "through the immanent presence and power of [God's] transcendent Spirit."[17] In this view, the *spirit* of humanity is not thought of as some third entity in the constitution of the human (as in 'body, soul and spirit'), but rather as "a dynamic correlate to the Spirit of God."[18] It is "the creaturely pole of the spirit/Spirit relation."[19] The human spirit is not some "spark of the divine" humans possess; rather, it is "the ontological qualification of his soul and indeed of his whole creaturely being."[20] On this basis, the human spirit is a way of referring to the ontological (and therefore structural) constitution of human beings: creatures who require the Holy Spirit in order to be what they were made to be as *imago Dei*.[21]

For Torrance, this perspective of the human constitution is a profound and radically generative theological concept. By locating the spirit/Spirit relation at the center of the human being as a unitary whole, Torrance is able to define human existence in onto-relational terms, analogous to the trinitarian relations in God. Torrance asserts that this onto-relational trinitarian doctrine of God (i.e., the love relations existing between the persons of the Trinity belong essentially to the ontology of the Father, Son, and Holy Spirit) actually gave rise to the concept of person. That is, "'Person' is an onto-relational concept."[22] Understood trinitarianly, personal being is constituted by

---

16. *S&PTP*, 106.
17. *G&DMCT*, 310.
18. *S&PTP*, 110.
19. *G&DMCT*, 310.
20. *S&PTP*, 110.
21. Torrance makes particular mention of the relevant exposition of Karl Barth and Ray Anderson. Cf. CD III.2, 344–66; and Ray S. Anderson, *On Being Human, Essays in Theological Anthropology* (Grand Rapids: Eerdmans, 1982), 207ff.

the giving and receiving of love. Thus Torrance asserts, "love belongs to the essential equation of the personal but love in the profound ontological sense that derives from the Holy Spirit, the love between persons which belongs to what personal beings really are."[23]

If *person* is a concept which originates out of the doctrine of God, in which God is understood as "the fullness of Love and of Personal Being,"[24] then human personhood is solely possible by the presence of the divine Spirit in the human creature.[25] Torrance suggests that this understanding of the human being "turned the basic concept of man inside out," because the approach to human existence and nature was now "governed by a transcendental determination of man to an objective other, primarily in God but also in his fellow man."[26] In fact, in a manner which reflects the onto-relations of the divine persons, Torrance maintains that within inter-human relations, the relations between persons also belong to what the persons really are.[27] This understanding of human personhood involves "an inherent relatedness" or "community-ness" among human beings, which reflects the "transcendent relatedness or 'community-ness' inherent in God."[28]

From this standpoint, Torrance's anthropology does not have a logical category or place for humanity in isolation from "a transcendental relation" to God and therefore also to fellow humanity.[29] Human attempts at self-governing existence do not produce autonomous persons definable by their independence or freedom; rather, the self-defined human is now distinguished by its lack of personal being or in the language of the Gospel of Luke, as one who is *lost*.[30] In Torrance's thought, there is no such thing as

---

22. Thomas F. Torrance, *The Christian Doctrine of God: One Being Three Persons* (Edinburgh: T&T Clark, 1996), 157. Hereafter, *CDG*.
23. *G&DMCT*, 320.
24. Ibid.
25. Cf. CD II.1, 284.
26. *S&PTP*, 112.
27. *GGT*, 173; *CDG*, 103.
28. *S&PTP*, 115.
29. *G&DMCT*, 319.
30. This theme dominates Luke 15 with its parables of the lost sheep, the lost coin, and the lost son, but is also used to describe 'lost' Israel in Matt 10:6, 15:24, 18:14, Luke 19:10, and John 18:9.

the "pure human"; there is only the human-in-communion-with-God or the human-alienated-from-God. Thus, to be a person—that is, to be properly personal—is to live a sort of *enhypostatic* existence; "for the existence of authentic personal being" requires "a transcendent relation of openness to what is beyond it."[31] Torrance asserts "it is precisely this kind of openness that is created through the intensely personalizing interaction of the triune God" upon the human creature.[32]

Having established human beings as irreducibly onto-relational beings, we can view participation in the life of God and human agency in this light. The essential framework for any positive description of human agency is determined by and takes place through the humanity of Christ.

The Ontological Space for Participation in Grace— the Humanity of Christ

In Torrance's theology of Grace, the onto-relational constitution of human being depends upon Christ's incarnational union with humanity. This union functions as the ontological anchor which identifies humans as the creatures determined to glorify God as his image-bearing children. It also marks the being of the human creature as a dynamic human *becoming*—a creature continually moving towards or away from union with Christ. Such creaturely union with Christ is the subjective event in our own spatio-temporal existence, in which we participate in Christ's objective incarnational union with us. Torrance describes these two unions as *correlated*: the way of Christ's union with us is also the way of our "participation in grace."[33] For Torrance, this principle by which the relation between the Grace of God and the faith of human beings is "*proportionaliter* to the relation of Man and

---

31. Thomas F. Torrance, *Reality and Scientific Theology* (Eugene, OR: Wipf and Stock, 2001), 192. Hereafter, *R&ST*. Cf. John Zizioulas, "Human Capacity and Incapacity: A Theological Exploration of Personhood," *SJT* 28, no. 5 (1975): 401–47. Whereas Boethius had defined the person as an individual substance with a rational nature, Zizioulas turns the Boethian approach on its head by asserting that the hypostasis (substance) of the person lies in *ekstasis*.
32. Ibid., 192.
33. *TRn*, 186.

God in hypostatic union in Christ Jesus" sets the terms within which human actions take place.[34] As "the central relation and union . . . of which every other relation must partake," this is the only "true and valid analogy," which can accurately refer to the God-human relation.[35] Thus, analogous to the *anhypostasia* and *enhypostasia* of Christ's humanity, our humanity has no independent existence apart from God's creative activity. That is, both unions are related to the rhythm of the *an/en-hypostasia*, and both are realized through one and the same Spirit. While the historical event of Christ's union with us has become an objective and universal truth encompassing and embracing all humanity, our union with Christ is an event that happens personally, and in our own spatio-temporal history. *Precisely because* human participation corresponds to the *an/en-hypostasia*, it does not abrogate our creaturely being; all the benefits of Christ—his sonship, new humanity, new creation, adoption, justification, sanctification, regeneration, the divine life and love—are shared through our union with him in his *human* (not divine) nature.

The ontological barrier of the *an/en*, which protects the Creator-creature distinction, is significant. Sharing in the life of God through the Son can easily drift into a kind of vertigo-inducing form of transhumanizing deification. As a result, Torrance has specifically resisted the impulse to apply the language of *perichoresis* to human relations, either between humans or of humans with God. However, this terminological restraint is not reflected by some of his interpreters. Kye Won Lee, Myk Habets, and Dick O. Eugenio in their respective doctoral theses on Torrance's theology of union in Christ, *theosis*, and trinitarian soteriology all import the term *perichoresis* into Torrance's discussion of *theosis*, where Torrance himself refrains from using it; and none call attention to the fact that Torrance himself does not apply the term *perichoresis* to human relations at any point or on any level.[36] This is a surprising oversight for some of Torrance's

---

34. Ibid., 114.
35. Ibid.; Thomas F. Torrance, "Predestination in Christ," *Evangelical Quarterly* 13 (1941): 127. Hereafter, *PiC*.
36. See Lee, *Union*, 207, and Habets, *Theosis*, 145, and Eugenio's entire last chapter and conclusion

foremost recent interpreters, and it suggests the far-reaching importance of understanding Torrance's doctrine of Grace if one is to understand his overall thought. For his own part, Torrance believed the doctrinal development of *perichoresis*, from its beginnings as a christological category to its eventual usage in reference to the Triune relations, to be an irreversible historical development. A development which "had the effect of defining [perichoresis] in such a way that it may not be applied to the hypostatic union of divine and human natures in Christ without serious damage to the doctrine of Christ."[37] This is of utmost importance for Torrance, for *perichoresis* has no correlate concept like *anhypostasia* to clarify the uni-directionality of the relation. Thus, creatures do not exist in any form of unmediated *perichoretic* relations with one another or with God. *Enhypostasia* apart from *anhypostasia* would in fact be a denial of Grace, for Grace establishes an irreversible relation between the Creator and the creature which is inexplicable from the side of the creature, and this is precisely the point *anhypostasia* affirms. Concisely put, *anhypostasia* asserts the unconditional priority of Grace; *enhypostasia* asserts that "God's grace acts only as grace."[38]

Torrance himself is quite explicit that creaturely participation, communion and *koinonia* in the triune life are "analogous to and grounded in," *but not the same as*, "the communion which [God] has eternally in himself."[39] Accordingly, Torrance deems the term onto-relations entirely appropriate with respect to inter-personal relations among human beings, but does not transgress the Creator-creature distinction by blurring the boundaries between divine and creaturely being.

(*Soteriology*, 141–89, especially 158–68). Eugenio, in what is an otherwise very well-structured and well-crafted thesis, makes mediated *perichoretic participation* the core descriptor of humanity's destiny (179). In similar fashion, in the realm of the hypostatic union, rather than the Trinity *per se*, Lee is also guilty of importing the specific Chalcedonian language (inconfuse, immutabiliter, indivise, and inseparabiliter) into Torrance's description of union with Christ understood according to the hypostatic union—again, making an extensive move where Torrance himself does not (Lee, *Union*, 204).

37. *CDG*, 102; cf. *GGT*, 173; *TS*, 214–18.
38. *TS*, 217.
39. *Incarnation*, 179.

The Ontological Space of Human Agency

The onto-personal structure of human beings also provides the essential framework for any positive description of human agency. Human agency is understood within this context of human personhood grounded in the humanity of Christ.

Because human beingness bears an onto-personal structure, the corruption of our relation to God entails the corruption of that image. As such, we are slaves to the self-will of our estranged human nature, and our human agency is now pervasively corrupted. The freedom-less perversion of our spiritual depravity is continually re-enacted in human creatures who have become enemies in our minds and turned the truth of God into a lie.[40] Sin is the irrational activity born of an alienated (and thus irrational) mind, which Torrance describes as the *hegemonikon*, or governing principle, of a human being.[41] Accordingly, sin is "properly of the mind,"[42] for the mind involves "a total relation to the person": when the natural gift of reason becomes corrupted, human subjectivity is set adrift and the whole human nature becomes degenerate. Because the mind holds this portal position in the constitution of the human creature, Torrance freely attributes to the mind all aspects, or descriptors, of human fallenness: its onto-personal being is twisted and distorted, alienated and estranged, hostile, resistant, biased, depraved, fallen, wayward, and diseased in its inner structure.[43] The essence of this perverted "hostility to grace" is expressed passively in ingratitude and actively in the "sinful motion of pride and self-will."[44]

Under the guidance of the mind, human agency is enacted by the will, which is the seat of desired action within the human creature. While the will is equally subject to the destructive power of sin, it nevertheless opens up an ontological space within which a degree of indeterminacy is exercised.

40. *MOC*, 40.
41. Cf. ibid., 39.
42. *CDM*, 117, 107, quoting Calvin's commentary on Rom 2:1. Cf. *Atonement*, 438.
43. *Atonement*, 438.
44. *TRn*, 109.

In order to ground and orient the theological and ontological space in which human agency takes place, we must return once again to Torrance's Christology, and more specifically to the way his theology of Grace bears upon the doctrine of the two wills of Christ. It is, in fact, the christological doctrine of two wills in one Person which provides the ontological basis needed for the dynamic exercise of Christ's divinity in the midst of his fallen humanity. To elaborate, the doctrine of two wills recognizes that Christ's will was not "bare like ours";[45] that is, it did not exist in isolation from God, but was at every point shaped by God's will.

While Torrance does not offer much description as to *how* the incarnate Son wields his will, it is clear the means of agency is relationally, not substantially driven. Ian McFarland offers helpful elucidation which is consistent with Torrance's framework when he points out the "ontologically odd status of the will as the feature of human nature that gives this nature a kind of indeterminacy":

> The will is not a power we have over our natures. . . , but rather identifies the fact that we live out our nature as agents. . . . In short, human nature is indeterminate in the sense that a human being is some*one* rather than some*thing*, and thus not adequately or fully described in terms of *what* they are.[46]

McFarland goes on to suggest the human being's will exists on the border of whatness and whoness, teetering between the ontologically-determinate features of earthly existence prior to glory (i.e., hunger, mortal fear, exhaustion, etc.) and our identity as beloved children of God. In the case of Jesus Christ, because his *hypostasis* (i.e., *who* he is) is the second person of the Trinity, its mode of operation is unique. As McFarland explains,

> In brief, while we sin because we are sinners, Christ does not sin because, as the divine Word (i.e. a *hypostasis* of the Trinity), he is not a sinner. . . . Whereas sinful wills are turned away from God, Christ's will is at every

---

45. Quoted in McFarland, "Fallen or Unfallen?," *IJST* 10, no. 4 (Oct 2008): 409. This particular phrase comes from Maximus the Confessor, *Opuscula Theologica et Polemica 20* (PG91:236D).
46. Ibid., 410.

point turned toward God, so that his willing is shaped by God's will for him.[47]

From this standpoint, the only difference ontologically between Christ's will and ours is his unique relation to God.

Since the mind with its will is the source or location of the human problem, it is also "right there the gospel tells us that we require to be cleansed by the blood of Christ and to be healed and reconciled to God."[48] Thus, the Son of God truly and personally laid hold of our hostile and alienated orientation in "the inner recesses of the human mind," that he might redeem it and effect reconciliation at the very heart of the rational center of human being.[49] Thus, Christ's will can still be considered "the will of estranged man in estranged adamic human nature;" and, as such, can face both temptations and sufferings resulting from all the natural passions of human existence (e.g., hunger, weariness, suffering, and death).[50] However, while we are slaves of our nature, Christ was not; and by his will he was able to continually redirect his fallen nature towards faithfulness to his Father. Christ's divine *hypostasis* is not subject to the corrupted human nature to which he united himself, but vice-versa.[51] Because his human will belonged to the one person of God the Son, its on-going mode of operation is one of communion with God. As a human therefore he is not *incurvatus in se*, but proceeds forth in a new direction: as the human-creature who finally answers the summons of the Creator, and thus as the New Man.

This description of Christ's holy life suggests implications for the doctrine of sanctification. In short, sanctification is not to be thought of as moral perfection, in the sense of some already-arrived-at state of freedom from moral struggle. While it is true that Jesus's *hypostasis* is that of the divine Son, that ontological reality is not metaphysically static, but is dependent upon its actualized *enhypostatic* fulfilment.

47. Ibid., 411–12; cf. *Incarnation*, 212.
48. *Atonement*, 438.
49. *TF*, 188; cf. *MOC*, 39.
50. *Incarnation*, 212.
51. Cf. McFarland, *Fallen or Unfallen?*, 412.

Sanctification is descriptive of Jesus's *lived* history. It is the situation of an agent who exists in intimate fellowship with God and who hears and answers the summons to be the image of God—the true Son of the Father. Within this understanding, sanctification as Torrance describes it is best recognized as a lived orientation (a position*ing*), rather than a static condition (a position). Additionally, Christ's sanctification of his fallen humanity does not thereby make him *unfallen*, for his holiness is recognized as a *continuous* (whilst unbroken) work. Consequently, his fallenness and his holiness persist in tension and yet within this tension, the fallen quality of his humanity is relativized by the Graced nature of his (divine) person. Thus, Christ's life is one of "continuous *kenosis*," throughout which he refuses to transgress the limits of his creaturely human nature, as he continuously offers his life up to the Father in obedient faithfulness.[52]

By viewing the concrete location of personal agency in the will, that is by viewing the will as a realm of self-determination, space is opened up for a relational ontology of personhood. Because Torrance gives priority in human ontology to relational over metaphysical categories, the will emerges as a borderland realm of self-determination, the nexus of person-formation. Together with the mind, the will determines whether the movement of the human being is either with or against Grace, either towards or away from communion with God.

In this section, a trinitarian basis for an onto-relational understanding of human personhood has been developed. Along the way, we have observed the central role of the Holy Spirit in constituting human beings as human persons, where love and communion belong to the basic equation of personhood. We explored Christ's incarnational union with humanity, which provides a christological anchor point and an analogy for union with Christ within our own spatio-temporal histories, whereby we share by the Spirit in the life and love of God. Upon this foundation of the onto-personal structure of human beings, the beginnings of a positive description of human agency grounded in the divine-human humanity of Christ, was

52. *Incarnation*, 187.

attempted. Our next task is to attend to this onto-personal structure of humanity as *co-humanity*, followed by the participatory implications of the human being as *imago Dei*.

Co-Humanity as the Structure of the Human Creature

I have already begun to unpack the community-ness which exists among human beings who cannot be extracted from their existence as persons-in-relation. Before moving on to consider Torrance's vision of the *imago Dei* proper, one more basic component of the human constitution needs to be put in place: humanity *as man and woman*. With an exposition that bears a clear resemblance to that of Karl Barth, Torrance views male and female *co-humanity* as basic to the onto-relational and functional structure of humanness.

The basis of Torrance's argument depends heavily on the unity of soul and body in the human being and on the teachings of Jesus on marriage. Since sexual differentiation is not "merely adventitious or accidental" but is actually "intrinsic to the human soul," Torrance asserts that "the human soul . . . is either male or female."[53] Gendered existence is ontologically constitutive, such that the "man-woman relation generates a dynamic ontological relationship within human existence."[54] Thus, "the essential human nucleus . . . is neither man by himself nor woman by herself, but only man and woman."[55] Torrance considers the *not good* of Genesis 2:18 a disclosure of the fundamentally sexual or gendered character of humanity's isolation. Torrance's concept of sexually differentiated co-humanity fittingly integrates with his holistic understanding of the human being as an onto-relational physical and rational creature designed for communion—with both God and one another. In this sense, the structural reality of sexuality functions as an innate drive toward bonding and also as a need to find completion in another human

53. *S&PTP*, 108–9.
54. *G&DMCT*, 311.
55. *S&PTP*, 109.

person which would complement and match our basic onto-relationality as persons.

Thus, as creatures structurally endowed as male or female, humans are inextricably *onto-personal* beings. Yet for Torrance the male-female inter-human relation is not simply structural, but functional as well. This "basic inter-human relation . . . is made to reflect in its creaturely difference a transcendent relation within God and also, to exhibit the basic covenant-partnership between God and mankind."[56] The reciprocity and complementarity of the "man-and-woman" relation images a "unique analogical relation to God."[57]

The *Imago Dei* as Participation in Grace

We finally come to a direct discussion of Torrance's understanding of the *imago Dei*. Yet we do not leave behind our discussion of the human being as an onto-relational creature, existing in a Spirit-relation with God, and addressed as differentiated co-humanity. On the contrary, we will see that Torrance's conception of the *imago Dei* embraces and integrates all these aspects in an orderly and cohesive whole, aligned around the motion of Grace. To this end, Torrance finds Calvin's mirror metaphor for understanding the *imago Dei* to be profoundly illuminating.

The *Imago Dei* and the 'Proleptic Self'

The[58] basic downward two-fold movement of Grace is noticeably evident in the following description:

> Within the single thought of *imago Dei* there is included a two-sided relation, but it is a relation which has only one essential motion and rhythm. There is the grace of God, and man's answer to that grace. *Such an answer partakes of and subsists in the essential motion of grace*—for even man's answer is the work of the Holy Spirit who through the Word forms the image anew in man, and forms his lips to acknowledge that he is a child of

---

56. *G&DMCT*, 311–12.
57. Ibid., 312.
58. Cf. Habets, *Theosis*, 43 who borrows the phrase, 'Proleptic Self,' from S.J. Grenz, "The *Imago Dei* and the Dissipation of the Self," *Dialog* 38 (Summer 1999): 187.

the Father. The *imago Dei* is thus the conformity of an intelligent being to the will and Word of God.[59]

While this quote is Torrance's attempt to summarize Calvin's thought on the *imago*, it is clear that he is incorporating Calvin's approach into his own framework. The image is constituted by two sides or factors, which give it an objective and subjective basis: the objective basis is God's beholding or regard of the human creature as his child; and the subjective basis is the human response or answer to God's gracious decision to regard him/her as his child.[60] In this description there is nothing static nor purely metaphysical about the *imago*. It is "not a dead but a living image,"[61] a dynamic reflection of active response to the will and word of God. Furthermore, the subjective human response is also objective in Jesus Christ. In the life of Christ, God images himself back to himself.[62] In Christ, the incarnate Son perfectly faces the Father; and the Father beholds his image in the Son, while the Son's joyful answer perfectly mirrors the love of the Father.

The fact that the *imago Dei* has its source and ground in Christ's imaging relation with the Father carries several implications. First, since the *imago Dei* itself is fundamentally a product of God's beholding the work of his Grace in human creatures—it is not tarnished or dragged down by human rebellion. Rather, the *imago Dei* "continues to hang over man as a destiny which he can realize no longer, and as a judgment upon his actual state of perversity."[63] In this sense, the christological vision of the *imago Dei* can be said to function as a *sentinel* standing over humanity and as such is 'the divinely given law and truth' of our being.[64] God's original intention for humanity to be his image-bearers is not dropped, but maintained in spite of the Fall.[65] Thus, the *imago Dei* continues to function as a calling and promise of what we shall become and also as a judgment upon what

59. *CDM*, 80. Italics added.
60. *TRn*, 105.
61. *CDM*, 71.
62. Ibid., 42.
63. *TRn*, 107.
64. *G&DMCT*, 376.
65. *TRn*, 107.

we presently are. Existence as the image of God is not only *not* an achievable existence apart from God, it is also *only* a concrete reality in the person of Christ. Christ alone is the *Archimedean Point* by which the *imago Dei* is measured.[66] As such, Christology—indeed, the living Christ—provides the foundation by which undergirds, empowers and motivates the *imago* in the creature. Torrance writes, "[T]he original intention of God becomes an event in man's existence only by the Word, and the *imago* is possessed only in faith and hope until we see Christ as he is and become like him."[67] True humanity is not discovered by examining our origins in Adam, but our destiny in Christ in whom the image of God is fully realized.[68]

Second, Christ is not only the reference point and reality of the image, but the source of the restoration of the *imago* in fallen human creatures. Jesus Christ is the "Archetypal and Dominical Man," from whom all that is truly human is derived and to whom all humanity must be referred. Technically speaking, humans are "the image of the image," and Christ is "the unique image-constituting Image of God."[69] Apart from Christ, human nature "goes out of tune."[70] Through the Spirit, Christ continually personalizes and humanizes the rest of humanity. As Habets points out, within Torrance's theology, "the movement within the salvation of men and women is from human being, a biological fact, to human person, a moral, theological fact."[71] We are *persons-in-becoming.*[72] God is the fullness of personal being who personalizes human beings.[73]

Torrance describes this humanizing and person-forming process as "the constant and continuous repetition of His pure grace."[74] This repetition of Grace is the humanity of Christ—the image of

---

66. *G&DMCT*, 318.
67. *TRn*, 109.
68. Cf. McFarlane, *Irving*, 74f.
69. GDMCT, 317.
70. Thomas F. Torrance, "Immortality and Light," *Rel Stud.* 17 (1981): 152. Quoting Georges Florovsky.
71. Habets, *Theosis*, 55.
72. Cf. ibid., 45.
73. Thomas F. Torrance, *The Soul and Person of the Unborn Child* (Edinburgh: Handsel Press for the Scottish Order of Christian Unity, 1999), 18. Hereafter, *S&PUC*.
74. *CDM*, 61.

God—coming to expression in his people through the renewing activity of the Spirit. The human spirit as we have noted is the aspect of the human creature which has been regenerated to bear the image of God: "Whatever in man is created anew in the image of God is called *spirit*. 'That which is born of the flesh is flesh; that which is born of the Spirit is *spirit*.'"[75] Calvin also calls this the *inner man*, renewed after the likeness of God. This inner renewal, or regeneration, or spiritual communion with God, is the Spirit in our hearts crying, "Abba Father." The distinctive thing is that human beings are created to enjoy this relation: to "give ear to the Word," knowing they are creatures who have been called into being by God; knowing that God has set his love upon them in order to assume them into the divine fellowship as children of the heavenly Father. They retain their life "only by a continuous thankful acknowledgement of this gracious calling of God," where no independence of life is presumed in themselves, but all is received as "the pure gift of God."[76] On this basis, Torrance will have nothing to do with second causes. There is no human act in which God is not also active. Through the Spirit's constant activity, the mirror (*imago*) is placed upon the human. It is the having of the *spirit* as well as the presence of *the Spirit* that differentiates humans from all other creaturely beings as those who are made *ad imaginem Dei*. Consequently, the human creature "may be understood not from an independent centre in himself but only from above and beyond himself in his transcendental relation to God."[77] Apart from the continual activity of the Spirit sent by the Father with the Son the image of God in the world would be an ineffective and vain reflection. Human life is but an "empty image" unless it is kept close to God. When it is, it becomes a "vital life."[78]

The third implication has to do with the onto-relational nature of the *imago*. As the image is a reality effected and brought into being

---

75. Ibid., 54.
76. *TRn*, 104. Torrance cites Calvin repeatedly in making this point: *Inst.* II.2.1; II.2.10; *Comm. On Gen.* 2.9; 3.6; *Serm. On Job* 28.10f.
77. *S&PTP*, 113.
78. *CDM*, 65, on Eph 4:18.

by God's loving beholding of the creature, it is also an image that fundamentally is perceptible only by God himself. God beholds the image which he images. It is this foundation of God's beholding of the creature and God's determination to remain in relation to the creature that enables the creature to turn by Grace towards God. Whatever imaging we achieve is the result of God's active gifting: "The image of God is basically that which God sees and fashions by His Grace."[79] The metaphor here is intentionally and inextricably relational. God's seeing of the creature is a way of describing God's loving orientation towards and for the creature. It is this orientation of God towards the creature which has a transforming effect upon human beings, effectively calling them into the responsive being. No one other than God himself can 'read' the image of the creature, for the essence of the image is the activity of the Word and Spirit calling the creature into existence.

Because of its fruitfulness, Torrance praises the brilliance of Calvin's use of the mirror metaphor:

> Only while the mirror actually reflects an object does it have the image of that object. There is no such thing in Calvin's thought as an *imago* disassociated from the act of reflecting. He does use such expressions as *engrave* and *sculptured*, but only in a metaphorical sense and never dissociated from the idea of the mirror.[80]

Yet Torrance's interpretation of Calvin's doctrine of the *imago Dei* has been critiqued and characterized as mere "correlative response," which exclusively highlights "creaturely incapacity."[81] Julie Canlis repeats Engel's critique that Torrance offers a "totalizing perspective" which fails to take proper note of the fact that in a very real sense, the *imago* is also preserved or substantial. Canlis writes, Torrance's "emphasis on the 'mirror' metaphor fails in that it is a metaphor that is limited to reflection only with little room for participation."[82] Yet this critique fails to recognize the dynamic and personal nature of

---

79. Ibid., 43; see *Inst.* 3.17.6.
80. Ibid., 36.
81. Canlis, *Calvin's Ladder*, 78–80.
82. Ibid., 80–81.

Torrance's understanding of human response and the manner in which he employs the mirror metaphor to that end.[83]

For Torrance, the mirror metaphor is far from passive. In fact, Torrance perceives the *imago* to involve a continuous motion of re-orienting or turning towards the proper object. The *imago* only reflects God when it faces God. Because of his onto-relational understanding of personhood, Torrance views the relations between persons as belonging to what persons actually are. Whatever we turn toward in faith is what will shape us. Thus, depending on the dynamic direction one faces, the human is always either *incurvatus in se* or *excurvatus ex se*. To a greater or lesser extent, one will set one's face toward the Son or one's stance will be set upon idols. While the former object of orientation (the Son) possesses the ontological weight of the incarnate Creator and Redeemer, the latter (idols) are ontologically-vacant legends of our own making. Here the critical realism of Torrance's concept of onto-relations comes into view as it illuminates the fundamental reflectivity of human existence. Ontology is not *given*; it is *caught* (personally communicated) or more properly shared in.[84] As human creatures take their stand in the Spirit and face the Father through the Son, they reflect God's glory by bearing witness in their very beings to the filial purpose for which they were created. In this sense, the image "is essentially a supernatural gift grounded in grace and possessed only in faith."[85]

Imago Dei as Participation in Christ's Ministry

Torrance perceives both an objective and a subjective aspect to the image evidenced in the scriptures. Objectively speaking, human beings are creatures uniquely addressed by God as his beloved children; as such, they are constituted "from without" by relations with God and other humans who are *ontopersonal*.[86] Subjectively speaking, human

---

83. Cf. *CDM*, 64-66.
84. For a parallel argument around the metaphor of light, see Torrance, "Immortality and Light," *Rel Stud.* 17 (1981): 159.
85. *TRn*, 105.
86. *S&PTP*, 109-10.

beings are gifted with both—great dignity and great responsibility—in their existence before God. The christological and pneumatological grounding of the image entails that "it must be *a life-answer* such that it characterizes the whole of man's being and action."[87] This intelligent "life-answer" is narrated by a particular kind of covenant-partnership between God and humans in which by Grace we are given to participate in the priestly and kingly ministry of Christ.[88] In this covenant partnership, we whose existence is mediated by our great high priest, share in his life as creaturely *mediators of order* and *priests of creation*. The work to which humans are called as stewards (mediators), who exercise dominion over the earth, is not the work of masters or servants but the work of participants. The organizing endeavors of humans are most truly understood as enactments of communion, such that the human creature is essentially "a witness-bearing image evoked by the wonderful grace of God in calling man into communion with Himself."[89] Torrance describes the quality of this witness as "an intelligent motion in answer" to the movement of divine Grace, which involves knowledge, thankfulness, consciousness of dependence, obedience, witness and faith.[90] In the motion of thankfulness, the grateful child reflects God's glory back to God. "Only thus can we image the glory of God."[91]

As priests of creation, humanity's task is to represent the creation before the Creator in a joyous and worshipping response. This representative function is expressed in bearing witness to the rational order and beauty of creation and in bringing "forth forms of order and beauty of which it would not be capable otherwise."[92] Men and women are the *stewards* and *keepers* of the garden of creation and as such humanity is "an essential member of the creation."[93] This perspective explains Torrance's life-long passion for science: the study of which

---

87. *CDM*, 64.
88. Torrance's idea of covenant partnership consists of both stewardship and communion.
89. *CDM*, 71.
90. *TRn*, 101; cf. *CDM*, 32.
91. Ibid., 105.
92. *DCO*, 130.
93. Thomas F. Torrance, *Reality and Evangelical Theology: The 1981 Payton Lectures* (Philadelphia: Westminster, 1982), 25, 26. Hereafter, *R&ET*.

he considered to be "part of man's religious duty, for it is part of his faithful response to the Creator and Sustainer of the cosmos."[94] Habets observes striking similarities between Torrance's view of humanity as the priest of creation and some Eastern Orthodox teachings. Staniloae for instance "uses the same expression as Torrance when he considers the world as God's gift to humanity in order that humanity may gift it back to God. In this way, argues Staniloae, the sacrifice offered to God by men and women is a Eucharist, making every person a "priest of God for the world."[95]

We have been attending to the way Torrance perceives the constitution of human beings as participants in Grace. To this end, we have noted the multi-faceted way in which human creatures are the *imago Dei*: as those who are addressed and called into an onto-relational existence as co-humanity through a continual Spirit-relation to God, and who thus thankfully participate in Christ's ministry in the world. Yet, graced by Grace upon Grace as we are, human creatures insanely hazard their being as sons and daughters of God for a surd-like autonomous existence. It is to the reality of this insanity and its disastrous results that we now turn.

The Shaky Constitution of Fallen Humanity

One of the important procedural starting points for Reformed theology in addressing the issue of human sin and depravity is to *begin* from the fact of Grace. Sin and evil are irrational realities that cannot be understood on their own terms but "only as a corollary of the doctrine of grace."[96] However, a correlation does not suggest either symmetry or direct opposition. In fact, sin and Grace are not even in the same category. Grace is an eternal reality and as such "grace does not rely on sin to exist."[97] Rather, sin relies on Grace to exist, for sin by definition

---

94. STR, 179–80.
95. Habets, *Theosis*, 46. Quoted from Dumitru Staniloae, "The World as Gift and Sacrament of God's Love," *Sobornost* 9 (1969): 662–73, and *Teologia Dogmatica Ortodoxa*, Vol. 1 (1996): 389.
96. TRn, 106.
97. Frost, "Sin and Grace," in *Trinitarian Soundings in Systematic Theology* (London: T&T Clark, 2005), 105.

is the denial of Grace. Thus, for Torrance, sin and disorder should always be approached from within the all-embracing framework of Grace and cannot be properly understood apart from that context.[98] If faith is the essential motion which corresponds to the motion of Grace,[99] then lack of faith (distrust, the will-to-autonomy) is the motion which contradicts Grace. Sin is the inversion of Grace.

In this section, we will demonstrate the way Torrance addresses sin as a motion contrary to Grace and thus destructive of the *imago Dei*. We will discover that even though sin itself is a movement whose intention is the rejection of Grace, it too is caught up in and thus defeated by the triumph of Grace. To this end, this section has two tasks: *first*, we will establish the double character of Torrance's teaching of sin as both sin and guilt; and *second*, this will prepare us to discuss God's wrath and judgment as further expressions of the motion of Grace.

The Double Character of Sin

We have already discussed the double character of sin in our analysis of Torrance's doctrine of Atonement. There we noted that sin involves both human rebellion against God and God's resistance to that rebellion. Torrance differentiates this double character through the language of *sin* and *guilt*. Together, sin and guilt constitute 'the utter chasm between self-willed humanity and God.'[100] Whereas sin refers to the relation of humanity to God, guilt refers to the relation of God to humanity.

Sin and Human Rebellion

Torrance views sin as profoundly and irreducibly personal and relational. As such, his interests lie in sin's actual existence within the dynamic and personal life-relation that creatures have with God, not in historical questions regarding original sin as an inherent hereditary or fatalistic determinate of our nature.[101] His concerns are the concrete

---

98. *CDM*, 83.
99. Ibid., 82.
100. *Incarnation*, 247.

consequences of sin and how sin is manifested in human beings as "an active perversity": a "positive contradiction," which "maintains itself in an active opposition."[102]

Torrance would concur with McFarland, who states that original sin does not refer to an act but to "the ground of all our acts apart from the transforming power of grace."[103] Original sin represents a profound dis-orientation of our life-relation in communion with God. What separates human creatures from God is that men and women have turned their face away from God; and it is this turning away, this separation, which causes "intrinsic damage" to our nature and irreversibly and inextricably locates us as "fallen." It is in this context that terms such as "total depravity" and "original sin" have their meaning.[104] A "constitutive change" has taken place which involves the whole person and in which the whole person is involved. By turning away from our Maker, the mirror image which we were created to be is literally "de-faced."[105] We have a "sinning being" and therefore all repeat our original sin. Isolated acts of sin "are but the outward manifestation of this perversion at the very roots of human being."[106] Torrance's relational ontology makes it entirely compatible both with a doctrine of *theosis* and one of healing from sin.

Descriptively, Torrance frequently uses the metaphorical language of *distance* to depict the destructive and tragic effects of sin. The fact of the incarnation itself reveals that humanity is "far away from" and "cut off from" God.[107] Yet, it would be a mistake to construe this distance metaphysically. Rather, "the distance between man and God is due to the nearness of God! That distance is a moral one."[108] For Torrance, to

---

101. Cf. Cass, *Condemned*, 242–43.
102. *CDM*, 113.
103. McFarland, *Fallen or Unfallen?*, 414.
104. *Incarnation*, 232. Torrance describes the function of the doctrine of Original Sin as a way of naming "the radical discontinuity between man and God" (Torrance, "The Call for a New Discussion on the Doctrine of Grace," Box 21: Auburn Lectures, 1938–1939, 29). Hereafter, *CNDDG*. In interpreting evil, we must "let the Cross and resurrection of Christ be the fixed point by reference to which we may chart in our understanding and expectation the fulfilment of God's redemptive will for the whole creation" (*DCO*, 139).
105. Ibid., 115.
106. Ibid., 253.
107. Thomas F. Torrance, *Doctrine of Jesus Christ* (Eugene, OR: Wipf and Stock, 2002), 159. Hereafter, *DJC*.
108. Ibid.

describe human beings as *alienated* and estranged from both God and themselves is to speak of an incompatibility of immanence. That is, it indicates the profound "antagonism between God's holy will of love and our sin." This difference is exposed in bold relief at the coming near of God in Jesus Christ. "Sin presupposes the nearness of God."[109] It is the distance of differentness, the "clash of wills," the gap created by opposing desires and the incompatibility of loves between the human creature and the central reality of their existence—namely, their life-unity with the Creator.[110] Thus, when Torrance defines sin as the motion contrary to Grace, he is not setting sin up as Grace's opposite (for that would be impossible); he is exposing both the personal nature and the utter emptiness of sin. Sin is not sin against an impersonal law, but is a crime against Grace itself—against God's loving, holy will and being.[111] Consequently, Torrance refuses to allow moralistic categories to drive his description of human fallenness. Sin 'is not sin simply because it is against love or goodness or even against man but because it is ultimately against God himself."[112]

Guilt and Divine Judgment

From what has been said thus far, one would not be surprised to discover that Torrance rarely discusses sin in isolation from guilt. While indeed coordinated, the force of these relations is not equal. He writes, "the relation of man to God . . . is less than half the truth, for it is the relation of God to humanity that is the important thing in life and in humanity's rebellion against him in sin."[113] Thus, while sin is subjectively real from the point of view of human beings, it is objectively real from the point of view of God. "The innermost gravity of sin" is the very real judgment of God against it, and against the

---

109. *Incarnation*, 247.
110. Cf. *DJC*, 159; Luke 5:8.
111. *Incarnation*, 156. Cf. CD III.2, 274ff: Sin is always "an inconceivable revolt."
112. Ibid., 250 (Ps 51:4).
113. Ibid., 248. The downward movement of grace overarches all facets of the divine-human relation.

human person who sins.[114] What makes guilt so terrible according to Torrance,

> is that at the back of it there is the full force of the divine resistance to sin . . . a black abyss, a gulf whose reality has been produced by man and is under the divine judgment upon sin—that is the meaning of hell. And Christ must descend into that hell in order to save and redeem man. He the Mediator must descend into the blackness of man's alienation from God to save him; he must unite in his own Person man and God and bear the guilt of man before the presence of God.[115]

The opening up of this chasm—this distance between God and the creature—is not only interpersonally destructive, it is also and inescapably *personally* destructive. Participation in sin is not simply external to the agent, nor is the enslaving condition of sin simply a relational, moral or legal problem. It is a matter of our *being*. "The will to be independent and autonomous" from God, which lies at the core of sin, results in a corresponding distancing of the self.[116]

Sin is not simply describable as a personal affront to God, a childish disregard for honoring the Creator with the respect he deserves; rather, sin is a form of ontological suicide.[117] Human existence and fellowship with God are created as counterparts—the one (existence) cannot be without the other (fellowship with God).[118] Since "the creature requires relation to the Creator in order to be a creature," the creature's very existence is called into question.[119] Thus, by definition, the self-defined, self-justified, self-made, autonomous creature is alienated, estranged and isolated from the Creator and from Grace; for the gift and the Giver cannot be separated. To reject Grace is not merely to reject an optional extra to creaturely existence or to consign oneself to living as one who is 'merely human." Rather, the pursuit of life apart from God is to become estranged from life itself.

Torrance's language is fraught with the onto-personal consequences

---

114. Ibid., 252.
115. *DJC*, 163–64.
116. *Incarnation*, 254.
117. Ibid., 242.
118. Ibid., 247.
119. Ibid.

of human rebellion: "threatened with chaos and negation," we "hazard our being," which is tenuous in nature and the life-relation with God is broken. It is personally destructive, opening a chasm, a breach, a divide, a separation, a contradiction within our being, and a split in our souls. The fall of humankind is a falling out of our constitutional center and we become *ec-centric*.[120] Without the light of the Spirit, natural gifts are corrupted and spiritual gifts are replaced by vanity, impurity and blindness.[121] "In sin, the very central point in human being is altered," and this affects the whole of the human being's relation with God, such that now "he or she *is* a sinner."[122]

Because sin is essentially a loss of personhood—we are depraved because we are *selves-in-isolation from God*—Torrance refuses to speak of depravity or sin-nature in non-personal categories. Sin is this turn away from the source and the attempt to become our own center and possession. Bending into ourselves, seeking to realize ourselves apart from God, we actually undo ourselves; and once undone there is no way back. "We are trapped within that rift" and cannot transcend it, heal it or re-socialize it, for it lies in our very selves.[123]

> Because sin now characterises the nature of man as fallen. . . . Their self-will is their free will, and they cannot escape out of their self-will. The more they strive in their self-will to save themselves, the more they sin—in fact that is the very movement of sin at its subtlest and in its very worst form, self-justification.[124]

This entanglement of self-will with free-will, along with the personal destruction which inter-personal estrangement necessitates, is also expressed in the way that Torrance envisions the state of the human conscience. Post-Fall, in their semi-independent state from God, men and women are able to distinguish between good and evil. Yet, this state of knowing is accompanied by a tension within human existence

---

120. Ibid., 248. Torrance uses this term in this context in a way uncharacteristic of his normal usage and the way the term is generally (and more positively) used when discussing human personhood.
121. Cf. *CDM*, 119.
122. *Incarnation*, 253.
123. *A&MO*, 251; cf. *Incarnation*, 39.
124. *Incarnation*, 253.

between the *is* and the *ought*; and this tension serves as a constant reminder of humanity's distance from the will of God. We know we are not what we ought to be and this rupture in our existence cannot be disentangled from any of our relations—whether between God and humanity, man and woman, or within each person.[125] The tension this situation creates within the human person, Torrance notes, is the source of all kinds of anxieties and disorders.

This guilt, which is felt in the conscience of the sinner, is the subjective side of our objective guilt before God. Felt guilt is merely the "subjective counterpart" which "echoes the objective reality of God's judgment upon sin."[126] Yet, the accusing condemnation of the conscience is only a faint and warped echo of the handwriting of God which is against us (Col 2:14).[127] Thus, while conscience makes us aware of the distance between our *ought* and our *is*, conscience too is subject to the corruption of fallen existence. It too needs to be "cleaned by the blood of Christ," for otherwise it will be a slave of sin.[128] Even though the law has divine sanction, in the hands of fallen and fearful creatures, the guilt of the conscience paradoxically serves to maintain and uphold sin in a "strange contradictory existence," by shielding the sinner from direct relation to God. In our presumptuous self-righteousness, we interpret the conscience as the voice of our own better selves, rather than accepting that our lives are not our own. Motivated and twisted by self-will, the guilty conscience, provoked by the law, stands between the sinner and God, thus keeping God at a distance.

Wrath, Judgment and the Motion of Grace

In the light of Grace, how are we to understand the biblical concept of the wrath of God? Throughout this book, we have observed that one consistent characteristic of Torrance's exposition is the thorough manner in which he understands God's action as personal. Because God is personal in all he does, even in his judging and condemning of sin

125. Ibid., 39.
126. *DJC*, 94.
127. Ibid., 163.
128. *A&MO*, 252.

174

God acts personally. Thus, sin "is met in personal relation and is judged in personal action . . . for sin is a personal act against the very person of God."[129]

Wrath as a Cognate of God's Faithfulness

Torrance states that the existence of human sin means "a real 'change' in God's mind and attitude toward man."[130] Yet, this change in God's mind and attitude arises paradoxically from the fact that God does not change at all. As a personal and objective agent, God is inflexible in the sense that he refuses not to be who he is. God has always been and ever remains the "I am who I am" and the "I will be who I will be." (Exod 3:14) His faithfulness and love are constant. If there is a law which God himself obeys, it is "the Law of his own divine Being and Activity"—and God's divine being and activity is intrinsically holy love.[131] God is faithful, God is love, God is truth; and because God *is* these things, he *remains* these things unswervingly in his relations with creatures. As the law of his own divine being, God's holy, lawful, divine love is inflexibly opposed to all that is not love or to anything that resists the fulfilment of God's love in his creation. Accordingly, Torrance approaches God's judgment and wrath as a conceptual cognate to God's faithfulness and love.[132] It is "in the steadfastness of his love [that] he judges man's sin and inhumanity, [and is] opposed to all that is opposed to his own being and nature as holy love."[133] The hell which is God's rejection is not his ceasing to love but precisely the faithfulness of his love "rejecting all that rejects love."[134] The ones who turn their backs upon Christ and deny him will shatter themselves against the love of God. Hell is the prison of one's refusal to be loved. Thus, wrath is the accidental result of God's refusal to withhold or limit his love, or to accept anything less than a complete response of love to

129. *Incarnation*, 252; Ps 51:4.
130. Ibid., 248.
131. *CDG*, 213.
132. Cf. *DJC*, 93.
133. *Incarnation*, 249.
134. *SOF*, cxvi.

his love.[135] It "withstands and negates all that is contrary to God's Love, judges all that resists it, and inexorably condemns it."[136] In love, God personally opposes that which opposes his Grace.

As an expression of the divine love and faithfulness, Torrance argues that wrath ought to be viewed as "a sign of hope" and "not of utter destruction." The fact that the "wrath of the lamb" is also "the wrath of redeeming love" means that Christ's death is a sign that "we are sons and daughters, and not bastards."[137] From this standpoint, Torrance identifies God's wrath as an integral part of atonement and new creation, "for it is his reaffirmation of his creature in spite of its sin and corruption. . . . God's very wrath tells us that we are children of God."[138] In wrath, God asserts his ownership of the creature and his refusal to allow the creature to cast itself off into nothingness. This is true even in death. God will not let his creature go—"even though he ultimately refuses Jesus Christ, even though he make his bed in Hell, the hand of God grasps him there."[139]

Because God is committed to his creature, human beings are bound eternally in an "existential relation to God."[140] Accordingly, Torrance rejects equating God's final judgment with annihilation. In an effort to root final judgment and reprobation biblically, he develops the Old Testament concepts of *the curse* of God and *sheol*. In being cursed, the reprobate are given up to their own uncleanness, separated from the face of God and banished from creation into "outer darkness." But, fundamentally, this is "a banishment to their own denial of their being in God."[141] It is the confirmation of their choice to exist outside of the covenant of God, as those who do not belong to it.[142] Whereas *sheol*, as Torrance expounds it, is this state of existence "in darkness

135. A&MO, 248.
136. CDG, 213.
137. Incarnation, 249; cf. Torrance, The Apocalypse Today: Sermons on Revelations (London: James Clarke and Co., 1960), 58–59.
138. Ibid., 250.
139. From a sermon Torrance preached on 1 Cor 2:1–5, date unknown. Thomas F. Torrance Manuscript Collection, Special Collections, Princeton Theological Seminary Library, Box 38: Sermons, Lectures and Addresses, in Scotland and Abroad.
140. Incarnation, 250.
141. Ibid., 251.
142. Here Torrance alludes to Rom 1:24, 26, 28.

behind God's back . . . in man's self-chosen perversity and blindness."[143] *Sheol* is a kind of suspended darkness, that already casts its shadow over all sinners as their self-chosen destiny, yet awaits God's final acts of judgment. The *curse* then is God's ultimate and final judgment in which those who cast themselves upon God's wrath and judgment will be justified; and those who choose to remain in their alienation will be utterly banished. Torrance describes hell as "the chasm that separates man from God in the very existence of sinful man," who is conditioned and determined by sin and guilt. Hell is not an abstract place, nor is it the no-thing of nothingness. Hell is the personal and concrete existence of the human being in alienation from God. It is the sinner choosing isolation from God's love. As such, the alienation of hell is always a possibility—for both the living as well as for the living dead. For those whose "ultimate reaction" is to deny God's claim upon them, they will bear the pain of a continued existence of "utter and final judgement within existential relation to God."[144] God gives sinners the freedom to deny his claim upon them, yet his claim remains nonetheless.

Implications for Understanding the Cross

Viewing God's wrath from the perspective of God's personal faithfulness to the creature he ceaselessly loves carries important implications for understanding the event of the cross. First, the very fact that God's faithfulness to his creature calls for a crucifixion event highlights the utter severity of the human predicament in alienation from God. Second, it allows the concept of *satisfaction* to be recognized as God's fulfillment of his own covenant of love with human creatures. Finally and perhaps most notably, is its compatibility with Torrance's consistent resistance towards logico-causal, one-to-one mechanistic rationales for *how* or *why* the life and death of Christ atones.

First, the righteousness humans receive through Christ is forged at extreme cost to God himself, as the cross event starkly reveals. The

143. *Incarnation*, 251.
144. Ibid., 250.

judgment of God against sin and therefore sinners is real—as real as God himself—and Christ takes upon himself that judgment. Christ on the cross is "God's attack of love upon the inhumanity of mankind."[145] Descending into the black pit of human alienation, Christ the mediator "bridges the chasm of hell in his own incarnate person."[146] Torrance locates the significance of this, not in the multitude of human sins which Christ bore but in the judgment of God in all his majesty, which was directed against Christ. The abyss is real, for humanity's very being is "threatened by annihilation" through separation from God.[147] The hell he bears is "not only in his bodily suffering, but . . . in the fearful pain and judgment which he bore on his soul."[148]

Second, the cross must be understood as a positive event with which God is rightfully *satisfied*. As noted in chapter 2, since the death of Christ is an act of love performed by God himself, it cannot be perceived in purely negative terms. The bearing and bearing away, of human sin by Christ is at the same time the positive offering of a full and complete human response of love to the love of the Father. Thus, Torrance argues that the penal element in God's judgment cannot be reduced to a mere fulfilling of the law. The cross is God's total *"no"* to our sin (our *"no"*); but even more so it is God's *"yes"* to, or God's *satisfaction* in, a personal response of love. The cross is not only a bare judgment upon a passive victim but also the active offering of Christ's holy life. The pouring out of Christ's blood symbolizes (according to Leviticus) his *life* willingly offered to the Father in our place. The sacrifice is chiefly the offering of atoned and atoning *life*, rather than the sacrifice of a *death*. It is akin to an act of new creation, which takes place not only in the historical life and activity of Jesus Christ but also in the very being of the Holy Trinity.[149]

Torrance vigilantly resists the temptation to supply a logico-causal, one-to-one mechanistic rationale for *why* the life and death of Christ

---

145. *Incarnation*, 256. Cf. Matt 27:46; Luke 23:34.
146. Ibid., 255.
147. Ibid., 256.
148. Ibid., 255.
149. *MOC*, 112f.

atones and observes that neither the Old Testament nor the New Testament ever gives an explanation for *why* atonement for sin involves the blood of sacrifice. As is his custom, the ultimate reason to which Torrance appeals is personal: the atonement takes place "within the incarnate mystery of the union of divine and human nature in Jesus Christ the Mediator between God and man," and as such is an "ineffable inexplicable mystery hidden in God himself."[150] God himself is his own reason: "Just as God's love, so God's atoning act, knows no 'Why?'"[151] For Torrance, to put a logico-causal explanation on God's forgiveness or the inexplicable nature of the "bottomless chasm" of evil, is tantamount to blasphemy: "like the Holy Trinity the atonement is infinitely more to be adored than expressed."[152] Torrance's personalism casts him back upon a confident apophatism: "All rests on his ordinance of grace."[153]

In light of critiques that Torrance underplays forensic atonement metaphors, it should be pointed out that his entire theology bears a legal or forensic tenor in the sense that he takes very seriously the reality of God's opposition to and thus judgment upon sin. However, the means by which this legal judgment is carried out is not purely legal. Torrance argues that neither the Pauline doctrine of justification, nor the priesthood of Christ expounded in Hebrews, is legalist in nature. Both have a legal sense to them in that both are concerned with law and righteousness and legal ordinances; yet both move *beyond and through* those forensic categories. With the one, the law is eschatologically suspended through the freedom of the resurrection; with the other, the unity of priest and the sacrifice in the person of Christ effectively break through the veil and open up a way for reconciled creaturely participation in the heavenly life of God.[154] In the propitiation effected by Christ's priestly atonement, the two sides of the God-human relation are healed as God turns away from his wrath

150. Ibid., 114.
151. Ibid.
152. *A&MO*, 256.
153. *Atonement*, 88.
154. *TRn*, 157.

in forgiveness and humanity turns away from rebellion and draws near to God in love. It is worth noting that Torrance is particularly critical of John McLeod Campbell (whom he otherwise highly praises) and at just this point, he remarks that Campbell's seminal work, *The Nature of the Atonement*, "fell down rather badly both in its failure to appreciate the element of judgment in atonement and also in a fundamentally Pelagian element in its conception of the vicarious penitence and priesthood of Christ."[155]

Thus, the act of atonement cannot be considered *in abstracto*. Nor can Jesus Christ's bearing of our sin be viewed abstractly as an external transfer of sins. What Christ does must be understood as an outflow of the filial love of the Father and the Son. Rather, by locating the forensic, juridical or penal relations of the doctrine of the atonement within the context of the Father-Son relation and what took place in the ontological depths of Christ's atoning life and death, Torrance believes they are actually "intensified, deepened and refined in their import."[156]

The Place of the Moral and Legal Order in the Light of the Cross

Another implication for God's judgment in the light of Grace concerns the place of the moral and legal order. The redemptive work of Christ encompasses not only humanity but "the whole created universe of space and time, including all things (*ta panta*) visible and invisible, earthly and heavenly alike."[157] Accordingly for Torrance, Christ's headship and the centrality of his atoning life, pointedly apply to the rational and moral order. In this, he offers a strong critique against Western theology, which as he perceives it has generally formulated its doctrine of atonement "within the parameters of the moral law as its stands, without any recognition that the whole moral order had to be redeemed and be set on a new basis through the atonement."[158] This oversight is symptomatic of what Torrance describes as the "dualist

---

155. *GCM*, 91.
156. *A&MO*, 253.
157. Ibid., 249.
158. Ibid.

way of understanding and interpreting the message of the gospel," when, in fact, the gospel itself is "a relation internal to the being of the Godhead."[159] In light of the inner ontological relation between Christ and God and also between Christ and humankind, Torrance asserts that an understanding of the atonement cannot be construed "merely in terms of a moral or legal framework external to the incarnation, for that is itself part of the actual state of affairs between man and God that has suffered disruption and needs to be set right."[160]

By setting the moral and legal order within the realm of what is set right through the blood of Christ, the justification of the ungodly is realized—not through the law, but simply "through the justification of God."[161] As Torrance points out, if the moral order were to continue to stand, it would judge the substitutionary death of Christ as morally wrong. Thus, justification ultimately comes "apart from the law."[162] This situation effectively renders any form of self-justification an impossibility because the legal and moral order upon which self-justification might take its stand has been eliminated. The whole legal/moral order has been fulfilled in Christ and is now transcended by direct and personal relations between God and the human person. It has been superseded by the logic and relation of Grace.

Justification and atonement "apart from the law" has radical implications. Torrance describes the "radical nature" of this justifying act of God in Christ as a "soteriological suspension of ethics," for it establishes "a new moral life that flows from grace," and in which "external legal relation is replaced by inner filial relation to God the Father."[163] Torrance is not championing antinomianism but a new motivation for obedience, which is not driven by self-justification but grounded upon a filial relation with the Father established in Christ. This opens up "an altogether new way of life for us resulting from our

---

159. Ibid.
160. Ibid., 250–51.
161. Ibid., 251. Torrance cites Rom 3:21. Cf. A&MO, 253ff.
162. Ibid., 252; TF, 160; Gal 4:3f; Rom 3:20f.
163. Ibid., 252. On the use of the phrase, Torrance comments that he has in mind Kierkegaard's reference to a "teleological suspension of ethics" in Fear and Trembling (USA: Penguin Classics, 1986), 75ff; cf. TF, 160–61.

being translated out of the bondage of law into the freedom of the children of God."[164] Through the presence of the Spirit within, "this new life is ruled by the indicatives of God's love rather than externally governed by the imperatives of the law."[165]

Within this new moral order, a detached imperative no longer bears down abstractly and externally upon the believer.[166] Rather, moral action has its ground and source in the obedient Sonship of Christ; in him the split between the *is* and the *ought* has been transcended and our relations with the Father have been healed and reconciled. For the free children of God, moral activity takes place in union with Christ through sharing in the communion of the Spirit; the Spirit sheds the love of God into our hearts, informing our lives with the very mind of Christ, the obedient Son of the Father.[167]

Conclusion

Throughout this chapter we have been aware of the movement or activity of Grace. From the four-fold constitution of the human creature as the *imago Dei*, to the shaky constitution of fallen humanity and God's loving judgment against our sin, Grace has been a constant thread. Indeed, the movement or activity of Grace provides a dynamic yet consistent pattern throughout all the diversity and chaos that we know as human existence. We might call this pattern "the constancy of Grace"; for God's love and word of Grace do not change, grounded as they are upon the fact that God "cannot and does not cease to be who he eternally is in his Holiness and Love."[168] We have seen that this constancy is interrupted neither by human hostility towards Grace nor by the divine judgment upon sin, for God's judgment is itself Grace in motion and as such is neither retributive nor penal, but restorative. The divine life seeks human fellowship.

In chapter 6 we will look more closely at the actual dynamics of

164. Ibid., 253.
165. Ibid.
166. Ibid., 253–54.
167. Ibid., 254.
168. *DJC*, 94.

human subjective participation in union with Christ. However, individual participation always and only takes place within the community, which has been made one body with Christ. It is to that corporate form of *koinonia* in Christ through the Spirit that we now turn in chapter 5.

5

The Ecclesiological Form of Grace

The Christian Church is what it is because of its indissoluble union with Christ through the Spirit, for in him is concentrated the Church and all ministry. . . . [T]he Church is what it is through sharing in his life and ministry.[1]

In addressing the doctrines of Church and Christian living, this chapter and the next constitute two aspects of the same subject. As those who exist in the time of the resurrection, a new ground of being has been established in the person of Jesus Christ. This new humanity, which dwells in the "new time" of Christ, encounters and challenges those who live in the "old time." Each human being is already implicated by this new reality and must "give an intelligent life-answer to grace."[2] Given the all-embracing framework of Grace in which we exist, the terms of this "life-answer" are set by Grace: that is, they are determined by, and fall within, the essential motion of Grace we find in Christ. The location of response is the Church and its form is a movement of faith.

---

1. Thomas F. Torrance, *Theology in Reconstruction* (Grand Rapids: Eerdmans, 1965), 208. Hereafter, *TRn*.
2. Ibid., 116.

According to Torrance himself, his writings on ecclesiology were a *parergon* to his primary interests in Christology and soteriology; however, by sheer volume they arguably constitute one of his primary areas of development and focus.[3] Even so, Torrance is explicit that at no point should ecclesiology displace Christology. The humanity of Jesus is theology's "real text."[4] Thus, "the whole life and work of the Church in history must be subordinated to the content of the Gospel," which is "the saving person and work of Jesus Christ."[5]

Torrance's Christocentricity certainly creates a tension as Stamps observes, "between making every theological issue a statement of Christology and allowing Christology to comment upon and emerge as finally decisive in all these issues."[6] However, even as a *parergon*, Torrance's sustained attention to ecclesiology offers an ample foundation on which to build a more detailed application of his theology to human creatures.[7] Given the focus of this book, we will not be attempting an exposition or analysis of Torrance's entire ecclesiology; rather, our purpose is to lift up several core foundations which undergird and frame his doctrine of the Church within the realm of Grace. In this chapter, our concern is to display and analyze Torrance's understanding of the Church, (1) as constituted by Christ to be the body of Christ in the communion of the Spirit; (2) nurtured by Christ through that same Spirit in Word and sacrament; and so, (3) empowered by the Spirit to enter the Eucharistic rhythm of Grace and participate in the continuing ministry of the risen Jesus. As the body

---

3. Thomas F. Torrance, *Conflict and Agreement in the Church*, vol. 1 (London: Lutterworth, 1960), 7, 19. Hereafter, *C&A1*.

4. Thomas F. Torrance, *The Mediation of Christ*, rev. ed. (Edinburgh: T&T Clark, 1992), 78. Hereafter, *MOC*.

5. Thomas F. Torrance, "Introduction to Calvin's Tracts and Treatises on the Reformation of the Church," in *Tracts and Treatises on the Reformation of the Church, no. 1*, by John Calvin (Grand Rapids: Eerdmans, 1958), viii. Cf. *C&A1*, 17.

6. Robert J. Stamps, *The Sacrament of the Word Made Flesh* (Rutherford House, 2007), 26; cf. Habets, *Theosis*, 266.

7. Torrance's published writings on ecclesiology began in earnest in the 1960's and include: *Theology in Reconciliation: Essays Towards Evangelical and Catholic Unity in East and West*. Reprint (Eugene, OR: 1997), hereafter, *TiR*; *C&A1*; *Conflict and Agreement in the Church, vol. 2: The Ministry of the Sacraments of the Gospel* (London: Lutterworth, 1959). Hereafter, *C&A2*; *Royal Priesthood* (Edinburgh: T&T Clark, 1993), 3. Hereafter, *RP*; *The Trinitarian Faith: The Evangelical Theology of the Ancient Catholic Church* (Edinburgh: T&T Clark, 1995), 252–301. Hereafter, *TF*; *TRn*, 192–284.

which receives its existence and ongoing life from the Triune God, the life of the Church *is* this participation in the continuing ministry of Jesus.

The Body of Christ in the Communion of the Spirit

When theology finally arrives at the doctrine of ecclesiology, it can be tempting to abandon this taxonomy in favor of a more sociological, institutional or even historical description of the way divine and human relations ought to proceed. Torrance, however, is adamant that his theology of Grace not veer off course, particularly regarding the Church. One might say his theology of Grace even *intensifies* with respect to ecclesiology, for the Church has no existence outside its Grace-relation in Christ.[8] As such, Torrance's ecclesiology is thoroughly ontologically-minded. The Church does not create itself; its being and reality do not reside in its sociological visibility, institutional structures, or organizational marks. The Church is the product of Grace and lives only in Grace. Through his hypostatic and atoning union, Christ is the Head and King of a new body of humanity, which he constitutes through his Spirit.

Created and Ordered by Christ and the Spirit

The Church is God's Creation

The Church like all God's works *ad extra* is a Triune act. Constituted by Christ in a creative event in which all three persons of the Trinity are active, the Church has its source in the eternal purpose (*prothesis*) of God and is grounded in their eternal communion of love.[9] As such, the Church is no merely human institution:

> . . . the union in which the Church is implicated is characterised by ontological depth reaching back into God himself. Through the communion of the Holy Spirit the Church is united to Christ and grounded

8. Thomas F. Torrance, *Gospel, Church and Ministry, Thomas F. Torrance Collected Studies I*, ed. Jock Stein (Eugene, OR: Pickwick, 2012), 108–9. Hereafter, *GCM*.
9. *TF*, 252.

in the hypostatic union of God and man embodied in him, and through Christ and in the Spirit it is anchored in the consubstantial union and communion of the Father, Son and Holy Spirit in the Holy Trinity.[10]

The doctrine of the Church has its dogmatic home within the doctrine of the Spirit. The Church only exists as "the empirical correlate of the *parousia* of the Spirit in our midst."[11] As such, the Church is a kind of *event* of the Spirit in which the incarnation of the Word of God is repeated or reflected in the Church.[12] The Church reflects Christ as through the Spirit Jesus Christ "constitutes and organizes the members of the Church into one" and gives them "to participate in the oneness between the Father and the Son through the Holy Spirit."[13]

The source of the Church determines the form of the Church. Because the Church is grounded "in the self-communication of the Holy Trinity," Torrance argues that any legitimate ecclesiology must make the trinitarian movement, "from the Father, through the Son and in the Spirit, and to the Father, through the Son and in the Spirit," the regulative center of all its worship, faith and mission.[14]

Christ is the Substance of the Church: The Body in Whom the Church Shares

The union established between Christ and humanity through his incarnation and crucifixion continues in his resurrection and ascension. This union effected by the Son and the Spirit is the basis and source of the Church's existence. Because of the resurrection and ascension, Torrance views the union between Christ and the Church as more than a metaphor: it is an *ontological fact* and the union is therefore somatic as well as spiritual.

Of the many metaphors or analogies for the Church found in the New Testament, Torrance believes one best captures the multi-faceted,

---

10. Ibid., 278.
11. Ibid., 252.
12. Cf. Thomas F. Torrance, *Royal Priesthood* (Edinburgh: T&T Clark, 1993), 25. Hereafter, *RP*. Torrance remarks that the language of *reflection* and *analogy* are better terms than *repetition*, and notes the same recognition in Barth (CD 4.1, 768–69).
13. Thomas F. Torrance, "The Mission of the Church," *SJT* 19 (1966): 141. Hereafter, *Mission*.
14. *TF*, 263.

intimate and ontological relation between Christ and the Church—"the body of Christ." Indeed, while Torrance certainly employs other biblical metaphors for the Church, for example: temple, building, vine, bride, Israel, new Jerusalem, city, holy nation, royal priesthood, people of God, household of faith, and family of God, the body of Christ is for him the "central and all-important conception" of the Church in the New Testament, for it is far more comprehensive and christologically-oriented than any other.[15] As Lee points out, its uniqueness lies in its conjoint application to both Christ and the Church, whereas other metaphors cannot have this conjoint reference.[16] Thus, "the 'Body' of Christ has a double reference—the Body of the risen Christ and the Church mystically adopted as his Body, which can never be confused nor regarded as identical."[17]

Torrance emphasizes again and again in his writings that the very substance of the Church lies in the humanity of Christ and he bemoans the contemporary Church's lack of "a Christology with genuine substance in it."[18] While Torrance recognizes that language identifying the Church as Christ's own body is surely figurative and analogical, it is *not only so,* "for a relation in *being* between Christ and his Church is clearly entertained."[19] For Torrance, the central 'mystery' of the Church has to do with "its profound ontological relation to Christ."[20] Torrance reiterates this crucial point from multiple angles: Jesus Christ comprises as "one new man"—both our humanity and his own—"that is the very heart of the doctrine of the Church";[21] our bodies are *connate* with his and as such "receive out of his fullness and have that body as the root of our resurrection and salvation";[22] and that Christ is the living source of the Church's life, such that "the Church has no

---

15. Thomas F. Torrance, *Royal Priesthood* (Edinburgh: T&T Clark, 1993), 29. Hereafter, *RP.*
16. Lee, *Union,* 225.
17. Ibid.
18. Thomas F. Torrance, "The Church in the New Era of Scientific and Cosmological Change," in *Theological Foundations for Ministry,* ed. Ray Anderson (Edinburgh: T&T Clark, 2000), 767. Hereafter, *New Era.*
19. *TF,* 291.
20. Ibid.
21. *SOF,* cix–cx. Quoting Craig's Catechism.
22. *TF,* 266.

independent existence . . . apart from what is *unceasingly communicated* to it through its union and communion with Christ who dwells in it by the power of the Spirit."[23] He goes so far as to say, "*Christ is the Church, for the Church is Church only in Him.*"[24]

When body of Christ is understood within the context of the continuing humanity of Christ, the image is properly understood as one of inclusion, yet differentiation. While the visible Church is included in the risen humanity of Christ and as such is one body with him, it is at the same time differentiated from the invisible ascended Christ and in no way serves as a replacement, substitute, or extension of her incarnate Head. As will be evident later in this chapter, Torrance was critical of "High Church" understandings of historical structures, arguing that the true significance of the Church as the body of Christ is only through her relation to her head, Jesus Christ. This is a relation of distinction in which Christ is head and the Church is body. At the same time, it is a relation of eschatologically conditioned *koinonia*. As such, the Church participates in the *wholeness* of Christ and "because that *wholeness* is already whole, there can be no talk of an extension of the Incarnation or historical continuity of the Body of Christ" (*C&A1*, 51, for more).

For Torrance, *Body of Christ* language appropriately follows *covenant* language as the expression of its fulfillment. While the concept of Covenant "must not be forgotten . . . it is filled in with the concept of the Body of Christ."[25] This side of the resurrection, "Covenant-union with God is fulfilled in communion with Christ through the Spirit." On this basis, Torrance concludes that we should regard the Church ontologically, "as hid with Christ through his Spirit in God the Father."[26]

Christ is the *Orderer* of the Church's Order

Because Torrance's theological ontology is anything but static,

23. *TRn*, 205.
24. *C&A1*, 108.
25. *Tracts and Treatises*, xxiii–xxiv.
26. *TF*, 268.

ontological description is always accompanied by corresponding activity. Accordingly, Torrance's deep rooting of his doctrine of the Church in the organic/ontological relation between Christ and Church results in a comprehensively dynamic ecclesiology centered in the humanity of Christ. Also formative for our discussion is the concept of *order*, which Torrance often uses as a cognate for the *Body of Christ*.

As with the body metaphor, the language of *order* functions usefully for Torrance as a way of speaking about two things at once: the *active ordering* of the Church by Jesus Christ, her Head; and the *actual order* which constitutes the necessities of daily life and ministry in the Church. This dual-reference enables Torrance to forge the closest linkage possible, whereby order in the life of the Church is apprehended as a direct result of "participation in the ordered life of Jesus Christ."[27] Thus, while "the Church must conform to Christ in the whole of its life and work,"[28] this conformity (ordering) is not dead imitation or mimicry but conformation "*through participation* in the obedience of Christ."[29]

Order in Jesus Christ

Torrance regards the "new order" constituted by the obedience of Jesus Christ as God's way of restoring his house of creation to order. "The covenant purpose of God in creation has been fulfilled and more than fulfilled. . . . Here in the new humanity in Jesus Christ nothing is out of order, or out of proportion."[30] As the divinely provided fulfilment of the law-covenant, Jesus Christ is "the new Adam," "the head of the new creation." God's will and human response are not related to one another as polarities, but in and through Jesus Christ, "the third dimension."[31]

Torrance locates the essence of the new order, in Jesus's own life

---

27. *GCM*, 96.
28. *Tracts and Treatises*, viii.
29. *GCM*, 93. Italics added.
30. Ibid., 95.
31. Ibid., 96. Cf. Thomas F. Torrance, *God and Rationality* (Edinburgh: T&T Clark, 1997), 151. Hereafter, *G&R*; *MOC*, 74; *C&A2*, 15.

of prayer and unbroken fellowship with the Father. "[F]rom out of our disobedience," he offers "a prayer of obedience." The whole life of Jesus is his prayer—"it was prayer without ceasing, lived prayer."[32] This bond of fellowship, confidence and trust was forged in the midst of our rejection and was the focus of all the attacks upon Jesus by the powers of evil.[33] While all other human beings are absorbed by their own self-willed activity, Jesus's life was one of continual "worshipping and praying obedience."[34] It is precisely here Torrance asserts that "the great *palingennesia*, the great conversion of humanity to God" took place.[35] Through his own filial life, Jesus was re-establishing the *imago Dei* and "restoring true sonship to our humanity."[36] Through his life of obedience and prayer, he converts our "house of bondage" into the house of God the Father, and brings us into "the freedom of God's sons and daughters" who rejoice "in the love and faithfulness of God the Father."[37] Every act of healing and mercy by Jesus is part of this movement, in which God "affirms as good what he has made and assumes it into communion with himself to share in his own divine life and glory."[38] Thus for Torrance the new order of the new humanity of Christ is essentially an order defined by joyful love and faithfulness: "the praise of creation for the Creator."[39]

Order through Jesus Christ

Torrance's understanding of Christ as the ontological substance of the Church and his perception of the somatic relation the Church has with Christ combined with his vision of a "new order" established in the risen Christ, function as core concepts within Torrance's theology of Grace. Christ is the order who orders, the new human who heads up a new humanity. Within this ordering, human responses to God are also

---

32. Thomas F. Torrance, *Incarnation: The Person and Life of Christ*, ed. Robert T. Walker (Nottingham: Intervarsity, 2008), 118. Hereafter, *Incarnation*.
33. Ibid.
34. Ibid., 119.
35. Torrance is referring to the Greek word for 'rebirth' as used in Matthew 19:28 and Titus 3:5. Ibid.
36. Ibid., 121.
37. Ibid., 121–22.
38. Ibid., 242–43.
39. *GCM*, 95.

ordered; that is, they have a particular *order* which they receive from their source in Christ and which is not arbitrary or self-determined.

Perhaps at this stage of our analysis it is becoming clearer how this language functions within Torrance's overall theology. Divine address and human response have become one in the new humanity of Jesus Christ. This is a vicarious humanity; it "represents" and "substitutes" for ours "in all our relations with God, including every aspect of human response: such as trusting and obeying, understanding and knowing, loving and worshipping."[40] As "the divinely provided response" and "the all-significant middle term,"[41] Jesus's vicarious humanity is the "sole norm" and "law," and "sole ground of acceptable human response to God."[42] For Torrance, this radically shifts the focus of concern from obedient but autonomous response, to *sharing in* the obedience of Christ through the power of the Spirit. The new order established in Christ, the true *imago Dei*, sets the standard and norm for all acceptable human response to God—whether that order be an ordering of its daily life, daily worship, daily fellowship or daily mission. Hence, the response to which humanity is summoned "is not some arbitrary self-determination or independent self-expression on his part, but one derived from, grounded in, and shaped by the very humanity of the Word."[43]

The Church is the place where knowledge of the Triune God becomes grounded in humanity and where union and communion with the Holy Trinity become embodied with the human race. This ontological relation of the Church to Christ becomes actualized in the Church's concrete existence by virtue of a Triune act. Habets observes the way Christology and pneumatology inform Torrance's ecclesiology differently, noting that Torrance develops his ecclesiology christologically as "the body of Christ," and pneumatologically as "the fellowship of the Spirit." Habets summarizes the way this trinitarian approach is integrated: "the church is the sphere of God's deifying

40. Ibid., 145.
41. Ibid.
42. Ibid., 146.
43. *G&R*, 146.

193

activity of believers in which the Spirit unites us to Christ and through Christ with the Father so that this community becomes *"the place in space and time where knowledge of the Father, the Son and the Holy Spirit becomes grounded in humanity, and union and communion with the Holy Trinity becomes embodied within the human race."*[44]

The Double Nature of the Church's Participation in Christ and Spirit

The Church has a two-fold communion, a double relation, to Christ through the Spirit.[45] This double-relation is reflected differently depending on the mode of speech Torrance is using. Robert Stamps in his excellent study of Torrance's theology of the Eucharist observes that Torrance systematically constructs his sacramental thought around two primary incarnational models or patterns.[46] While Stamps's immediate concern is Torrance's eucharistic theology, his observations apply equally to Torrance's ecclesiology as a whole.

The first pattern focuses on *union with Christ*. This is a single union, which nevertheless has two distinct *moments*: Christ's union with us in the incarnation and the Church's pneumatic and sacramental union with Christ.[47] Through the gift of the Holy Spirit who unites earthly and heavenly realities, the Church's pneumatic union with Christ is realized because of and out of his incarnational union with us. The second pattern Stamps observes, focuses on the *mediation of Christ*. Here the emphasis is upon "the reciprocal movement of Christ's priesthood," that is, his movement as God to humanity, and as humanity to God.

It would be a distortion of Torrance's thought to force these two patterns or models together or to collapse them. It is better to recognize the first as foundational for the second, for both arise from the same center.[48] The focus of the first model is primarily the

---

44. Habets, *Theosis*, 226. Quoting *TF*, 256–57 (italics mine).
45. *TF*, 265.
46. Stamps, *Sacrament*, 27–29.
47. *MOC*, 101.

hypostatic union of divine and human natures in Christ. The second model is concerned with the Church's sacramental and pneumatic union with "the inter-relations immanent in [Christ's] divine-human person."[49] The first explicates the incarnation according to its *parts*, while the second considers the incarnation from as it were within "the dynamic life of that mystery itself."[50] The second model has the advantage of being a more overtly internal and active metaphor but it presumes, requires and builds upon the underlying assertions of the first.[51] Neither model is static or external to the person of Christ. Each illumines the downward two-fold movement of Grace, though with slightly altered emphasis—the first highlighting the *downward*; the second the *two-fold*.

Attention to these two incarnational models will prove helpful in our discussion of how Torrance speaks of the relation of Christ and the Church. On the one hand, Torrance speaks of Christ and the Church as two entities, separated by the distance of the ascension and united by the Spirit: on the other hand, he speaks of the Church having its existence solely through participation in the mediatorial presence and priestly sacrifice of the person of Christ.

The Invisible and the Visible Church

Because of the ontological relation the Church has to Christ the crucified and ascended Lord, the Church bears a 'double nature.'[52] Torrance refers to these two dimensions of the Church as the visible 'Church in Christ,' and the invisible presence of 'Christ in the Church.' The *invisible* Church refers to the ascended Lord who is no longer

48. Thomas F. Torrance, *The Ground and Grammar of Theology* (Charlottesville: University Press of Virginia, 1980), 165. Hereafter, *GGT*.
49. Stamps, *Sacrament*, 28.
50. Ibid.
51. Stamps suggests that the second model demonstrates well a growing preference within Torrance's thinking for doing theology in conformity with the *inner relations* and the *interior logic* of the living objective reality of God himself. He notes that the concept of the mediation of Christ, while a fundamental theme in Torrance's epistemology from early on (Cf. *RP*, 15; *TS*, 45; *TRn*, 130), "does not in fact find its way into his sacramental theology until the mid 70s" (*Sacrament*, 29).
52. See *RP*, 43ff; Torrance, *Space, Time and Resurrection* (Edinburgh: T&T Clark, 1998), 141. Hereafter, *STR*, 156f; *C&A1*, 44, 113f.

visible in history, while the *visible* Church is that earthly community which is empirically observable throughout history in space and time. The latter is observed historically and has been passed on through the apostles; the former is a supernatural relation through the Holy Spirit and, as such, is "a mystery, a sacrament."[53] The ontological reality of the invisible Church is eschatologically realized through the visible Church's pneumatic and sacramental participation in Christ.[54]

Torrance points out that, while the Church does have *marks* (the preaching of the Word, the right administration of the sacraments, and true discipline), "the Church can never be defined in terms of its marks," for that would be to confuse the invisible and the visible aspects of the Church.[55] The Church may appeal to historical succession or its obedience to the apostolic tradition but her being, or reality, is not defined by these visibilities. Rather, the Church must be defined "in terms of Christ Himself, that is, as His Body." Her only security rests upon "the new covenant that Christ has made with [the Church] in his body and blood."[56] The fact that the ontology of the Church lies elsewhere—in the resurrected and ascended body of Christ—and means that the Church can never autonomously possess her own Being. The Church cannot justify herself by any means other than Christ's Grace alone.[57]

Since the ontology of the Church is inseparable from her ongoing union with Christ, who is her head, the Church is most properly recognized as an object of faith. *Church* is not a product for which consumers shop; she is a gift only children receive. Torrance finds it significant that the creed states, *credo* (not *video*) *sanctam ecclesiam*, for "faith is the evidence of things not seen."[58] Torrance further observes,

---

53. *C&A1*, 43. Cf. ibid., 26.
54. Ibid., 66.
55. Ibid.
56. *GCM*, 108.
57. Torrance critiques "High Church" understandings of historical structures for failing to recognize that the true significance of the Church as the Body of Christ is only through her relation to her head, Jesus Christ. It is a relation of distinction, in which Christ is head and the Church is body. At the same time, it is a relation of eschatologically conditioned *koinonia*. As such, the Church participates in the *wholeness* of Christ, and "because that *wholeness* is already whole there can be no talk of an extension of the Incarnation or historical continuity of the Body of Christ" (*C&A1*, 51).
58. *C&A1*, 66.

"The clauses on the Church do not constitute an independent set of beliefs but follow from belief in the Holy Spirit, for holy Church is the fruit of the Holy Spirit—the result of his sanctifying activity in mankind."[59] In short, the "'one holy Church' is . . . the complement of the 'one Holy Spirit.'"[60] In fact, none of the attributes of the Church attested by the creed (one, holy, catholic, apostolic) refer to independent qualities of the Church *per se*; they affirm her nature as it participates in Jesus Christ. They are realities which have their being only in *koinonia*. As a result, those fundamental creedal attributes of the Church are only discernible to the eyes of faith.

The Church as *Body* Participates in the Ascended Christ's Ministry

We have seen that the Church is constituted by Christ to be one body with Christ in the communion of the Spirit. As Christ's body, the Church is properly an object of faith, for its true substance (Christ) is invisible (ascended). Since the substance and head of the Church is ascended to the right hand of the Father, the order of the visible Church is ordered by the ascended invisible Christ. In order to understand Torrance's theology and his concept of Grace in particular, it is essential to recognize the supreme significance he ascribes to the doctrine of the ascension. In many ways, he considers it the great theological divide: "In my view it is the main issue which divides all theologies and strikes them apart to the one side or to the other. Are we to take the humanity of the risen Jesus seriously or not? Or are we to teach a Docetic view of the risen and ascended Jesus?"[61]

Torrance's approach to the continuing humanity of Christ is both thoroughly personal and thoroughly objective. The incarnate risen Christ is not just a placeholder: occupying a seat in heaven, yet with no real function. Instead, Christ continues to be himself in word *and* in act. The new human supervenes over a new humanity; the risen Lord

---

59. *TF*, 252.
60. Ibid., 257.
61. *C&A1*, 98; cf. *RP*, 43.

orders the Church's order; "the mediator continues to mediate." We do not only "look to Jesus," we "look to what Jesus is doing."[62]

This attention to 'what Jesus is doing' is especially relevant to how Torrance conceives of the Church's participation in the ongoing ministry of Christ.

The Church has a Triangular Relation to *the Whole* Christ

Torrance posits a *triangular relation* between Christ the head and his body on earth. This triangular relation is "to the historical and crucified Christ, to the risen and ascended Christ, and to the advent Christ who comes to judge and renew his creation."[63] Yet, because Torrance holds the person and work of Christ together, this triangular relation is expressed at many levels and in many dimensions throughout Torrance's writings on the church. As a result, while it may not always come in a systematised form, the trifold shape is nearly always evident. The taxis are many and diverse:

- Father, Son, Spirit;
- consubstantial communion, hypostatic communion, communion of the Spirit;
- king, priest, prophet;
- past, present, future;
- historical Christ, ascended Christ, advent Christ;
- universal family of God the Father, community of the reconciled, communion of saints;
- ontological, sacramental, eschatological;
- incorporation, participation, service.

---

62. Sandra Fach, pre-published version of thesis, "Answering the Upward Call: The Ascended Christ, Mediator of our Worship." Kings College London, 2008. Chapter 2, p. 12.
63. *Atonement*, 372. Cf. *GCM*, 109–10.

Most of the time, Torrance prefers to weave various themes together rather than to speak abstractly of one aspect in isolation from the others. This is because any splitting up, dividing or isolating from their inter-relations has the result of stripping Christ himself and also Grace, of their essential meaning and logic.

Consequently, when speaking of Christ's continuing ministry in his heavenly session, Torrance frequently employs Calvin's three-fold office scheme, yet with a certain free-flowing style. Torrance's concern throughout is to shine light on the *whole* Christ, so as to illuminate the fullness of who Christ is for us in his humanity and divinity and in the unity of his person. This approach gives Torrance's exposition a dynamic, integrative style that focuses more on the coinherence of act, being and relations than on tight definitions and categories. Thus, kingly, priestly and prophetic functions intersect and overlap as they should when the emphasis is focused on a real, living person more than a schemata. There is ultimately only one office (*munus*) with three differentiable elements or aspects (*triplex*). Each element of Christ's office is essentially him being himself. As Prophet, "he is in himself the Word he proclaims just as he is himself the King of the Kingdom and the Priest who is identical with the Offering he makes."[64]

This is not to suggest that all structure is abandoned. An appropriate ordering remains but the taxis always serves the person. Thus, as Torrance observes, while Christ's kingly office was always present in his earthly ministry, it remained in the background to his prophetic and priestly functions. However, with the ascension, Christ's kingly ministry is supreme and his ministries as priest and prophet are brought to their fullness in the consummation of his kingship, for "the priesthood of Christ is a Royal Priesthood, and the proclamation of Christ is a Royal Proclamation."[65]

64. *STR*, 119.
65. Ibid., 107.

The Church as the Eschatological *Place* where
Heaven and Earth Intersect

The triangular taxis is a helpful tool for remaining cognizant of the wholeness of the Christ-Church relation; it is also consistent with Torrance's commitment to approach his ecclesiology in a thoroughly christological manner. Because ecclesiology is christological it is also eschatological, for "eschatology is the application of Christology to the Kingdom of Christ and to the work of the Church in history."[66] Furthermore, because Christology orders ecclesiology eschatologically, Torrance views all order in the Church as essentially eschatological.[67] The ordering of the Church then involves ordering its place and time on earth "in obedience to its share in Christ's heavenly place and ... Christ's heavenly time."[68] The life and ministry of the Church are nothing less than the place where heaven and earth intersect and they must be ordered accordingly. Until the final advent and the renewing of the creation, "the Church shares in the real presence of the new man and the real time of the new creation."[69] As the Head, Lord and King of the body, Christ came to be obedient to the Father from *within* the Church so that the Church might share in an obedience not its own, not as a mere "imitation of his obedience, but a ... participation in Christ's obedience."[70] The Church then is the *place* where the vertical relation of mutual knowing between the Father and the Son enters

---

66. *RP*, 43. See Stanley MacLean's recent study of the eschatological nature of Torrance's theological outlook.
67. Differing perspectives on the relation of eschatology and ecclesiology has significant ramifications for inter-Church relations. Matthew Baker points out that Torrance and Vladimir Florovsky's differing convictions regarding intercommunion are rooted in their respective understanding of eschatology and its relationship to the Church in history. Torrance viewed the relationship primarily as a "negative dialectic" in which "the kingdom of God pronounces a judgment on all claims of history." Florovsky, on the other hand, viewed the Church in history as a "proleptic eschatology" which is constituted in the sacraments (Matthew Baker, "The Correspondence between T. F. Torrance and Georges Florovsky (1950–1973)," in *T. F. Torrance and Eastern Orthodoxy: Theology in Reconciliation*, ed. Matthew Baker and Todd Speidell [Eugene, OR: Wipf & Stock, 2015], 288). For Florovsky, eschatology should not ignore historical structures, for eschatology is mediated through history which inevitably involves structures (ibid., 314). History matters, and so too do the structures embedded in history. Structural distortions or losses, where they exist, "should be recovered or healed" (ibid., 317).
68. *GCM*, 107.
69. Ibid.
70. Ibid., 97.

our creaturely horizontal plane of existence; and where through the Spirit the Church creates for itself a corresponding personal fellowship among human beings in their relations with one another.[71] Thus, for Torrance—even in the midst of the current space-time form of this fallen world—"the actual space of the Church, its physical place in this world, has to be regarded as the trysting place of Christ on earth."[72]

Thus, within this spiritual union, Christ's own sonship is made to echo consciously within his people through their obedience to God and also through the "supernatural fellowship" they share with one another, which reflects the communion of the Spirit shared by the Father and Son.[73] Through the Spirit, the life and love he is and gives is generated in his people.[74] This is the Church's true joy: to be "rendered ever more transparent to the love that is eternal life."[75]

Ambiguous Structures

Because the Church in history is the place where heaven and earth intersect, the structures of the Church will carry within them an eschatological tension between the old creation and the new creation, between the past/present and the coming future. While the Church's basic order originates in the new humanity in Christ—the *Eschatos*—the Church continues to live out its existence in the midst of the old creation and its disorder.[76] This invests the Church's existence with a double-relation involving two *times* and two *places*. Thus, "true order in the Church of Christ" will point "above and beyond" its present forms to the new order of the risen Christ, which will be fully and finally manifested in the future new creation. Torrance perceives these two orders or ages as "overlapping"—distinct, but not separated—meaning that "all order in the Church is thus ambivalent and provisional."[77]

71. *R&ST*, 186–87; *TF*, 278; *SOF*, cxviii.
72. *GCM*, 108.
73. *SOF*, cxviii.
74. *Atonement*, 373.
75. Holmes, *Ethics in the Presence of Christ* (London: T&T Clark, 2012), 136. Hereafter, *Ethics*.
76. Eschatology for Torrance is not so much about the last things (*eschata*), or the end times, but about the Last One (*Eschatos*). Thomas F. Torrance, *The Apocalypse Today: Sermons on Revelations* (London: James Clarke and Co., 1960), 13. Hereafter, *Apocalypse*.
77. *GCM*, 98.

The Church, existing in this double-relation to Christ expresses itself in an order which is still subject to sin and brokenness. This double-relation to Christ necessarily calls the Church to continuous repentance. "She must ever be shedding her outward garments, putting off the old and putting on the new, refusing to be built into the fabric of orders fashioned to suit human selfishness or some naturalistic ideology."[78] Yet even while the Church remains caught up in the old creation and subject to the "fallen order" of human agents, the Church is still the heart of the new creation.[79] It is the Spirit who enables the Church to exist within this tension of the intersection of heaven and earth. The Spirit pulls the Church upward and forward, doing so in such a way that the Church's earthly existence is opened up and transformed into signs of the kingdom and the "redeemed order" of the incarnate Christ.[80] As such, the Church is given the task within humanity to be the *mediator of order* or the *priest of creation*.[81] The mission of the Church in the world is defined by this task and vocation. When the Church is true to this prophetic and priestly role—to this eschatologically ordering work of the Spirit—it is the most revolutionary force on earth.[82]

Implications for Ministry and Leadership in the Church

Torrance clearly struggles "to state precisely" the relation "described as participation" between the ministry of the Church and the ministry of Christ.[83] However, this descriptive challenge is similar to previous ones, in that the basic structure continues to be the form of Grace. It is "a movement . . . downward" from the head to the members of the body, such that "the Church's ministry . . . participates in the motion of grace from God to man, and ministers in the same direction as moves."[84]

---

78. *Apocalypse*, 155.
79. Ibid., 152.
80. Cf. Flett, *Persons, Powers, and Pluralities: Toward a Trinitarian Theology of Culture* (Cambridge: James Clarke, 2012), 134. *GCM*, 106.
81. Cf. *R&ST*, 114ff.
82. *Apocalypse*, 71.
83. *RP*, 37.

When speaking of the relation that exists between the ministry of the Church and the ministry of Christ, Torrance gives as much attention to clarifying what the relation is *not* as he does to clarifying what it *is*. The relation for example is not a relation of identity.[85] Nor are the two of the same genus, so the Church's ministry cannot properly be described as *incarnational*, as if it were a kind of *extension* of the incarnation.[86] However, while the relation is radically asymmetrical, the ministry of the Church is also not *another* ministry, different or separable from the ministry of Christ. Stated positively, while all ministry is Christ's ministry, the Church shares in the mission and ministry of Christ by sharing in his sonship and participating in his priesthood.[87] Accordingly, Torrance's foundational starting point is that "there is only one ministry, that of Christ in his Body."[88]

The central mark of Christ's ministry is loving service. As "the supreme Diakonos," Christ the Lord of the Church has "made *diakonia* an essential mark of the Church,"[89] with he himself "the creative ground and source of all such *diakonia*" service.[90] In Christ's command to serve "he gives what he commands and commands what he gives." Thus, "he commands a service of love, and he gives the love that empowers that service,"[91] even "imparting [mercy] where there is no mercy, until it begets mercy even where it has been scorned."[92]

The Church participates in Christ's ministry as servant, recognizing that the pattern for her life and work finds its significance only in directing the world's attention towards her risen and ascended Lord. As his body, the Church serves "Him who is Prophet, Priest, and King,"[93] and "exercises in obedience to Him, a prophetic, priestly, and kingly ministry."[94] The Church's ministry is participatory from

84. Ibid., 38.
85. Ibid., 37.
86. Ibid.
87. *GCM*, 119; *RP*, 22.
88. *TRn*, 208.
89. *GCM*, 151.
90. Ibid., 145.
91. Ibid., 142.
92. Ibid., 146.
93. *RP*, 37.
94. *C&A2*, 195.

beginning to end: it worships and serves *with* Christ, *in union with* Christ, *in the communion* of the Spirit. Throughout the whole ministry of the Church, Christ himself "presides"; but he also "summons the Church to engage in *His* ministry by witness (*marturia*), by stewardship (*oikonomia*), and by service (*diakonia*)."[95] The (prophetic) witness is to the gospel of reconciliation and the advent of the new creation. The (priestly) stewardship is stewardship of the sacramental mysteries, by which Christ feeds, blesses and renews his body. The service is obedience to the crucified and risen king according to the gifts he gives. In this way, the forms of the Church's life and ministry effectively "become the signs of the new divine order that already breaks in upon the Church in history."[96] Thus, the Church participates in Christ's own triplex ministry and its own life and ministry are ordered accordingly.[97]

This claim—that in the Church "there is only one ministry, that of Christ in his Body"[98]—carries significant implications for how the Church understands professional ministry. Though we participate in this ministry, our service is always empowered: no part of it is ever handed over to us to realize, actualize or make effective. Torrance claims that the early Church regarded Christ "in the absolute and proper sense, as the only Minister of the Church before God, the only One who was appointed and anointed (*Christos*) for office in the Kingdom of God."[99] This ontology of ministry renders all who minister in the Church as essentially, the scaffolding God uses as Christ and Christ alone, gives growth and increase by his Spirit.[100]

Church Nurtured by Word and Sacrament

Before launching into Torrance's approach to Word and Sacrament, it is worth noting that Torrance's position locates him at the Catholic

95. *RP*, 38.
96. *GCM*, 106.
97. Cf. *RP*, 38.
98. *TRn*, 208.
99. Ibid., 207.
100. *RP*, 97.

end of the Reformed spectrum and in many ways distinguishes him from his predecessor, Karl Barth. Writing from a Catholic perspective, Douglass Farrow observes that "Protestants can learn from Torrance something that Barth cannot teach them: a degree of respect for liturgy and sacraments and even for episcopal ministry."[101] Torrance's approach to the sacraments can be described as highly sacramental without the sacramentalism and highly personal without the sentimentalism. During most of his teaching career, Torrance was heavily committed to the work of the Scottish Church Society whose goals included liturgical renewal, a more frequent celebration of the Lord's Supper and an account of the real presence of Christ in the Eucharistic elements.[102] David Ferguson suggests that it was Torrance's association with these circles that enabled him "to move beyond Karl Barth in some important respects."[103] In the ensuing section we will note in more detail some of the specific ways in which Torrance distinguishes himself from Barth, most notably in his theology of baptism.

The Church has been created and ordered by Christ to participate in his ascended ministry and as such occupies a central place, and

101. Douglass Farrow, "T. F. Torrance and the Latin Heresy," *First Things* (2013): 12.
102. Torrance's efforts to further this strand of the Reformed tradition consumed much of his efforts throughout the 1950's, most notably in a series of bilateral and multilateral theological dialogues. Torrance's own contributions were later gathered into the two volumes of Conflict and Agreement in the Church. In 1957, he was a promoter of the so-called Bishops' Report to the General Assembly of the Church of Scotland which would have prepared the way for the union of the Church of Scotland with the Church of England by introducing bishops into presbyteries. The depth from which Torrance's commitment to church union around a 'higher' sacramentalism is reflected in the dedication Torrance chose for his 1955 book, *Royal Priesthood: A Theology of Ordained Ministry*: "To the Church of England, the church of my mother and my wife, and to the Church of Scotland, the church of my father, in the earnest prayer that they may soon be one" (Edinburgh: Oliver & Boyd, 1955). The book is dedicated. A second edition was published in 1993.
103. "Torrance as a Scottish Theologian," *Participatio*, vol. 2 (2010): 82. Ferguson notes that in particular it was Torrance's commitment to the continuing ministry of the ascended Christ made present by the Holy Spirit that theologically funded his more robust ecclesiology, sacramentalism and eschatology than what one finds in Barth. Torrance, in fact, criticizes Barth (in their very last conversation together, no less!) for this shortcoming, "I then ventured to express my qualms about his account of the ascended Jesus Christ in CD IV/3, in which Christ seemed to be swallowed up in the transcendent Light and Spirit of God, so that the humanity of the risen Jesus appeared to be displaced by what he had called 'the humanity of God' in his turning toward us. I had confessed to being astonished not to find at that point in Barth's exposition a careful account of the priestly ministry of the ascended Jesus in accordance with the teaching of the Epistle to the Hebrews about the heavenly intercession of the ascended Christ" ("My Interaction with Karl Barth," in *Karl Barth: Biblical and Evangelical Theologian* [Edinburgh: T&T Clark, 1990], 134).

describes the inner circle of the Triune God's identification with humanity. The Church is "a supernatural fellowship" in the midst of creation in which "[Christ's] own Sonship toward the Father is made consciously to echo within mankind in a filial relation of obedience to God the Father."[104] Together, Word and Sacrament are the means by which through the Spirit Christ continues to guide and rule his Church.

By Word

Christ rules his Church by his Word and Spirit. He unites himself to his creation in the incarnation; but that union, which involves the whole of creation, is concretized as a living reality only within the realm of the Church—that is, wherever the Name of Christ who sends the Spirit is heard and gathered under. The proclamation of the Gospel "is the scepter by which the ascended Lord rules both his Church and the nations."[105]

A Dynamic Rule—through the Mind of Christ

Torrance envisions this union, effected by the rule of Christ in intensely dynamic terms. This rule through Word and Spirit works itself out through the subjection of the Church to the mind of Christ. The mind of Christ is actually a broad concept which includes the whole of the Son's incarnate life (mind, heart, and will), in obedient and faithful response to the Father.[106] In this sense, the mind of Christ is the "sanctified humanity of Christ" and, as such, represents for Torrance "the fulcrum of all mediation."[107] This is Jesus Christ himself "as a worshipper of God, and worshipper in our place."[108]

Torrance has much to say about the way the mind of Christ became embodied in the formation of the New Testament scriptures.[109] For the purposes of this book, some very brief remarks will suffice. Through

---

104. *Mission*, 134.
105. Thomas F. Torrance, "The Mission of Anglicanism," in *Essays in Anglican Self-Criticism*, ed. David M. Paton, (London: SCM, 1958), 207.
106. Cf. *TiR*, 117–18, 139–214; *Atonement*, 376–78.
107. Stamps, *Sacrament*, 194.
108. *TiR*, 211.
109. Cf. Thomas F. Torrance, "The Deposit of Faith," *SJT* 36 (1983).

the Spirit, in whom Christ himself is personally present and active, the mind of Christ was enshrined in the mind of the apostles.[110] Out of this unique relation, three basic traditions became the source and norm of the apostolic church: the canon of Holy Scripture; "the Rule of Faith" (i.e., the structure of doctrine and worship laid out in the Apostles' Creed); and the functions and gifts of the apostolic ministry. Torrance views these three basic traditions as mutually dependent upon, and inseparable from, one another.[111] Through the apostles's faithfulness to their functions of preaching and teaching, ministering Word and Sacrament, and pastoral oversight—along with the gifts of the Holy Spirit, sent down by the ascended Lord upon His Church—the *kerygma* and the *didache* of Christ are gathered up and handed on.

Through the written word handed on from the apostles, Christ himself continues to be present through his Spirit: sharing his mind with his people and constituting them as one, holy, catholic Church in him. Indeed, by being "continuously occupied with the interpretation, exposition and application of Holy Scripture" the Church is rejuvenated in its apostolicity.[112] For Torrance, neither the handing on of the scriptures nor their reception, are passive activities. In hearing the Word, the Church is confronted with the very being of God and a response to the living Word is demanded from it. Torrance therefore emphasizes that the Word is to be *heard* in the words. Through the working of the Spirit, the words of the Church are opened up, thus operating as a sign, pointing to the reality to which they refer.[113] Through the living Word speaking through his own written word, the Church is formed in and by Jesus Christ. As the Church actively engages this Word, it grows to have the mind of Christ; that is, it learns to obediently trust and offer itself as praise to the Father. This is a creative, personal, relational and continuous process, whereby Christ and his Spirit use human instruments to "reveal and shape" the form

---

110. Torrance describes this as a *shaliach* relation. *C&A1*, 37ff.
111. *C&A1*, 27ff.
112. *TF*, 288.
113. For Torrance's discussion of the subjective and objective pole of existence statements, see *TRn*, 60–61.

of the Church into the form of Christ.[114] When the Church obeys the Word, it participates in the mind of Christ; when it disobeys, it is alienated from him. Even as we offer up our theological statements, the Spirit can be at work: re-creating us and re-creating our statements to bear true relation to the reality to which they refer. As the Spirit performs this creative work, he also re-creates our mind and our understanding. Thus, as we pray, our speech, our mind and our very humanity are being recreated, for our prayer is truly a participation in Christ's prayer; so even in our praying we hear the gospel again and again—and Jesus is our teacher.[115]

The Sacrament of the Word Preached

Torrance envisions the closest possible connection between the Word and the sacraments, such that they are truly inseparable and must therefore be thought together. The Word is present in the enactment of the sacrament and is in fact a sacrament itself. The "solemn proclamation of the Word is essentially sacramental." It is in fact "sacramentalizing event."[116] Torrance writes, "*Kerygma* may be defined . . . as objective sacramental preaching with an eschatological result, such that the original event, Christ incarnate, crucified and risen, becomes event all over again in the faith of the hearer."[117]

In a sermon on 1 Cor 2:1–5, Torrance describes in detail how he understands Christ's presence in the preaching:

> Christ is the message we preach, but here is the extraordinary thing about it. It is such a message that in it Christ is actively alive; He meets us and confronts us face to face. He leaps, as it were, out of history into the present, out of eternity into the here and now, out of the pages of this Holy Book into our hearts and minds. This is unique preaching, such that the original deed of our salvation, Christ crucified, becomes active among us. It becomes deed all over again in us and for us. We can help ourselves to understand that by remembering that *true preaching is a sacrament*.[118]

114. *Mission*, 142.
115. Cf. *GCM*, 150f.
116. Thomas F. Torrance, "The Mission of Anglicanism," 206.
117. *C&A1*, 41.
118. Unless otherwise indicated, all quotes in this section are from a sermon on 1 Cor 2:1–5

Torrance goes on to draw a comparison between the bread and wine of Communion and the preaching of the scriptures. He points out that the living presence of Christ is not conveyed by "the goodness of the bread or the fineness of the wine"; that God can use "the poorest, blackest bread and the most insipid wine." Similarly, "no enticing words, no excellency of speech can convey the testimony of God or communicate the Word made flesh." There is no human action by which we can "make Christ real." Christ must come himself. Yet, "behind the human action at the Table of the Lord there is the immediate and almighty action of the living Christ." Torrance continues: "So it is in preaching. It is a sacramental act in which the words of the preacher are like simple bread and wine which he takes and puts into our mouths. When this is done in the Name of Christ He Himself comes into our midst."

However, lest the motion of Grace be forgotten, Torrance shifts from considering the God-humanward movement to considering the nature of human action in response to God:

> Let us think again of the sacrament of the Lord's Supper. There are two sides to it all. We act and we break bread and pass it from hand to hand and eat it. These are our actions. But the real thing, the significant thing, is Christ's action. He Himself comes and enacts salvation in us and gives us to participate in Himself. *It is as we act that the miracle takes place in and through our act.*

As we act in faith, our "personal act of decision . . . answers the Word of God" and "Jesus Christ becomes alive within [us]." While it is true that we choose Christ, "you know that you have not chosen Him. He has chosen you." In this encounter,

> . . . each man is made to stand on his own feet before God in Christ, as the man loved by God to the uttermost, the man for whom Christ died and rose again, the man who through the love of God poured out upon him by the Spirit is enabled to say "He loved me and gave himself for me," and so in Christ to say "Abba, Father."[119]

(unpublished sermon, "Thomas F. Torrance Manuscript Collection." Box 38, labeled "Sermons, Lectures and Addresses, in Scotland and Abroad"). Italics added.

119. *Mission*, 135.

Word and the Two Sacraments cannot be Separated from One Another

In both Word and Sacrament, it is Christ himself who comes through his Spirit and enlivens faith. In, through, and with these acts and signs of the Church, the objective reality of Christ is present and active on our behalf. He is present in the wholeness of himself, in his divinity and his humanity; and he is present in the wholeness of his ministry towards us and for us, as prophet, priest and king. Through the unity of Christ's person and work, his vicariously inclusive life is at work in and among his Church.[120]

Jesus Christ is "the whole substance" of both the outer and inner form of the New Covenant. The sacraments are the *outward form* of this covenant; but its *inward form* is the Communion of the Spirit, "through which believers are taken up to share in the life and love of the Father and the Son and the Holy Spirit."[121] Consequently, there is only one sacramental relation between Christ and his Church, for there is only one Christ-event, defined as it is by Jesus's whole life and ministry. Accordingly, a theology of the sacraments, like all doctrines, must be traced back to its ground in the incarnation: that is, to "the vicarious obedience of Jesus Christ in the human nature," which he took, sanctified and offered to the Father. They are not merely human responses to the Word; the sacraments actually "enshrine" the action of the Word and as such, are "charged" with the power of the resurrection.[122] Torrance clarifies that the sacramental relation is a speaking-hearing relation, such that the inanimate element is always and only an "instrument" of Christ's real presence and not a "bearer" of it.[123] The relation between Christ and created instruments is dynamic, not static. The Word always remains transcendent to and differentiated from these "created mediations."[124]

---

120. Alasdair Heron refers to Christ's work as "vicarious but also inclusive, substitutionary but also incorporating" (Heron, *Table and Tradition*, [Philadelphia: Westminster, 1983], 169).
121. *Mission*, 136.
122. Cf. Hunsinger, *Dimension of Depth*, 15.
123. *C&A2*, 188.
124. Cf. *TS*, 149–50; *SOF*, lii; *TiR*, 132.

The relation which Torrance posits between the Word and the sacraments is complex and, because of the double meaning of *Word*, can lead to confusion. As already noted, Torrance comes very near to designating preaching as a third sacrament but in fact never goes that far.[125] According to Torrance, Word and sacraments are related as unified elements in the one movement of Grace, which is a single mystery with two moments; not as three separate entities that mutually affect each other and need to be coordinated together.[126] There is for Torrance technically only one sacrament: Jesus Christ himself.[127] Baptism and Eucharist are sacraments of the Church only because Jesus Christ makes them so, by *sacramentalizing* the sacraments.[128] As such, they point away from themselves toward Christ, who is "the primary *mysterium* or *sacramentum*"—the "all-inclusive Sacrament of the Word made flesh" who through the Spirit creates and forms the Church "in sacramental union" with himself.[129] A discussion of the function of *kerygma* in Torrance's epistemology will clarify the way he envisions Christ and Spirit at work in and through, the actions of the Church.

In his 1952 article, 'Eschatology and the Eucharist,' Torrance treats the New Testament concept of *kerygma* as the way in which Word and sacrament are held together conceptually. He begins by noting that the meaning of the "Christ-event" is "the Word made flesh," the *mysterion* of the hypostatic union in Jesus Christ, and that it refers to both the "eternal Truth" and "the act of the Eternal in time."[130] In Jesus Christ, "Word and act [preaching and miracles] are inseparable and complementary," such that the Word that is spoken is not just an idea or "a word spoken into the air," but is also enacted.[131] It is

---

125. The one exception to this rule takes place in the context of a sermon on 1 Cor 2:1–5 in which Torrance declares, "true preaching is a sacrament" (unpublished sermon, "Thomas F. Torrance Manuscript Collection." Box 38, labeled "Sermons, Lectures and Addresses, in Scotland and Abroad").

126. *RP*, 74–75. Torrance prefers the term mystery rather than sacrament, due to the connotation associated with sacrament "which lays the stress not on what God has once and for all done for us, but on our responsibilities and our vows of response." *C&A2*, 92.

127. *C&A2*, 156; *TS*, 150.

128. *RP*, 75.

129. Ibid.

130. *C&A2*, 157.

this two-fold sense to which kerygma refers: "*Kerygma* means both the thing preached and the preaching of it in one. It is the proclamation of the Christ-event, but such proclamation that by the Holy Spirit it becomes the actualization of that event among men. . . . " "*Kerygma* is the Word . . . that cannot be conveyed in mere speech."[132] Thus, "*kerygma* is in the fullest sense the sacramental action of the Church through which the mystery of the Kingdom concerning Christ and His Church . . . is now being revealed in history."[133] Torrance then draws a parallel between the signs and miracles of Christ and the sacraments of baptism and Eucharist. Each is part of, and inseparable from, the *kerygma*. Thus, "Baptism, *kerygma* and Eucharist together form a whole—the sacramental life and action of the Church."[134]

The depth of the interrelationship of Word and Sacrament must be recognized and taken into account.[135] Together these are caught up in a *sacramental* or genuine relation with God in which he makes them "the instrument of his purpose in revelation and reconciliation."[136] The Word proclaimed and the sacraments celebrated are equally priestly acts which become assimilated to Christ's own self-offering before the Father.[137] In the sacramental acts of the Church, Jesus Christ himself—the living Word—continues to rule and govern his Church as king and head. "God's Word in sermon and sacrament is one and the same Word, what he proclaims himself to be as Word in the former he proclaims himself to be as action in the latter."[138]

In either case—Word or Sacrament—the Gift is the same: it is Christ himself.[139] The purpose of the sacraments is not simply to present visually what cannot be expressed in words. Nor are the sacraments merely illustrations, or "pledges," of the preached word. As Stamps

---

131. Ibid.
132. Ibid., 158.
133. Ibid.
134. Ibid., 165. Torrance references Jesus' final commission to his disciples from Matthew 28:18–20 to demonstrate the link between kerygma, baptism and eucharistic communion.
135. Ibid., 160.
136. *SOF*, lii; *TS*, 150.
137. *GCM*, 265ff.
138. Stamps, *Sacrament*, 72; cf. *G&R*, 160.
139. Cf. *G&R*, 160.

notes in his description of the relation of knowing and being in Torrance's thought, "This is not a deference of 'the language of words' to 'the language of vision,' but the deference of knowledge as purely rational comprehension to knowledge as relation."[140] What the sacraments uniquely offer is an event, which we engage in by faith that particularizes our union with Christ within the "time-form" of this world, while we are living on this side of the "veil of sense" and the "veil of time."[141] As such, Christ's presence is manifest in the sacraments in a special "intensity."[142] That is, the sacraments "will not allow us . . . to respond to the proclamation of the Word only in some intellectual or merely Spiritual way, for in and through them the movement of faith reaches its fruition as lived and acted response to the coming of the Word of God into our space and time."[143] The sacraments remind us that Christ "insists on actualizing in us the promises of redemption and regeneration."[144] Through Word and Sacraments together, Christ meets and rules his Church.[145]

By Sacrament

While the sacraments are indeed acts which the Church *does*, they are explicitly not sacraments of what *the Church* does. They are, rather the divinely instituted forms of human response, vicariously provided by Jesus Christ, who is the one Word of God to humanity and of humanity to God.[146] Through Christ and in the Spirit, these creaturely elements "participate sacramentally in the mystery of Christ," who as noted above is himself the one true Sacrament.[147] Their function is to manifest and bear witness to Christ, yet they do this *not* through any inherent power of their own.[148] To the extent that the sacrament

---

140. Stamps, *Sacrament*, 8.
141. *STR*, 152.
142. "Why then is the Sacrament appointed? Not that you may get any new thing, but that you may get the same thing better than you had it in the Word" (Thomas F. Torrance, *The Mystery of the Lord's Supper: Sermons by Robert Bruce* [Reprint. Edinburgh: Rutherford House, 2005], 59).
143. *G&R*, 161.
144. Ibid., 160.
145. *Mission*, 142.
146. *MOC*, 90.
147. *TS*, 150.

effects what it signifies, it is only because "what it signifies, Christ does."[149]

Torrance goes against the traditional Reformed view (received from Augustine) that the Sacrament is a sign (*signum*) that corresponds to a thing (*res*): he argues instead that it is a sign which is "essentially an event"—the Christ-event in history.[150] As such, Sacraments are not "an outward expression" of the believer's inward piety; they are the Church's present participation in the life of the risen and glorified Christ. The act of the Church thus serves the primary action of Christ, and "directs us away from itself to Christ."[151]

Thus for Torrance, the sacraments make no sense apart from our *present* relation to Christ. "Because the Sacraments are Sacraments of the Word made flesh, they are nothing apart from the Word."[152] Most properly then the sacraments "have to be understood as concerned with our *koinonia* or participation in the mystery of Christ and his Church through the *koinonia* or communion of the Holy Spirit."[153] The sacraments are concrete, symbolic enactments of this eschatological relation, which as we have observed is the mystery of Christ and his Church. It is both "once and for all" and also "abiding and enduring," and these two moments are expressed in baptism and the Lord's Supper.[154] "Baptism . . . may be spoken of as the Sacrament of Justification, which is not to be repeated. The Eucharist is the Sacrament of our continuous participation in Christ and may be spoken of as the Sacrament of Sanctification, which is regularly to be repeated, until Christ comes again."[155] Thus, baptism is into Christ, into a life of communion with the Father through the Son in the Spirit and the

---

148. *RP*, 75. Recall the discussion in the previous section of Christ's prophetic self-proclamation in the kerygma.

149. Thomas F. Torrance and Ronald Selby Wright, eds., *A Manual of Church Doctrine According to the Church of Scotland*, H.J. Wotherspoon and J.M. Kirkpatrick, 2nd ed. (London: Oxford University Press, 1960), 18–19. Torrance considered the statement on the theology of the Eucharist in Wotherspoon and Kirkpatrick's Manual as thoroughly representative of his own view (Stamps, *Sacrament*, 71).

150. *C&A2*, 161.

151. *TiR*, 107.

152. *RP*, 75.

153. *TiR*, 82.

154. *C&A2*, 163.

155. *STR*, 150. Cf. *RP*, 74–75.

Lord's Supper is the continual feeding and renewal in that life of communion. As appointed signs, the sacraments themselves are participatory events: in baptism we participate, by the Spirit, in the vicarious baptism of Christ; in the Lord's Supper we participate, by the Spirit, in the life of the ascended Christ, our high priest, in memory and communion. In both, truth and being cohere dynamically. Because the Eucharist presupposes baptismal incorporation, Torrance views intercommunion as completely appropriate, for "He who is sacramentally incorporated into the body of Christ is already participant in sacramental communion."[156] Based upon the same reasoning, Torrance is also critical of the common church practice of waiting for confirmation until one's baptism is considered complete, arguing that this contradicts the once-for-all character of the sacrament and usurps the lordship over the Eucharist "which by right belongs to Christ alone."[157]

Together, the two sacraments reflect the form of Grace: downward and two-fold. The summons to the Church is to live in the light of her true reality, by entering the movement of Grace.

Baptism—One Body

Torrance suggests that in order to view baptism in its proper *dimension of depth*, three pictures must simultaneously be held together, "stereoscopically."[158] Jesus's entire life must be understood as a kind of

---

156. *C&A2*, 187; cf. *C&A2*, 166ff. "Surely a clear and high doctrine of Holy Baptism forbids us to allow any wedge to be driven between Baptism and Eucharist" (*C&A2*, 192). Torrance had strong feelings about intercommunion and was not hesitant to speak his mind. Erecting barriers to Intercommunion "would be to sin against the Incarnation, to fight against the Cross, to deny the Resurrection, the quench the Holy Spirit" (*C&A1*, 262). "[W]ho are we to deny" those incorporated into the body of Christ by baptism "renewal of their incorporation in the Body of Christ?" Since the real continuity of the Church is found, not "on the plane of historical relativity but in the continuous act of God," "to refuse the Eucharist to those baptized into Christ Jesus and incorporated into His resurrection-body amounts either to a denial of the transcendent reality of holy Baptism or to attempted schism within the Body of Christ" (*C&A2*, 191). For Torrance, the stakes could not be higher: "the road to the unity of the Church and to the evangelization of the world lies through *Intercommunion*, so that all who are baptized into the one Body of Christ may be healed of their dividedness through Eucharistic Communion and in the reconciliation thereby effectively enacted in their flesh and blood show forth to the whole world the death of Christ until He come" (*C&A1*, 262).
157. *C&A1*, 73. On the relation of infant baptism to confirmation, Torrance also found himself at odds with Karl Barth who famously said, "Is not infant baptism only half a baptism?" (CD IV/4, 188).

baptism[159] (Mark 10:38–39): it begins with the baptism of Jesus in the Jordan (baptism in water) and is fulfilled first, in the Son's obedient life and death (baptism in blood) and finally, in the baptism of the Church at Pentecost (baptism by Spirit), when "the Church was assimilated to Christ as his Body and made to share in the baptism with which he was baptized."[160] In Christ, these three baptismal moments—water, blood, Spirit—are one baptism in him.[161]

Torrance understands Jesus's baptism vicariously. Jesus in his baptism received the Spirit not for his own sake, but for ours. "Our baptism in the name of the Trinity . . . is to be understood as a partaking through the Spirit in the one unrepeatable baptism of Christ."[162] However, Christ's baptism for us refers to what he underwent, not just in the Jordan River, but throughout his life, death and resurrection on our behalf. If this is "the structure to which baptism belongs," it should not be interpreted "in the flat," as only an event that has meaning in itself, but "in a dimension of depth," where it is "grounded so objectively in that work that it has no content, reality or power apart from it."[163] If baptism is not objective but only subjectively lodged in us, then "the only meaning we can give to it will be in terms of what we do or experience, or in terms of the efficacy of its valid performance as a rite."[164] Certainly, ritual act and ethical response have a place in baptism "but baptism itself is focused beyond those acts upon the one saving act of God embodied in Jesus Christ."[165] Just as in the *kerygma*, Christ "is both its material content and its active agent."[166]

Torrance's profoundly trinitarian understanding of baptism is grounded in his conviction that we are enabled by the Spirit to participate in the Son's incarnate relation with the Father. The first

---

158. *TiR*, 88.
159. Ibid., 83. Torrance suggests that the New Testament coinage of the term *baptisma* rather than utilizing the more common *baptismos* is a demonstration of their intention to express Christian baptism in a unique objective sense.
160. Ibid., 104.
161. Ibid., 92; see 1 John 5:6.
162. *TF*, 293.
163. *TiR*, 83.
164. *TF*, 294.
165. *TiR*, 83.
166. Ibid., 99; cf. Torrance, *Karl Barth: Biblical and Evangelical Theologian*, 134–35. Hereafter, *KBBET*.

principle Torrance argues for is that "the act of God in baptism is to be understood in terms of the reciprocity between divine and human agency which he has established for us" in Christ and which he continues to maintain in us through his Spirit.

An important cognate concept to "reciprocity," for Torrance, is the idea of an "overlapping" of responses, in which we find ourselves caught up in a "circle of relation" within which our human responses are given their reality and substance. This relation, enacted in its two-fold mode in Christ and in the Spirit and embodied in the doctrine of baptism "establishes the polar relation between God and man which we find in all our relations with God, in faith, knowledge, obedience, freedom, etc."[167]

However, Torrance argues that dualistic thinking tended to separate the rite of baptism (*baptismos*) from the objective reality of baptism (*baptisma*) in the Incarnation. This disconnection meant that the rite received a heightened profile in order to increase its magical effectiveness. Torrance identifies an early tendency in Church history towards a more anthropological than christological approach to baptism. This involved an emphasis on human psychological response rather than on the divine promise, with the result that a huge and awful responsibility was laid on the baptized in a *pactum fidei*.[168] This "latent synergism," Torrance believes, led Augustine to place an emphasis on subjective, instrumentalist notions of sacraments, such as: 'means of grace,' 'containing grace,' 'causing grace,' 'conferring grace,' 'causal efficacy,' 'baptismal regeneration,' and the like. Within this synergistic and instrumentalist framework, *Grace* was demoted to the status of an intermediate reality between God and humanity, and was distinguished from Christ himself. Humans were given merely an "indirect participation in the divine."[169] Torrance believes that "the effect of this was to build into the basic fabric of Western thought a hidden deism which knocked out any notion of an intuitive apprehension of God in his own living reality and made the concept

---

167. Ibid., 101.
168. Torrance calls out Tertullian and Origen for critique, but praises Irenaeus (ibid., 96).
169. Ibid., 99.

of any direct act of God within the space-time structure of this world rather problematic."[170]

Here one observes an important difference between Torrance and Karl Barth. While Barth and Torrance both agree that *sacramentalism* (the idea that the sacraments themselves mediate supernatural Grace between God and humanity) is to be rejected, they proceed forward along different paths. Torrance charges Barth guilty of harboring "vestiges" of dualism in his understanding of the sacraments, most noticeably in the polarizing separation he draws between water and Spirit baptism.[171] Torrance on the other hand would press divine activity in Spirit baptism and human activity in water baptism more nearly together, for "God is a living God who acts here and now in our world."[172] Torrance's concern and thus the demonizing charge of dualism, is the sharp distinction that Barth's position makes between subject and object, or knower and the thing known. Such a dualistic epistemological stance coincides with an equally dualistic approach to divine and human activity. As such, Torrance critiques Barth's theology of baptism as "a return to a sacramental dualism between water-baptism and Spirit-baptism in which the meaning of baptism is found not in a direct act of God but in an ethical act on the part of man, made by way of response to what God has already done on his behalf."[173] In other words, God's activity falls on one side and human activity on the other, each operating in its own sphere parallel to the other.[174] Torrance's solution is integration according to the downward

---

170. Ibid.
171. Karl Barth, BET, 138; see also *TiR*, 100.
172. W. Travis McMaken, "The Sign of the Gospel: Toward an Evangelical Doctrine of Infant Baptism after Karl Barth" (Minneapolis: Fortress Press, 2013), 53.
173. *TiR*, 99.
174. Whether Torrance's criticism of Barth sticks is a matter for debate. Torrance's conclusion that Barth is "deeply inconsistent" (*TiR*, 99) at this point is not shared by John Webster and Paul Molnar (McMaken, "The Sign of the Gospel: Toward an Evangelical Doctrine of Infant Baptism after Karl Barth" [Minneapolis: Fortress Press, 2013], 53n144). Regardless of whether Torrance understands Barth rightly, he is concerned about the right thing. McMaken offers a fascinating discussion on the distinction between Barth and Torrance as rooted in their respective handling of theological dialectic. Whereas "Barth's theology makes use of an actualistic dialectic," which "prevents the theologian from taking anything for granted. . . . Torrance generally tries to build the dialectic into his theological position" (ibid., 261n84). This explains why Torrance is able to boldly state, "when the church baptizes in his name, it is actually Christ himself who is savingly at work," (*TiR*, 83) while Barth is less willing to offer such a guarantee. For Barth, as McMaken points

two-fold movement of Grace where the living God "interacts with what he has made in such a way that he creates genuine reciprocity between us and himself."[175]

For Torrance, these "false problems of sacramental dualism and monism that have constantly troubled the Church,"[176] and wrongly separated water and Spirit baptism are overcome by a proper understanding that "there is essentially one baptism common to Christ and his Church."[177] Within this "one baptism" model, "Christ and his Church participate in the one baptism in different ways—Christ actively and vicariously as Redeemer, the Church passively and receptively as the redeemed Community."[178] Here as one would expect the contours of the downward two-fold motion of Grace are evident. The Church participates *receptively*, as those who have been redeemed by Christ's vicarious and redemptive baptism in our place and on our behalf. In his vicarious life he took up our humanity and made it his own, "sharing to the full what we are that we may share to the full what he is."[179]

As a movement of Grace, the dynamics of this one baptism from the Church's side are two-fold. As in all aspects of the divine-human relation, God is the initiator; yet human agency is not bypassed. Baptism reflects the divine initiation, the downward movement of God's love, in its concrete sign by "setting forth" the covenant of what Christ has done *for* us. This reflects our once-and-for-all union with Christ. It corresponds to the substitutionary more than the representative aspect of atonement, for in this one baptism we die to ourselves and Christ takes our place. Baptism thus expresses the fact that our faith is implicated in the faith and faithfulness of Christ.

out, the union of the act of God and the action of human beings "always remains a subject of the church's confident and expectant but no less prayerful hope rather than a foregone conclusion" (ibid., 261n84). McMaken's proposal to view the relationship of divine and human activity in Barth's theology in terms of "paradoxical identity" offers an insightful way forward between Barth and Torrance.

175. *TiR*, 100.
176. Ibid., 104.
177. Ibid., 86.
178. Ibid., 87.
179. *TF*, 294.

The point of baptism (in its death imagery) is that we rely upon the vicarious faith of Christ; and this Grace "anticipates, generates, sustains and embraces the faith granted" to those who are baptized.[180] Baptism proclaims that we belong to Christ and it is this belonging from which faith originates and out of which faith continues to grow.

Fundamentally, this is visible in the fact that we do not baptize ourselves. Torrance writes, "Baptism is thus not a sacrament of what we do but of what God has done for us in Jesus Christ, in whom he has bound himself to us and bound us to himself, before ever we could respond to him."[181] Baptism is an ordinance whose primary focus is upon "what God has already done in Christ, and through His Spirit continues to do in and to us. . . . Baptism is administered to us in the Name of the Triune God, and our part is only to receive it, for we cannot add anything to Christ's finished work."[182]

Torrance on this basis strongly affirms infant baptism.[183] Accordingly, it is important and significant that the same baptism—both in doctrine and in form—is administered to adults as to children: "it is only as little children that we enter into this inheritance of the Kingdom freely bestowed upon us in the New Covenant . . . and we enter into it relying not upon ourselves in any way but solely upon Him who has already laid hold of us by His grace."[184] Both forms of baptism stand upon the same basis of the vicarious humanity of Christ.[185]

---

180. *MOC*, 91. See Eph 2:9–10.
181. *TiR*, 103.
182. Ibid., 88.
183. *C&A2*, 125.
184. Ibid., 125.
185. The vicarious responsibility of Christ in baptism is superbly represented in the declaration contained in the French Reformed baptismal tradition, which Bryan Spinks relates as follows:

> N . . . ,
> For you Jesus Christ came into the world:
> for you he lived and showed God's love;
> for you he suffered the darkness of Calvary and cried at the last, "It is accomplished";
> for you he triumphed over death and rose in newness of life;
> for you he ascended to reign at God's right hand.
> All this he did for you, N . . . ,
> Though you do not know it yet.
> And so the word of Scripture is fulfilled:
> "We love because God loved us first."

Yet, while "baptism tells us that it is not upon our act of faith or on our own faithfulness that we rely but upon Christ alone and his vicarious faithfulness," the baptized are not left as spectators, passively inactive. Baptism is not only a sacrament of what God has done for us in Christ "before ever we could respond to him"; "it is also the sacrament of what God now does in us by his Spirit, uniting us with Christ in his faithfulness and obedience to the Father and making that the ground of our faith."[186] The vicarious activity of Christ is for our inclusion—not as a separate act—but as an inclusion included in the substitutionary act itself. Torrance describes this mystery: in the freedom of his Spirit, "God makes himself present to us and binds us creatively to himself in such marvelous ways that not only is faith called forth from us as our own spontaneous response to the grace of God in Christ, but it is undergirded and supported by Christ and enclosed with his own faithfulness and thus grounded in the mutual relation between the incarnate Son and the heavenly Father."[187]

Eucharist—One Sacrifice/Offering

Torrance's eucharistic theology receives its force and form from its grounding in the incarnate Christ. He writes, ". . . the mystery of the Eucharist is to be understood in terms of our participation through the Spirit in what the whole Jesus Christ—the incarnate, crucified, risen and ascended Son—is in himself, in respect both of his activity from the Father towards mankind and of his activity from mankind towards the Father."[188] For Torrance, this understanding of the relation of Christ's *whole life* to reconciliation is non-negotiable. *"Only when we are able to give the human nature of Christ the saving significance it occupies in the New Testament . . .* will we be in a proper position to understand what it

(Bryan D. Spinks, "Reformation and Modern Rituals and Theologies of Baptism: From Luther to Contemporary Practices" [Aldershot, UK: Ashgate, 2006], 190–91). A simple change of the third line from the end to, "having chosen you in Christ before the foundation of the world" (see Eph. 1:4) would allow the declaration to properly address baptizands of any age (cf. McMaken, "The Sign of the Gospel: Toward an Evangelical Doctrine of Infant Baptism after Karl Barth" [Minneapolis: Fortress Press, 2013], 280–81).

186. *TiR*, 103.
187. Ibid., 103–4.
188. Ibid., 117.

means to eat and drink the body and blood of Christ, and understand what the real presence actually means."[189]

Within Torrance's "whole Christ" perspective, the Eucharist is both God-humanward and human-Godward. It is the Sacrament of the real presence of Christ upon whom the Church feeds and also the Sacrament of Christ's offering of himself to God on our behalf, and us, in him. In this second sense, the Church offers Christ eucharistically to the Father as our only true worship and Christ takes that offering and assimilates it into his own self-offering. Consequently, in the Eucharist the Church does two things befitting its form—two things which define our identity as those who share one body with Christ: (1) we *feed* on Christ, recognizing and enjoying our communion with him through the Spirit; and (2) in union with Christ's eternal self-offering, we *worship* the Father in the Spirit through the Son, in whose vicarious self-offering we are included. Both our feeding and our worship take place on the basis of our union with Christ through the Spirit. Through this two-fold movement, the Lord's Supper proclaims that "we live unceasingly not from a centre in our selves or our doing but from a centre in Christ and his doing."[190]

These two movements (God-humanward and human-Godward) within the one motion of Grace in the incarnate Mediator form the central framework of Torrance's eucharistic theology. We will explore them in turn, in each case noting first the common errors which Torrance critiques before expositing Torrance's own correctives.

The God-Humanward Movement: the *Feeding* of the Church

With regard to the God-humanward movement, the central issue is the nature of God's self-giving in the real presence of the Eucharist. Torrance's dynamic and relational understanding of time and space enable him to move past the stalemate of long-standing debates on the eucharistic presence. In contrast to eucharistic theologies which

---

189. Thomas F. Torrance, "Doctrinal Consensus on Holy Communion," *SJT* 15, no. 1 (March 1962): 10 (italics added). Hereafter, *Consensus*.
190. *MOC*, 91.

THE ECCLESIOLOGICAL FORM OF GRACE

essentially refract the inherent oneness of the Giver and the Gift, Torrance grounds the real presence in God's self-giving to us in Christ. Torrance identifies two common errors in how the presence of Christ is defined in the Sacrament. He refers to these as "sacramental dualisms" and locates their source in a fundamentally damaged understanding of the relation of God to the world. Both refractions are expressed in this phrase, embedded in the Augustinian tradition: "an outward sign of an inward and invisible Grace."[191] As Torrance sees the problem, transubstantiation and memorialism are two sides of the same dualistic coin.[192] Transubstantiation is an ontological dualism; it defines the real presence in a "phenomenalist, physico-causal way" and leads to an over-profiling of the eucharistic rite in which *Grace is assimilated to causality*.[193] Memorialism is a kind of epistemological dualism; it operates with a symbolic and inward understanding of the sacraments, and "a merely spiritual interpretation of the real presence," with the effect that *Grace is subjectivized*.[194] Torrance argues that the dualistic perspective inherent in both errors damages our understanding of God's relation with the world, actually dividing the Gift from the Giver.[195] The Catholic tendency is to focus on the Gift "as inhering in the Eucharist as such."[196] The Protestant pietistic tendency focuses on the receiver over against the Giver; as such, it encourages us to rely on ourselves "to effect our own 'Pelagian' mediation with God by being our own priests and by offering to him our own sacrifices."[197]

191. *TiR*, 122.
192. Ibid., 137.
193. Ibid., 123.
194. Ibid.
195. Ibid., 131.
196. Ibid., 132. Paradoxically, yet coherently, Torrance characterizes the Roman doctrine of the Mass as "an extremely low doctrine" for "it does not teach a doctrine of the real presence." "Christ's presence comes only half-way, and the worldly element is divinized or raised up by transubstantiation to meet it. This was precisely what Nicaea denied . . . but the Church did not go on to apply that correction to the shape of the liturgy or the form of the Church" (*C&A1*, 45).
197. Ibid., 134.

Emphasis on the Rite as such (Outward Extrinsicism)

The Catholic side of this sacramental dualism places the emphasis on the *outward sign* in such a way that the Eucharist is perceived objectively to enshrine the Gift. In this approach, the bread as the *corpus Christi* functions as a "substitute-Christ," itself containing the divine mystery through transubstantiation. Here, "attention was directed *at* the Eucharist itself rather than *from* or *through* the Eucharist to its real ground in the paschal mystery of Christ which gave it its real meaning."[198]

Torrance diagnoses transubstantiation as a "docetic error," born of a monophysite Christology which effectively flattens out the Chalcedonian mystery.[199] Rather than there being a genuine union (but not confusion) of divinity and humanity in Christ, God and creaturely realities are deemed inherently and impossibly incompatible. Since God cannot be truly present to creatures, other created intermediaries are necessary. As Torrance sees it, this monophysite error warps many aspects of Roman ecclesiology beyond the Eucharist itself.[200]

Torrance's charge of over-profiling the outward sign is not just against Roman eucharistic theology, but Lutheran as well. He describes the Lutheran *Hoc est corpus meum* as "the great ontological clamp" which attempts to hold the two kingdoms together.[201] Here, the rite replaces the objective reality of the divine promise with the net effect that the rite takes up an intermediary role between an essentially deistic God and a sinful people. The eucharistic rite is attributed with a created kind of magical effectiveness, conveying created Grace to a fallen people who left to themselves would be without hope. Torrance counters, "the New Testament . . . clearly tells us . . . in the Gospel stories of the Transfiguration and of the Emmaus manifestation that by our human institutions . . . we cannot perpetuate in the continuity of space and time the risen Jesus Christ. He inevitably vanishes out of

198. Ibid., 122.
199. *TRn*, 184.
200. *C&A1*, 151. He mentions the Roman position on Mary, the priesthood, and church unity through a common baptism (cf. *RP*, 106). See *C&A2*, 150–62 for Torrance's account of the assumption of Mary.
201. *TiR*, 127.

our sight at that point."[202] For Torrance, to identify the sacrament itself *rather than Jesus Christ himself* as the source and strength of the Grace given through the Eucharist, is commensurate with usurping Christ's person for a mere creaturely activity.[203]

Emphasis on the Experience of the Participant (Inward Pietism)

The other side of sacramental dualism places the stress on the subjective aspect of the "inward or invisible grace." Here the emphasis in the Eucharist falls upon the receiver, over and against the Giver. The basic function of the Eucharist is to stimulate in the believer deeper subjective spiritual consciousness and awareness.

This low church approach replaces the *hoc est* by a *hoc significant* with the effect of splitting the two kingdoms apart for good. Torrance traces this move towards a moralistic and existentialist phenomenology to Reformation reactions against Luther's physicalist ontology (and *vice-versa*). This would eventually give way to a reinterpretation of the eucharistic presence based on the categories of practical reason in which acts of God were considered completely detached from both divine and creaturely being.[204] The fall-out of this spiritualized interpretation of the eucharistic presence of Christ was this: the emphasis shifted more and more toward a pietistic focus on the inwardness and immediate loving response of the participant.

Whether Protestant or Catholic, Torrance's overall analysis is that these characteristic orientations toward the Eucharist "ultimately stem from the same source, a damaged understanding of the relation between God and the world," which affects the doctrines of creation and incarnation.[205] Torrance starkly presents the two problematic options which the Church has too often chosen: "[T]he Eucharist is regarded either as a holy mystery in itself enshrining and guaranteeing the divine mystery of the Church in the host or as the appointed

---

202. C&A1, 45–46.
203. "It would be just as wrong to speak of many graces as many Christs, or of sacramental grace as of a sacramental Christ, or of created grace as of a created Christ" (*TRn*, 183).
204. *TiR*, 127–28.
205. Ibid., 131.

ordinance which occasions and stimulates deeper spiritual consciousness and awareness in believers."[206]

The Real Presence of Christ through the Spirit

Torrance's remedy to sacramental dualism in the God-humanward
movement of the Eucharist is the gospel of Grace, which is most
fundamentally expressed in an immediate self-giving of God to the
Church, in Jesus Christ and through the Holy Spirit.[207] Torrance
emphasizes, "this is a real presence of Christ to us, creating a union
between himself and us, and us and himself in the Spirit—the Spirit
who comes to us from the Father through the Son and who gives us
access through the Son to the Father."[208] As noted in previous chapters,
the movement of Grace requires and implies certain ontological
conditions. Here we include just two of the most relevant examples:
the freedom of God to be transcendently present within his creation
without compromising the integrity of creaturely realities; and the fact
that Christ is both Lord over his presence and is present as Lord.

The Freedom of God and his Transcendent Presence

In chapter 3, we observed that Torrance does not view transcendence
and immanence as mutually exclusive predicates of God.[209] The
presupposition of the freedom of God plays a foundational role in his
approach to the real presence of Christ in the Eucharist. As a result,
Torrance fundamentally rejects receptacle/container notions of space,
for these lead to thinking in exclusivist terms. Thus, with regard to
the Eucharist, Christ's presence is either confined within the bread
and wine, or confined in heaven as the ascended Lord.[210] For Torrance,
discerning Christ's presence requires that we focus our attention *from*
or *through* the Eucharist to its real ground, rather than *at* the Eucharist

---

206. Ibid.
207. Ibid., 132.
208. Ibid.
209. Cf. Stamps, *Sacrament*, 44–45.
210. *STI*, 32.

itself. The form is not determinative of the reality. Thus, Torrance distinguishes the "Eucharistic form" of Christ's real presence from his "unveiled form" or his "historical form." In each case, Christ's real presence is just as real. The same one is present, but his presence is not the same. Stamps states the foundational presupposition of Torrance's position succinctly: "The real presence for Torrance is a christological reality before it is a sacramental reality."[211]

Given this priority, Torrance refuses to explain the real presence in the sacrament causally and keeps the focus on *who* is present rather than *how* Christ is present. Torrance does view the *action* of the sacrament as significant; but he has no interest in controversies over consecrating words or moments whose purpose is to designate precisely where and when the Church finds the presence of Christ in the sacrament. For Torrance, these are simply the wrong questions, for they betray an incipient dualism. He relies on no analogy other than the hypostatic union itself.[212] How Christ is present "transcends any kind of explanation which we can offer," and it is "only explicable from the side of God."[213] Based on the analogy of the hypostatic union, God in his freedom can use created intermediaries as instruments for his purposes. The fact that God deigns to use creaturely realities does not transubstantiate them into a "substitute-Christ," but simply demonstrates the lordly freedom of God through the Holy Spirit, to be present to his creatures in an immediate self-giving through Jesus Christ. Through the Spirit, Christ's presence in the sacrament is that of "a mediated immediacy."[214]

The Whole Christ is Present as Lord of His Presence

Christ's eucharistic presence is not the presence of "a naked Christ," but of "Christ clothed with his gospel . . . in the unique reality of

---

211. Stamps, *Sacrament*, 120.
212. *TiR*, 126–27.
213. Ibid., 119.
214. This phrase is originally that of John Baillie, but is quoted by J.B. Torrance in his article, "The Vicarious Humanity of Christ," *The Incarnation: Ecumenical Studies in the Nicene-Constantiopolitan Creed AD 381*, ed. T. F. Torrance (Edinburgh, Handsel, 1981), 136 (cf. Stamps, *Sacrament*, 169).

his incarnate Person."[215] This is the one who is fully divine and fully human, clothed with his gospel and with the power of his Spirit, in the fullness of his person and his work: the one who was, who is, and who is to come. Torrance writes that this *eucharistic parousia* is the real presence "of *the whole* Christ . . . crucified, risen, ascended, glorified, in his whole, living and active reality and in his identity as Gift and Giver."[216] Jesus can no more "cast aside" the clothing of his atoning life and work than he can shed his own essential nature.[217]

Two implications of the presence of the whole Christ in the midst of his Church deserve to be highlighted. **First**, because this really is the presence of Jesus Christ, it is the presence of **the Lord**: "it is a presence over which we have no kind of control, ecclesiastical, liturgical or intellectual."[218] In his personal self-giving, Christ witnesses to himself. Torrance stresses with emphasis, that "*Jesus does not need to be made real.*"[219] Therefore, the Church's *anamnesis* does not consist in the Church concentrating her mental and spiritual powers upward, in an attempt to call down Jesus's presence. Rather, the living Lord "stands behind the Church's . . . *anamnesis*, so that it is really Christ in the Eucharist who represents to the Church and makes effective for the Church His own atoning deed of sacrifice."[220] Here Torrance's doctrine of the ascension of Christ plays a key role, for "the Ascension of Christ is not in order to an absence, but in order to a presence, the real presence."[221] In this sense, "[t]he Eucharist is the sacrament which God has given to us as the counterpart of the ascension."[222] In his ascension, Christ withholds his *visible* presence, for otherwise the unveiling of his full power and glory would mean the final judgment and renewal of all things. In his mercy, he gives us time to repent and proclaim the gospel until that final unveiling. In the meantime, he comes among his Church "in the form of His Humility"; yet as the one who overcame

---

215. *TiR*, 119.
216. Ibid. Cf. *C&A2*, 142; *TiR*, 120.
217. *Consensus*, 13.
218. *TiR*, 120.
219. *Consensus*, 12.
220. *C&A2*, 179.
221. *Consensus*, 13.
222. *C&A2*, 173.

all corruption and mortality, he comes not only in the power of his crucifixion, but also in the power of His resurrection.[223] The central truth here is this: the one who has completely fulfilled and finished his salvific work "remains [an] enduring and everlasting reality, continually and really present in the Church as its Lord and Master giving it to participate in the *fulfilled efficacy* of His atoning reconciliation."[224]

Second, because this is really the presence of Jesus Christ, it is *a creative and personal presence*: it is a presence "specifically and intensely" given in the appointed sacramental act.[225] God personally acts through a eucharistic presence in which "Word and Work and Person are indissolubly one," such that "he creatively effects what he declares, and what he promises actually takes place: 'This is my body broken for you,' 'This is my blood shed for many for the remission of sins.'"[226]

Thus, while the Eucharist remains an action performed by the Church, it is foremost an action of God's in which we share derivatively and obediently by virtue of the real presence of Christ.[227] It is a movement of *Grace*; the Church's place in the divine action is one of *inclusion* by the Spirit, in and *with Christ*, in his response to the Father. The emphasis then is not on *us receiving* a presence, but on *that presence* receiving and acting upon us in our worship of God.[228] The Eucharist is thus understood as *participation* in this sense: the Spirit unites the Church's sacramental act to the vicarious act of God in Christ, such that we really do "share in the life of God"[229]—and appropriately call it, "The Sacrament of the Holy Communion."[230]

223. *Consensus*, 14.
224. *SOF*, lviii, italics added.
225. *TiR*, 120.
226. Ibid.
227. *C&A2*, 145.
228. Cf. Stamps, *Sacrament*, 158; *GT*, 10.
229. *SOF*, 145.
230. Stamps, *Sacrament*, 117. Torrance and Florovsky exchanged many letters over the issue of the intercommunion, yet neither was swayed by the arguments of the other. In a letter dated January 25, 1950, Torrance states that while he understands the theological significance and earnestness of defection from a united Eucharist, he believes that a trust in the presence and activity of God should overcome our human limitations. "If the real presence of the Lord, the Son of Man, the Eschatos, the Lamb of God, is with us in the Eucharist . . . , then I am ready to put the Lord and

The Human-Godward Movement: The Worship and Service of the Church

In the God-humanward movement, the central issue was the nature of God's self-giving in the real presence of the Eucharist. With regard to the Human-Godward movement, the focus shifts to the nature of Jesus Christ's self-offering in the eucharistic sacrifice. In chapter 2, we observed that Torrance understands Christ's entire life as a vicarious offering on our behalf. What Christ does he does *for us* in our name as both substitute and representative. Absolutely fundamental to Torrance's eucharistic theology is the union of worshippers with Christ's eternal self-offering before the Father. "In the humanity of the ascended Christ there remains for ever before the Face of God the Father the one, perfect, sufficient Offering for mankind."[231] Thus, Christ is present, presenting himself, before the Father as the Redeemer, the one who has united himself to humanity and become our brother and eternal substitute in our place (Word of God to humanity). He also represents humanity before the Father as those who are included in him and, therefore, are consecrated, or perfected, together with him; as such we join in his offering, offering ourselves and adding our voices to the chorus of praise to the Creator (Word of Humanity to God).

As we examine Torrance's concept of the human-Godward movement in the Eucharist, we will discover in contrast to eucharistic theologies which refract the inherent oneness of the offerer and the offering that Torrance grounds the offering of the Church in the incarnate Son's self-offering to the Father.

Head of the Church before Church Order, before Doctrine, before Tradition" (Matthew Baker, "The Correspondence between T. F. Torrance and Georges Florovsky (1950–1973)," in *T. F. Torrance and Eastern Orthodoxy: Theology in Reconciliation*, ed. Matthew Baker and Todd Speidell [Eugene, OR: Wipf & Stock, 2015], 298). In his 1952 paper on "Eschatology and the Eucharist," prepared for the World Conference on Faith and Order, his language is even stronger: "The Church can never manage the Eucharist or exercise any lordship over it unless it wishes to be like the kings of the Gentiles that exercise lordship and authority over them and are called benefactors" (*C&A2*, 190).
231. *STR*, 115.

The Danger of "A Pelagian Priesthood of All Believers"

Within Torrance's all-embracing framework of Grace, it is critical that the priestly offerings of the incarnate Christ not only be representational acts in our name, but also *substitutionary* acts *in our place*. However, when Jesus's human priesthood is set within a damaging dualistic context—either Nestorian or Apollinarian in type—"it becomes only a representative and no longer a vicarious priesthood."[232] If Jesus's self-offering is only demonstrative and no longer substitutionary, the uniqueness of his priesthood is abandoned, and becomes *de facto* an exemplary form of our own priesthood and our own self-offerings. In this case, we are thrown back on ourselves to be our own Pelagian priests, offering our own Pelagian sacrifices.[233]

In parallel fashion to the distortions associated with the eucharistic presence, the refraction of the offering in the God-human relation also manifests itself in an over-blown 'outward extrinsicism' and 'inward pietism.' Outwardly, the focus centers upon the value, importance and sacrificial worth of our own priestly offerings; while inwardly attention is reduced to the subjective pietistic feelings of love in ourselves as the offerers. In either case, worshippers are exhorted to make their offerings *for Christ's sake* and *motivated by him*, but not necessarily *with him* and *in him*. As a result, as our own personal Pelagian mediators, we have "no access *through him* into the immediate presence of God." In the last resort, the worshipper can have "no boldness before the throne of grace but only fear and trembling before the consuming fire of God's holiness and majesty."[234] Since these distortions were delineated in the previous section, there is no need to repeat them, but only to reinforce Torrance's understanding of the significance of Christ's continuing, eternal, high priestly and vicarious self-offering. We will come to see that here in particular Torrance's concept of Grace has its greatest practical impact upon the Church.

---

232. *TiR*, 133.
233. Ibid., 134.
234. Ibid.

Christ's High Priestly Vicarious Self-Offering

As a Reformed Protestant, a unique feature of Torrance's eucharistic theology is his understanding of the Eucharist as sacrifice. In this regard, he is not only unique but also bold, for as Stamps points out, "over half Torrance's eucharistic writings are devoted to the concept of eucharistic sacrifice for the Church."[235] Torrance insists we "must not seek to avoid the notion of Eucharistic sacrifice," for to the extent that the Church's act is a *re-actio* to Christ's *sacrificial actio* it "partakes of" a "sacrificial character."[236] It is important to recognize that Torrance does not use the language of *sacrifice* and *offering* univocally of God and the Church.[237] The difference between the two is one of kind, not merely degree.[238] As Torrance puts it, the Church's offering is "not the actual and literal offering of the sacrifice but an action proclaiming a sacrifice once offered and eternally valid before the Father."[239] That is, what the Church *offers* and *sacrifices* in the Eucharist is most properly "under the rubric of proclamation."[240] The Eucharist echoes the unique sacrifice of Christ as "the sacramental counterpart," and only in that derivative sense is it "a sacramental sacrifice."[241]

---

235. Stamps, *Sacrament*, 248.
236. *C&A2*, 178–79; cf. *Consensus*, 15; *MOC*, 100.
237. Ibid., 180.
238. Ibid., 182.
239. Ibid., 180.
240. Ibid.
241. Ibid. In a 2013 article in *First Things*, Catholic theologian Douglass Farrow argues that Barth (and those who follow in his wake, like Torrance) who subscribe to an actualist ontology falsely conflate the person and work of Christ, and this conflation hinders them from any deep appreciation of the Catholic tradition. This "theological oversteer," Farrow argues, "puts Christology into the ditch on the Eutychian side of the road." Where Farrow as a Catholic desires to ascribe to the Church some reconciling or mediating function of its own, Barth and Torrance locate the Church primarily and fundamentally as a community of witnesses, participant in what already is the case in and through and because of Jesus Christ. For Farrow, this position lacks "sacramental concreteness." "The Church," he critiques, "in its pastoral function as in its proclamation, points to the reality that is Christ, but it only points. It possesses nothing" (Douglass Farrow, *First Things*, 2013.12, "T. F. Torrance and the Latin Heresy"). Farrow concludes his appraisal of Barth and Torrance, not by rejecting them, but advocating for further wrestling with these issues so that participation in the life of Christ by the Church can have a clearer role for the Holy Spirit in the life of the new covenant community. However, strangely missing from Farrow's account is any acknowledgement of Torrance's robust conception of the formation of the New Testament Cannon through the apostles and the deposit of faith which transcends Farrow's critique. This, as well as Torrance's theology of the high priesthood of Christ, suggest that Torrance holds an important, though contextualized, place for human participation in the ongoing activity of God on this historical plane.

The Eucharistic Rhythm of Grace

The motion of Grace provides the order by which the Lord's Supper is to be understood. Torrance notes that there are *two moments* to the Church's union and communion with Christ in the Lord's Supper.[242] These two moments refer to two tangible ways in which the Church shares in the benefits of Christ through her participation in him.[243]

Feeding/Receiving and Participating/Offering

The first moment is the Church's reception of Christ's gift of himself and of all that he has done on its behalf, this "receiving is effectuated through our communion in His Body and Blood."[244] As the Church in faith and thanksgiving receives Christ by feeding on him, it communes in him and is renewed in its faith and assurance that it is incorporated into Christ's body. In confidence the Church "draws near," "takes shelter," "pleads the merits of Christ," "testifies," "holds up," and "sets forth" his all sufficient self-offering on its behalf.[245] By feeding on Christ in this way, we in the Church "live continually out of our true centre in him and not out of a centre in ourselves."[246] This kind of abiding in Christ is not introspection but the spiritual discipline of looking away from ourselves. On the basis of this confident remembrance of our Mediator and Advocate, we are called to "lift up our hearts in praise and thanksgiving for His triumphant resurrection and for His ascension."[247]

However, the Church does not simply commune (*receive* and *feed*); her communion also involves a union (a second moment) with Christ "in the whole of His obedient Self-oblation to the Father."[248] Torrance describes the first moment, which primarily has to do with the death of

---

242. Cf. ibid., 92; 170–71.
243. Torrance places the word 'moments' in inverted commas to convey that, while the emphasis may differ, both 'moments' occur simultaneously in the Eucharistic celebration and mutually assume one another.
244. *C&A2*, 147.
245. Cf. *Consensus*, 16.
246. *MOC*, 97.
247. *C&A2*, 147.
248. Ibid.

Christ, as a "memorial in thanksgiving" of his once and for all sacrifice. The second moment, which has to do with the resurrection of Christ, is one in which "we lift up our hearts in responsive obedience to his ascension and are made to sit with Christ in heavenly places."[249] In receiving, feeding and communing in Christ, the Church gives thanks for Christ's self-giving, self-impartation, and self-bestowing on the cross once and for all. This is complemented by the Church's responsive obedience, in which it participates in the whole of Christ's obedient life-prayer before the Father.

Here Torrance envisions more than a formal liturgical act. In this eucharistic memorial or sacrifice, "we present our bodies to Him as a living sacrifice, holy and acceptable unto God," "pour[ing] ourselves out in the service of others for whom Christ died."[250] In this way, "the sacrifice we call eucharistic" is not restricted to the supper itself, but opens more widely to "all the offices of charity."[251] "The Church that goes to the Lord's Table, and is renewed there in the humanity of Christ, must live and act according to His humanity in the midst of the inhumanity of the world."[252] The sacrifice is ultimately a sacrifice of love in accordance with Christ's life of love and its form and mode is prayer in accordance with Christ's prayer of obedience. As such, the prayer and communion of the Table flows outward as the Church continues to "participate in the prayer of His obedient life on earth."[253] This is how "we show forth His death and give Him thanks," and come to be called "a royal priesthood."[254]

Remembrance and Proclamation

Torrance adds depth to this two-fold eucharistic movement of the Church by invoking the apostle Paul's liturgy of *remembrance* ("do this in remembrance of me") and *proclamation* ("ye proclaim the Lord's

---

249. Ibid., 148.
250. Ibid., 149; Rom 12:2.
251. Ibid., 149.
252. *C&A1*, 100.
253. *C&A2*, 147. The significance of "obedience as prayer" will be drawn out more extensively in the following chapter.
254. Ibid., 149; quoting from Calvin *Institutes* IV, xviii, 16, 17.

death till he come").[255] In the remembrance (*anamnesis*), the Church receives/remembers the past event in such a way that "through the eternal Spirit . . . the past is made a present reality."[256] By continually setting before itself the atoning sacrifice of Christ, the Church appropriates by the power of the Spirit that once-and-for-all sacrifice. In other words, because the action of the Church is the *anamnesis* of an act that is not only once-and-for-all but also eternally enduring before the heavenly Father, "it is the living echo of that act." True, it may be only a "splintered reflection"; but it is, nonetheless, a Spirit-lifted "*Amen*, the counterpart on earth, to the eternal oblation in heaven."[257]

Similarly, Torrance observes that we find the same sacramental reflection, or *echo*, in eucharistic proclamation as in the *anamnesis*. Like the *kerygma*, the eucharistic proclamation is "sacramentally contrapuntal to the continuing work of the risen Lord."[258] Here, Torrance envisions more than an ecclesial action objectively grounded upon a past Christ-event. What he has in mind is "more than a parable"; it is "the actual *homoioma*" of the Christ-event in its "*objective duration*."[259] The analogical relation in the sacrament is not simply with regard to its Christological content, but to its action as well "it is an *active analogy*."[260] Eucharistic proclamation is essentially attestation, by way of the Church's voice, of Christ's own self-proclamation. As such, sacramental participation is "the kind by which we are conducted upward to spiritual things, and are more and more raised up to share in the life of God."[261] While the Church's proclamation is certainly not identical with *the mysterion*, neither can it be separated from it: "it is sacramentally and analogically derivative from it, but as such it is analogically different."[262] What unites the Church's eucharistic action and the ascended Lamb before the Father is the *koinonia* of the eternal Spirit, "through whom Christ offered Himself to the Father,

255. *C&A2*, 175; 1 Cor 11:25–26.
256. *C&A2*, 176.
257. Ibid.
258. Ibid., 177.
259. Ibid., 177–78.
260. Ibid., 145.
261. Ibid.
262. Ibid., 178.

and through whom we are given to participate in that oblation made on our behalf."[263] This demonstrates why the Eucharist is of such central importance to the life of the Church. In it,

> the presence of the living Lord in the Church, which is the very essence of the Church . . . is the living action appropriated by the Church in its continuous action of proclamation. In such proclamation the Church declares that its anchor is cast within the veil, that its being is grounded beyond itself in the ascended Lord, that its real life is a divine gift, and . . . opens *the door in the Church for the incoming of that ultimate reality from beyond*.[264]

Indeed, the Church's proclamation cry of "*Maranatha!*" is being fulfilled in its eucharistic act.

In both, in the Church's *anamnesis* and proclamation, "the living Lord stands behind" the Church's acts, "so that it is really Christ in the Eucharist who represents to the Church and makes effective for the Church His own atoning deed of sacrifice."[265] Thus eucharistic proclamation set as it is within the context of the presence of the living Lord and High Priest, "points to the divine action as the heart of it all."[266] "The Risen Lord Himself is the true Celebrant."[267] The Eucharist does not "make Christ present"; rather, Christ's presence gives the Church the Eucharist.[268] We may bring our best, but in the end it is God himself who provides a sacrifice for himself. His sacrifice alone bears judgment and is propitiatory, and "cannot be repeated in [the eucharistic sacrifice] in any sense."[269]

The 'new thing' that takes place in the eucharistic sacrifice is this: the Church 'answers' Christ's atoning act, which was for us and in our place, with "the acceptance of Him as the One who has taken our place, the acceptance of His Self-offering as our offering to God."[270] As an action which proclaims another action, the Church's sacrifice is its

---

263. Ibid.
264. Ibid., 179. Italics added.
265. Ibid., 180.
266. Ibid.
267. Ibid., 178.
268. *RP*, 3.
269. *C&A2*, 181.
270. Ibid., 182.

anamnesis in which the Church does not just recollect the Christ-event, but *declares* it through an action. In this sense, neither the Church's proclamation nor its *anamnesis* is merely "outwards" to the world, but "upwards to God."[271] In approaching God in this way, the Church acknowledges and proclaims the truth that there is no other oblation than that of Christ himself.[272]

The *Sursum Corda*

Since the defining center of the God-human relation is located in the exalted person and work of Jesus Christ, the liturgical *sursum corda* is the paradigmatic summons to the worshipping community. In the *sursum corda*, the Church is called to look upwards to *who* Christ is and what he is doing and to offer her "Amen" to Christ's vicarious offering on her behalf. For Torrance, the *sursum corda* resides at the very heart of the Eucharist, calling the Church to recognize its proximity and access to *the very same mystery* involved in the incarnation, virgin birth and resurrection of Christ. Here we catch a glimpse of the height of Torrance's sacramentology. He writes, "Parallel to [the virgin birth and resurrection], Baptism and the Eucharist are the miraculous signs through which the divine Word enters into the Church it has called out of the world, in Self-impartation, and yet ever remains identical with Himself."[273] While recognizing the correspondence to be "analogically related in the Holy Spirit," Torrance asserts: "in the Eucharist there takes place an actual *katabasis* of the living Lord, and an actual *anabasis* in which He bears the Church up with Him to the throne of God."[274] It is on the basis of this high sacramentology that Torrance can affirm that "in the Eucharist . . . the Church really becomes the Church."[275]

The emphasis in the Eucharist Torrance argues is not upon a static union or a substantial transformation of the created elements of the bread and wine, but upon the *action* of the sacrament. By the dramatic

271. Ibid., 180.
272. *RP*, 14; cf. *G&R*, 161.
273. *C&A2*, 189.
274. Ibid.
275. Ibid.

actions of the sacrament—taking, breaking, pouring, sharing—the minister and people outwardly and sacramentally attest to the real and current presence and activity of Christ.[276] The concern of the Church is not to be with the science of Christ's presence, but the activity of Christ's ministry. That is, the attention in the Eucharist is to be on: what is Jesus *doing*?

For Torrance, the *sursum corda* witnesses to the assertion that the Church's union with the risen and ascended Christ remains operative over the eucharistic presence; it thus opens a way for real participation, through the Holy Spirit, in the self-consecration and self-offering which Christ made—and still makes on our behalf as the ascended Lord.[277] The *sursum corda*, then, reminds the Church that the sacraments are "vital signs" of an *event* which *is* a present reality. The Christian life is a life centered not in ourselves, but in Christ (Gal 2:20). We in the Church participate in that life by looking up to him and away from ourselves. Faith is not a human achievement but an expression of the union that already exists and which was already accomplished in Christ. Even the *sursum corda* itself is not something that *we* in the Church do independently, for it too is already fulfilled in Jesus Christ. The *sursum corda* which we make is simply a participation in the *sursum corda* which Christ has already made, through the same Spirit. Through the Spirit, "Christ in his real presence with us realizes his manward and Godward acts."[278]

The way Torrance conceives of the *sursum corda* reveals just how critically realistic he is about Grace. Grace is no concept or principle in his theology. It is *the living center*, bursting forth with life-giving reality into every facet of the Church's life. The Church's existence and continuity in the world are not her own doing, but that of the ineffable God. Consequently, "the Church through its ministry can no more exercise its authority over the Eucharist than Joseph could exercise

---

276. Ibid., 185. For a description of how Torrance differs from Luther by underlining the instrumental character of the sacrament and the transcendence of Christ's presence, see Stamps, *Sacrament*, 184n200.
277. *TiR*, 128.
278. Lee, *Union*, 207.

his authority over the virgin birth." Like Joseph, the Church can only "stand aside at the miracle . . . even in the Eucharist where it is ordained to serve."[279] Like the disciples at the Last Supper who had to submit to Jesus washing their feet, the Church is trained to forswear all lordship—such is the radical and all-encompassing nature of Grace. Literally every aspect of theology must be re-thought in the light of the living water and new wine that is the person of the ascended and reigning Lord Jesus Christ, who refuses to be without his Church. Like Mary, "it belongs to the Church in the Eucharist humbly to *receive* (*Take ye, eat ye*) the eternal Word as the ground of the Church's being."[280]

Conclusion: One Sacrifice Common to Christ and to His Church

Since Christ offers himself eternally before the Father as both substitute for and representative of the Church, Torrance asserts that there is just one sacrifice common to Christ and his Church. It is not an overstatement to suggest that this assertion represents the pinnacle of Torrance's theology of Grace as it applies to the Church.[281] Here the "new and living way" opened up by Christ the "only Priest and Mediator" of the Church is set forth in Christ's vicarious and inclusive life before the Father.[282] Here, the all-encompassing framework of Grace renders the act of the Church an act in Christ's name, "which serves the act of Christ and directs us away from itself to Christ."[283] The following chapter will explore the practical outworking of this conviction, which has to do with the heart of the nature of Grace itself.

---

279. *C&A2*, 190.
280. Ibid; cf. *Consensus*, 17.
281. George Hunsinger considers this claim and its dogmatic exposition "the highpoint of Torrance's teaching" (*The Eucharist*, 155).
282. *TiR*, 107.
283. Ibid.

6

Formation through Participation: Identity and Movement

We must give an intelligent life-answer to grace in such a way that our
existence is ours only as we re-live our grace-existence in a thankful and
knowledgeable motion in answer to the Word of grace.[1]

Christian formation, while obviously a theme the Church has thought
long and hard about since its inception, has experienced a significant
revival of interest and attention in the last forty years. Yet, even with
the significant effort expended in this area, by and large the theological
foundations for Christian formation have been exceedingly thin. Into
this gap, Torrance's trinitarian approach to Grace and participation
offers an important corrective as well as a biblically and theologically
grounded framework for how Christian formation could fruitfully and
faithfully be understood and pursued. The purpose of this chapter is
to trace some of the contours of such an endeavor within Torrance's
overall scheme.

---

1. Thomas F. Torrance, *Theology in Reconstruction* (Grand Rapids: Eerdmans, 1965), 116. Hereafter,
TRn.

One of the central arguments and laments of this book is that discourse surrounding human activity too often represents an abandonment of theology proper and in particular of a trinitarian theology, which reserves a central and defining place for the continuing mediatorial role of the incarnate Jesus. In lieu of careful attention to trinitarian objective reality as revealed in Christ, discussions of Christian formation[2] are invariably reduced to an exercise in moral effort to become the persons we ought to be. What Torrance so refreshingly offers is an approach to human activity which begins, proceeds and culminates *in* and *from* the side of Christ who instills, in the words of Christopher Holmes, "the power, truth and love of himself into us and is as such the obedient answer to that power, truth and love, an answer which takes us up, rendering us correspondent to it."[3] More simply, Christian formation is not our own undertaking but a participation in a "life-relation." In the simple yet profound and radical language of the apostle Paul, Christian formation takes place *in* Christ. As such, the mediation of Christ in the pursuit of Christian formation cannot be treated as an afterthought.[4] As we noted in the previous chapter, Christ dwells in his Church through his Spirit; yet the Church also finds that its very existence is caught up in and "encircled by Christ."[5] Our purpose is to explore more specifically the contours of such an encircled life. Specifically what is the nature, character and shape of the 'graced' life and how can it be embraced, nurtured and deepened? We will also seek to answer clearly the question, "*How* does Torrance's theology of Grace offer a way of conceptualizing Christian formation as *participation*, rather than *imitation* per se?"

Since Christian formation encompasses the entirety of Christian

---

2. In this essay we will use the general language of *Christian formation* as a summary phrase for what might also be described as Spiritual formation, Christian living, Spiritual growth, etc. From Torrance's perspective, a more descriptive phrase would be *trinitarian participation in Christ*.

3. Holmes, *Ethics in the Presence of Christ* (London: T&T Clark, 2012), 13. Hereafter, *Ethics*.

4. Cf. ibid., 57.

5. Torrance was fond of quoting John McLeod Campbell's phrase that the life of the Church takes place "properly within the circle of the life of Jesus Christ." Thomas F. Torrance, *Theology in Reconciliation: Essays Towards Evangelical and Catholic Unity in East and West* (Eugene, OR: 1997), 211, 109. Hereafter, *TiR*.

existence, it necessarily bears upon the totality of the human being's being, doing and relating. Accordingly, we will approach it by examining the *identity* of those who are in Christ and then the *movement*, or activity, which corresponds to, flows from, and participates in Jesus Christ.

Identity: The Ontological Church

Torrance understands Christian existence in Christ to be an objective ontological reality. Each Christian is brought within the circle of the life of Christ to share in the Son's communion with the Father through the Spirit. Whether we recognize it or not, the reality of who we are is not the sum of our individual acts and personal virtues, but the fact that we are hid with Christ in God. "Strictly speaking," Torrance remarks, "Christianity is quite invisible."[6] Whatever the Church does is never independent of the reality of the covenant response fulfilled in Jesus Christ. Drawing on the apostle Paul's teaching in Galations 2:20, Torrance argues that:

> [the one who is] the ground of man's existence from beyond his existence has now become also the ground of his existence within his existence . . . in such a way as to establish his reality and meaning as human being and to realize his distinctive response toward God in the fullness of his creaturely freedom and integrity.[7]

Christian existence does not take place in a vacuum but is a participative reality.

Who we are is defined by whose we are; thus, as those who are in Christ, we are one body with Christ. From this relation of union, communion and participation, Torrance argues successively that there is *one body, one worship, one ministry*—in short, one *existence* "common to Christ and his Church." As a result, who we are before God and what we offer to God are inseparable from Jesus Christ.

---

6. Sermon on Colossians 3:3, unpublished sermon delivered at Beechgrove Church, Scotland (November 1948), "Thomas F. Torrance Manuscript Collection" Box 47, under "Subseries 1: Sermons 1940–1951," 6.

7. Thomas F. Torrance, *God and Rationality* (Edinburgh: T&T Clark, 1997), 144. Hereafter, *G&R.*

Since the life of the individual believer takes place within the body of Christ, everything that is true of the body is true of the individual. Accordingly, Torrance offers three fundamental identity descriptors that follow from the fact that the Church is one body with Christ: the Church is a corporate body into which individuals are incorporated; a "supernatural fellowship" of reconciliation; and outwardly oriented towards the world.

A Corporate Body Adopted into Sonship

That there is just one body common to Christ and his Church implies that **Christian identity is corporate before it is individual.**[8] The fundamental existence of the Church is "as a whole," since Christ himself is "a whole"; so the relation particular individuals have with Christ is derivative from Christ's primary relation to the whole.[9] On this basis, Torrance finds the language of 'the priesthood of all believers' problematic for it implicitly downgrades the "universal bishoprick" of Christ in whose one priesthood we are given to share.[10] To emphasize this point Torrance suggests that the Church can be understood as "a corporate Communion . . . of mutual participation through the Spirit in Christ and His graces, and a personal Communion which each may have with Christ within the corporate Communion."[11] In this way, everything that is true of the body is true of the individual in the body, by way of participation.

Incorporation into Christ by the Spirit is through adoption. Habets observes that while the themes of adoption and sonship are discussed by Torrance on a number of occasions, there is no fully developed doctrine of adoption worked out in his theology. This gap may be attributed as Habets suggests to the fact that "most of what can be said

---

8. Cf. Thomas F. Torrance, *Conflict and Agreement in the Church, vol. 2: The Ministry of the Sacraments of the Gospel* (London: Lutterworth, 1959), 151. Hereafter, *C&A2*.
9. Thomas F. Torrance, *School of Faith* (London: Camelot, 1959), cxvii. Hereafter, *SOF*.
10. Thomas F. Torrance, *Space, Time and Resurrection* (Edinburgh: T&T Clark, 1998), 118. Hereafter, *STR*; cf. Torrance, "Introduction to Calvin's Tracts and Treatises on the Reformation of the Church," in *Tracts and Treatises on the Reformation of the Church, no. 1*, by John Calvin (Grand Rapids: Eerdmans, 1958), xv. Hereafter, *Tracts and Treatises.*
11. *SOF*, cxxiv.

regarding our adoption as 'sons' has already been said in relation to the vicarious humanity of Christ."[12] Even so, it could still be argued that adoption represents the most profound metaphor correlative to Torrance's theology of Grace. Adoption by definition is an explicitly trinitarian metaphor. Adoption expresses the fact that salvation by Grace involves a double movement: *from* the Father, who loves, elects and sends the Son and Spirit; and *to* the Father, who joyfully receives human children into the family of God as sons and daughters.[13] Again as Eugenio states "adoption refers to the dynamic relationship between humanity as brothers of Christ in the fellowship of the Holy Spirit with the loving and electing Father."[14] Thus while Christ alone is the Son, believers become children of God by being incorporated into him by the Spirit (Rom 8:14, 17).

A benefit of highlighting the adoption metaphor in our understanding of Grace and Christian identity is that it is thick with ontological connotations. If the church is to inhabit a vision of her existence as a shared reality—that is, she has her being in another—then the church needs an ontological understanding of her existence which allows for that possibility and is grounded in an understanding of the person as *person-in-relation*. Construed onto-relationally, as Torrance would have it, adoption locates the believer's relation to Christ through the Spirit as an activity of *koinonia* with the triune God. Rather than a legal transaction between two individuals, the person-in-Christ is constituted by the Spirit as a new creation—or more precisely as the person-in-relation-to-the-Father-through-the-Son-in-the-Spirit. As adopted children of the Father through the Son, we live out a *koino*-existence, which the Church expresses in the sacramental acts of baptism and the Eucharist.[15] Thus, the Spirit's primary work (as the Spirit of adoption) is to remind us over and over

---

12. Habets, *Theosis*, 162. Cf. *STR*, 69–70; Thomas F. Torrance, *The Trinitarian Faith: The Evangelical Theology of the Ancient Catholic Church* (Edinburgh: T&T Clark, 1995), 264–68. Hereafter *TF*; Thomas F. Torrance, *The Mediation of Christ*, rev. ed. (Edinburgh: T&T Clark, 1992), 115–17. Hereafter, *MOC*.
13. Cf. chapter 3 of Eugenio's important thesis (*Soteriology*, 79–105) presents a well-balanced description of the three persons of the Godhead specifically in relation to soteriology.
14. Eugenio, *Soteriology*, 161.
15. Thomas F. Torrance, *Royal Priesthood* (Edinburgh: T&T Clark, 1993), 33. Hereafter, *RP*.

of the new reality which onto-relationally redefines our identity: in union with Christ and through the communion of the Spirit, we are children; and as children we cry, "Abba!" (Rom 8:14–16).

A "Supernatural Fellowship" of Reconciliation

That there is just one body common to Christ and his Church also implies that the Church reflects the reconciling ministry of Christ, by embodying *a "supernatural fellowship" of reconciliation.*[16] In the Church, the "vertical" communion of love shared between the incarnate Son and the heavenly Father is translated on the "horizontal" level through the Spirit. The Spirit sets up this vertical relation "within our social or interpersonal existence . . . as a created counterpart or reflection of the trinitarian Communion of Love within the Life of God."[17]

The communion of the Spirit "is not only the bond of unity between the three divine Persons in the one being of God but the bond of unity between God and human beings as they are baptized into the one Lord and are united with him and one another in one faith."[18] As members of the body participate through the Spirit in Christ and his graces, they also commune with one another.[19] Torrance describes this as the doctrine of the Church as the communion of saints: "In that Communion no one can live for himself alone, or believe or worship alone, for he is nothing without his brother for whom Christ died, and has no relation to Christ except in Christ's relation with all for whom He died."[20]

Having been a pastor for ten years himself, Torrance knows all too well that far too often the 'communion of saints' seems anything but that. Instead of the Church "allowing the divisions of the world to penetrate back into the life of the Church," Torrance pleads that the

---

16. *SOF,* cxviii.
17. Thomas F. Torrance, *Reality and Scientific Theology* (Eugene, OR: Wipf and Stock, 2001), 186–87. Hereafter, *R&ST;* Thomas F. Torrance, *The Trinitarian Faith: The Evangelical Theology of the Ancient Catholic Church* (Edinburgh: T&T Clark, 1995), 278 (italics mine). Hereafter, *TF; SOF,* cxviii.
18. *TF,* 292.
19. Cf. *SOF,* cxxiv.
20. Ibid.

Church "should live out in the midst of a broken and divided humanity the reconciled life of the one unbroken Body of Jesus Christ."[21] Echoing Christ's prayer for communion enacted through love, Torrance exhorts: the Church "cannot offer healing to mankind without being healed in its own body. It cannot minister reconciliation to humanity in its bitter divisions and hostilities without being reconciled in its own membership and purged of its internal bitterness and strife" (John 17:23).

Outward Oriented toward the World

Finally, that there is just one body common to Christ and his Church implies an *outward orientation of Christ's body in service and ministry to the world*. The great *telos* of the Church is in fact union with God. The most basic truth of the Church is that it belongs to Christ and exists for him. Therefore, it is a reductive distortion to suggest as some have that "the Church exists for mission." And yet, as the body of Christ, the mission "belongs to the nature of the Church."[22] The Church is what it is because it is that portion of humanity in the midst of the whole world who participate in the reconciling work of Christ. becoming itself "a fellowship of reconciliation . . . sent out into the divided world with the message of reconciliation for all men. Therefore the Church must proclaim the reconciliation by which it lives and live out the reconciliation it proclaims."[23]

The outward orientation of the Church in both its breadth and depth is fundamentally without borders. As Christ poured himself out for all people, so the communion of the Spirit is equally broad.[24] If the Church is to be properly *catholic*, it must reach out as far and wide as the Spirit's activity so that everywhere that the Spirit is active, the communion of the Spirit might be known and realized. The "irresistible compulsion" of the Spirit is to turn "outward to all for whom Christ became

21. Thomas F. Torrance, *Gospel, Church and Ministry, Thomas F. Torrance Collected Studies I*, ed. Jock Stein (Eugene, OR: Pickwick, 2012), 160. Hereafter, *GCM*.
22. Thomas F. Torrance, "The Mission of the Church," *SJT* 19 (1966): 141. Hereafter, *Mission*.
23. Ibid.
24. *SOF*, cxxiv.

incarnate and lived and died that they might be gathered into the life of God. Thus the Church cannot live to itself."[25]

When speaking of the depth of the Church's call to minister in Christ's name, Torrance's approach is particularly rich theologically. As Christ himself ministered God's mercy to humanity at the deepest point of need and misery even where humans were bitterly hostile and resentful of mercy, so Torrance asserts must the Church, if it is to reflect the fact that it is one body with him. "Jesus met the hostility of man by making it the supreme object of his compassion, by accepting it and bearing it in himself and then by making an end of it in his own death."[26] So too the Church is called to direct its witness "above all to the deepest point of man's misery in his guilty alienation from God" and as such to "witness in the face of resistance and even persecution."[27]

This rich, christologically-rooted approach perceives a direct correlation between the reconciliation of the saints, and ministry/ service to the suffering and most needy in society. With this approach, Torrance is not simply encouraging social action, nor does he advocate ministry and service as a transactional, or hierarchical form of mere giving. He is advocating the very gospel of reconciliation and therefore ministry and service that are always in the relational form of meeting and sharing. As the Church serves the poor and the outcast, Christ "clothed with his gospel" meets "Christ clothed with the need and affliction of men," and the reconciliation of Christ is manifest on earth as it is in heaven:[28]

> Christ is to be found wherever there is sickness or hunger or thirst or nakedness or imprisonment, for he has stationed himself in the concrete actualities of human life where the bounds and structures of existence break down under the onslaught of disease and want, sin and guilt, death and judgement, in order that he may serve man in re-creating his relation to God and realizing his response to the divine mercy. It is thus that Jesus Christ mediates in himself the healing reconciliation of God with man and

25. Ibid.
26. *GCM*, 153.
27. Ibid., 159.
28. Ibid., 160–61.

man with God in the form, as it were, of *a meeting of himself with himself in the depths of human need.*[29]

Unless Christ meets himself in the depths of human misery and there proclaims himself, the church cannot be recognized as his. The church that bears Christ's image and likeness most clearly will not seek to serve itself, but Christ, who clothes himself with both his gospel *and* "the misery of men." The commission to the church is "to seek and to pray for their meeting and so to be in history the bodily instrument which Christ uses in the proclamation of the divine mercy to mankind and in prompting their responses to that mercy."[30] If the disbelieving world is to be reconciled, then these divisions must be reconciled—both within the body of the saints itself and in Christ's ministry in the world, where the proclaiming Christ (clothed with the towel of service) and the miserable Christ (with dirty feet), meet and are reconciled.[31]

Movement: Christ's Inclusive Life

The Christian life, patterned after the way of the triune God manifest in Jesus, transcends the dualisms of being and action. While Christian identity is being *in Christ*, the reality of this identity is inseparable from a *movement* of life which corresponds to it and participates in it. The Christian life is an onto-relational humanizing movement as we come to live in greater fidelity to our identity as beloved adopted children of God. As we embrace this movement, the gap between our *ought* and our is progressively narrows.

As creatures, we are "strung out in time," and word and act "do not coincide in the unity and power of our person"; yet with God this is not so, for his Word and Act belong to the self-subsistence of his Person.[32] In Christ, the Word (in which word, act and person are one) entered our space and time (in which word, act and person are

29. Ibid., 150 (italics mine).
30. Ibid., 151.
31. Ibid., 160–61.
32. *G&R*, 141.

stretched out); in this overlap, the Word gathers 'within its embrace the differences between person, word and act in the creature."[33] Here we have a genuine, authentic, real man for the first time.[34] Word and act, being and action, cohere in his person and the alienation of dualism is overcome. In Jesus Christ, true integrity (integration) of our personhood takes place.

Throughout this book I have argued that for Torrance the basic motion of Grace is downward and two-fold—a movement initiated from *above* in which God meets human beings where we are and takes us to where he is. Within this framework, the basic motion of Christian formation is participation in "the mind of Christ" through love and so, sharing by the Spirit "in the life and love of the Trinity."[35] For the individual believer, the movement of Grace is one of personalization (rather than sanctification): we take on the mind of Christ through a continuous motion of faith, in which "we, through [passively] sharing in his self-offering, may [actively] offer to God through him a holiness from the side of man answering his own."[36]

The *Telos* of Formation

It is important to recognize that Christian formation is not an end in itself. Formation is not for the sake of formation. Formation into the image of Christ is very simply conformity to the law of our being. Torrance describes this law as the *telos* embedded in our "ontological substructure," which constitutes who we are as eschatological beings.[37] We were made for union and participation with God and formation into Christ's image is the manner in which we live into who we truly are.[38] Thus, to the extent that we live in congruence with the *telos* or substructure of our being—to the extent that our *doing* matches

---

33. Ibid., 142.
34. Ibid.
35. *MOC*, 66.
36. *TiR*, 117. The implication here is that what Christ accomplished objectively, we share in passively; and what he accomplished subjectively by the Spirit, we share in actively by the same Spirit.
37. *R&ST*, 115ff.
38. *MOC*, 66.

the reality of our *being* in Christ—our personal being will be sustained rather than subverted.[39]

Practically speaking, Christian formation involves the basic disciplines of prayer, worship, obedience and service. These disciplines must be recognized *not as ends, but as means toward participation*, for their basic motion is looking away from the self towards Christ, in whom true human life is found. Over time, personalized by communion in and with Christ, the Christian is freed from the self-enclosed "ring of the self" and "freed to spontaneously love in freedom."[40] This is growth: learning to love and live consciously and faithfully "within the circle of the life of Christ."[41]

Thus, Christian formation is both a personalizing reality here and now, and the beginning of our sharing in the eternal reality of communion in the life of the triune God. The purpose of the one is to enter more fully into the other. There is no higher goal or purpose for human creatures than union and communion, through Christ and his Spirit, with the life, light and love of the triune God. Torrance refers to this movement as *theosis* and suggests it is experienced as a sense of "transparency." The goal of *theosis* is to reflect God's uncreated light fully and completely, without spot or blemish, and ultimately to mirror God absolutely. This perfect image-bearing is found only in the incarnate and ascended Lord, whose transparent light "continues to bear directly, personally, intimately upon the ontological depths of our human existence, searching, judging, cleansing, healing and renewing, and remains for ever [sic] the one light-bearing and life-giving Life for all mankind."[42] As we participate in his transparent incarnate life, we share in his *theosis*, and are "transformed into the same image from glory to glory" (2 Cor 3:18).[43]

39. Cf. Flett, *Persons, Powers, and Pluralities: Toward a Trinitarian Theology of Culture* (Cambridge: James Clarke, 2012), 186. Hereafter, *Culture*.
40. *MOC*, 66. Torrance's reference to "the circle of the life of Christ" might be contrasted with his description of Cartesian philosophy which "has consciously enclosed itself within the ring of the self," *CNDDG*, 31.
41. *TiR*, 109.
42. Thomas F. Torrance, *Christian Theology and Scientific Culture* (Belfast: Christian Journals, 1980), 97. Hereafter, *CTSC*.
43. Torrance attributes the influence of Florovsky in forcing him to reconsider his position on several

The Process of Formation: Necessary, Possible, Shaped

Torrance makes it clear that formation and participation in the life of Christ are not optional: "We *must* give an intelligent life-answer to grace."[44] *Jesus's union with us* in becoming human requires a corresponding union with him, in which we offer God all of our worship [and service] in Christ. [45] God's Grace does not displace, but actually *intensifies*, the necessity of human response to God. Within the logic of Grace, *"all of grace means all of man."*[46] As a "mode of their freedom," and a "movement of their love," service "is not something that is accidental to the Christian, but essential to him, for it is rooted in his basic structure of existence as a slave of Jesus Christ."[47]

Accordingly, Torrance asserts that living into Grace requires a *continuous* motion of faith. Apart from "this motion of grace, then every step . . . can only be from alienation to alienation in the continued assertion of self-will; instead of from faith to faith, in the continued receiving of grace for grace, in which the true life of man consists."[48] There is no fence or middle ground here: we either face towards Christ, or we gaze upon idols; and "[f]reedom is only possible

theological points. Apparently, Florovsky made a similar comment with respect to Torrance. ("The Relevance of Orthodoxy," *T. F. Torrance and Eastern Orthodoxy*, ed. Matthew Baker and Todd Speidell [Eugene, OR: Wipf & Stock, 2015], 292). This is particularly the case in Torrance's view of the Greek patristic teaching on *theosis*. In his doctoral dissertation, Torrance echoed the Harnackian view: "The idea of deification was taken up even by such good theologians as Irenaeus and Athanasius. Nothing could be more characteristically Hellenistic" (*The Doctrine of Grace in the Apostolic Fathers* [Eugene, OR: Wipf and Stock, 1996], 140n3). Later, in a 1950 letter to Florovsky, Torrance again registers his rejection of *theosis*, describing it as "un-Hebraic and un-biblical" ("Correspondence between Torrance and Florovsky," *T. F. Torrance and Eastern Orthodoxy*, ed. Matthew Baker and Todd Speidell [Eugene, OR: Wipf & Stock, 2015], 296). However, by 1964, Torrance is making a plea "for a reconsideration by the Reformed Church of what the Greek Fathers called *theosis*" (*TRn*, 243). Matthew Baker points out how Torrance eventually embraced Florovsky's concept of the "Christian Hellenism" of the Fathers in which "in making use of Greek thought-forms Christianity radically transformed them" (*TF*, 68; "Correspondence between Torrance and Florovsky," *T. F. Torrance and Eastern Orthodoxy*, ed. Matthew Baker and Todd Speidell [Eugene, OR: Wipf & Stock, 2015], 294-95). Torrance writes, "I myself learned, I think, from the Orthodox more than from any other [ecclesiastical tradition]" ("The Relevance of Orthodoxy," reprinted in *T. F. Torrance and Eastern Orthodoxy*, ed. Matthew Baker and Todd Speidell [Eugene, OR: Wipf & Stock, 2015], 333).

44. *TiR*, 116 (italics mine).
45. *TRn*, 111.
46. *MOC*, xii.
47. *GCM*, 141.
48. *TRn*, 116 (italics mine).

face to face with Jesus Christ."[49] In his exposition of Calvin regarding the *imago Dei*, Torrance notes the inherent appropriateness of the reflective aspect of the *imago Dei* metaphor. We reflect the glory of God only as we are in fellowship with Christ; and we live into the *imago Dei* through a relentless "obedience of the mind toward God."[50] This does not take place in a single day. We must constantly listen to the Word in order to be formed. We must "wear the glasses of the Word all the time . . . continually transcending our judgments."[51]

Of course, a *must* without a *means* leads to despair. Unlike the law in which the *is* must conform to the *ought*, participation in Christ is based upon an obedience (an *ought*) which is grounded on an already existing reality (an *is*). As such, Christ also *"conveys in Himself the active possibility"* of the same: Jesus "carries in Himself the vicarious actuality . . . of true and faithful response on the part of all men to God's Word."[52] In other words, the nature of the objective ontological reality of our redemption in Christ *includes within it* our subjective participation. Christ is not only the ground of humanity's existence in creation; in redemption he also grounds human existence *from within humanity's existence*. [53] Torrance's language of "participation in" or "sharing in" the life of Christ refers to human faith standing on the foundation of the faithfulness of Jesus. This inclusion of our subjective participation as part of Christ's objectivity does not override or deny *our* subjective response; on the contrary, *in his objectivity, our subjectivity is recreated and reaffirmed*.[54] Only then do we rise with our humanity recreated, the *imago Dei* imprinted upon us and our mind and will filled by its proper Object.

Torrance describes the architecture of this movement of Grace and faith:

> We must say then that there is a kind of hypostatic union between Grace and faith, through the Holy Spirit, a kind of *communion quaedam*

49. Thomas F. Torrance, "Predestination in Christ," *Evangelical Quarterly* 13 (1941): 123. Hereafter, *PiC*.
50. *CDM*, 128.
51. Ibid., 174.
52. *G&R*, 138.
53. Ibid., 144.
54. *TRn*, 237.

consubstantialis! Faith has no independent existence apart from the initiative of Grace, nor is it in any sense the produce [sic] of human activity working independently of the Word. It is WE who believe, and we come to believe in a personal encounter with the living Word. Faith entails a genuine human decision, but at its heart there is a divine decision, which, as it were, catches up and makes it what it is, begotten of the Holy Ghost.[55]

Thus for Torrance while faith is most definitely a human act, it is our human act *undergirded by* (grounded in) the vicarious faithfulness of Jesus. The effect of Jesus's acting on our behalf, and in our place, is not to destroy our responses, but to *establish them.* Christ provides, in himself, a basis and foundation for all our responses. As such, inclusion *in* Christ does not necessitate competition *with* Christ.

Yet Christ is not merely the ground and means for our participation; he is also its *normative pattern.* As such, Jesus is the way, the truth and the life of our every response. That Christ has already made "the true and faithful response" implies the exclusion of all other patterns (rules, systems, programs, etc.), that might attempt to displace Christ as our ultimate pattern.[56] Participation in the pattern of Christ's life of vicarious obedience entails a downward movement of mortification in which we humbly follow the way of Christ in his death.[57] This demands radical repentance and renunciation of everything in and among us that contradicts his cross-shaped life. In the "self-emptying of faith," we "stretch out an empty hand," "placing nothing in ourselves" and laying aside all self-assertion, self-will and self-justification.[58]

Then, through an "acknowledgement of thankfulness," we are carried out beyond any capacity we have in dependence entirely upon the movement of Grace,[59] and the Spirit mysteriously "forms the ear to hear and the mind to understand" . . . "and our hearts to submit to its yoke."[60] As we yield and respond to the Spirit's movement in our lives,[61] our acts "in his name" are assimilated and identified with his

---

55. *PiC*, 130.
56. This includes an idealized vision of 'the good' or some other transcendental.
57. *G&R*, 152–53, *CDM*, 145.
58. Cf. Molnar, *Theologian of the Trinity*, 75f.
59. *TRn*, 115.
60. *Inst.* 2.2.20, 21; *Comm. On Luke* 24:45.

vicarious acts "in our name," such that we become "a form of the life of Jesus Christ."[62] Thus, the Son is made to reverberate (echo) in our hearts and lives. With the apostle Paul, we discover that "the life I live is not I alone."[63]

The Eucharistic Shape of Formation

We began this chapter by introducing the basic structure of Torrance's understanding of participation and formation in Christ. This, unsurprisingly, involves an identity determined by the downward movement of God's objective inclusion of humanity in Christ and an active participation in the movement of Grace as defined by the *imago* himself—Jesus Christ.

Now we examine in greater detail the contours of what it means for Christ and his Church to be one body in terms of offering. Here we move beyond the affirmation that "there is just one body common to Christ and his Church," to a second affirmation that "there is just one sacrifice common to Christ and to his Church."[64]

One of Torrance's preferred modes of expressing the human response to God is the eucharistic actions.[65] We will approach Torrance's concept of "just one sacrifice common to Christ and his Church" by attending to the Eucharistic form, or shape, of this offering. This enables us to develop Torrance's understanding of sanctification as personalization, nurtured and expressed in the Church's sharing in the worship and prayer of Christ by the Spirit, and thus sharing in the ongoing ministry of Christ.

61. *CDM*, 137.
62. *TiR*, 109.
63. Ibid., 111.
64. The parallelism of this phrase with Torrance's affirmation re. baptism is Hunsingers gloss, based on similar statements (*The Eucharist*, 155). Most closely, "It is his one sufficient and once for all offering of himself for us that is our only sacrifice before God," *STR*, 117; cf. *TiR*, 134, 212.
65. *G&R*, 159–61.

The Shape of Faith: Eucharistic Worship

While Torrance's descriptions of the "normative pattern" which would "make room" for Christ are not prescriptive, a certain pattern, or rhythm, does seem to emerge. As we might expect, this pattern follows the movement embodied in Christ's incarnate life, death, resurrection and ascension, and is reflected in the eucharistic actions of the Church. In fact, as the uniquely appointed and repeating anamnetic action of the Church, the Eucharist plays a paradigmatic role in the Christian life and therefore in Christian formation. As such, a eucharistic orientation enshrines, or embodies, the Godward movement of the Church as the Church in Christ.[66]

The Church's Liturgy of Life

Torrance draws a strong connection and correspondence between liturgy, life and the Eucharist. The mode of the Church's life is fundamentally characterized as worship. As Torrance reads Paul, the ministry of the Church is a "liturgy of life"—an act of "rational worship," of *logike latreia* (Rom 12:1)—which is "acted out in the life of the one body that bears about the dying of the Lord Jesus, that the life of the Lord Jesus may be made manifest in our mortal flesh."[67] Consequently, Church proclamation (Word) and service (witness to the Word) are understood *within* the rhythm of the Eucharist; that is, as an enacted "liturgy of the Lord's Supper."

Torrance regards the liturgical *actions* of the Church in the Eucharist as the paradigmatic enactment of the Church's union and communion with Christ. Yet the Eucharist is more than enactment; it is also *an active analogy* which reflects a *real* communion.[68] The One who is the "ultimate reality from beyond" comes and acts *as the Church acts.*[69] The Church's acts of taking and blessing, of breaking and giving, the bread

---

66. *TiR*, 118.
67. *RP*, 10; cf. *Atonement*, 97.
68. Cf. *C&A2*, 177f, 145; *TiR*, 111; Torrance, *Conflict and Agreement in the Church*, vol. 1 (London: Lutterworth, 1960), 291. Hereafter, *C&A1*.
69. *GCM*, 107.

and cup, are participative acts of *koinonia*. The movements of this "holy analogue" parallel the very movements of the incarnate Son's self-offering: he *takes up* our fallen humanity in a condescending act of self-giving; he *blesses* and transforms our humanity, assimilating us in mind and will to himself through his sanctified and consecrated life, lived in grateful communion with the Father; he *breaks* the wayward drift of our fallen humanity, condemning sin in the flesh in and through his long and faithful obedience, which culminated in his self-offering on the cross; and, once he is lifted up to the closest union with the Father, *he gives* this New Humanity to his Church that she might share in the Son's communion with the Father through the Spirit.

These basic eucharistic actions, which reflect so comprehensively the movement of God's self-giving in Christ also express the shape of the whole life of the Church in her living liturgy of worship, prayer, ministry and service. The Eucharist then is a reflection of the Church's holistic participation with, in and through Christ. Through the indwelling communion of the Spirit, all the Church's actions are made to echo Christ's. In this Eucharist shaped "liturgy of life,"

> When the Church worships, praises and adores . . . it is Christ himself who worships, praises and adores the Father in and through his members, *taking up, moulding and sanctifying* the prayers of his people as they are united to him through communion in his body and blood. . . . And when the Church at the Eucharist intercedes in his name for all mankind, it is Christ himself who intercedes in them, doing in them what he has done for all mankind in his own Person. Thus the eucharistic intercession is not so much what we do, or even do by the aid of God's grace, for the Spirit of Christ who dwells in us intercedes in us, making the heavenly intercessions of Christ inaudibly to echo in our intercessions on earth.[70]

Thus, the sacraments truly represent the *outward form* ("the pledges of God's faithfulness in Christ, the signs and seals of His fulfilled promise") of the new covenant—a covenant that has its *inward form* in the "*koinonia* of the Spirit through which the Church is given to share in the Love and Life of the Trinity."[71] The sacramental act not

---

70. *TiR*, 134 (italics mine). Torrance's 4-actions echo Gregory Dix's, *The Shape of the Liturgy* (Westminster London: Dacre, 1945), 103ff.

only complements the historical act of Christ; it is a real sharing in the eschatological reality of Christ's present self-offering (self-consecration, self-presentation) on our behalf to the Father. It is an act of the Church that takes place as Torrance says at the intersection of heaven and earth as a *real* act of union and communion. As a response within the response which Christ has already made "toward the love of the Father" for us, it is *genuine fellowship* within the "reality of the new time of the new creation," and not merely an imitation or symbol of fellowship.[72] Furthermore, because the offering of worship by the Son to the Father is perpetual, believers are invited to shift their focus from a myopic fixation on the perfect tense of salvation's surety, to salvation's enduring validity and perfection.

We are now in a position to draw together several strands of Torrance's thought on the Christ-Church relation. Taken together, these give a fuller picture of the tapestry that informs his view of the Church's proclamation and service. The Church's priestly act of proclamation is a movement of Christ "clothed with his gospel," in which the living Word stands behind the Church's words, so that the act of proclamation is—paradoxically—primarily in the mode of reception and communion. Similarly, the Church's priestly act of service is a movement of "Christ clothed with the need and affliction of men," in which the sacrifice, service and ministry of the Church are primarily in the mode of thanksgiving and worship.[73] Eucharistically conceived, the "word, deed, and life" of the Church are irreducibly participatory in nature—a eucharistic feeding on, and proclamation of, the living Word, and a eucharistic service joined to the ultimate offering of the Son to the Father in the Spirit.

The Church's calling is to follow and serve Christ's ministry of healing reconciliation, as both the proclaiming Christ and the misery-

---

71. *C&A1*, 26.
72. *GCM*, 107; cf. Robert J. Stamps, *The Sacrament of the Word Made Flesh* (Edinburgh: Rutherford House, 2007), 129.
73. Ibid., 160–61.

laden Christ, in a kind of "meeting of himself with himself."[74] Torrance writes,

> The Word must be done into the flesh, the priestly liturgy must be enacted in life and obedience. . . . The pattern of [Christian] liturgy and priesthood derives from the Suffering Servant and is to be enacted in the Body. That is our rational worship.[75]

Christ clothed with his gospel meets Christ clothed in the misery of humanity. This is the irreducible form of Christ's body wherever and whenever it is found: in its historical form in the incarnate Son; in its exalted form at the right hand of the Father; and in Christ's Church as it bears his image and conforms to the pattern of his life on earth as it is in heaven.

Christ's Priestly Mediation of the Offered Life of the Church

Torrance's consistent application of the vicarious humanity of Christ results in radical implications for the life of the church. Paul Molnar describes this aspect of Torrance's theology as a "massive" achievement: "By focusing on '*God as Man rather than upon God in Man*,' Torrance embraces a high Christology which concentrates on the *humanity* of the incarnate Son of God and a view of eucharistic worship and life in which 'the primacy is given to the priestly mediation of Jesus Christ himself.'"[76] What Molnar observes is of central importance to Torrance's theological framework and thus to his conception of Grace itself. As the ascended new human, our priest and mediator, Jesus Christ himself is *eternally* our prayer before the face of the Father. "He lived in our human nature in such a way . . . that his whole life formed itself into worship, prayer and praise which he offered to the Father on our behalf."[77] Now, as "High Priest of our souls," he has "ascended to the Father to be the Leitourgos of the heavenly Sanctuary and the

---

74. Ibid., 150.
75. *RP*, 22.
76. Molnar, *Theologian of the Trinity*, 321; quoting *TiR*, 135.
77. *TRn*, 211.

Mediator of our worship in mind and soul and body in union with him."[78] Jesus Christ is no partial mediator, but one who

> acts with us and for us and on our behalf towards the Father in all our distinctive human experiences as children of God, such as confession, penitence, sorrow, chastisement, submission to the divine judgment, and faith, obedience, love, prayer, praise, adoration, that we may share with him what he is in his ascension and self-presentation before the Father as the beloved Son in whom he is well pleased.[79]

It is only as "we are made partakers of his worship" that we genuinely worship God in Spirit and in truth.[80] Practically speaking, this means the Church comes to God in worship and prayer, *in the name of Jesus*—empty-handed except for the body and blood of Christ, his life and death offered for us and in our name.[81] The fundamental motion of the Church is acquiescence before the complete and inclusive substitutionary act of Christ. As Stamps says, "the voice of the Church's act is changed from active to passive"[82] as she concedes primary action to Christ's offering.[83] The Church's basic sacrifice is the sacrificing of her privilege to make her own sacrifice. Thus the Church prays but it prays only "in his name," on the basis of the prayer which Christ makes before God "in our name."[84] Everything the Church does, she does "within the circle of the life of Christ."[85] Within this 'ring,' the Church's acts are *sanctified by, assimilated into* and *identified with* Christ's acts towards the Father, such that the Church's acts become "a form of the life of Jesus Christ ascending to the Father."[86] This is what Torrance means by "Eucharistic worship."[87] By the Spirit whom

---

78. *TiR*, 114. Torrance bemoans the loss of emphasis upon Christ's high priesthood within the liturgical life of the Church (ibid., 115f) This tendency towards "liturgical monophysicism." in which Christ's mediatorship was assimilated to his Lordship is historically chronicled in Josef Andreas Jungmann's study, *The Place of Christ in Liturgical Prayer* (London: Chapman, 1965).
79. Ibid., 134.
80. Ibid., 139. Cf. *STR*, 116; *TiR*, 109, 130, 134, 211, 175ff.
81. Ibid., 212. Cf. *TRn*, 115.
82. Stamps, *Sacrament*, 233.
83. Ibid.; cf. *C&A2*, 250; *TRn*, 212.
84. *MOC*, 97. Cf. Thomas F. Torrance, "The Church in the New Era of Scientific and Cosmological Change," in *Theological Foundations for Ministry*, ed. Ray Anderson (Edinburgh: T&T Clark, 2000), 773. Hereafter, *New Era*.
85. *TiR*, 109, quoting Campbell.
86. Ibid.

Christ imparts to us, the "Abba, Father" of Christ is echoed in us.[88] As Torrance himself asserts, this is undoubtedly a "profounder doctrine" of the Church's life or worship than most ecclesiologies might attempt. Thus, Torrance writes,

> It is in fact the eternal life of the incarnate Son in us that ascends to the Father in our worship and prayer through, with and in him, in the unity of the Holy Spirit. While they are our worship and prayer, in as much as we freely and fully participate in the Sonship of Christ and in the whole course of his filial obedience to the Father, they are derived from and rooted in a source beyond themselves, in the economic condescension and ascension of the Son of God. The movement of worship and prayer . . . is essentially correlative to the movement of the divine love and grace, from the Father, through the Son and in the Spirit.[89]

Note the explicit link Torrance draws between: the Spirit of the Son in the Church; the worshipping life of the incarnate Son; and the movement of the love and Grace of the triune God. The worshipping life of the Church, which encompasses her whole life of faith, obedience and service, is participation in the Godward movement of the incarnate Son. As such, the Church cannot ignore that her starting point is always Christ, her high priest and mediator. To do so is essentially to opt out of her entire onto-relational reality as one body with Christ. To approach God other than in, through and with the humanity of Christ is to venture into the groundless realm of self-justification and idolatrous projection.

Again, we are reminded of Molnar's remark regarding the massive primacy Torrance ascribes to the priestly mediation of Jesus Christ in the Christian life. As the ascended, vicarious, new humanity, Jesus Christ is, the "Mediator of our salvation in mind as well as body, Advocate who represents us continually before the Father," and the "High Priest who prays in our place and on our behalf."[90]

---

87. Ibid.
88. Ibid., 114.
89. Ibid., 212.
90. *New Era*, 773.

The Sanctification Process:
Personalization in and through *Koinonia*

We began this chapter by re-stating Torrance's assertion that "there is just one sacrifice common to Christ and his Church." Now, having traced the relationship between the actions of the Eucharist, the incarnate life of Jesus and the living liturgy of the Church, we proceed to examine Torrance's understanding of sanctification as *personalization*. This will prepare us for the final section, which will focus on how personalization comes to expression in the Church as godliness, which is the fruit of sharing in the Son's relation with the Father through the Spirit.

Eric Flett, in his doctoral thesis on Torrance's understanding of culture, observes that "the terms personalization, humanization, and sanctification are nearly synonymous" in Torrance's usage.[91] In contrast to the moralistic way sanctification is often understood, Torrance's dynamic and christological starting point leads him to take account of Christ's humanity as well as his divinity. While it is true that Jesus's hypostasis is that of the divine Son, Torrance argues that ontological reality is not metaphysically static, but is dependent upon its actualized enhypostatic fulfillment. In other words, sanctification as Torrance conceives of it involves Christ's consistent dedication in fulfillment of the divine vocation. In short, sanctification is relational fidelity. This perspective reorients sanctification, shifting it from a merely moral category to an onto-relational one. The sanctified person is not free from moral struggle but the one who faithfully faces God.[92]

Returning again to Flett's insightful study, we examine the logic behind this understanding of sanctification as 'continuous facing' or *personalization*. Flett presents a four-point description of how human

---

91. Flett, *Culture*, 40. Flett notes that Torrance tends to speak of the "work of the Spirit as 'sanctification' when referring to the created order in general, and as 'humanization' or 'personalization' when speaking of human creatures in particular" (44).

92. Thomas F. Torrance, *Incarnation: The Person and Life of Christ*, ed. Robert T. Walker (Nottingham: Intervarsity, 2008), 187. Hereafter, *Incarnation*. Cf. chapter 4, "The *imago Dei* and the 'proleptic self'."

formation takes place from an onto-relational anthropological standpoint. To summarize: (1) human development continually progresses along a path which moves from a particular orientation/ positioning, which we actively (or passively) serve; (2) to a becoming/ forming in line with that orientation; (3) to a constructing of our outer environment accordingly; (4) to effects that are increasingly humanizing or de-humanizing.[93]

This approach to Christian formation is thoroughly grounded in personal and relational categories. As we turn and face and trust Christ, "personal forms of reflection are begotten in us as we are obedient to Him."[94] In other words, sanctification is an onto-relational process, in which the "personalizing Spirit" makes us "personalized persons," by drawing us into genuine relations with the triune God and everything he has created.[95] Torrance concludes: "Far from crushing our creaturely nature or damaging our personal existence, the indwelling presence of God through Jesus Christ and in the Holy Spirit has the effect of healing and restoring and deepening human personal being."[96]

Torrance emphasizes that we are summoned to give "an intelligent life-answer to grace" by a "re-living of our grace-existence."[97] This too is the language of participation; and it is important to recognize that for Torrance there is no other appropriate way to speak of human obedience or sanctification than from within this framework ("the all-embracing framework of grace"). Just as for Torrance "there is just one sacrifice common to Christ and his Church,"[98] the same is true with regard to sanctification. There is no Christian form of sanctification that is not also in Christ and therefore participatory. Where Barth would turn to the category of *vocation*, Torrance plunges deeper into the mystery of *participation*. He is reticent even to speak of human

---

93. *TS*, 207.
94. Ibid.
95. Thomas F. Torrance, *The Christian Doctrine of God: One Being Three Persons* (Edinburgh: T&T Clark, 1996), 160. Hereafter, *CDG*; *G&R*, 188.
96. *TF*, 230.
97. *TRn*, 116.
98. Hunsinger, *The Eucharist*, 155.

activity in terms which could be construed as autonomous; and, while vocation certainly maintains the divine initiative, it does not adequately ground the human response in the vicarious ascended humanity of Christ—as a *koinonia* in the Son's *koinonia* with the Father in the Spirit.

In sum, human sanctification is the personalizing result of living in fidelity to the movement of participative Grace over time. Human existence is relational through and through; sanctification therefore takes place as we share in the *koinonia* of the Son with the Father through the Spirit. Accordingly, we will now reflect on its dynamics within the apposite structure of the love of God, the Grace of Jesus Christ and the fellowship of the Holy Spirit. By this three-fold way, the life of Christ echoes in our hearts, while our voices are added to the mighty angelic chorus of antiphonal praise, just on the other side of the veil.[99]

Personalized by the Love of God

Christian sanctification takes place by the love of God. For Torrance, the triune life and love of God is the most objective reality that exists. Accordingly, the gracious movement of this life "from the Father, through the Son, in the Spirit" is the "healing source of all true objectivity."[100] Consequently, human transformation takes place through an encounter with the sheer objectivity of the Divine Subject—through whom, and in whom, all creaturely subjecthood derives.

For Torrance, knowledge requires love of the truth—i.e., loving an object in accordance with its nature. Thus, "we cannot know God without love,"[101] nor can we know ourselves without love. True and proper love is taught and learned (1 John 1:9). The logic of this is straightforward: in being loved, we learn to love; that is, we learn to see and treat ourselves and others in accordance with their nature.[102]

99. *TiR*, 212.
100. *TRn*, 233.
101. *MOC*, 25–26.
102. *TRn*, 232.

Love begets love; therefore Grace—whose content is simply love in action—begets love. Christian love is simply the reciprocal echo of God's love. Knowing and experiencing the love of God is an incredibly personifying and humanizing experience, for the love of God establishes the human creature and sets him "on his feet" as a genuinely "free and spontaneous subject."[103] This love is the center of Christian sanctification. As Augustine observed: "the beginning of love is the beginning of righteousness; progress in love is progress in righteousness; great love is great righteousness; perfect love is perfect righteousness."[104]

Within this context, it becomes clear that holiness *per se* is not the heart, sum, or goal of sanctification but a means to sanctification. The goal and end of holiness is *love* and love comes only in and through personal encounter.[105] Recognizing this, Tom Noble describes Torrance's overall theology as "a theology of love."[106] The negative aspects, such as purification from sin, are purely for the sake of receiving the positive—the love of God. Grace has its eternal source and ground in love and its ultimate fulfillment is also realized in love. From this standpoint, as Noble helpfully points out, sanctification is impossible for the detached observer: we must commit ourselves to the truth, through love, in order to know it; and we must know it through love in order to become it.

Personalized by the Grace of Jesus Christ

Christian sanctification takes place through the Grace of Jesus Christ. The Grace of God is not a principle or a force, but a personal, dynamic, *divine* presence. Through the Spirit, the love of God in Christ confronts each individual person 'face to face' with Grace, and in doing so calls for an ultimate decision.[107]

---

103. *G&R*, 188, 189.
104. *On Nature and Grace*, 84, 70.
105. *TRn*, 233.
106. Tom Noble, Didsbury Lectures, "Christian Holiness and the Holy Trinity" (Nazarene Theological College, Manchester, 2012).
107. Thomas F. Torrance, "Universalism or Election," *SJT* 2.3 (1949): 315. Hereafter, *UE*.

Torrance identifies the locus of this meeting with the mind, the crucible for the conflict of ultimate decision. Human subjects, in their autonomous subjectivity, invariably drift either towards the impersonal or towards false objectivities. In the former, we reduce ourselves and those in our sphere (including God) to causal and mechanical forces. In the latter, we objectify our own subjective states and conditions, giving them absolute authority.[108] In either case, we shut ourselves off from subject-to-subject relations and this incapacity is the root of human alienation.

Since the mind is the source of the problem, it is also the locus of the solution.[109] It is this hostile and alienated mind that God laid hold of in Jesus Christ and inverted. In this vein, Torrance echoes Cyril of Alexandria and John McLeod Campbell, liberally employing the phrase *the mind of Christ* to refer to the sanctified union and communion Christ enjoys with the Father.[110] If we are to be formed into the image of Christ, we must take the "way of Christ"s humanity," in which Christ had to "work out his salvation with fear and trembling (blood and tears)."[111] The same "basic soteriological inversion," which Christ wrought by entering our perverted order and re-ordering it, "must be pushed through the whole region of the mind" until we are reschematized and inverted in "the whole of our mental system."[112] As we face Christ, taking up and sharing in his relation with the Father and learning from him—our mind along with the heart and will like Christ's—is oriented toward the Father step by step.[113] Practically, this involves offering ourselves daily to God by continual, repentant re-thinking, and unceasing prayer. Through study of Scripture, meditation and prayer, we tune in to the mind of God incarnate in Jesus

---

108. Unsurprisingly, this diagnosis parallels the sacramental dualism which Torrance identifies in both Romanism and memorialism. See chapter 5, "The God-humanward movement: the 'feeding' of the Church."
109. See chapter 4, "The ontological space of human agency."
110. *TRn*, 212.
111. Ibid., 115–16.
112. Ibid., *Comm. On Col* 1.21; *Inst.* II.15.9.
113. Matt 11:28. While Torrance also uses the term *heart* parallel to *mind*, his preferred metaphor for the seat of human hostility or fidelity towards our Creator is the mind. Cf. *MOC*, 39; *Atonement*, 438.

Christ. In doing so, we experience the fruit of our union with Christ: minds that are healed, renewed and sanctified in him.[114]

Personalized by the Fellowship of the Holy Spirit

Christian sanctification takes place in the fellowship of the Holy Spirit. Those who have been encountered by the love of God and confronted by the Grace of Jesus Christ are given to live their lives according to a new way—the way of communion. In chapter 3, we argued that the Spirit is continuously active in the incarnate Son, preserving his full and faithful humanity. Likewise, we too require the continuous activity of the Spirit in order to actualize our full and proper humanity.

In the New Testament, Jesus's life of faithfulness and obedience is described less as the display of a Herculean feat of will power and more as communion—the manifestation of his Spirit-led love for the Father worked out in every aspect of his life. From this standpoint, obedience is the flower of communion, not its root. The nature and posture of this communion-driven relationship are given expression in the biblical language which contrasts slaves and hirelings to sons and friends. The difference between these two human orientations is the Spirit, sent from the Son into our hearts. The Spirit who preserved the humanity of Christ is given to us in such a way that our humanity is also preserved and enhanced, as we participate in Christ. In contrast to the mind centered in ourselves and governed by our own autonomous reason in isolation from God, the Spirit teaches us the mind of Christ through which we learn to think, worship and serve in a God-centered way. That is, through his Spirit, we are now able to have *koinonia* with Christ in which we truly "share with him his mind"[115] (Col 1:19–22; Phil 2:5, Rom 12:1–2), drawing near to the Father with no other oblation, prayer, faith or love and no other response other than that of Christ himself. This reality locates human agency firmly within the category of participation. That which we offer to the Father through the Son is a form of the life of Christ in us.[116] Through the Spirit, we live not so

---

114. See "The Reconciliation of Mind," in *Atonement*, 437–47.
115. *TiR*, 113.

much *to* God, as *in* and *with* God. We live out of identities constituted by communion, for there is no true following of Christ that is not also fellowship with him. This is the life of faith.

Torrance's solution to alienated minds is the gracious intervention of the personalizing Spirit. The picture Torrance paints of this fellowship or communion is one in which the inner circle of the self is not only broken into from without, but is also emancipated and recreated from within; our sheer existence is undergirded by the substitutionary, vicarious movement of God in Christ. [117]

This is a movement Torrance also describes as *theosis*.[118] By coming into us, the Spirit opens us up for a "corresponding act" which entails the renunciation of ourselves, "that the divine love may have its way with [us] in a self-less objectivity."[119] Torrance offers a concrete and penetrating description of this self-renunciation. It is:

> a relentless objectivity in which you do not love your neighbour because love is a form of your self-fulfilment, in which you do not think out of your own self-centeredness but out of a centre in the incarnate Word who summons you to leave all and follow Him, and in which you do not pray or worship God in your own name or in your own significance but only in the name and significance of Jesus Christ . . . in which you do not feed upon yourself but feed only upon the Body and Blood of the Lord.[120]

To summarize Torrance in plainer language: we only become ourselves in him and the only way to be 'in him' is to be 'out of ourselves.' But we cannot get out of ourselves by ourselves; so God the Spirit comes into us to open us out for God,[121] so that we might "find our life *not in* ourselves but *out of* ourselves, *objectively in him*."[122] God himself is the one who "creatively brings about within us . . . faith, hope and love," by opening us to acceptance of his self-impartation to us.[123]

---

116. *TRn*, 111; Gal 2:20.
117. Humanity's "reception of the Holy Spirit is itself a creative work of God" (ibid., 243).
118. Ibid., 244.
119. Ibid., 238.
120. *G&R*, 70.
121. *TRn*, 238.
122. Ibid.
123. Thomas F. Torrance, *Trinitarian Perspectives: Toward Doctrinal Agreement* (Edinburgh: T&T Clark, 1994), 99. Hereafter, *TP*.

Thus, while faith is not a human work, it does involve our creaturely "Amen!" Faith is the obedience of reason to the nature and reality of God. Accordingly, the decision of faith is more properly construed in the mode of *acceptance* and *obedience* than in the mode of *achievement*. In faith we feed on what God has given, rather than strive for what we do not have. Thus, a non-believer or a believer who doesn't live in the communion-generated qualities of faith, hope and love is denying and resisting reality. This constitutes rejection of their humanity by going against its grain and refusal of its benefits and its true end in a right relationship with God. In this sense, sin is sin against one's own self, and God opposes us when we are opposed to ourselves. What is required is *metanoia* (repentance), in which we allow the Spirit to train us away from sin's prison of guilt, fear and anxiety, and into the humanizing and personalizing qualities of faith—hope and love.

Summary

Thus far in our treatment of *the movement of Grace*, we have expounded Torrance's argument that sanctification as an on-going process is an experience of personalization in and through communion. This personalizing process is also eucharistic in form, for it participates in the life of Jesus, whose pattern of life is expressed in the liturgical rhythm enacted in the Eucharist. In this movement, the downward two-fold motion of Grace, together with its humanward and Godward aspects, is manifest. Within this context we have also noted that the life of the Church is irreducibly participatory in nature, so that its "rational worship"—its living liturgy of prayer, worship, ministry and service—is understood as a response within a response.

As high priest, advocate and mediator, Christ represents and substitutes for us in all aspects of human experience as children of God. The Church responds with thankful praise and lives into her new humanity by participating in his filial obedience. Through the communion of the Spirit, who dwells in the Church, the Church's actions are made to echo Christ's. Grace begets Grace, as the motion of Grace from God draws us into the circle of his abundant life and love.

Christian sanctification takes place by the love of God, through the Grace of Jesus Christ, in the fellowship of the Holy Spirit. Encountering the reality of the Father's perfect love recreates us with the capacity to love God for his own sake, and our neighbors for theirs. Sanctification—and thus holiness—begins and ends in love. The presence of Jesus Christ, the eloquent, ascended, vicarious embodiment of God's Grace, confronts our *incurvatus* alienated minds and frees us to share in the filial obedience of the mind of Christ. The *koinonia* of the Spirit continually teaches us to live in communion with God and in God, such that our obedience is an ongoing "Amen, yes!" to God, expressed through God-centered faith, hope and love.

This trinitarian-framed description of sanctification as a personalizing encounter has *not* been an exposition of what is in effect three different activities, or steps in a process of sanctification. Rather, it is the one true God who in his triune coactivity frees us from our self-enclosed selves to become our true selves as his children—children who live in his presence and thus out of a center in Christ, with him, for the sake of others.

Eucharistic (Sacramental) Living

Our final task in this chapter of this book is to focus on how personalization is nurtured and expressed in the Church: sharing as it does in the worship and prayer of Christ and thus in the ongoing ministry of Christ.

Included in the Son's fellowship with the Father through the Spirit, the Christian is called to participation in that fellowship and in the sacrificial life, which flows from it. Participation defined as such is not something Christians 'make real'; it is something to which we are faithful. Fidelity or faithfulness is to submit to and participate in the Eucharistic movement of the divine *koinonia*. Our welcome and embrace of this movement in the Spirit opens up human existence to a way of being that bears a eucharistic shape. As Torrance repeatedly emphasizes, the activity of the Church "in worship, ministry, and life . . . is essentially eucharistic."[124]

Eucharistic or "sacramental living,"[125] as we are calling it, is essentially a way of describing Torrance's understanding of the Christian life as a sacramental participation in the way of Grace through love. To live sacramentally, is to be a sign that reflects and echoes the active presence through the Spirit of the ascended Jesus. It is to live consciously aware that one participates in the objective reality of Christ's vicarious life of faith, prayer, worship, thanksgiving and self-offering to the Father.[126] The Christian life, construed as such, "is *sursum corda* through the Son in the Spirit to the Father."[127]

Objective Spiritual Participation versus Subjective Moral Formation

Torrance achieves this trinitarian vision by combining a profound commitment to and integration of two dynamics: the *objectivity* of critical realism, and the *koinonia* of personal relations and indwelling. The result is Christian formation that is grounded in and determined by an objective reality, while also being personal and dynamic. Within Torrance's framework, Christian virtues such as obedience, faithfulness and holiness are understood as irreducibly communal, or 'koinonial,' realities: for the life of Christ draws a circle around our life, including our response of faith inside his "ring of faithfulness."[128] "Christ's faithfulness undergirds our feeble and faltering faith and enfolds it in His own."[129] Encircled by the life of Christ, our faith and obedience are a manifestation of our participation in the faithful response of Christ. Through the Spirit, the risen Lord is present as both substitute and representative, drawing his people "into the sphere of [his] effective operation"; and in this way Jesus is "the creative ground and normative pattern for the actualization of every response to God on our part."[130] This approach views Christian formation as essentially

---

124. *RP*, 17.
125. The phrase *sacramental living* is not Torrance's term, but it evokes the sense of what Torrance advocates.
126. *TiR*, 109, 209.
127. Lee, *Union*, 206n38. Cf. *TRn*, 251.
128. *TiR*, 109.
129. *G&R*, 154.

participatory knowing and personal indwelling in which knowledge inspires loving and loving reveals knowledge. It is a form of *theosis*, of becoming like God by dwelling in God and its most fundamental motion is worship and prayer.

While *theosis* is intensely personal, this does not compromise its objectivity. In fact, its very personalness is what grounds *theosis* in reality. *Theosis* by definition is ontologically-grounded in the particularity of the triune God, whose Personal Being is the objective ground of all personal being. It is the basis in reality which makes the *sursum corda* more than a mere psychological act, and turns it into a transformative encounter. As Torrance says,

> . . . through the Spirit God is able to take possession of his creatures and to be present to them in such a way that they are lifted up to the level of participation in God where they are opened out for union and communion with God far beyond the limits of their creaturely existence—which is another way of describing *theosis*. To *be* in the Spirit is to *be* in God, for the Spirit is not external but internal to the Godhead.[131]

Critical realism combined with personal indwelling makes Torrance's framework for Christian formation more than mysticism; yet also much more than a tidy theological construct which works well on paper but has no on-the-ground practical import. Life in Christ is utterly comprehensive and concrete and encompasses and transforms all things.[132]

Given this trinitarian and soteriological foundation, what Torrance offers in terms of Christian formation is most properly termed **'Objective Trinitarian Participation.'** It is *objective* because the primary agent is the living, ascended Christ. It is *Trinitarian* because its activity has its origin and continuation in and through the Holy Spirit sent by the Father with the Son. It is *participation* because we are included: through our engagement in specific practices, habits and

---

130. Ibid., 153.
131. Ibid., 238–39. Italics original.
132. The far-reaching breadth of Torrance's concern is demonstrated by the areas he specifically addresses: natural goodness, natural knowledge, church tradition, order and polity, pastoral ministry, service and worship. *TRn*, 166.

attitudes, the Holy Spirit continually leads us, through Christ, to the Father in every area of life. Throughout, the focus and concern of Christian formation is that the Father-Son relation be translated into the daily life of the children of God through the Spirit.[133]

The critical realism of Torrance's theology of Grace radically critiques the common version of Christian formation we encounter today—what we might more accurately call **'Subjective Moral Formation.'** This version of Christian formation is *subjective* because the primary agent is ourselves, rather than the ascended Christ. It is *moral* because its goal is development in virtue and other socially idealistic behaviors. It is *formation* because it assumes that we can train ourselves—through specific practices, habits and attitudes—toward the achievement of predetermined behaviors and qualities which imitate Jesus.[134]

The contrast between these two approaches could not be more far-reaching. Torrance's commitment to critical realism insists that the risen Christ—who lives forever before the Father, as well as among us through his Spirit—must always be at the center.[135] Through our participation in this man, we learn to see, think and act in truly and properly human ways.

133. *A&MO*, 254.
134. See figure 1.
135. Cf. Molnar, *Theologian of the Trinity*, 170.

Objective Trinitarian Participation vs.
Subjective Moral Formation

Objective Trinitarian Participation

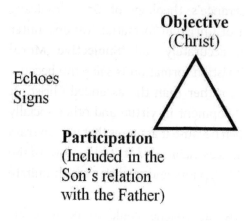

Objective
(Christ)

Echoes
Signs

Participation
Sharing

Participation
(Included in the
Son's relation
with the Father)

Trinitarian
(through the Holy Spirit,
sent by the Father with
the Son)

Subject Moral Formation

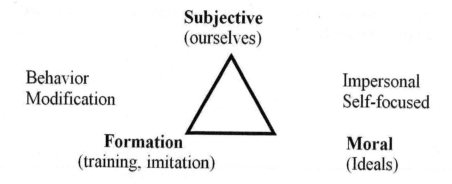

Subjective
(ourselves)

Behavior
Modification

Impersonal
Self-focused

Formation
(training, imitation)

Moral
(Ideals)

The Insidious Drift Toward Self-Justification

Given our propensity toward non-relational, self-justifying approaches
to Christian living, Torrance is deeply concerned about how Christian
action is understood. In particular, he worried that preoccupation

with the human subject would devolve into a psychological or sociological abyss, obscuring and swallowing up the objectivity of the living, reigning Lord.[136] Christ is the new humanity, and this new humanity commands the displacing, denying and de-centering of our alienating attempts to be our own priests before God. The ascended and advent Lord is a perpetually present reality and cannot be relegated to the past. Thus to *begin* with Christ is not enough; we must *stay* with Christ and seek to be present to Christ who is continually present to us.[137] At *no point* in the Christian life is Christ not central—beginning, middle, or end. Faith, when understood within an onto-relational framework, is not faith in faith, but faith *in Christ*. Yet faith usurps the central place of Christ anytime self-justification and self-reliance seep in. [138] Consequently, any activity that does not arise from faith in Christ "is self-willed and indeed it represents a form of self-justification." [139]

For all these reasons, significant challenges are inherent in giving an account of the moral life. Our tendency toward self-justification rather than faith in Christ is evident in much of our common religious language. Far too often unexamined religious language does the Church a disservice by casting us back upon ourselves, and obscuring the divine logic of Grace. The ubiquitous language of *application*, *example, extension* and *growth* are a number of such examples.

Application (versus Obedience): Conceptually, to speak of 'applying the work of Christ' or of 'applying the Bible' to our lives is problematic. This is because the posture of application is profoundly objectivistic and suggests an inert subject matter. Scripture is not a record of commands which must be *applied*, as if it were up to the

---

136. Shortly after his year as moderator of the Church of Scotland, Torrance wrote an article in Life and Work in which he railed against the poor quality of training for parish ministers, especially concerning the core of the Christian message: "Pious chatty moralism displaces proclamation and teaching of the Word of God, and justification by social righteousness replacing justification by the grace of the Lord Jesus Christ only bores and repels the man in the pew" (Torrance, 'A Serious Call for Return to Devout and Holy Life' [July 1979]).
137. As Christopher Holmes point out, the ascended and advent Lord is reality, and "reality . . . cannot be applied. It can only be heard and so be obeyed" (Ethics, 148; cf. 144).
138. G&R, 154. Cf. TRn, 160–62.
139. Molnar, Theologian of the Trinity, 75; TRn, 162.

reader to stand-over the text in the role of conferrer of authority or relevance. Rather, Holy Scripture is address, which we are summoned to *hear* and *obey*. Its authority is not conferred upon it by the reader, but is derivative of an authoritative presence.

Exemplarism (versus Participation): *Exemplarism* is insensitive to what God is doing in the world, for it reduces Jesus current relevance to an example from the past. While Torrance affirms that the historical Jesus is the "normative pattern" for our every response to God to end there or to emphasize the exemplary nature of Jesus's life without embedding our following after him in his present tense command would be Torrance points out to vacate the Christian life of all its power and joy.

Christopher Holmes describes the fundamental problems of exemplarism well: exemplarism is "the idea that Jesus himself is an example or an instantiation of something that lies beyond himself. He becomes the paradigm for instance for talking about social justice or . . . personal piety. . . . What matters . . . is not so much who he is . . . , but what he can point us toward."[140] However, Jesus is not a dead man whom Christians imitate for his exemplary virtues. To speak in this way suggests God is an utterly passive player in the God-human relation. We do not *make* Christ relevant; rather, it is he who continuously summons us to be relevant to him.[141] Given the reality of the present and ministering Christ, Holmes reframes well the proper mode of questioning: "What does the 'situation' ask of me in the light of Christ's very definite presence and concrete activity in relationship to it?"[142]

Extending the Incarnation (versus Serving the Present, Risen Lord): Accounts of Christian action, which speak of the need to extend the teachings and ministry of Jesus or to incarnate Christ in the present, or to 'adapt the insights of Jesus's into our own historical contexts, only serve to reinforce the idea of an inert Jesus. Within a Christian framework, informed by the reality of the heavenly session

140. Holmes, *Ethics in the Presence of Christ* (London: T&T Clark, 2012), 24. Hereafter, *Ethics*.
141. Ibid., 5.
142. Ibid., 147.

of Christ, none of this makes sense. The job of the Spirit is not to help Christians "make Christ present."[143] Rather, through the Spirit, Jesus *is* present, "but in a different way."[144] "The resurrection . . . does not decay into the past"[145] as if the risen Jesus did not have a present ministry.[146] The ascension of Christ makes the material content of his historical life available for immediate actual encounter.[147]

Growth (versus Fidelity): Torrance also detects a drift toward self-justification in the way that sanctification is often equated with the idea of spiritual growth. Since we are already sanctified through union with Christ in the Spirit, Torrance argues that the challenge of the Christian life is not to become more and more sanctified, but to live according to our sanctification.

Thus, we do not strive for a sanctification we lack; we give our attention to the one who is present as our sanctification. When we strive after something that we already possess, the attention that belongs rightly to Christ is displaced by our anxious selves and by the quality of our own behavior. Sanctification is simply the continual realization and renewal of justification in our personal histories, the "manifestation of what has already happened."[148]

Furthermore, Torrance perceives in the ideology of growth an implicit assumption that the trajectory of the Christian life is the way of glory rather than the way of the cross. He is particularly critical of popular notions of church growth and would remind us that the sacramental marks of the Church are baptism and Holy Communion, not enlarged membership rolls and budgets. God's people have always been "subject to judgment and . . . plunged into disaster and death . . . in order to show . . . that the Kirk in all ages has her life and continuity . . . in being constantly called out of death into life."[149]

Torrance judges each of these terms as problematic for in their

---

143. Quoted in ibid., 8–9.
144. *Atonement*, 305.
145. Ibid., 245.
146. Cf. Purves, *The Resurrection of Ministry* (Downers Grove: Intervarsity, 2010), 59.
147. *Atonement*, 305.
148. *C&A2*, 131; cf. *C&A1*, 65.
149. *C&A1*, 62.

popular use they relate to the living Lord as if he were an inert and impersonal subject matter. Each in its own way suggests that *we* are the center to which all else must refer. Each in its own way implicitly ignores or actively resists the personal summons of the living, ascended Lord to hear and obey in faith.

Shared Sanctification

To state the argument positively, trinitarian participation as the way of Christian formation takes place by way of *inclusion* and *sharing*. Sanctification then is the believer's nourishment "with the new humanity of Christ … which is the fundamental reality of his Christian being."[150] Or to put it differently, sanctification is the continuance of Jesus's first century ministry into our present in a dynamic and personal sense because it has been contemporized by his resurrection and ascension.[151] It is a participation in Christ's accomplished work through surrender to the Spirit's ongoing actualization of Christ's work in our lives.

Terms such as 'inclusion' and 'sharing' emphasize human passivity over human activity. As human beings we certainly are involved in our Christian formation but our agency is always secondary.[152] What we can do and must do with regard to our sanctification is rejoice in it, repent of our infidelity, and indwell the reality of our filial identity through Christ. As we joyfully confess our inclusion in Christ and live in fidelity to it (and to him), our lives manifest and continuously demonstrate, the truth of our regeneration.

Stepping back a bit, we can see that the basic movement of Christian formation is *from* identity *to* fidelity/obedience; not the other way round. In a culture where identity is routinely constructed by amassing personal achievements or slavish dependency upon the opinions of others, this calls for a radical reorientation. Rather than striving, our mode of participation is the confident peace of those

150. Ibid., 65–66.
151. Cf. *Atonement*, 136, 170; Holmes, *Ethics*, 19.
152. Cf. Holmes, *Ethics*, 13.

whose identity is securely grounded in the fact that we belong to Christ. As we fix our eyes on Jesus, attending day by day to the risen Lord's ministering and commanding presence (*sursum corda*), we discover that we are regenerated: not abstractly or externally but from the inside—through Christ in whom our life is hid; through Christ who is "present in such a way as to evoke activity that is correspondent to and participant in what he as the truth is and is now doing." [153] Christ's presence in us and to us is "generative of a response. And that response, that corollary, is ethics." [154]

Torrance recognizes that this way of thinking is radically new for us—so much so that the average person reacts to it "like a cow staring at a new gate." [155] As a result he remarks, "We need to learn and learn again and again that salvation by Grace alone is so radical that we have to rely upon Christ Jesus entirely in everything and that it is only when we rely on him alone that we are really free to believe: 'Not I but Christ'," for "it is Christ who lives in me." (Gal 2:20).[156]

The Cultivation of Godliness

As we have observed, framing obedience and human response within the context of participation qualifies the moral and ethical life as an act of *faith*. 'Ethics,' however, is a term loaded with cultural and philosophical assumptions, which is why Torrance prefers the biblical language of 'godliness' (*eusebeia*) when speaking of the moral life of the Christian. [157] Unlike virtue-ethics, godliness receives its definition solely in reference to Jesus Christ and therefore cannot be separated from him. This locates the moral life (alongside Christian formation) as taking place firmly within a dynamic (onto)-relational mode of operation. As we will see, the implications of this approach are far-reaching; and they certainly call into question much of the language, as

---

153. Ibid., 95. (Heb 12:1–2; Phil 3:8–9).
154. Ibid., 96.
155. *G&R*, 71. Torrance is using Luther's phrase here.
156. Thomas F. Torrance, *Preaching Christ Today: The Gospel and Scientific Thinking* (Grand Rapids: Eerdmans, 1994), 37.
157. *TF*, "Faith and Godliness," 13–46.

well as many of the practices, of large swaths of the Christian Church today.

As Torrance understands it, the New Testament concept of godliness (*eusebeia*) is more or less a technical term for the living embodiment of the faith as found in Jesus Christ, the Son of God incarnate: "Jesus Christ himself defined for Christians what true godliness is."[158] In him, godly living, godly worship and godly thinking are combined and embodied.

Thus for Torrance godliness and godly living are thoroughly christological and as such find their ontological reality in him. Since godliness is essentially the life of Christ—a life which eternally endures at the right hand of the Father—it is not an achievement of the Church. The 'ought' toward which the Church is called, already 'is' by virtue of the one who is present in the Spirit in the power of his Grace. Even so, by the same Spirit, godliness does become "embodied in the Church as [Christ's] godly counterpart."[159] As such, godliness defines and determines the entire sphere of the life of the Christian. Every aspect of the Christian life—faith, knowledge, prayer and worship, ethics and so on—is either a movement of godliness or a movement of ungodliness.[160]

In keeping with our overall purpose, we will examine how godliness is expressed in the specific areas of Christian knowledge and Christian morality.

Godliness and the Mind of Christ

Torrance defines knowledge of God (faith) as an "objectively grounded persuasion of the mind, supported beyond itself by the objective reality . . . of God's own being."[161] Thus, *faith* is fundamentally a motion of receptivity to an objective ground beyond ourselves. It is in other words a movement of godliness.

158. Ibid., 39.
159. Ibid., 30.
160. Thomas F. Torrance, *Reality and Evangelical Theology: The 1981 Payton Lectures* (Philadelphia: Westminster, 1982), 138. Hereafter, *R&ET*.
161. *TF*, 19.

Torrance argues that the early Church regarded theology (*theologia*) and godliness (*theosebeia* or *eusebeia*) as mutually conditioning of each other: "Godliness and theology, worship and faith, went inseparably together"—so much so that Athanasius could say, "faith and godliness are connected and are sisters."[162] This pairing of knowledge of God and godliness is also how Torrance (via Origen) understands Paul's references to having or knowing through *the mind of Christ*.[163] To have the mind of Christ, or to know through the mind of Christ, is to know *with* God. Through the communion of the Spirit we participate in the truth embodied in the vicarious human mind of Christ, where *theologia is eusebia*.[164] Thus, theology is not simply knowledge *about* God, nor is godliness simply doing things *for* God; rather, the mind of Christ is both theology and godliness, united through abiding with Christ and being present to Christ. As we attend and listen and dialogue with God, our knowledge and understanding increasingly are shaped and formed through the mind of Christ. More specifically, *by abiding in Christ, and being present to Christ who is present to us through his Spirit, we come to share and participate in Christ's relationship with the Father.* This is the essence of godliness: in faith to correspond to the Son's filial receptivity to the Father. As we give our full, ongoing attention to Jesus's communion with the Father, we learn to think, worship and serve in a God-centered way (Col 1:19-22; Phil 2:5, Rom 12:1-2). We learn from Jesus *how* to be sons and daughters of the Father—how to abide in the Father's love. Here, from this secure identity as beloved children of the Father, we find our existence and identity 'inside the circle' of triune Grace. Faith that is "in Christ" involves a shift of centers, a cognitive recalibration—from thinking that is centered in the inward-turned alienation of human reason, toward thinking that is caught up in the unswerving faithfulness and reliability of the love of God.[165] From this place, abiding in the mind of Christ, the Spirit

---

162. *TF*, 17; cf. 38; *Ep.*, 11.9-11. Torrance notes that this is what was later known in the Church as "*lex orandi - lex credendi.*" *TF*, 41.
163. *TF*, 39. Torrance references several biblical passages: 1 Cor 2:16; Rom 8:5-27; Rom 12:2; Phil 2:2-8; Col 3:2.
164. *CDG*, 74.
165. "That transformation in our inner self in which we learn to think from a centre in God rather

calls forth from us the will to will God's will. There is no such thing as godliness apart from god*wardness*, that is, fellowship (*koinonia*) with the Father through the Son in the Spirit.

Torrance also describes theological knowledge as a kind of *kinetic thinking* in which being and action, cognition and communion, go hand in hand.[166] Since knowledge of God is "con-scientia" (*knowledge with*) it cannot be passive.[167] We do not do theology as spectators, objectively distanced from the triune God. Before we even begin, we are antecedently and irreversibly in the midst of a relation. Consequently, Torrance argues what is required for true knowledge of God (and thus for our authentic formation) is not simply a "movement of thought," but "a movement of personal response and commitment in worship, obedience and love in which a transformation of our mind or a spiritual reorganization of our consciousness of God takes place."[168] In knowledge of God we certainly ask questions, but our questions themselves are questioned in return,[169] along with our very selves. We cannot know the Father if we are not open to corresponding to the Father; and such correspondence always involves a change (*metanoia*) in our thinking—that is, *repenting*. Our personal subjectivities must be conformed to the Father's personal objectivity. Repentance is a function of the personal presence of the living God invading our lives and calling us to himself in grace and mercy. God addresses us, *and so we respond*.[170] The basic movement of the Christian is to hear and

than from a centre in ourselves is the basic reorientation that takes place in the church of Jesus Christ. Christian discipleship is the disciplined habit of thinking and acting *in Christ*" (Torrance, *Atonement*, 376).

166. *G&R*, 177; cf. *TS*, 47.

167. Torrance appropriates Calvin's concept of "shared knowledge" (*con-scientia*) with God. Knowledge of God requires agreement with the divine judgment. Thus, to think Christianly is to allow God to preside in all our judgments (Thomas F. Torrance, *The Hermeneutics of John Calvin* [Edinburgh: Scottish Academic Press, 1988], 164).

168. *CDG*, 88.

169. Ibid., "The Nature of Scientific Activity," 120–40.

170. Thomas F. Torrance, *Christian Doctrine of God*, 88. As Eugene Peterson memorably reminds us, all our speech in relation to God is most properly *answering* speech: "God's word precedes [our] words: [our] prayers don't seek God, they respond to the God who seeks us." "What is essential in prayer is not that we learn to express ourselves, but that we learn to answer God" (Eugene Peterson, *Answering God*, 5–6).

obey, thereby learning to live in alignment with the humanizing will of God.[171]

Thus, we repent, but we do not repent alone. Christ's mediatorship matters profoundly. In fact, the whole point of repentance is that we turn away from our non-God-centered patterns of thinking and doing. For us to repent in our own strength is not to repent at all! By definition then, repentance is not something we are able to generate under our own power or through our own wisdom. Repentance is a function of Christ's mediatorship. Such a movement is both personal and God-dominated in both directions (humanward and Godward). It is "initiated by God informed by his personal address to us in his Word and sustained through the presence of his Spirit in our personal response to his Word."[172] Godliness or ethics "does not take place in a vacuum but *in* Christ."[173]

Thus, to take on the mind of Christ entails a constant conversion, in which our independent ways of knowing are judged, healed and reconciled to the movement of Grace. Mindsets which contradict the life and love of God are exposed as impersonal and self-isolating rejections of the mind of Christ. As such, abiding in the love of God in Christ involves a "two-fold involution,"[174] correspondent to the movement of Grace, of dying to self and living to Christ. These two motions of faith (dying and living, hearing and obeying, repenting and believing) correspond to the invitation and command that permeate all of Jesus' teaching about life in God's kingdom. The one and only appropriate response to God's personal presence is to be always repenting and always believing (Mark 1:14-15).[175]

At this point Torrance calls for sober caution. His grave concern is his recognition that at any and every point we are susceptible to taking knowledge we have *about* God and then attempting to do things

---

171. *MOC*, 72.
172. Ibid.
173. Holmes, *Ethics*, 57.
174. *TS*, 153.
175. It is significant that the verbs, normally translated as 'repent' and 'believe', are present imperatives which indicates that Jesus is calling those who would follow him to *constant* repenting and believing. A more accurate, though awkward, translation of Mark 1:15 would be "the kingdom of God has come near, *be repenting* and *be believing* in the good news."

for God. We are continually tempted to trade *Objective Trinitarian Participation* for *Subjective Moral Formation*—or at least to drift from one to the other. This trade—or drift—occurs anytime we bypass relationship with the triune God and fast-track to activity (John 15:5). We exchange our identity in Christ, our personal participation in the triune life, and our life of faith, for the impersonal assumptions, demands, and efforts of moralism and self-reliance. Such an exchange may remain undetectable on the surface of our lives, at the level of outward appearances. Yet inwardly the move is of seismic proportions: it is a shift from actions that are contrapuntal to the present ministry of Christ—and that participate in the present ministry of Christ—to actions that merely imitate a dead Christ and correspond to an ethical ideal.

The defense against this reversal, this drift toward self-reliance, is faith *in Christ*. To practice godliness is to live consciously aware that we participate in the objective reality of Christ's vicarious life of faith, prayer, worship, thanksgiving and self-offering to the Father.[176] It is to also recognize the fact that there are some actions which point toward Christ's ways and conform to Christ's rule. Understood in this way, the Christian life is defined as a life lived present to Christ and participant in his mission. In this way—creaturely and fallen beings though we are—we can be signs that reflect and echo the active presence of God through the Spirit of the ascended Jesus. In Torrance's own words, ethics, or "Christian discipleship," is simply "the disciplined habit of thinking and acting *in Christ*."[177] Out of this basic movement of godly faith, Torrance says, flow all properly Christian ethics, ministry and mission.

In summary, as Torrance understands it, 'godliness' (or 'ungodliness') is the way the pastoral epistles describe our participation with (or against) the human-Godward movement of Christ—a movement that expresses itself as filial obedience to the Father and is spurred by the Father's love, which the Spirit pours into

---

176. *TiR*, 109, 209.
177. Thomas F. Torrance, *Atonement*, 376.

our hearts. By our godly participation in the Son's relation with the Father, our lives refer beyond themselves to the triune God. Ethics or "Christian discipleship" is simply "the disciplined habit of thinking and acting *in Christ*."[178] This reality is expressed in the sacraments and mirrored in the life of faith through its movements of gratitude, repentance, and obedience.

The task of the Christian in the world is to articulate and socially embody the life of Christ in creatively contrapuntal and open-textured ways.[179] Given the completely new environment of Christian existence, it should be no surprise to discover that the all-embracing framework of Grace requires a complete reorientation to ethics.

The Ethics of Grace

In his approach to moral theology, Torrance locates ethics within the larger and primary context of 'godliness.' In doing so, he actually places ethics at the center of the Gospel. These ethics however are not the prescriptive ethics of legalism, but the freedom of dwelling in a right relation to the Truth in which godliness is the fruit. From the standpoint of ontology, Torrance's approach to ethics is built upon a different understanding of what grounds and upholds the moral order.[180] In sharp contrast to anthropocentric, virtue-based systems of Christian formation, he argues for a "soteriological suspension of ethics," and in its place the establishment of the proper foundations for "a moral life that flows from grace"—a life in which the Father-Son relation is translated into the daily life of the children of God.[181] As Christopher Holmes describes it, this is "an account of ethics that understands itself to be the human response to the question 'What is Jesus now doing?'"[182]

One of the noticeable differences between Torrance's theological writings and many others including Barth's is the limited attention

178. *Atonement*, 376.
179. Cf. *R&ST*, 99; Flett, *Culture*, 161–67.
180. *A&MO*, 254.
181. Ibid., 253. Cf. *TF*, 160–61.
182. Holmes, *Ethics*, 3.

he gives to spelling out a concrete Christian ethic. It would be a misreading of Torrance to consider this an oversight or an indication of disinterest, for as with most of his decisions, Torrance's reasoning is strongly theological. In an unpublished paper entitled 'The Call for a New Discussion on the Doctrine of Grace,' Torrance lays out his early thinking on ethics.[183]

He begins with the observation that the very idea of an ethic trades upon a particular anthropological assumption: that humans are beings with particular ends, "which take shape as ideals" and become identified as the "true self."[184] However, as soon as the ideal receives ethical formulation, any concrete ethical actions are now judged in relation to an 'ought,' a 'law,' or 'the good,' which stands outside of men and women in the role of judge.[185] Thus, "the essential nature of the 'ethic' is what St. Paul called 'the curse of the Law,' for by the law no flesh can possibly be justified."[186] Torrance would later call this humanity's "inescapable sense of obligation."[187]

For Torrance, the fatal flaw in the idea of a *Christian* ethic is that it "reduces the theocentricity of Christianity to a basic anthropocentricity" by "crushing . . . the transcendent into finite and human thought-forms."[188] In this case, a personal God is replaced by abstract truth, and "legalism or formalism once again take the field over against the personal approach of God in a Word of Grace."[189] This is why for Torrance "there can be no half-way house between Grace that is Transcendental and personal and Grace that is immanent and natural," for "to pursue the good even for the sake of the good is to seek the good in the very place of God!"[190]

Torrance suggests that the demand for abstract ethics and "even the idea of goodness for goodness' sake" is a form of "aesthetic desire."

183. Cf. A&MO, 252ff.
184. Thomas F. Torrance, "The Call for a New Discussion on the Doctrine of Grace," Box 21: Auburn Lectures, 1938–1939), 23. Hereafter, CNDDG.
185. Cf. Atonement, 111–12.
186. CNDDG, 24; Gal 3:13; cf. Atonement, 253–34.
187. Atonement, 254.
188. CNDDG, 25.
189. Ibid., 25–26.
190. Ibid., 33.

Yet in concrete actuality none of these laws, ethics or values is, in fact, *true* goodness. Torrance defines "true goodness" as "the spontaneous products of a free spirit," which is "genuine and not disguised forms of selfishness or egoistic cravings." Consequently, "Christianity means . . . the setting aside of the Law, but at the same time it means the fulfilling of the Law."[191] Torrance's advocacy for Christian spontaneity is not a plea for carelessness, but for a life of self-giving service that "is emancipated from the necessity of having to supply its own intelligible ground"; for "loving service looks for no reward . . . and looks for no thanks."[192]

The pure self-giving of God in Jesus Christ takes us behind and beyond good and evil, puts a new Spirit within, and relates us personally to God

> in such a way that goodness is a spontaneous growth. He [Jesus] himself, the law alive, enters our hearts and so fulfils the law for He is Love. He issues no commands, promulgates no new ethic, sets up no new standards of life. What He does is rather to bring a completely new orientation that is as different from the old as death is to life, a new orientation in which He and not the human 'self' is the central point of reference, a new Orientation grounded in His Love which is guided by no external law but creates itself in the exigencies of the occasion the forms in which Love shall act.[193]

This does not mean that ethics are purely relativistic and subjective; quite the opposite, in fact. Ethics finds its ultimate objectivity in the law of Christ, which is to say in Christ himself. Yet Christ himself is not a principle: Christ *lives*. This One who lives as the commander of the 'ought' '*is*' also the 'ought' which he commands. Christ *is* the true human whose being action and relations have perfect integrity; as such Christ also generates true humanity in those who abide in him and abiding share even his 'mindset.'

Through the Spirit, he perfects and finishes in his people what he has pioneered and authored in himself. His command to us is not to

191. Ibid., 32.
192. *G&R*, 162.
193. *CNDDG*, 33.

follow a law but to live in harmony *with* himself, who is present as the law he *is*. God's will for us is none other than *Christ himself*—that we might live *in* and act *on* the basis of his living reality.[194] By his presence, he actively draws men and women into the realm of his reconciliation and makes us to become what we are in him—to live according to the ultimate reality which he alone is. He summons us to be present to his presence and action and lordship,[195] and so to participate in his ministry. In other words, the ascended Jesus comes to us by his Spirit so that we might become Christians again and again. That is, subjectively *be becoming* that which we already are objectively in him.

As we indwell the triune communion, we come to listen as God listens, to hear what God hears, to love what God loves, and therefore to do what God does. This is the true fruit of *theosis* and the source of all true sanctification and godliness. We turn toward him and "learn to think from a centre in God" in which we "no longer live unto [ourselves] but unto him"; as we turn toward Christ in this way, we flourish [196] and our humanity comes to its "proper expression": fully human and fully alive in Christ.[197]

This is Torrance's passionate concern: the personalization (and thus humanization) of our humanity through Grace which is onto-relational, personal, dynamic, and free. What may look like antinomianism in Torrance is actually anti-idealism or anti-abstractionism. The law was given by the Lord, not for its own sake, but as an instrument of fellowship and communion. One cannot obey God impersonally and be the humans we ought to be.[198] Thus he writes, "What Christ wants is not goodness, but you."[199] We must *listen*, so that our doing flows from our relating. As those who *hear* and obey, we will not be able to determine 'logically' and in advance what it looks like to love as God loves in any particular situation—for the love of God is not a principle but a Person. No principle, system, or model

194. Holmes, *Ethics*, 43.
195. Barth, *CD IV/2*, 323.
196. *Atonement*, 376.
197. *CNDDG*, 33.
198. Ibid. For the same argument in biblical, rather than philosophical, terms, see *Atonement*, 112–13.
199. Ibid., 33–34. Torrance's theology (like Barth's) is the abolition of abstract ethics.

can determine in advance what the proper response will always be.[200] Instead, through the Spirit which Christ breathes, we live "in the Truth."

Through the Spirit sent by the Father and the Son, Christ perfects and finishes in his people what he has pioneered and authored in himself. Of course, we never get this 'right'—for our correspondence to the love, truth, and Grace of Christ is of a stumbling nature. Like the disciples who return to their fishing, we too fail to recognize that we are caught up in a real movement—a movement defined by the presence and activity and lordship of Christ. Christopher Holmes catches the spirit of Torrance's ethical thought well in his description of ethics as essentially "our fumbling response to Jesus' contemporary ministry."[201] And yet, stumbling and fumbling though we are, by his Spirit we are given to share in Christ's obedience. We are given ears to hear the commanding Christ.[202] His command, "Follow me," is a summons to remain present to him. His command is an invitation born of love—that we might be those who love him and correspond to the love that he is.[203] His faithfulness is the basis for our faith, and the 'is' of his presence becomes a 'thou shalt' to ours, for his Spirit is the power to obey what he commands. His living identity functions imperatively and effectively, forming us into people of truth,[204] calling us to be about what he is now doing. "The love he is and gives, he calls forth in the power of the Spirit."[205] Thus, the command of the gospel—to follow—is truly good news. It is about living, "not to an ethic of a person, but rather in harmony with a person who is present and active in his Spirit as the love he is."[206] In this sense, ethics are essentially a function of Christ's own presence and ministry, which are "continually operative in reconciling intervention...within all the affairs of humanity."[207]

200. A&MO, 253.
201. Holmes, Ethics, 13. I have been tremendously helped by the excellent work of Christopher Holmes who is an excellent and faithful interpreter and extender of the ethical trajectory of Torrance's thought.
202. Ibid., 136.
203. Ibid., 125.
204. Ibid., 100–101.
205. Ibid., 135.
206. Ibid., 125–26.

Once again, we reiterate that Torrance's vision of the moral life is far more rigorous and unconditional in its obligations than any version of virtue ethics could ever be. He presents an approach to the doctrine of Grace which takes "the road of real responsibility," for it calls for the courage and surrender of a "life of spontaneous love."[208] Torrance concludes his lecture on ethics by emphasizing a difficult truth: that "the way to this new life of the spontaneous Good, in which the fruits of the spirit blossom freely like flowers on a tree, is one that lies under the shadow of the Cross."[209] The way of resurrection passes through Good Friday where we must face not an ethical ideal but the surrender and humiliation of the cross.[210] The risen Jesus continues to bear the scars of his suffering; he continues his ministry among the poor and the powerless, the hurting and the broken. Accordingly, as long as the Church continues to exist on the plane of history, "the cross is still in the field."[211] Jesus's contemporary disciples who like the apostle Paul, know the power of the resurrection (Phil 3:10–11), also share in his suffering and become like him in his death. From Easter faith they choose to follow Christ; to enter into his continuing Good Friday ministry to the least of these (Matt 25:31–46), yet in confidence and hope that all sin and suffering will be transformed into resurrection glory.[212]

Conclusion

In this chapter we have reflected upon the theological grounding which Torrance's theology of Grace provides for the actual practice of Christian formation within the Church. We have endeavored to put to the test Torrance's claim that, within the logic of Grace, "all of grace does not mean nothing of man" but, rather, "*all of grace means all of man.*"[213] We have argued that Torrance's approach intensifies, rather

---

207. Thomas F. Torrance, *Atonement*, 170; cf. Holmes, *Ethics*, 23f.
208. CNDDG, 35.
209. Ibid., 34.
210. Ibid.
211. Thomas F. Torrance, *The Apocalypse Today: Sermons on Revelations* (London: James Clarke and Co., 1960), 75.
212. Andrew Purves develops this concept in his excellent book, *The Resurrection of Ministry*, 117f.

than lessens, the necessity of human response to God in sacrificial and Christ-like service. Finally, we have noted that this human response is nothing more—*and nothing less*—than a movement of love,[214] for it has its creative ground and source in Christ himself.

We have also observed that for Torrance the work of the Spirit in God's people is always a movement toward greater *humanization*. The Christian life is relational and personal through and through. Sanctification describes the personalizing effect which results from living in fidelity to the movement of participative Grace over time. Christian living is a *participation in Grace* in which formation takes place through participation in the love of God, the Grace of Christ, and the *koinonia* of the Spirit. Accordingly, all desirable qualities such as faithfulness, growth, and spiritual maturity are defined in Torrance's framework, not according to legalistic boundary markers, or even by adherence to strict spiritual disciplines. They are defined, rather, by a continuous motion of faith, which expresses itself in "the continued receiving of grace for grace, in which the true life of man consists."[215] As such, the *telos* of Christian existence is the humanization of God's *imago*-bearers through communion with the worship, prayer, and ministry of the Son before the Father.

In sum, what Torrance advocates is a vision of Christian existence which is 'encircled,'—whose fundamental environment is "within the circle of the life of Jesus Christ."[216] No sector of humanity, no realm of human experience, falls outside his life and love. The summons to disciples of Jesus is to be opened to this gift of Grace and to participate in the movement of his life and love through the Spirit. In the church which Christ creates, there is only one body, one sacrifice, one ministry—all of which are visibly expressed in the Eucharist. This reality makes the whole life of the Church a kind of *living liturgy* of eucharistic participation. As those who have been eucharistically transformed by Christ's claim upon us, we are unafraid of losing our

213. *MOC*, xii.
214. *GCM*, 141.
215. *TRn*, 116.
216. *TiR*, 211, 109.

lives and therefore freed from the need to strive jealously and selfishly to save them. In Christ we are liberated to bless all we encounter, through lives broken and poured out for the sake of the world that God loves.

Conclusion

This book accomplishes two things. It presents Torrance's doctrine of Grace in an explicitly trinitarian and participatory way, and it demonstrates the centrality of his concept of Grace in the unfolding of his theology across the dogmatic spectrum.

First, it articulates Torrance's distinctive trinitarian and participatory understanding of Grace. Torrance argues that the New Testament concept of *charis* is a neologism with "no theological point of contact . . . in classical and Hellenistic Greek."[1] In light of its uniqueness, *charis* "cannot be interpreted in terms of antecedent roots or ideas."[2]

Grace for Torrance is the event of God's self-giving in Christ and through the Spirit for human salvation and participation in the life and love of God. Although finite and fallen, we are included in the Son's relation with the Father. As a reality inextricably grounded in the trinitarian life, Torrance steadfastly rejects any attempt to treat Grace sub-personally: as a force, energy, spiritual power, supplement, aid, or spiritual medicine. Likewise, Grace can never be reduced to a "private possession" of the believer, as a "deposit" held by the Church,[3] or as a naturalized principle subject to legal and causal definitions and controls.[4] In contrast to these more common approaches, Torrance

---

1. Thomas F. Torrance, *The Doctrine of Grace in the Apostolic Fathers* (Eugene, OR: Wipf and Stock, 1996), 21. Hereafter, *DGAF*.
2. Ibid., 20.
3. Quoted in Torrance, *Theology in Reconstruction* (Grand Rapids: Eerdmans, 1965), 76. Hereafter, *TRn*.
4. *TRn*, 179.

argues that Grace always acts upon men and women in an intensely personal manner—"as personal as Christ Himself."[5]

Second, this study demonstrates the consistent manner in which Torrance's own theology is determined by his doctrine of Grace. Torrance both claims and delivers a theology in which the doctrine of Grace provides the interior logic characterizing the whole.[6] This study has shown that the thread which guides the whole and which provides the material dogmatic norms around which all doctrines can cohere and dovetail together, is "how God deals with us in Jesus Christ" or more simply, "the doctrine of grace."[7] Thus, rather than reducing his doctrine of Grace to a subcategory within a larger doctrine of justification, this study shows that Torrance's doctrine of Grace informs and determines the shape of the rest of his theology.

Central Questions and Challenges

The intent and purpose of this study has been to demonstrate and illuminate the logic of Grace which flows through Torrance's theology and therefore it does not engage deeply with secondary critiques. However, it is worth revisiting what is conceivably the most important criticism and challenge to Torrance's theology of Grace: *the nature of the relation between the Creator and the creature.*

This critique and the multiple concerns which accompany it comes in various forms and arises in the midst of engagement with numerous doctrines. Thus when Torrance vigorously asserts that "'all of grace' does not mean 'nothing of man,' but the very reverse,"[8] the question is posed as to whether this statement is sustainable or even coherent. Again, when Torrance asserts there is only "one sacrifice common to Christ and his Church," is he not guilty of conflating the believer and Christ? In what sense, if at all, does Torrance's christological ontology

---

5. *DGAF*, 32.
6. Thomas F. Torrance, "Predestination in Christ," *Evangelical Quarterly* 13 (1941): 127–28. Hereafter, *PiC*.
7. Ibid.
8. Thomas F. Torrance, *The Mediation of Christ*, rev. ed. (Edinburgh: T&T Clark, 1992), 95. Hereafter, *MOC*.

facilitate the mediation of Grace through creaturely means? Or does Torrance identify Grace so thoroughly with Christology that its working is purely and solely immediate, bypassing created instruments altogether? These questions and others like them expose a significant theological divide, one which Torrance himself acknowledged and sought to bring out in the open.

For his part, Torrance identified the key issue with the hypostatic union. As noted in chapter 2, this theologumen functions as a sort of category—the Chalcedonian *logic of Christ*—which determines the form and logic of all doctrines that involve a divine and human component. For Torrance, "the other doctrines of the faith, the Church, the Sacraments, man and the last things, etc., all have their place and their truthfulness by reference to this central point in Jesus Christ."[9] Unsurprisingly, the hypostatic union is also at the center of his concept of Grace. Torrance writes, "If grace is God's self-giving to us in Christ, then grace must be understood in terms of his human as well as his divine nature."[10] In Torrance's scheme, it is the careful articulation of this tension that allows for a kind of participation of humanity in the triune life, which does not slip into either *methexis* or extrinsicism.

What makes Torrance's doctrine of Grace particularly potent and radical, is his commitment to applying the hypostatic union to the ascension. In fact, one cannot truly understand or even rightly engage with Torrance's thought without appreciating the supreme significance he ascribes to the humanity of Christ in the doctrine of the ascension. He writes, "In my view it is the main issue which divides all theologies and strikes them apart to the one side or to the other. Are we to take the humanity of the risen Jesus seriously or not? Or are we to teach a Docetic view of the risen and ascended Jesus?"[11]

Torrance orders the relation between God and creatures by means of a thorough integration of the vicarious humanity of Christ, the

9. Thomas F. Torrance, *Theological Science* (Oxford: Oxford University Press, 1969), 216. Hereafter, *TS*.
10. *TRn*, 183.
11. Thomas F. Torrance, *Conflict and Agreement in the Church*, vol. 1 (London: Lutterworth, 1960), 98. Hereafter, *C&A1*; cf. Thomas F. Torrance, *Royal Priesthood* (Edinburgh: T&T Clark, 1993), 43. Hereafter, *RP*.

hypostatic union, the doctrine of the ascension, and the *homoousion* of Grace. By means of this set of central theological tools, Torrance presents a vision of Christian existence which is a personal, dynamic, downward two-fold movement of Grace. This being the case, critiques which address the Creator-creature relation in Torrance's theology draw attention not so much to a potential weakness or deficiency in Torrance's thinking as they do to the deliberate choice of a different path and a corresponding set of convictions. In other words, this represents a basic fall line; and therefore, *criticisms or misunderstandings of Torrance will normally gather themselves around this fundamental theological divide.*

For his part, Torrance refuses to fill the distance left by the ascended Christ with human forms of mediation. He vigilantly criticizes this tendency wherever he finds it, beginning with the Arian and Pelagian notions of created and merited Grace which found their way into the early Church.[12] For Torrance, Grace is always mediated but never created. In other words, the mediation of Grace takes place by the immediate presence of Christ in the Spirit—it is "the one indivisible self-giving of God in Christ."[13] Creaturely being in the form of the Church never takes over Christ's eternal position as mediator and Torrance's approach to participation does not blur this line. Far from conceiving of humanity's participation in the triune communion as some kind of substantial metamorphosis, redeemed humanity actually communes with God in a manner which humanizes their humanity and personalizes their personhood. Torrance writes,

> The exaltation of human nature into the life of God does not mean the disappearance of man or the swallowing up of human and creaturely being in the infinite ocean of divine Being, but rather that human nature, remaining creaturely and human, is yet exalted in Christ to share in God's life and glory.[14]

---

12. *TRn*, 225, where Torrance references *De Spiritu Sancto* 9.23.
13. Ibid. Cf. ibid., 190.
14. Thomas F. Torrance, *Space, Time and Resurrection* (Edinburgh: T&T Clark, 1998), 135. Hereafter, *STR*.

Thus, Torrance understands the ascension of Christ to signify the concrete establishment of the human race once and for all.

While Torrance's formulation is profitable on many counts, it is far from ideal and justified concerns abound. *First, Torrance's technical employment of a few core theological concepts can border on the formulaic.* One of the most integral and apparent features of Torrance's theological method is his expansive usage of the *an/en-hypostasia* couplet across the dogmatic spectrum. This couplet functions as Torrance's key to walking through the tensions inherent in the divine-human relation in a manner which would "deliver the Chalcedonian doctrine of Christ from the tendency involved in the Greek terms to state the doctrine of Christ statically and metaphysically."[15] However, one might argue whether a formulaic mode is the most effective approach for the kind of personal dynamism Torrance seeks. Has he chosen a mode of reasoning more akin to abstract mathematics than the logic of personal relations? Furthermore, since the *an/en-hypostasia* originate historically as specifically christological terms, one wonders if their employment as descriptors of human agency in general results in a dangerous loss of christological precision. Whether the hypostatic union can indeed bear such weight is an important question to consider. Could not the same work be achieved through an appeal to creation and creatureliness, since creatures have their being in and so far as they receive it from the hands of God? Whether the *an/en* formula does much more than function as an algebraic shorthand for the Creator-creature order and distinction remains to be seen and calls for more critical engagement. If not, a more thorough reliance on creation and creatureliness that is more narratival than formulaic would protect the uniqueness of the incarnation event, which it is the true purpose of the *an/en* to illuminate.

Torrance himself is aware of this danger and warns against the temptation to turn the doctrine into an ideological truth "and use it as

15. Thomas F. Torrance, *Incarnation: The Person and Life of Christ*, ed. Robert T. Walker (Nottingham: Intervarsity, 2008), 85. Hereafter, *Incarnation*.

the masterful idea of a system of thought."[16] He would be the first to remind us that the important thing is the reality (Jesus Christ), not the doctrine. "[W]e must respect the importance and indeed the necessity of formal logic, but we cannot allow it to usurp the authoritative place occupied by the Truth Himself or be a substitute for the material logic that inheres in what He reveals to us of Himself."[17] Torrance is well aware that once theological statements get detached from their referring function they become merely non-sensical caricatures of themselves.[18] Theology must be transposed into "the living and actual forms of personal being," or it is merely "theologistic."[19] Paper-logic, whatever the mode of expression, is not master of the Truth. In the end, the Truth is something "more to be adored than expressed."[20]

Second, **and more significantly,** *Torrance's exposition lacks* *significant concrete description.* His *total substitution* understanding of the vicarious and atoning exchange can lead to an undervaluing of humanity's contingent freedom, either rendering it unnecessary or overpowering it altogether. Alongside the towering ontology of the vicarious humanity of Christ, there is the threat that we get lost in the shadows. This can be seen in Torrance's reticence to describe or even speak of conversion in a subjective sense. His keen awareness that "our free-will is our self-will" renders him extremely hesitant to give much time to the subjective side of faith.[21] While Torrance's intent is that Christ's solid and enduring ontology would give our weak creaturely ontology a place where it can be established, the specific and concrete manner in which such faith might be generated and sustained remains somewhat vague and under-described. The authentic human response of spontaneity and freedom which Torrance anticipates remains an ambiguous "miracle of the Spirit."[22]

In his book *Christ and Culture*, Graham Ward speaks to this concern

16. *TS*, 217.
17. Ibid., 219.
18. Ibid., 268.
19. Ibid., 269.
20. Ibid., 220.
21. *MOC*, 85.
22. Ibid., xii.

as it shows itself in Barth's theology. Ward makes the point that while Barth speaks a lot about participation, he does not give an account of the process (or economy) of redemption in a way that makes the relations between God and human beings appear to be anything other than "autocratic."[23] Ward writes,

> What is missing from Barth's account of faith is the experience and practices in which faith becomes operable and evident: the formation of the one who is being faithful. What is missing is a sociology and a phenomenology of believing. On its own, 'by faith' is simply a theological abstraction.[24]

Without some concrete account of the economy and productions of faith, discipleship and personal formation, or of the process by which love is received and responded to, Ward suggests that in the end Barth's dialectic leads to a 'non-identity' of both Christ and the human person. "Barth"s Christology," Ward writes, "is a negotiation of what Gillian Rose called 'the broken middle.'"[25] We are left with a Christ we can't touch, and an *us* that cannot act agentially in any participative way as the body of Christ. While Ward's critique is aimed at Barth, we must ask whether this critique might also apply to Torrance. Functionally speaking, does Torrance leave us with a 'broken middle,' a no man's land Christology where humanity has no real place in practice? While Torrance's onto-relational approach and stronger doctrine of the ascension give more substance and texture to his understanding of participation, the details remain absent.

It is true that Torrance has not left us much in the way of specifics on ethics, public policy, or models of spiritual formation; and while Torrance's pneumatology is particularly strong in its trinitarian integration, other important aspects are left undeveloped. For example, Torrance has little to say about the specific moral-ethical implications of the Pauline concept of life in the Spirit.[26] More attention to the ethical narrative of Jesus of Nazareth with particular

23. Graham Ward, *Christ and Culture* (Oxford: Blackwell, 2005), 8.
24. Ibid.
25. Ibid., 22.
26. Ray Anderson has sought to extract the practical implications of Torrance's pneumatology. Cf.

consideration of the way the Spirit empowered his faithful and obedient life, along with a correspondingly concrete description of our own call to walk in the Spirit, would be welcome additions to his oeuvre. Torrance's legacy would be bolstered by a more robust account in these areas. Thus, in spite of Torrance's careful theological description of the place of human action and his explicit rejection of a Christology which might render human response irrelevant, this lack of concreteness threatens the coherence of his arguments.[27]

A *third critique* against Torrance builds upon the shortcomings described by the first two and accuses *Torrance's theology of a fatal flaw when it comes to the place of human agency*. Stamps, for example, ends a discussion entitled "As to the Abiding Integrity of Man's Individual Response via-a-vis the All-Embracing Vicarious Response of Christ" with the following cryptic question:

> In his attempt to separate the subjectivity of God from our own, to make the subjectivity of Christ and not our own that which is determinative, and finally to remove all assertiveness from our own subjectivity, has Torrance in effect removed not only our significance salvifically speaking, but our significance altogether?[28]

Again, Stamps asks, "Does this way of thinking make God 'so absolute that man is relativized to the point of vanishing[?].'"[29] Stamps's verdict is clear: "Everything in Torrance's theology militates against a positive answer to these questions."[30] Another example is Thomas Smail who queries, "If Christ acts so decisively on our behalf in regard to our response to God what room is left for our own response to God?"[31]

Stamps's and Smail's questions and damning conclusion are examples of how a lack of appreciation for Torrance's onto-relational

---

"The Practical Theology of Thomas F. Torrance," *Participatio* 1 (2009): 49–65; and "Reading T. F. Torrance as a Practical Theologian," in *The Promise of Trinitarian Theology*, 161–83.

27. As Morrison writes, "vigorous assertion does not overcome incoherence" (Morrison, *Knowledge of the Self-revealing God*, 253).

28. Robert J. Stamps, *The Sacrament of the Word made Flesh* (Edinburgh: Rutherford House, 2007), 269.

29. Ibid., quoting James Quinn, review of *Theology in Reconstruction*, ThSt 28 (1967): 389ff.

30. Stamps, *Sacrament*, 268.

31. Smail, review of *Mediation of Christ*, SJT 38 (1985), 243. Note Smail's choice of the word 'room' in his quest for legitimate human agency which betrays the container notion of the God-human relation which guides (and limits) his reasoning.

and downward two-fold approach to Grace can sabotage our ability to recognize actual participation when we see it. It is the argument of this book that Torrance has been misunderstood and misrepresented on the point of human participation. These critiques are typical and fail to do justice to the logic which undergirds his language of *theosis*. As such, they miss the point that it is the very distinction and ontological separation of the Creator and the creature, which functions as one of the necessary ingredients for actual participation. According to the logic of these critiques, *all of God* necessarily (or, logically) means *nothing of man*; therefore, election and faith are polar opposites and cannot coexist.[32] By contrast, Torrance's approach to Grace transcends such dualistic bifurcation and makes *theosis* truly possible.

Within the matrix of distinction-yet-participation delineated by the hypostatic union, human activity takes place within a circle of relation in which human response and the divine self-giving overlap with one another. Torrance writes,

> In the activity of the Spirit . . . God unites us with Christ in such a way that his human agency in vicarious response to the Father overlaps with our response, gathers it up in its embrace, sanctifying, affirming and upholding it in himself, so that it is established in spite of all our frailty as our free and faithful response to the Father in him. But here a continuous circle of relation, from God to man and from man to God, is thrown around us, reconciling and uniting human agency and divine agency.[33]

This non-competitive co-existence of human and divine freedom is formulaically described by Torrance through the *an/en* couplet. Yet, perhaps this relation could be visually described as well particularly since part of our problem stems from an imagination restricted by a container notion of space. Rather than conceptualizing agency as a zero-sum game where the creatures and the Creator vie for domination and sovereignty, Torrance allows an onto-relational approach grounded in the triune life to define the relation.

---

32. Cf. Thomas F. Torrance, "The Mission of the Church," *SJT* 19 (1966).
33. Thomas F. Torrance, *Theology in Reconciliation: Essays Towards Evangelical and Catholic Unity in East and West* (Eugene, OR: 1997), 103.

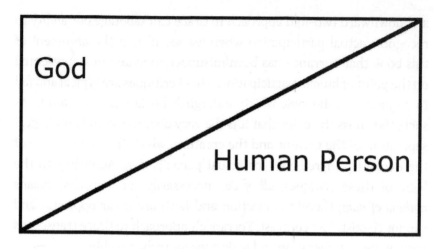

Figure 1.

Rather than dualism determining the framework in which we live and move and have our being [figure 1], Torrance locates human freedom within the circle of God's freedom [figure 2].[34] In this way, the freedom of the one does not restrict the freedom of the other, but rather enhances it and provides it with meaning. Since who human beings are is who they are in Christ, their exercise of freedom (choices) either affirms reality by participating in harmony with it or denies reality by scratching out a tiny space [see figure 1] for human sovereignty and autonomy. True humanity in the fullness of its freedom is found in Jesus Christ, who never sought to find his own life on his own apart from his relation to the Father with the Spirit. Within the circle of the triune life and love, more of God means more space for humanity to expand into its full and true self.

---

34. The basic contours for this figure are derived from a presentation given by Garry Deddo at the T. F. Torrance Retreat at Firbush, Nov. 2012.

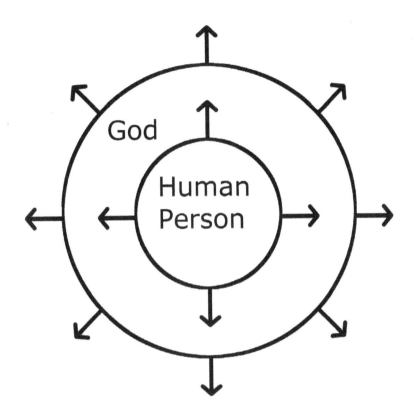

Figure 2.

Thus, contra to Stamps' accusation, what Torrance rejects is not the reality, validity, or even necessity of human response, but the notion of it having any independence to it.[35] Because the covenant will of God for human beings is completely fulfilled in Jesus Christ, the focus of human action shifts from obedient but autonomous response, to *sharing in* the obedience of the Son through the power of the Spirit.[36]

---

35. Thomas F. Torrance, *God and Rationality* (Edinburgh: T&T Clark, 1997), 146.
36. Thomas F. Torrance, *Gospel, Church and Ministry, Thomas F. Torrance Collected Studies I*, ed. Jock Stein (Eugene, OR: Pickwick, 2012), 96.

Contributions

This book makes at least three contributions to wider Torrance studies. *First*, **it fills a significant gap in Torrance scholarship to date. Until now, no single monograph has existed which focuses attention specifically on the development and scope of Torrance's language and theology of Grace.** While this lacuna is understandable given the fact that Grace *per se* does not form a specific locus of doctrine for Torrance, it does leaven the whole of Torrance's theological thinking and serves as the subject of his own doctoral studies.

Second, **in addition to filling an important gap, this study has also demonstrated the critical import of Torrance's concept of Grace for understanding Torrance's overall theology.** It has been my contention that reconciliation through union with Christ is informed and undergirded by the more determinative doctrine of Grace within Torrance's theology. Furthermore, this study has shown that a misunderstanding of Torrance's approach to Grace will lead to a misunderstanding at nearly every level of his theological thought. Because Grace provides a controlling metaphor that gives coherence to the disparate themes of Torrance's soteriology, 'getting Grace right' is critical for the present and future of Torrance scholarship, and also for those who seek to extend Torrance's thinking into further areas of knowledge and practice.

Third, **this book has shown that Torrance is a valuable resource in furthering and rooting the conversation on contemporary ecclesial practices of Spiritual Formation.** Within a cultural context where the relation of God and human beings is always drifting toward either fusion or detachment, Torrance offers a vision of the moral life which does not cast human persons back upon themselves. He accomplishes this important task by a thorough and consistent emphasis upon the humanity of the ascended Christ and of Christian existence as life in and through this One. As such, all service and ministry in the Church are understood as shared and mediated by our eternal high priest who makes the whole life of the Church a kind of living liturgy of eucharistic participation.

Torrance's theology deserves to be understood before it is judged. By lifting up and bringing to the fore Torrance's unique approach to the doctrine of Grace, here it is presented as a valuable resource in the theological conversation. In a Christian culture in which the doctrines of Grace are used in quite diverse ways by Catholics and Protestants alike, Torrance (and the Athanasian tradition which he seeks to represent) stands apart as a consistent, robust, trinitarian and practical approach worthy of much wider appreciation and practice.

Bibliography

Thomas F. Torrance's Works: Books

Torrance, Thomas F. *The Apocalypse Today: Sermons on Revelations.* London: James Clarke and Co., 1960.

_____. *Atonement: The Person and Work of Christ.* Edited by Robert T. Walker. Milton Keynes: Paternoster, 2009.

_____. *The Being and Nature of the Unborn Child.* Edinburgh: Handsel Press for the Scottish Order of Christian Unity, 2000.

_____. *Calvin's Doctrine of Man.* London: Lutterworth, 1949.

_____. *The Christian Doctrine of God: One Being Three Persons.* Edinburgh: T&T Clark, 1996.

_____. *The Christian Frame of Mind: Reason, Order and Openness in Theology and Natural Science.* New enlarged edition. Colorado Springs: Helmers and Howard, 1989.

_____. *Christian Theology and Scientific Culture.* Belfast: Christian Journals, 1980.

_____. *Conflict and Agreement in the Church I: Order and Disorder.* London: Lutterworth, 1960.

_____. *Conflict and Agreement in the Church II: The Ministry of the Sacraments of the Gospel.* London: Lutterworth, 1959.

_____. *Divine and Contingent Order.* Reprint. Edinburgh: T&T Clark, 1998.

_____. *Divine Meaning: Studies in Patristic Hermeneutics.* Edinburgh: T&T Clark, 1995.

_____. *The Doctrine of Grace in the Apostolic Fathers*. Reprint. Eugene, OR: Wipf and Stock, 1996.

_____. *The Doctrine of Jesus Christ*. Eugene, OR: Wipf and Stock, 2002.

_____. *God and Rationality*. Reprint. Edinburgh: T&T Clark, 1997.

_____. *Gospel, Church, and Ministry: Thomas F. Torrance Collected Studies I*. Edited by Jock Stein. Eugene, OR: Pickwick, 2012.

_____. *The Ground and Grammar of Theology*. Charlottesville: University Press of Virginia, 1980.

_____. *The Hermeneutics of John Calvin*. Edinburgh: Scottish Academic, 1988.

_____, editor with introduction. *The Incarnation: Ecumenical Studies in the Nicene-Constantinopolitan Creed AD 381*. Edinburgh: Handsel Press, 1981.

_____. *Incarnation: The Person and Life of Christ*. Edited by Robert T. Walker. Nottingham: Intervarsity, 2008.

_____. *Karl Barth: Biblical and Evangelical Theologian*. Edinburgh: T&T Clark, 1990.

_____. *Kingdom and the Church: A Study in the Theology of the Reformation*. Reprint. Eugene, OR: Wipf and Stock, 1996.

_____, and Ronald Selby Wright, editors. *A Manual of Church Doctrine According to the Church of Scotland*, by H.J. Wotherspoon and J.M. Kirkpatrick, 2nd ed. London: Oxford University Press, 1960.

_____, ed. *The Mystery of the Lord's Supper: Sermons by Robert Bruce*. Reprint. Edinburgh: Rutherford House, 2005.

_____. *The Mediation of Christ*. Revised edition. Edinburgh: T&T Clark, 1992.

_____. *Preaching Christ Today: The Gospel and Scientific Thinking*. Grand Rapids: Eerdmans, 1994.

_____. *Reality and Evangelical Theology: The 1981 Payton Lectures*. Philadelphia: Westminster, 1982.

_____. *Reality and Scientific Theology*. Eugene, OR: Wipf and Stock, 2001.

_____. *Royal Priesthood: A Theology of Ordained Ministry*. Edinburgh: T&T Clark, 1993.

_____. *The School of Faith*. London: Camelot, 1959.

_____. *Scottish Theology: From John Knox to John McLeod Campbell*. Edinburgh: T&T Clark, 1996.

_____. *Space, Time and Incarnation*. Reprint. Edinburgh: T&T Clark, 1997.

_____. *Space, Time and Resurrection.* Edinburgh: T&T Clark, 1998.

_____. *Theological Science.* Oxford: Oxford University Press, 1969.

_____. *Theology in Reconciliation: Essays Towards Evangelical and Catholic Unity in East and West.* Reprint. Eugene, OR: 1997.

_____. *Theology in Reconstruction.* Grand Rapids: Eerdmans, 1965.

_____. *Transformation & Convergence in the Frame of Knowledge: Explorations in the Interrelations of Scientific and Theological Enterprise.* Grand Rapids: Eerdmans, 1984.

_____. *The Trinitarian Faith: The Evangelical Theology of the Ancient Catholic Church.* Edinburgh: T&T Clark, 1995.

_____. *Trinitarian Perspectives: Toward Doctrinal Agreement.* Edinburgh: T&T Clark, 1994.

_____. *When Christ Comes and Comes Again.* Reprint. Eugene, OR: Wipf and Stock, 1996.

Thomas F. Torrance's Works: Published Articles

Torrance, Thomas F. "A Serious Call for a Return to Devout and Holy Life." *Life and Work* (July 1979).

_____. "The Apostolic Ministry." *Scottish Journal of Theology* 2 (1948): 190–201.

_____. "Aspects of Baptism in the New Testament." *Theologische Zeitschrift* 14 (1958): 241–60.

_____. "The Atonement and the Oneness of the Church." *Scottish Journal of Theology* 7 (1954): 245–69.

_____. "The Atoning Obedience of Christ." *Moravian Theological Seminary Bulletin* (1959): 65–81.

_____. "The Atonement: The Singularity of Christ and the Finality of the Cross: The Atonement and the Moral Order." Pages 225–56 in *Universalism and the Doctrine of Hell. Papers presented at the Fourth Edinburgh Conference in Christian Dogmatics.* Edited by Nigel De S. Cameron. Grand Rapids: Baker Book House, 1992.

_____. Review of Martin Heidegger, *Being and Time. Journal of Theological Studies*, 15 (1964): 471–86.

_____. "Bloesch's Doctrine of God." Pages 136–199 in *Evangelical Theology in*

Transition - Theologians in Dialogue with Donald Bloesch. Edited by Elmer M. Colyer. Downers Grove: InterVarsity, 1999.

_____. "Calvin's Catholic Christology." *Scottish Journal of Theology* 23 (1970): 92–94.

_____. "Calvin's Doctrine of the Trinity." *Calvin Theological Journal* 25 (1990): 165–93.

_____. "Cheap and Costly Grace." *The Baptist Quarterly* 22 (1968): 290–311.

_____. "The Christian Apprehension of God the Father." Pages 120–43 in *Speaking the Christian God: The Holy Trinity and the Challenge of Feminism.* Edited by Alvin F. Kimmel, Jr. Grand Rapids: Eerdmans, 1992.

_____. "The Church in the New Era of Scientific and Cosmological Change." Pages 752–76 in *Theological Foundations for Ministry.* Edited by Ray S. Anderson. Edinburgh: T&T Clark, 2000.

_____. "Concerning Amsterdam. I. The Nature and Mission of the Church: A Discussion of Volumes I and II of the Preparatory Studies." *Scottish Journal of Theology* 2 (1949): 241–70.

_____. "Creation, Contingent World-Order, and Time: A Theologico-Scientific Approach." *Theology and Natural Science* (2002): 35–60.

_____. "The Deposit of Faith." *Scottish Journal of Theology* 36 (1983): 1–28.

_____. "Doctrinal Consensus on Holy Communion." *Scottish Journal of Theology* 15, no. 1 (1962): 10.

_____. "The Doctrine of Grace in the Old Testament." *Scottish Journal of Theology* (1948):

_____. "The Doctrine of the Holy Trinity According to St. Athanasius." *Anglican Theological Review* 71 (1989): 395–405.

_____. "The Doctrine of the Virgin Birth." *Scottish Bulletin of Evangelical Theology* 12 (1994): 8–25.

_____. "The Foundation for Hellenism in Great Britain—The Orthodox Church in Great Britain" in Texts and Studies, Vol. 2, edited by Methodios Fouyas, 2:253–59. London: Thyateira House, 1983.

_____. "The Foundation of the Church: Union with Christ through the Spirit." *Scottish Journal of Theology* 16 (1963): 113–31.

_____. "From John Knox to John McLeod Campbell: A Reading of Scottish

Theology." Pages 1–28 in *Disruption to Diversity: Edinburgh Divinity 1846-1996*. Edinburgh: T&T Clark, 2001.

———. "The Goodness and Dignity of Man in the Christian Tradition." *Modern Theology* 4 (1988): 309–22.

———. "Hugh Ross Mackintosh: Theologian of the Cross." *Scottish Bulletin of Evangelical Theology* 5 (1987): 160–73.

———. "Immortality and Light." *Religious Studies* 17 (1981): 147–61.

———. "Incarnation and Atonement: Theosis and Henosis in the Light of Modern Scientific Rejection of Dualism." *Society for Ordained Scientists*, no. 7 (Spring 1992): 8–20.

———. "The Influence of Reformed Theology on the Development of Scientific Method." *Dialog* 2 (1963): 40–49.

———. "Introduction to Calvin's Tracts and Treatises on the Reformation of the Church." Pages xxvii-xxxiii in *Tracts and Treatises on the Reformation of the Church*, no. 1. By John Calvin. Grand Rapids: Eerdmans, 1958.

———. "Israel and the Incarnation." *Judaica* 13 (1957): 1–18.

———. "Justification: Its Radical Nature and Place in Reformed Doctrine and Life." *Scottish Journal of Theology* 13 (1960): 225–46.

———. "Karl Barth." *Scottish Journal of Theology* 22 (1969): 1–9.

———. "Karl Barth and the Latin Heresy." *Scottish Journal of Theology* 39 (1986): 461–82.

———. "The Kirk's Crisis of Faith." *Life and Work* (October 1990): 15–16.

———. "The Legacy of Karl Barth (1186-1986)." *Scottish Journal of Theology* 39 (1986): 289–308.

———. "The Light of the World." *Reformed Journal* 38 (December 1988): 9–12.

———. "The Meaning of Baptism." *Canadian Journal of Theology* 2 (1956): 129–34.

———. "The Meaning of Order." *The Church Quarterly Review* 160 (1959): 21–36.

———. "The Mission of the Church." *Scottish Journal of Theology* 19 (1966): 129–43.

———. "The Mission of Anglicanism." Pages 194–208 in *Essays in Anglican Self-Criticism*. Edited by David M. Paton. London: SCM, 1958.

———. "One Aspect of the Biblical Conception of Faith." *Expository Times* 68 (1957): 111–14.

_____. "The Origins of Baptism." *Scottish Journal of Theology* 11 (1958): 158–71.

_____. "The Ought and the Is: Moral and Natural Law." *Insights - Journal of the Faculty of Austin Seminary* (1994): 49–59.

_____. "Predestination in Christ." *Evangelical Quarterly* 13 (1941): 108–41.

_____. "Predestination in Christ." *Evangelical Quarterly* 13.2 (April 1941): 108–41.

_____. "The Problem of Natural Theology in the Thought of Karl Barth." *Religious Studies* 6 (1970): 121–35.

_____. "The Reconciliation of Mind: A Theological Meditation upon the Teaching of St. Paul." *TSF Bulletin* 10 (1987): 196–204.

_____. "Reformed Dogmatics, not Dogmatism." *Theology* 70 (1967): 152–56.

_____. "The Roman Doctrine of Grace from the Point of View of Reformed Theology." *The Eastern Churches Quarterly* 16 (1964): 290–312.

_____. "Salvation is of the Jews." *The Evangelical Quarterly* 22 (1950): 164–73.

_____. "The Soul and Person in Theological Perspective." Pages 103–18 in *Religion, Reason and the Self: Essays in Honour of Hywel D. Lewis*. Edited by Stuart R. Sutherland and T. A. Roberts. Cardiff: University of Wales Press, 1989.

_____. *The Soul and Person of the Unborn Child*. Scottish Order of Christian Unity. Edinburgh: Handsel (1999).

_____. "The Spiritual Relevance of Angels." Pages 122–39 in *Alive to God*. Edited by J. I. Packer and Loren Wilkinson. Vancouver, Canada: Regent College Publishing, 1992.

_____. "Spiritus Creator." *Verbum Caro* 23 (1969): 63–85.

_____. "A Study in New Testament Communication." *Scottish Journal of Theology* 3 (1950): 298–313.

_____. "The Substance of the Faith: A Clarification of the Concept in the Church of Scotland." *Scottish Journal of Theology* 36 (1983): 327–38.

_____. "Theological Realism." Pages 169–96 in *The Philosophical Frontiers of Christian Theology: Essays Presented to D.M. MacKinnon*. Edited by Brian Hebblethwaite and Stewart Sutherland. Cambridge: Cambridge University Press, 1982.

_____. "The Theology of Light: A University Sermon." Appendix. *The Christian Frame of Mind* (1989): 147–55.

_____. "Toward an Ecumenical Consensus on the Trinity." *Theologische Zeitschrift* 31 (1975): 337–50.

_____. "Truth and Authority: Theses on Truth." *The Irish Theological Quarterly* 38 (1972): 215–42.

_____. "The Uniqueness of Divine Revelation and the Authority of the Scriptures: the Creed Association's Statement." *Scottish Bulletin of Evangelical Theology*, 97–101.

_____. "Universalism or Election?" *Scottish Journal of Theology* 2 (1949): 310–18.

_____. "Where Do We Go from Lund?" *Scottish Journal of Theology* 6 (1953): 53–64.

_____. "Why Karl Barth Still Matters so Much." *Life and Work* (June 1986): 16.

_____. "The Word of God and the Nature of Man." Pages 121–41 in *Reformation Old and New: Festschrift for Karl Barth*. Edited by F. W. Camfield. London: Lutterworth, 1947.

_____. "The Word of God and the Response of Man." *Bijragen* 30 (1969): 172–83.

Thomas F. Torrance's Works: Unpublished Texts

All unpublished texts used and referenced here (unless otherwise stated) can be found in the Thomas F. Torrance Manuscript Collection, Special Collections, Princeton Theological Seminary Library.

Torrance, Thomas F. "The Call for a New Discussion on the Doctrine of Grace." (1938–1939): Box 21.

_____. "Christian Thinking Today," unpublished Moot Paper (1941), John Baillie Collection, New College Library, Edinburgh.

_____. "Dialogue de Gratia." Typescript notes. Box 36.

_____. "From a Christocentric to a Trinitarian Ecumenism: Ecumenical Suicide or Christocentric Renewal." The Oliver Tomkins Lecture, Worchester Cathedral (June 22, 1999): Box 84.

_____. "Minutes from the visit of the delegation from the World Alliance of Reformed Churches to the ecumenical patriarchate in Istanbul, July 26–30, 1979." Box 170.

_____. "Preaching as Sacrament." Sermon. Box 38.

_____. "Reconciliation through the Person of Christ." Sermon on Romans 5 (February 14, 1943): Box 45.

_____. "Relevance of the Doctrine to the Spirit for Ecumenical Theology." Reply of Professor Thomas F. Torrance to his critics. Edinburgh, Scotland (November 20, 1963): Box 135.

_____. "Reply to Donald Macleod," Tape 199, http://tapesfromscotland.org/Rutherfordhouseaudio.htm. Edinburgh: Rutherford House, 1999.

_____. "Sermon on 1 Corinthians 2:1–5," Box 38.

_____. "2 Corinthians 13:14," preached November 1940.

_____. "Sermon on Colossians 3:3," delivered at Beechgrove Church, Scotland (November 1948): Box 47.

_____. "That in Everything He Might be Preeminent." Sermon on Colosians 1:13, St. Giles', Edinburgh, Scotland. (May 24, 1977): Box 38.

_____. "Theology in Action." Lecture. (1938–1946): Box 22:

_____. "The Transfinite Significance of Beauty in Science and Theology". Lecture. Box 71.

_____. "What is God Like? – God in the Face of Jesus Christ". Advent series (December 6, 1964): Box 47.

_____. "What is God Like? – God in Judgment." Advent series (December 13, 1964): Box 47.

_____. "What is God Like? – God in Mercy." Advent series (December 20, 1964): Box 47.

Secondary Works

Anderson, David L. Review of T. F. Torrance, *Divine and Contingent Order*. Bloomsbury, 2005.

Anderson, Ray. *On Being Human, Essays in Theological Anthropology*. Grand Rapids: Eerdmans, 1982.

_____, ed. *Theological Foundations for Ministry*. Edinburgh: T&T Clark, 1979.

_____. "The Practical Theology of Thomas F. Torrance." *Participatio: The Journal of the Thomas F. Torrance Theological Fellowship*, vol. 1 (2009): 49–65.

Ayers, Lewis. "The Fundamental Grammar of Augustine's Trinitarian Theology." Pages 51–76 in *Augustine and His Critics: Essays in Honour of Gerald Bonner*. Edited by Robert Dodaro and George Lawless. London: Routledge, 2000.

_____. "Remember that you are Catholic: Augustine on the Unity of the Triune God." *Journal of Early Christian Studies* 8 (2000): 39–82.

Baillie, John. "Christian Thinking Today." Unpublished Moot Paper. John Baillie Collection, New College Library, Edinburgh, 1941.

Baker, Matthew. "The Correspondence between T. F. Torrance and Georges Florovsky (1950 - 1973)," in T. F. Torrance and Eastern Orthodoxy, edited by Matthew Baker and Todd Speidell, 286–324. Eugene, OR: Wipf & Stock, 2015.

_____. "Interview with Protopresbyter George Dion. Dragas regarding T. F. Torrance," in T. F. Torrance and Eastern Orthodoxy, edited by Matthew Baker and Todd Speidell, 1–18. Eugene, OR: Wipf & Stock, 2015.

_____. "The Place of St. Irenaeus of Lyons in Historical and Dogmatic Theology According to Thomas F. Torrance." *Participatio: The Journal of the Thomas F. Torrance Theological Fellowship*, vol. 2 (2010): 3–43.

Barkley, John. *The Worship of the Reformed Church*. London: Lutterworth, 1966: 70.

Barnes, Michel, "Rereading Augustine's Theology of the Trinity." Pages 145–76 in *The Trinity*, Edited by Stephen T. Davis, Daniel Kendall and Gerald O'Collins. Oxford: Oxford University Press, 1999.

_____. "Augustine in Contemporary Trinitarian Theology." *Theological Studies* 56 (1995): 237–50.

Barr, James. *The Semantics of Biblical Language*. London: Oxford University Press. 1961.

Barth, Karl. *Church Dogmatics: The Doctrine of the Word of God. Vol. 1, 1*. Edited and translated by G. W. Bromiley and T. F. Torrance. Edinburgh: T&T Clark, 1975.

_____. *Church Dogmatics: The Doctrine of the Word of God. Vol. 1, 2*. Edited by G.W. Bromiley and T. F. Torrance. Translated by G. T. Thomson and Harold Knight. Edinburgh: T&T Clark, 1970.

_____. *Church Dogmatics: The Doctrine of the Word of God. Vol. 2, 1*. Edited by G. W. Bromiley and T. F. Torrance. Translated by T. H. L. Parker, W. B. Johnston, H. Knight, and J. L. M. Harie. Edinburgh: T&T Clark, 1964.

_____. *Church Dogmatics the Doctrine of Creation: The Work of Creation. Vol. 3, 2*.

Edited by G. W. Bromiley and T. F. Torrance. Translated by H. Knight, G. W. Bromiley, J. K. S. Reid, R. H. Fuller. Edinburgh: T&T Clark, 1968.

_____. *Church Dogmatics: The Doctrine of Reconciliation. Vol. 4, 1.* Edited by G. W. Bromiley, R. J. Ehrlich. Translated by G.W. Bromiley and T. F. Torrance. Edinburgh: T&T Clark, 1974.

_____. *Church Dogmatics: The Doctrine of Reconciliation. Vol. 4, 2.* Edited by G. W. Bromiley and T. F. Torrance. Translated by G. W. Bromiley. Edinburgh: T&T Clark, 1967.

_____. *Dogmatics in Outline.* London: SCM, 1949.

Bauman, Michael. *Roundtable Conversations with European Theologians.* Grand Rapids: Baker Book House, 1990.

Betz, Hans D. *Religion Past and Present: Encyclopedia of Theology and Religion.* Leiden: Brill, 2007.

Canlis, Julie. *Calvin's Ladder: a Spiritual Theology of Ascent and Ascension.* Grand Rapids: Eerdmans, 2010.

Cass, Peter. *Christ Condemned in the Flesh: Thomas F. Torrance's Doctrine of Soteriology and Its Ecumenical Significance.* Saarbrücken, Germany: VDM Verlag, 2009.

Colyer, Elmer M. *How to Read T. F. Torrance: Understanding His Trinitarian & Scientific Theology.* Downers Grove: InterVarsity, 2001.

_____. *The Nature of Doctrine in T. F. Torrance's Theology.* Eugene, OR: Wipf & Stock, 2001.

_____, ed. *The Promise of Trinitarian Theology: Theologians in Dialogue with T. F. Torrance.* Lanham: Rowman & Littlefield, 2001.

Crisp, Oliver. "Did Christ have a Fallen Human Nature?" *International Journal of Systematic Theology* 6.3 (2004): 270–88.

Davidson, Ivor. "Pondering the Sinlessness of Jesus Christ: Moral Christologies and the Witness of Scripture." *International Journal of Systematic Theology* 10.4 (2008): 372–92.

Dawson, Gerrit Scott, ed. *An Introduction to Torrance Theology.* London: T&T Clark, 2007.

Deddo, Gary. "The Holy Spirit in T. F. Torrance's Theology." Pages 81–114 in *The Promise of Trinitarian Theology: Theologians in Dialogue with T. F. Torrance.* Edited by Elmer M. Colyer. Lanham: Rowman & Littlefield, 2001.

Dix, Gregory. *The Shape of the Liturgy.* Westminster London: Dacre, 1945.

Dodaro, Robert, and George Lawless, eds. *Augustine and His Critics: Essays in Honour of Gerald Bonner.* London: Routledge, 2000.

Dragas, George. "The Significance for the Church of Professor Torrance's Election As Moderator of the General Assembly of the Church of Scotland." ΕΚΚΛΗΣΙΑΣΤΙΚΟΣ ΦΑΡΟΣ LVIII, no. III–IV (1976): 214–31.

Eugenio, Dick. *Communion with God: The Trinitarian Soteriology of Thomas F. Torrance.* Eugene, OR: Pickwick, 2014.

Fach, Sandra E. "Answering the Upward Call: The Ascended Christ, Mediator of our Worship." PhD diss., Kings College London, 2008.

Farrow, Douglass. "T. F. Torrance and the Latin Heresy" in *First Things,* 2013.12.

Fergusson, David. "Torrance as a Scottish Theologian" in Participatio: Journal of the Thomas F. Torrance Theological Fellowship, Vol. 2 (2010): 77–87.

Flett, Eric G. *Persons, Powers, and Pluralities: Toward a Trinitarian Theology of Culture.* Cambridge: James Clark, 2012.

Frost, R. N., "Sin and Grace." Pages 101–12 in *Trinitarian Soundings in Systematic Theology.* Edited by Paul Louis Metzger. London: T&T Clark, 2005.

Gockel, M. "A Dubiojs Christological Formula? Leontius of Byzantium and the Anhypostasis-Enhypostasis Theory." *Journal of Theological Studies,* 51 (2000): 515–32.

Gunton, Colin E., "Being and Person: T. F. Torrance's Doctrine of God." Pages 115–37 in *The Promise of Trinitarian Theology: Theologians in Dialogue with T. F. Torrance.* Edited by Elmer M. Colyer. Lanham: Rowman & Littlefield, 2001.

_____. *The One, the Three and the Many: God, Creation and the Culture of Modernity/ The 1992 Bampton Lectures.* Cambridge: Cambridge University Press, 1993.

_____. *The Promise of Trinitarian Theology.* 2nd ed. Edinburgh: T&T Clark, 1997.

Grenz, Stanley. "The Named God and the Question of Being: A Trinitarian Theo-Ontology." In *The Matrix of Christian Theology,* vol. 2. Louisville: John Knox, 2005.

_____. *Rediscovering the Triune God: The Trinity in Contemporary Theology.* Minneapolis: Fortress, 2004.

_____. "The Imago Dei and the Dissipation of the Self." *Dialog* 38 (1999): 182–98.

Habets, Myk. *Theosis in the Theology of Thomas Torrance.* Farnham: Ashgate, 2009.

Habets, Myk, and Phillip Tolliday, eds. Trinitarian Theology After Barth. Eugene, OR: Pickwick, 2011.

Hardy, Daniel W., "Thomas F. Torrance." Pages 163–77 in The Modern Theologians: An Introduction to Christian Theology Since 1918, 3rd ed. Edited by David F. Ford with Rachel Muers. Oxford: Blackwell, 2005.

Heron, Alasdair I. C. Table and Tradition: Toward an Ecumenical Understanding of the Eucharist. Philadelphia: Westminster, 1983.

Hesselink, I. John, "A Pilgrimage in the School of Christ – An Interview with Thomas F. Torrance." Reformed Review 38.1 (Autumn 1984): 47–64.

Holmes, Christopher. Ethics in the Presence of Christ. London: T&T Clark, 2012.

Holmes, Stephen R. The Holy Trinity: Understanding God's Life. Milton Keynes: Paternoster, 2012.

Hunsinger, George, The Christ and Ecumenism: Let Us Keep the Feast. Cambridge: Cambridge University Press 2008.

_____. "The Dimension of Depth: Thomas F. Torrance on the Sacraments of Baptism and The Lord's Supper." Scottish Journal of Theology 54.2 (2001): 155–76.

_____. "Forward," in T. F. Torrance and Eastern Orthodoxy, edited by Matthew Baker and Todd Speidell, iii-iv. Eugene, OR: Wipf & Stock, 2015.

_____. How to Read Karl Barth: The Shape of His Theology. New York: Oxford University Press, 1991.

_____. "Robert Jenson's Systematic Theology: A Review Essay." Scottish Journal of Theology 55 (2002): 166.

Hunter, Harold. "Spirit Christology: Dilemma and Promise," Heythrop Journal 24 (1983).

Jenson, Robert W. Systematic Theology v. 2 The Works of God. Oxford: Oxford University Press, 1999.

Jungmann, Josef A. The Place of Christ in Liturgical Prayer. London: Chapman, 1965.

Kang, Phee Seng. "The Concept of the Vicarious Humanity of Christ in the Theology of Thomas Forsyth Torrance." PhD diss., University of Aberdeen, 1989.

Kapic, Kelly. "The Son's Assumption of a Human Nature: A Call for Clarity." International Journal of Systematic Theology 3.2 (2001): 154–66.

Kelly, Douglas. "The Realist Epistemology of Thomas F. Torrance." Pages 75–102 in *An Introduction to Torrance Theology: Discovering the Incarnate Saviour*, edited by Gerrit Scott Dawson. London: T&T Clark, 2007.

Kettler, Christian D. *The Vicarious Humanity of Christ and the Reality of Salvation*. Lanham: University Press, 1991.

Kierkegaard, Soren. *Fear and Trembling*. Translated by Alastair Hannay. Introduction by Johannes de Silentio. USA: Penguin Classics, 1986.

Kruger, C. Baxter. "The Doctrine of the Knowledge of God in the Theology of T. F. Torrance: Sharing in the Son's Communion with the Father in the Spirit." *Scottish Journal of Theology* 43.3 (1990): 366–89.

_____. "Participation in the Self-knowledge of God: The Nature and Means of our Knowledge of God in the Theology of T. F. Torrance." PhD diss., University of Aberdeen, 1989.

_____. "On the Road to Becoming Flesh, Israel as the Womb of the Incarnation in the Theology of T. F. Torrance." *Participatio: The Journal of the Thomas F. Torrance Theological Fellowship*, vol. 3. (2012): 64–91.

LaCugna, Catherine Mowry. *God For Us: the Trinity and Christian Life*. New York: Harper, 1993.

Lang, U. M. "Anhypostatos and Enhypostatos: Church Fathers, Protestant Orthodoxy and Karl Barth." *Journal of Theological Studies*, 49 (1998): 630–657.

Lee, Kye Won. *Living in Union with Christ: The Practical Theology of Thomas F. Torrance*. New York: Peter Lang Publishing, 2003.

Lunt, Ronald. Review of T. F. Torrance, *Theology in Reconciliation*. *Expository Times* 87 (1975–76): 379.

Luoma, Tapio. *Incarnation and Physics: Natural Science in the Theology of Thomas F. Torrance*. Oxford: Oxford University Press, 2002.

MacKay, Donald M. Review of T. F. Torrance, *Divine and Contingent Order*. *ChrG* 35, no. 2 (1982): 38–39.

Mackintosh, H. R. *The Person of Jesus Christ*. London: T&T Clark, 1912.

MacLean, Stanley. *Resurrection, Apocalypse, and the Kingdom of Christ: The Eschatology of Thomas F. Torrance*. Eugene, OR: Pickwick, 2012.

Man Kei Ho. *A Critical Study on T. F. Torrance's Theology of Incarnation*. Bern: Peter Lang, 2008.

McCormack, Bruce L. *Karl Barth's Critically Realistic Dialectical Theology: Its Genesis and Development in 1909-1936.* Oxford: Clarendon, 1995.

_____. *Orthodox and Modern: Studies in the Theology of Karl Barth.* Grand Rapids: Baker Academic, 2008.

McFarland, Ian, "Fallen or Unfallen? Christ's Human Nature and the Ontology of Human Sinfulness." *International Journal of Systematic Theology* 10.4 (2008): 409–12.

McGrath, Alister E. *A Scientific Theology: Volume I, Nature.* Grand Rapids: Eerdmans, 2001.

_____. *Thomas F. Torrance: An Intellectual Biography.* Edinburgh: T&T Clark, 1999.

McMaken, Travis W. *The Sign of the Gospel: Toward an Evangelical Doctrine of Infant Baptism after Karl Barth.* Minneapolis: Fortress Press, 2013.

Meyers, Ben, "The Stratification of Knowledge in the Thought of T. F. Torrance." *Scottish Journal of Theology* 61, no. 1 (2008): 15.

Molnar, Paul D. *Divine Freedom and the Doctrine of the Immanent Trinity: In Dialogue with Karl Barth and Contemporary Theology.* London: T&T Clark, 2002.

_____. "The Eucharist and the Mind of Christ: Some Trinitarian Implications of T. F. Torrance's Sacramental Theology." Pages 175–88 on *Trinitarian Soundings in Systematic Theology.* Edited by Paul Louis Metzger. New York and London: T&T Clark, 2005.

_____. *Incarnation and Resurrection: Toward a Contemporary Understanding.* Grand Rapids: Eerdmans, 2007.

_____. *Karl Barth and the Theology of the Lord's Supper: A Systematic Investigation.* New York: Peter Lang, 1996.

_____. *Thomas F. Torrance, Theologian of the Trinity.* Farnham: Ashgate, 2009.

Moltmann, Jürgen. *God in Creation: A New Theology of Creation and the Spirit of God,* translated by Margaret Kohl. New York: Harper and Row, 1985.

_____. *The Trinity and the Kingdom, The Doctrine of God,* translated by Margaret Kohl. New York: Harper & Row, 1981.

Morrison, John Douglas. *Knowledge of the Self-Revealing God in the Thought of Thomas Forsyth Torrance.* New York: Peter Lang, 1997.

Muller, Richard A. "The Barth Legacy: New Athanasius or Origen Redivivus? A Response to T. F. Torrance." *The Thomist* 54.4 (October 1990): 673–704.

Newell, R. J. *Participatory Knowledge: Theology as Art and Science in C. S. Lewis and T. F. Torrance*. Aberdeen University, 1983.

Pannenberg, Wolfhard. *Jesus - God and Man*. 2nd ed. Translated by L. L. Wilkins and D. A. Priebe, 337–44. Philadelphia: Westminster, 1975.

_____. *Systematic Theology, vol. 1*. Grand Rapids: Eerdmans, 1991.

Polanyi, Michael. *Personal Knowledge: Towards a Post-Critical Philosophy*. London: Routledge and Kegan Paul, 1958.

Prestige, G. L. *God in Patristic Thought*. London, 1952. Eugene, OR: Wipf & Stock, 2008.

Purves, Andrew. "The Christology of Thomas F. Torrance." Pages 51–80 in *The Promise of Trinitarian Theology: Theologians in Dialogue with T. F. Torrance*. Edited by Elmer M. Colyer, Lanham: Rowman & Littlefield, 2001.

_____. *The Resurrection of Ministry*. Downers Grove: Intervarsity, 2010.

Radcliff, Jason. "T. F. Torrance in the Light of Stephen Holmes's Critique of Contemporary Trinitarian Thought." *Evangelical Quarterly* 86.1 (2014): 21–38.

Rahner, Karl. *Foundations of Christian Faith: An Introduction to the Idea of Christianity*. Translated by William V. Dych New York: Seabury, 1978.

_____. "Theology and Anthropology." Pages 28–45 in *Theological Investigations, Vol. 9: Writings of 1965-1967*. Translated by Graham Harrison. New York: Herder and Herder, 1972.

_____. *The Trinity*. Translated by Joseph Donceel. New York: Herder and Herder, 1970.

Rankin, William. "Carnal Union with Christ in the Theology of T. F. Torrance." PhD diss., University of Edinburgh, 1997.

Robinson, J.A.T. "Universalism - Is it Heretical?" *Scottish Journal of Theology* 2.2 (1949): 139–55.

Sanders, Fred. "The Image of the Immanent Trinity: Implications of Rahner's Rule for a Theological Interpretation of Scripture." Thesis. Graduate Theological Union, 2001.

Sarisky, Darren. "T. F. Torrance on Biblical Interpretation." *International Journal of Systematic Theology* 11.3 (2009): 332–46.

Shults, LeRon. "A Dubious Christological Formula: From Leontius of Byzantium to Karl Barth." *Theological Studies* 57 (1996): 431–46.

Smail, Thomas. *The Giving Gift: The Holy Spirit in Person.* Lima: CSS Publishing, 1998.

_____. Review of "Mediation of Christ." *Scottish Journal of Theology* 38 (1985): 243.

Spinks, Bryan D. Reformation and Modern Rituals and Theologies of Baptism: From Luther to Contemporary Practices. Aldershot: Ashgate, 2006.

Stamps, Robert J. *The Sacrament of the Word Made Flesh: The Eucharistic Theology of Thomas F. Torrance.* Edinburgh: Rutherford House, 2007.

Staniloae, Fr. Dumitru. "The World as Gift and Sacrament of God's Love," *Sobornost* 9 (1969): 662–73.

Thorson, Walter R. Review of Thomas F. Torrance, *Reality and Scientific Theology.* PSCF 38, no. 2 (1986): 212–14.

Tomlin, Graham. *The Prodigal Spirit: The Trinity of the Church and the Future of the World.* Alpha International, 2011.

Torrance, Alan J. "What is a Person?" Pages 199–222 in *From Cells to Souls - and Beyond: Changing Portraits of Human Nature.* Edited by Malcolm Jeeves, Grand Rapids: Eerdmans, 2004.

Torrance, David W., "Thomas Forsyth Torrance: Minister of the Gospel, Pastor and Evangelical Theologian." Pages 1–30 in *The Promise of Trinitarian Theology: Theologians in Dialogue with T. F. Torrance.* Edited by Elmer M. Colyer, Lanham: Rowman & Littlefield (2001).

_____. *The Witness of the Jews to God.* Eugene, OR: Wipf and Stock, 2011.

Torrance, James B. *Worship, Communion, and the Triune God of Grace.* Downers Grove: InterVarsity, 1997: 50–57.

Walker, Robert. "Editor's Introduction." Pages xxi–lii in *Incarnation: The Person and Life of Christ.* Edited by Robert T. Walker. Downers Grove: InterVarsity, (2008).

Ward, Graham. *Christ and Culture.* Oxford: Blackwell, 2005.

Webster, John B. "Editorial" in *IJST*, Vol 10.4. Oct 2008, 369–71.

_____. "Thomas Forsyth Torrance, 1913–2007," *Biographical Memoirs of Fellows of the British Academy* 13 (2014): 417–36.

_____. *Word and Church: Essays in Christian Dogmatics.* Edinburgh: T&T Clark, 2001.

Weightman, Colin. *Theology in a Polanyian Universe: The Theology of T. F. Torrance.* New York: Peter Lang, 1995.

Zizioulas, John. *Being As Communion: Studies in Personhood and the Church.* Crestwood: St. Vladimir's Seminary, 1985.

_____. *Communion and Otherness: Further Studies in Personhood and the Church.* London: T&T Clark, 2006.

_____. "Human Capacity and Incapacity: A Theological Exploration of Personhood." *Scottish Journal of Theology* 28, no. 5 (1975): 401–47.

Index